ORGANISED CRIME AND THE LAW

Organised Crime and the Law presents an overview of the laws and policies adopted to address the phenomenon of organised crime in the United Kingdom and Ireland, assessing the degree to which these justice systems have been recalibrated, in terms of the prevention, investigation, prosecution and punishment of organised criminality. While the notion of organised crime itself is a contested one, States' legal responses often treat it and its constituent offences as unproblematic in a definitional sense. This book advances a systematic doctrinal critique of relevant domestic criminal laws, laws of evidence and civil processes.

Organised Crime and the Law constructs a theoretical framework on which an appraisal of these legal measures may be based, focusing in particular on the tension between due process and crime control, the demands of public protection and risk aversion, and other adaptations. In particular, it identifies parallels and points of divergence between the different jurisdictions in the UK and Ireland, bearing in mind the shared history of subversive threats and counter-terrorism policies. It further examines the extent to which policy transfer is evident in the UK and Ireland in terms of emulating the US in the reactions to organised crime.

CW00552294

Organised Crime and the Law

A Comparative Analysis

Liz Campbell

·HART·
PUBLISHING
OXFORD AND PORTLAND, OREGON
2013

Published in the United Kingdom by Hart Publishing Ltd
16C Worcester Place, Oxford, OX1 2JW
Telephone: +44 (0)1865 517530
Fax: +44 (0)1865 510710
E-mail: mail@hartpub.co.uk
Website: http://www.hartpub.co.uk

Published in North America (US and Canada) by
Hart Publishing
c/o International Specialized Book Services
920 NE 58th Avenue, Suite 300
Portland, OR 97213-3786
USA
Tel: +1 503 287 3093 or toll-free: (1) 800 944 6190
Fax: +1 503 280 8832
E-mail: orders@isbs.com
Website: http://www.isbs.com

British Library Cataloguing in Publication Data
Data Available

ISBN: 978-1-84946-122-1

Typeset by Hope Services, Abingdon
Printed and bound in Great Britain by
TJ International Ltd, Padstow, Cornwall

MIX
Paper from
responsible sources
FSC
www.fsc.org   FSC® C013056

ACKNOWLEDGEMENTS

I would like to thank Peter Duff, Ronald Goldstock, James Jacobs, Michael Levi and Dermot Walsh for their careful and detailed comments on previous drafts. Many other colleagues and friends over the years, especially Shane Kilcommins, provided stimulating and challenging insights on various aspects of my work.

I am grateful to the School of Law, University of Aberdeen, for supporting this project, and in particular for the valuable advice and guidance given by Peter Duff and Margaret Ross. I completed this book as a Fulbright Scholar at the University of Maryland Law School (2011–12), and I would like to express my appreciation for this support. My special thanks are extended to many colleagues there.

Last, but certainly not least, I would like to thank Cliff, Frances and Sarah.

TABLE OF CONTENTS

TABLES OF CASES

TABLES OF LEGISLATION

United States

European Union

INTERNATIONAL TREATIES
AND CONVENTIONS

1

Introduction

The threat posed by organised crime is a dominant concern for many citizens, communities and legislators in late-modern societies. Its centrality in political discourse and the fear it engenders in the public derive from the increase in rates of certain types of criminality, and the menacing depiction of criminal associations presented in the media and through popular culture. Organised crime, involving the systematic provision by criminal enterprises of illegal goods or services, or the planned group perpetration of certain grave crimes motivated by profit, seems to be worsening: gun-related crimes and the trafficking of illicit goods and even people grow more common, while homicides motivated by feuds between drug traffickers or rival gangs have moved from infrequent aberrations to regular occurrences. In addition, organised crime groups are seen as ever more sophisticated, and as assisted by modern technologies which provide rapid and impenetrable communication techniques and conceal the movement of assets and contraband. This compounds the widely held view that such offences merit robust and innovative legal reactions.

The inherent nature of organised crime – the ruthlessness of the actors, their illicit accrual of vast wealth, the pernicious effects of their actions for victims and witnesses, and the potential corruption of the political and judicial systems – is seen by policy makers as warranting radical legal responses. In essence, the dominant narrative in political and media circles is that the present criminal justice system, in particular the normal schemes of procedure and sentencing, is incapable of dealing with crime of this form and extent, and that some of the traditional processes actually preclude effective investigation or prosecution. It is believed that the police are constrained in attempting to detect crime and in subsequent investigations, and that the prosecution faces overwhelming obstacles if any such case reaches the courts. Moreover, the sentencing model in place is regarded as insufficiently punitive towards serious and organised criminals and as ineffective in terms of preventing further such offences. There is a perception that this renders organised criminals essentially immune from punishment. Overall, the prevailing attitude in the political sphere is that the justice system pays scant regard to the imperatives of crime control and public protection in relation to the danger posed by organised crime, and is entrenched unjustifiably in an anachronistic due process paradigm which is concerned excessively with the rights and liberties of the suspect or offender.

Thus, in the United Kingdom (the UK) and Ireland, the powers of the State and its agents have been modified during investigation and at trial, given these limitations of the justice system in its traditional guise. In a bid to improve the abilities of the State, alterations have been made to laws, policies and practices at all stages of the criminal process. Moreover, provisions have been enacted which reach beyond the traditional confines of the criminal process into the arena of civil law to address organised crime more effectively.

In the UK and Ireland, new substantive offences have been created. Considerable modifications have been made to the rules relating to police investigation: surveillance powers are considerable and used widely, and detention periods have been extended. In addition, procedural rights have been altered: the right to be tried before a jury has been eroded; the right to cross-examine witnesses has been diluted; previous inconsistent statements are admissible as evidence, and the evidence of accomplices and participants in witness protection programmes may now be relied upon. After conviction, robust and sometimes indeterminate sentences may be imposed, in addition to numerous ancillary orders. Moreover, the tactics adopted by the State have extended beyond the criminal process, with the establishment of agencies which may recover assets believed to be the proceeds of crime in civil proceedings, in addition to pursuing actions under taxation legislation.

In examining the legal reactions to organised crime across the different jurisdictions of the UK and in Ireland this book may impart a false coherence[1] to both the concept of organised crime and to the statutory measures introduced to deal with it. Though its conceptual boundaries may be questioned, organised crime as a phenomenon, however defined or conceived, has prompted considerable political concern and concomitant legislative reaction. While conceding and then analysing the nebulous nature of this type of crime, the primary focal point of this book is on the legal reactions to this type of criminality in a number of neighbouring common law jurisdictions, whether it is viewed as a determinate type of crime, or a rhetorical description, or a fluid yet useful label.

As Levi and Maguire note, only intermittently have law enforcement operations against organised crime been devised as part of a systematic reduction strategy.[2] In a similar vein but on a broader level, the legal responses in the UK and Ireland are not systematic or cohesive. Indeed, given the contested nature of the definition of organised crime itself, one cannot identify definitively those measures which pertain to this type of crime only. Many reactions to organised crime may apply to a broader range of criminality; nonetheless, what is explored here in a doctrinal, theoretical and normative sense is a range of the most critical legal measures which may and do address organised crime. The matters under consideration are predominantly procedural, and some substantive law is also examined, in addition to changes to sentencing practice and the use of civil means to deal with a crime

---

[1] M Levi, 'The Organization of Serious Crimes for Gain' in M Maguire, R Morgan and R Reiner (eds), *The Oxford Handbook of Criminology* (5th edn) (Oxford, Oxford University Press, 2012) 612.
[2] M Levi and M Maguire, 'Reducing and Preventing Organised Crime: An Evidence-Based Critique' (2004) 41 *Crime, Law & Social Change* 397, 451.

problem. The focus is not on the relevant criminal justice agencies or actors, nor on structural change to law enforcement, nor on policing practices, though laws facilitating the establishment of new agencies are considered briefly.[3] The focus here is on one particular dimension of the State's reaction to such crime, namely how the law has been constructed, amended and interpreted to address organised crime more effectively.

Though the selection may be challenged, the analysis here concerns those legal provisions which are focused on this category of crime and criminal actor and which are the most visible, the most publicised, and those most likely to affect civil liberties and individual rights. In a normative sense, the book adopts a liberal, due process stance, and this perspective shapes the choice of legal measures to be evaluated. While there are unquestionable difficulties in investigating and prosecuting organised crime, and though the threat posed by organised crime to witnesses, jurors and the administration of justice overall is a real one, the more complex matter is how to address the problem in a measured way that is cognisant of due process.

Throughout, reference is made to criminological scholarship and empirical research, but this book does not delve into the socio-economic, political, psychological or structural factors contributing to or explaining organised crime. Essentially, the focus is not on preventive or 'anti'-organised crime measures, but rather on legal 'counter'-organised crime strategies, and the ramifications these hold for traditional norms and protections in the criminal justice context.

I. The Comparator Jurisdictions

The principal jurisdictions on which this book concentrates are the constituent States in the UK and Ireland, although reference is sometimes made to other common law jurisdictions such as the United States (the US) and Canada. Comparing the neighbouring jurisdictions in the UK and Ireland is instructive due to their shared cultural and common law heritage, and the degree of criminal justice policy transfer between them, generally speaking. A comparative method of legal analysis highlights readily the points of commonality and divergence between geographically adjacent and historically bound jurisdictions in terms of the enactment, implementation and efficacy of laws against organised crime. 'Negative similarities',[4] such as lacunae in policy and law, exist between the comparator States, and sometimes, where equivalent laws exist, there are variations in effectiveness due to administrative and/or practical matters.

---

[3] For an analysis of the work of significant actors like prosecutors in dealing with organised crime see R Goldstock, *Organised Crime in Northern Ireland: A Report for the Secretary of State* (Belfast, Northern Ireland Office, 2004) 4.8 *et seq*.

[4] L Paoli and C Fijnaut, 'Organised Crime and its Control Policies' (2006) 14 *European Journal of Crime, Criminal Law and Criminal Justice* 307, 326.

In the reactions to organised crime in the UK and Ireland, there is evidence of policy transfer in a true sense involving purposeful imitative activity, as well as policy diffusion and convergence where the jurisdictions become more alike purely by the successive adoption of specific policy approaches.[5] In some respects, and indeed as is often the case in relation to criminal justice, counter-organised crime measures in the United States represent a prototype,[6] such as with the adoption of witness protection programmes. In addition, measures first used in England and Wales, such as anonymous witness evidence, have been emulated north of the border in Scotland, while post-conviction measures first adopted across the UK were imitated subsequently in Ireland. Against the usual flow of policy transfer, the use of civil measures to recoup the proceeds of crime in the UK derives from an Irish model, though is also influenced by US civil forfeiture mechanisms.

Many of the legal measures introduced to address organised crime are echoed across the comparator jurisdictions with readily identifiable parallels in policy and practice. On the other hand, despite geographical proximity, shared histories, and the overarching influence of the common law, a comparative analysis of domestic laws highlights some divergences, stimulated and maintained by cultural, social and legal contingencies. Certain historical factors have sensitised policy makers and the public to the dangers of expanded State powers, thereby dissuading them from the use of particular measures; conversely and simultaneously, legal precursors that developed in very different times may provide an example for contemporary laws. In the Republic of Ireland, the crucial historical contingency which facilitated the legal expansion of State powers is the terrorist legacy and the resultant restrictions on civil liberties. Thus, measures such as non-jury criminal courts and prolonged detention periods, with their antecedents in counter-paramilitary tactics, are welcomed in Ireland, while rarely if ever contemplated in Scotland, for example. Moreover, in Northern Ireland expansion of State powers prompted by the political situation has influenced counter-organised crime measures when compared with the rest of the UK. Conversely, the presence of a written Constitution and a robust rights-oriented jurisprudence in Ireland has guarded against certain measures, such as anonymous witnesses, in contrast to the situation across the UK.

---

[5]   C Bennett, 'What is Policy Convergence and What Causes it?' (1991) 21 *British Journal of Political Science* 215, 220–21.

[6]   See T Jones and T Newburn, *Policy Transfer and Criminal Justice: Exploring US Influence Over British Crime Control Policy* (Maidenhead, Open University Press, 2007); T Jones and T Newburn, 'Learning From Uncle Sam? Understanding US Influences Over UK Crime Control Policy' (2002) 15 *Governance* 97; T Newburn, 'Atlantic Crossings: "Policy Transfer" and Crime Control in the USA and Britain' (2002) 4 *Punishment & Society* 165.

II. The Legal Framework

The legal framework that exists in the comparator jurisdictions in the United Kingdom (that is, in England and Wales, Scotland and Northern Ireland) became rather more complex with the devolution of power that occurred at the end of the twentieth century and is significant in terms of the legal reactions to organised crime. Scotland has long had a separate legal and court system,[7] with autonomy in the context of the criminal process, except for matters that impact State security. In particular, Scotland has a distinctive criminal justice system, with a jury of 15, a 'not proven' verdict, a requirement of corroboration, and a marked reliance on common law definitions in substantive law.[8] Despite this separate legal system in Scotland, the United Kingdom had a single Parliament and an Executive consisting of the Prime Minister and the Cabinet until the late-1990s when considerable amendment to the constitutional structure occurred. Referenda were held permitting some executive and legislative powers to be devolved to the Scottish Parliament, the National Assembly in Wales and the Northern Ireland Assembly.[9] The Welsh Assembly originally had executive powers only, whereas now it has limited legislative competence but no law-making powers in the area of criminal justice.[10] In contrast, both Scotland and Northern Ireland possess powers that may affect the bid to address organised crime.

The Scotland Act 1998 provided Scotland with an Executive, and a Parliament which can legislate on areas not reserved to Westminster. Devolved subjects which are within the legislative competence of the Scottish Parliament include health, education and local government, and most critically for present purposes, most aspects of criminal and civil law, the prosecution system and the courts. Reserved matters include defence and national security, social security, immigration, financial and economic issues including money laundering, misuse of drugs, firearms, national security, interception of communications, official secrets and terrorism; many of these are germane to the legal reactions to organised crime.[11] Furthermore, although precluded from legislating, the Scottish Parliament may debate reserved matters that are deemed to be of public interest and importance.[12]

The Scotland Act 1998 does not affect the power of the UK Parliament to make laws for Scotland.[13] In other words, the Westminster Parliament may continue to legislate on devolved subjects; however this requires the consent of its Scottish

---

[7] See the Acts of Union 1707 and 1800.

[8] See P Duff and N Hutton (eds), *Criminal Justice in Scotland* (Dartmouth, Ashgate, 1999).

[9] Northern Ireland Act 1998; Scotland Act 1998; Government of Wales Act.

[10] Government of Wales Act 2006, sch 7. The Welsh Assembly has legislative competence in respect of certain aspects of agriculture, fisheries, forestry and rural development, culture, education, housing, sport, tourism, and health, which can cut across certain drugs issues.

[11] Scotland Act 1998, sch 5.

[12] D Arter, *The Scottish Parliament: A Scandinavian-Style Assembly?* (London, Frank Cass, 2004) 15.

[13] Scotland Act 1998, s 28(7).

equivalent. While not provided for in the Scotland Act 1998, it has become a convention that Westminster would not legislate on devolved matters in Scotland without the consent of the Scottish Parliament under what is now known as the Sewel Convention.[14] Thus, Sewel motions (otherwise referred to as legislative consent motions) were passed in relation to significant statutes like the Regulation of Investigatory Powers Bill, the Proceeds of Crime Bill and the Serious Organised Crime and Police Bill, permitting Westminster to legislate on matters that, strictly speaking, fall within the competence of the Scottish Parliament. As noted, Westminster solely legislates on financial and economic matters including money laundering, misuse of drugs, firearms, and the interception of communications.

In Northern Ireland, the devolution of powers has been suspended and restored a number of times since 1998 due to the political situation there. After suspension in 2002, the Assembly resumed in 2006 and devolution was restored in 2007.[15] Government powers are divided into reserved, excepted and transferred powers, with the Northern Ireland Assembly responsible for making laws on transferred matters such as education, health and agriculture. Excepted matters such as defence, taxation and foreign policy remain within the competence of the UK Parliament only.[16] Reserved matters include policing and criminal law.[17] The Assembly can legislate on reserved matters with the consent of the Secretary of State,[18] and at the time of enactment it was envisaged that such matters could, under certain circumstances, be transferred to the Assembly at a later date.[19] In March 2010, the Northern Ireland Assembly voted in favour of the transfer of policing and justice powers from Westminster,[20] and there is now a Department of Justice in Northern Ireland.[21]

Ireland is a common law country which, in contrast to the United Kingdom, has a written Constitution, *Bunreacht na hÉireann*. This was enacted by plebiscite in 1937, and is the primary legal document in the State and may be amended by popular referendum only.[22] Statute law, which is subordinate to the Constitution, is made by the two Houses of Parliament (the Oireachtas), the Dáil and the Seanad. Crucially, the Irish Supreme Court has the ability to declare legislation as unconstitutional and therefore invalid.[23] These particular legal traditions, struc-

---

[14] See P Bowers and C Sear, *The Sewel Convention*, Standard Note: SN/PC/2084 (London, Parliament and Constitution Centre, 2005).

[15] Northern Ireland (St Andrews Agreement) Act 2006.

[16] Northern Ireland Act 1998, Sch 2.

[17] Northern Ireland Act 1998, Sch 3.

[18] Northern Ireland Act 1998, s 8.

[19] See D Foster and O Gay, *The Hillsborough Agreement*, Library Standard Note SN/PC/05350 (London, Parliament and Constitution Centre, 2010) 2.

[20] ibid.

[21] The Department was established by the Department of Justice (Northern Ireland) Act 2010 and facilitated by the Northern Ireland Act 2009.

[22] Art 46.

[23] Arts 15.4.2° and 34.3.1°. The ability of courts to do so is criticised by some scholars who see this as anti-democratic. See, eg T Campbell, 'Human Rights: A Culture of Controversy' (1999) 26 *Journal of Law and Society* 6, 25; and C Gearty, *Can Human Rights Survive?* (Cambridge, Cambridge University Press, 2006) 69ff.

tures and documents in each of the comparator jurisdictions have influenced the nature of the reactions to organised crime.

III. The International Dimension

Organised crime is a cross-border phenomenon and consequently is far more than a national law enforcement problem.[24] The individuals and groups involved in organised criminality are not limited by State borders, and, in fact, often exploit national differences in laws, regulations, and taxes to establish illegal markets and generate profits. Moreover, the importation of controlled goods like drugs or weapons by definition is transnational in nature. Actors in the UK and Ireland may collaborate with or rely on colleagues in other countries or continents to import illegal materials, and may represent a part of or the final aspect of a lengthy, complex and international distribution chain. This international dimension both permits organised crime groups to increase the range and depth of their activities and also requires cross-border cooperation by investigating and prosecuting authorities. Thus, international agencies, like Interpol, and supra-national obligations and legal standards, such as the European Convention on Human Rights, European Union Directives and United Nations Conventions, all are crucial in respect of dealing with these types of crime.

The European Union (EU), as a supranational body whose laws take precedence over domestic legislation, has had a considerable effect on criminal law and practice in the UK and Ireland.[25] For instance, money laundering legislation was modified to ensure adherence to a number of EU Directives. Therefore, although these provisions may illustrate an innovative turn in adaptations to organised crime, these alterations have not been initiated by the Irish and UK States alone but implement compulsory pan-European measures. Moreover, the signing and ratification by Ireland and the UK of international measures such as the United Nations Convention Against Illicit Traffic in Narcotic Drugs and Psychotropic Substances[26] and the United Nations Convention Against Transnational Organized Crime[27] may influence the measures used to address organised criminality. As regards international law and conventions, both the UK and Ireland have dualist systems, which require the express translation of international measures into domestic law. Despite these binding and persuasive authorities, the primary impetus for legislative change remains local, and so the emphasis remains on national laws, though reference is made to EU and international measures.

---

[24] P Van Duyne, *Organized Crime in Europe* (New York, Nova Science Publishers, 1996).

[25] European Communities Act 1972. See Bunreacht na hÉireann, Art 29.4.3°, as inserted by the Third Amendment to the Constitution Act 1972.

[26] UN Convention Against Illicit Traffic in Narcotic Drugs and Psychotropic Substances, GA Res 47/97, 47 UN GAOR Supp (no 49) at 179, UN Doc A/47/49 (1992).

[27] UN Convention Against Transnational Organized Crime, GA Res 25, annex I, UN GAOR, 55th Sess, Supp no 49, at 44, UN Doc A/45/49 (vol I) (2001).

Moreover, the 'Europeanisation' of human rights, in particular in the context of crime control,[28] is significant for this project. The Human Rights Act 1998 made the rights protected by the European Convention on Human Rights (the ECHR), such as the rights to a fair trial, to liberty and to privacy, enforceable under national law in the United Kingdom, thereby facilitating challenge to acts of public authorities or to legislation in domestic courts on the ground that they infringe Convention rights. The courts may then make a 'declaration of incompatibility' if satisfied that legislation conflicts with a right under the ECHR.[29] In this dialogic approach,[30] Parliament has the ability to remedy the situation if it chooses to do so, or a Minister may make a remedial order to remove the incompatibility.[31] This maintains parliamentary sovereignty as the defining principle of the UK Constitution.[32]

As noted, the primary protective document for rights in Ireland is the Constitution, *Bunreacht na hÉireann*, which safeguards due process rights,[33] the right to liberty, equality,[34] and so on. In addition, the European Convention on Human Rights Act 2003, which incorporated the ECHR into Irish law, requires courts to interpret and apply the law, as far as is possible, in a manner compatible with the Irish State's obligations under the ECHR,[35] and organs of the State must perform their functions in a manner compatible with the ECHR unless there is a domestic law stating that this is not required.[36] Akin to the situation in the UK, the Irish courts may make 'a declaration of incompatibility' and there is no onus on the legislature or executive to react to this declaration.[37] While it may be argued that constitutional safeguards in Ireland mean that the ECHR does little in terms of supplementing the rights of the accused or the offender, it seems more accurate to say that in fact the Convention's incorporation enhances rights in the criminal process, in particular in the context of procedural rights,[38] since certain ECHR cases may involve a more extensive protection of individual rights than that promulgated by the Irish courts.[39]

---

[28] S Kilcommins and B Vaughan, *Terrorism, Rights and the Rule of Law: Negotiating State Justice in Ireland* (Cullompton, Willan Publishing, 2007).

[29] Human Rights Act 1998, s 4.

[30] See T Hickman, 'Constitutional Dialogue, Constitutional Theories and the HRA 1998' (2005) *PL* 206.

[31] s 10(2).

[32] J Goldsworthy, *The Sovereignty of Parliament: History and Philosophy* (Oxford, Clarendon Press, 1999); M Elliott, 'United Kingdom: Parliamentary Sovereignty under Pressure' (2004) 2 *International Journal of Constitutional Law* 545.

[33] Art 38.1 of Bunreacht na hÉireann provides that 'no person shall be tried on any criminal charge save in due course of law'.

[34] Art 40.

[35] s 2.

[36] s 3(1).

[37] European Convention on Human Rights 2003, Art 5.

[38] I Bacik, 'Criminal Law' in U Kilkelly (ed), *ECHR and Irish Law* (London, Jordans, 2004) 151.

[39] See, eg *Salduz v Turkey* (2009) 49 EHRR 19 regarding the right of access to a lawyer during pre-trial detention.

Undoubtedly, the threats posed by organised crime groups are not limited to and do not derive from a single jurisdiction, and arguably few legal responses may be regarded as truly local; nonetheless the focus here is on domestic law as affected by international trends and instruments, rather than constituting an international study, of either the laws or the actors, as such.[40] Whilst remaining cognisant of and incorporating consideration of international measures and transnational organised crime itself, this book examines principally the national definitions of organised crime and constituent offences, and advances a doctrinal and theoretical critique of the salient aspects of domestic criminal law, the laws of evidence, and financial regulations. Granted, the interaction between domestic and supranational law is important, however most of the responses to organised crime remain prompted by local concerns and enacted by domestic legal measures. So, the analysis here centres primarily on the substance and effect of domestic legislative and judicial reactions to organised crime in the UK and Ireland.

IV. The Theoretical Lens

Appraising the legal reactions to organised crime throughout the UK and Ireland indicates that these often map onto wider penological and criminal justice trends. Essentially, what appears to be occurring is the prioritisation of the demands of security and the resolution of crime, and the associated erosion of due process rights. This book adopts a rights' oriented perspective that is critical of many legal shifts which are animated by the imperative of crime control to the undue detriment of due process protections. Though there is no one logic to such developments in relation to organised crime, central overarching themes which contribute to this shift in the ethos of policy-making include the centrality of public protection, the aversion towards risk, the generation of a crisis discourse, and the diversification in crime control which involves the participation or 'responsibilisation' of a range of actors other than State agencies. Even so, failure to use the laws enacted, and application of such laws in a piecemeal or uncoordinated manner, suggests that ultimately the expressive aspects of the reactions to organised crime may be of more significance than their practical effect.

The legal measures used to address organised crime often embody a tension between the judicial and legislative arms of the State in terms of the competing demands of criminal justice. Judicial oversight may mitigate the momentum towards a pragmatic and results-oriented model of criminal justice in the drive to prevent and punish organised crime, by placing more stress on the significance of

---

[40] See, eg JD McClean, *Transnational Organized Crime: A Commentary on the UN Convention and its Protocols* (Oxford, Oxford University Press, 2007); A Edwards and P Gill (eds), *Transnational Organised Crime Perspectives on Global Security* (London, Routledge, 2003); T Obokata, *Transnational Organised Crime in International Law* (Oxford, Hart, 2010).

due process. Nonetheless, superior courts in the UK and Ireland have given constitutional or conventional imprimatur to other such provisions, indicating that a dichotomous interpretation, in which the judiciary act as enforcers and protectors of rights when compared with an authoritarian legislature, is unduly simplistic.

V. Structural Outline

This book presents a comparative exploration of the legal measures adopted across a number of jurisdictions to counter the threat of organised criminality, and critiques the diminishing concern for due process values in the creation of such legislation. Rather than adopting a criminological focus on the actors or an in-depth appraisal of particular aspects of methods of dealing with organised crime, this work assesses and then situates these laws as part of wider trends in the criminal justice realm. A distinctive contextualised approach is undertaken, firmly grounded in penological and criminal justice theory so as to enrich the doctrinal legal analysis. It identifies the different motivations and principles of the various agencies and institutions involved in dealing with organised crime and how this impacts on the construction and application of the law.

Before the doctrinal evaluation is undertaken, Chapters two and three unpack key definitional issues and theoretical propositions. Chapter two explores the scholarly, political and legal attempts to define organised crime, as a concept which may depict a type of criminality, may denote specific crimes, and may involve certain actors. It considers the gravity of the threat, and the extent to which this can be measured, given the ineluctable definitional problems. In a substantive sense, the criminalisation of organised crime itself, as well as constitutive crimes, is analysed, as are the several of the new agencies which have been established as a result.

Chapter three sets up the theoretical framework which underpins the doctrinal analysis in subsequent chapters. Legal reactions to organised crime exemplify the perceived conflict of ideologies and imperatives in criminal justice, with security being portrayed as compromised by undue concern about due process rights. The emphasis on public protection, the centrality of risk, the belief that the threat of organised crime constitutes a state of emergency, and the adaptations required by the nature and gravity of the problem explain the form and substance of the legislation introduced. This chapter then examines the dialogue between the arms of the State whereby the judiciary sometimes finds itself in opposition to policy makers and legislators, and motivated by conflicting concerns.

Chapters four to seven constitute the doctrinal analysis of the laws used to address organised crime in the UK and Ireland, informed by and drawing on the theoretical insights examined in chapter three. The laws and policies adopted to address organised crime are described and appraised legally and normatively, and then evaluated through a theoretical lens. Throughout, reference is made to the theoretical arguments which each initiative tends to support: for example, one legislative development might demonstrate the move towards risk while another might temper this potential with a greater emphasis on due process values. Moreover, the diverging perspectives and animating rationales of the different players and institutions involved will be noted, with the courts being much more concerned with due process than any other State institution.

Chapter four focuses on the pre-trial process, that is, the investigation of organised crime. This chapter explores the growing use of access and disclosure orders, suspicious activity reports, surveillance of various sorts, and controlled deliveries of illicit goods, and the effect that these have on investigative norms and practices. In addition, the extension of detention periods and the amendment of rules of interrogation are considered.

Chapter five concerns the prosecution of organised crime, and the changes that have been made to the criminal trial. Firstly, procedural law changes are examined, including the admissibility of surveillance evidence and accomplice testimony. This chapter also examines the range of measures employed to protect jurors and witnesses, such as non-jury trials, anonymous juries and witnesses, protective measures for witnesses, the use of prior inconsistent evidence, and witness protection programmes.

Chapter six examines the post-conviction stage of the criminal process and the means of punishing organised crime. It assesses the growing reliance on presumptive minimum sentences for certain quintessential organised crimes and the imposition of indeterminate sentences. The reduction of sentences in return for assistance is also examined. Various post-conviction orders are explored, such as confiscating or forfeiting property upon conviction, limitations on travel and registration requirements.

Chapter seven moves the analysis beyond the criminal process into the civil context, and focuses primarily on asset recovery. The historical predecessors for this radical approach are considered, as are the challenges posed to its legitimacy, and the contrasting success of the schemes that are in place across the UK and Ireland. Chapter eight maintains the focus outside the criminal process per se by considering the use of revenue powers and the taxing of organised crime.

The dominant narrative on organised crime is that the existing legal framework is not sufficient. The book concludes by reiterating scepticism regarding this depiction, and suggests that the implementation rather than construction or structure of the laws is the critical factor in reacting effectively to organised criminality. Given the threat posed to due process rights, the book closes with a call for caution in the introduction and expansion of legal responses to organised crime.

2

Organised Crime: Defining, Measuring and Criminalising the Problem

I. Introduction

Political discourse across the UK and Ireland emphasises the 'scourge'[1] of organised crime that 'blights'[2] communities. This is no mere rhetorical flourish, as in seeking to address this particular type of crime, legal changes are wrought, new agencies are established, and considerable resources are spent. Defining what organised crime is, and is not, is critical to determine firstly the extent of the problem, and then to ascertain if such new tactics are warranted. Policy documents and debates on proposed legislation adopt a range of terminology in referring to this type of criminality, from 'organised crime', 'organised criminals', 'criminal organisations', through to 'gangland crime'. Notwithstanding their common use in the political sphere, such terms are problematic in an analytical and legal sense, given the fluidity of their meanings and connotations. The remit of the terms is taken as given, or sometimes as unimportant, by policy makers and legislators in the UK and Ireland, and they are used to describe certain crimes, suspects and offenders, and, critically for present purposes, to justify the introduction of often radical, punitive and draconian legal provisions. Thus, this chapter seeks to determine if using the term 'organised crime', either as a rhetorical device or as a basis for policy development, is dubious.

This chapter first deals with the concept and definitional parameters of organised crime, and considers the extent of the phenomenon within the UK and Ireland. It then examines the criminalisation of organised crime as an enterprise in itself.[3] In addition to the widespread adoption of such terms in a policy sense, Scotland and Ireland have introduced statutory definitions on which are predicated offences such as directing organised crime, and failing to report organised crime. The problems in respect of these statutory measures are outlined, and con-

---

[1] Stage 1 of the Criminal Justice and Licensing (Scotland) Bill, Scottish Parliament, 26 November 2009, col 21574 per Justice Secretary Kenny MacAskill.
[2] Serious Organised Crime Debate, Scottish Parliament, 11 March 2010, col 24544 per Justice Secretary Kenny MacAskill; Home Office, *One Step Ahead: A 21st Century Strategy to Defeat Organised Crime* (Cm 6167, 2004) (London, The Stationery Office) 9.
[3] Such an approach was advocated by the Home Office, n 2, 43.

sideration is given to whether the existing law across the UK and Ireland relating to conspiracy is adequate and whether the new provisions are likely to be effective. In doing so, the rationales of the Scottish and Irish legislatures in particular will be unpacked, and an attempt made to conceptualise such political action. Then, a range of quintessential organised crimes, such as drug trafficking and firearms offences, is explored. The chapter concludes with an appraisal of the new agencies established to deal with organised crime specifically, and whose mandates often centre on this term.

II. Defining Organised Crime

This section attempts to tease out what is meant by, and what is excluded from, the term 'organised crime', which has been described as provoking an 'allergic reaction' in some scholars.[4] Despite its currency and popular use, there is no 'agreed-upon definition' of organised crime;[5] in fact many variants have been proposed in the academic, legal and political sense. Essentially, 'organised crime' may denote specific structures or organisations that are involved in criminality; the provision of illegal goods or services; or a certain type of crime which meets a given level of gravity.[6] In other words, the term may refer to both the 'who' and the 'what' of organised crime.[7]

The dominant conceptualisation of organised crime in the mid-twentieth century derived from Cressey's work on the Mafia,[8] which depicted formal command structures, internal stratification, and unified norms, symbols and collective identity.[9] Cressey's consultation by the US President's Commission Task Force on Organized Crime contributed to the generation of the American (and now global) popular perception of organised crime as a centralised criminal organisation (predominantly comprising persons with Italian roots) involved in profitable

---

[4] M Felson, *The Ecosystem for Organized Crime,* HEUNI Paper No 26 (Helsinki, European Institute for Crime Prevention and Control, 2006) 7 n 4.

[5] P Van Duyne, 'The Phantom and Threat of Organized Crime' (1996) 24 *Crime, Law and Social Change* 341, 343. See also F Varese, 'What is Organized Crime?' in F Varese (ed), *Organized Crime: Critical Concepts in Criminology* (London, Routledge, 2010) 1–33; FE Hagan, 'The Organized Crime Continuum: A Further Specification of a New Conceptual Model' (1983) 8 *Criminal Justice Review* 52; and Frank E Hagan, '"Organized Crime" and "organized crime": Indeterminate Problems of Definition' (2006) 9 *Trends in Organized Crime* 127.

[6] See L Paoli and C Fijnaut, 'Organised Crime and its Control Policies' (2006) 14 *European Journal of Crime, Criminal Law and Criminal Justice* 307, 308; N Hamilton-Smith and S Mackenzie, 'The Geometry of Shadows: A Critical Review of Organised Crime Risk Assessments' (2010) 20 *Policing and Society* 257, 261.

[7] M Woodiwiss, 'Organized Crime – The Dumbing of Discourse' (2000) vol 3 *British Criminology Conference: Selected Proceedings* (Liverpool, July 1999) 3–4.

[8] D Cressey, *Theft of the Nation: The Structure and Operations of Organized Crime in America* (New York, Harper, 1969) 72.

[9] See L Paoli, *Mafia Brotherhoods: Organized Crime, Italian Style* (Cary, NC, Oxford University Press, 2003) 4, 21, 220.

illegal markets.[10] Building on this understanding, the Omnibus Crime Control and Safe Streets Act of 1968 in the United States defined organised crime as 'the unlawful activities of the members of a highly organized, disciplined association engaged in supplying illegal goods and services, including but not limited to gambling, prostitution, loan sharking, narcotics, labor racketeering, and other unlawful activities of members of organizations'. Such a hierarchical interpretation of the structure of the groups involved is reiterated in the work of Abadinsky, amongst others, who also sees organised crime as involving a limited or exclusive membership and as being governed by explicit rules and regulations.[11]

Despite the common depiction of organised crime as comprising highly coordinated criminal organisations, this socially constructed image[12] is not borne out in empirical studies, either of Mafia groups like Cosa Nostra, the 'Ndrangheta and the Camorra, or of criminal activities in other Western countries, which are usually carried out by 'often ephemeral enterprises'.[13] On this basis, much scholarship indicates a shift in focus toward the illegality of the activities or enterprise undertaken, rather than or in addition to the nature and structure of the group responsible.[14] Drawing on this interpretation and methodology, Maltz proposed a typology in which organised crime includes four characteristics: violence, corruption, continuity, and variety in the types of criminality engaged in,[15] and these aspects have been reiterated by other scholars.[16] The provision of 'illicit goods that are in public demand' is stressed by Hagan,[17] while Levi speaks of profitable crimes that need organising, thus leading to a preference for 'the connotations of the verb "organizing crime"' to that of the noun organised crime.[18]

A return to the 'who' of organised crime in certain respects is proposed by Finckenauer, who argues that organised crime can only be committed by a criminal organisation.[19] He distinguishes between a criminal network which is a group working together to carry out a crime, and a criminal organisation, which is an advanced network whose members go beyond a single criminal opportunity to organise themselves to continue to commit crimes and view themselves as a criminal organisation, and which has durability, reputation and continuity. For Finckenauer,

---

[10] ibid 222.

[11] H Abadinsky, *Organized Crime* (9th edn) (Belmont, CA, Wadsworth, 2010) 3.

[12] See M Levi, 'The Organization of Serious Crimes for Gain' in M Maguire, R Morgan and R Reiner (eds), *The Oxford Handbook of Criminology* (5th edn) (Oxford, Oxford University Press, 2012).

[13] Paoli, n 9, 224; D Hobbs, 'Going Down the Glocal: The Local Context of Organised Crime' (1998) 37 *The Howard Journal of Criminal Justice* 407, 415.

[14] A Block and W Chambliss, *Organising Crime* (New York, Elsevier, 1981) 13; J Albini, *The American Mafia: Genesis of a Legend* (New York, Appleton-Century-Crofts, 1971); AK Cohen, 'The Concept of Criminal Organisation' (1977) 17 *British Journal of Criminology* 97, 98.

[15] M Maltz, 'On Defining "Organized Crime": The Development of a Definition and a Typology' (1976) 22 *Crime and Delinquency* 338.

[16] Abadinsky, n 11; FE Hagan, *Crime Types and Criminals* (Thousand Oaks, CA, Sage, 2010) 300; JO Finckenauer, 'Problems of Definition: What is Organized Crime?' (2005) 8 *Trends in Organized Crime* 63, 81.

[17] Hagan, n 16, 300.

[18] Levi, n 12, 597.

[19] Finckenauer, n 16, 75.

although some crimes may be extremely complex and highly organised in their commission, unless they are committed by criminal organisations they are not organised crime.[20] This binary depiction overlooks the fact that organised crime is better regarded as involving a spectrum of organisation.

Goldstock *et al* recognised that words are tools that are defined differently depending on the purpose for which they are designed to be used, and so 'organised crime' is thought of conceptually in at least three ways, as an enterprise, a syndicate or a venture. In the context of organised crime, an enterprise is a criminal group that provides on a regular basis either illicit goods or services or licit goods and services through illicit means (a criminal firm or business organisation); a syndicate is a criminal group that regulates relations between various enterprises; and may act as a cartel, a legislature, arbitrator and protector; while a venture is a criminal episode, usually conducted for profit by a group, and this qualifies as organised crime when members of the venture have ties to a syndicate.[21]

While some organised crime groups may replace or usurp the government and governance of a geographical area, this is not a central identifying or necessary feature. The evasion or neutering of State control and the corruption of officials may assist in the criminal enterprise; nonetheless the generation of profit and the control of illicit markets is the primary focus for organised crime rather than any grasping of power for political ends. This absence of ideology was focused on by Abadinsky and Finckenauer,[22] thereby ostensibly distinguishing organised crime from paramilitary or terrorist groups and activities. Like organised crime, the definition of terrorism remains elusive; nonetheless, it centres on violence motivated by political, ideological, or philosophical considerations, aimed at civilians so as to generate fear and cause damage, and thereby to coerce a government or organisation to act in a particular manner.[23] These aspects demarcate terrorism from organised crime. However, this distinction is becoming less clear, and increasingly there is a nexus in terms of the personnel involved, with the provision of illegal arms from one to the other, and the generation of funds for the latter through the sale of illegal goods and services. For example, terrorist groups may use drug smuggling to fund political campaigns; such 'narco-terrorism' is becoming more prevalent and ranges from facilitation to involvement in the actual trafficking itself.[24] Nonetheless, for organised crime the only true ideology or motivation is profit through the creation and monopoly of illicit markets.

Organised crime is different to crime committed by 'gangs'.[25] Though the terms organised crime, gangs and gangland are often used interchangeably in public

[20] ibid, 76.
[21] R Goldstock, GR Blakey and CH Rogovin, *Rackets Bureaus: The Investigation and Prosecution of Organized Crime* (Washington DC, LEAA, 1978).
[22] Finckenauer, n 16, 65.
[23] A Cassese, *International Criminal Law* (2nd edn) (Oxford, Oxford University Press, 2008) 167.
[24] Abadinsky, n 11, 6; T Makarenko, 'The Crime-Terror Continuum: Tracing the Interplay Between Transnational Organised Crime and Terrorism' (2004) 6 *Global Crime* 129.
[25] See A Wright, *Organised Crime* (Cullompton, Willan, 2006) 34ff.

and political debate in the UK and Ireland, analytically and practically one must distinguish between gangs and what could be called 'traditional organised crime groups'.[26] A gang has been described as an 'age-graded peer group that exhibits some permanence, engages in criminal activity and has symbolic representation of membership';[27] as a 'self-formed group, united by mutual interests, that controls a particular territory, facility, or enterprise; uses symbols in communications; and is collectively involved in crime';[28] or as an 'interstitial group originally formed spontaneously, and then integrated through conflict'.[29] Despite common depictions, gangs are not composed necessarily of teenagers or juveniles,[30] so it is not the age profile of the participants that differentiates them from organised criminals. Moreover, gangs also involve continuity, as do organised crime groups. Rather, it is the level of criminality, the absence of a systematic approach to provision of illegal services, and the absence of corruption of either officials or the administration of justice that distinguishes gangs from organised crime. There is no definite linkage between such entities, nor is there an inevitability that the former will develop or mutate into the latter.[31]

In addition, the terms 'gangland violence' and 'gangland crime' are used increasingly in political and popular discourse in the UK and Ireland.[32] Although the phrase has no legal basis, it imparts a certain moral opprobrium, usually regarding both the perpetrator and the victim, as well as the social context in which such behaviour occurs, and encapsulates the view of organised crime as occupying an 'underworld' and being perpetrated by certain types or classes of people only. Reference to 'gangland' killings in the media and political spheres denotes the assassination of persons suspected of involvement in organised crimes such as drug trafficking, usually occurring in certain geographical and socio-economic areas, while 'gangland crime' in general encompasses drug trafficking and other such organised criminality. Moreover, 'gangland' offences are seen to be carried out by certain types of people, generally young men from economically deprived areas, who are euphemistically referred to as 'known to the police',[33] or

---

[26] ibid, 39. SH Decker and B van Winkle, *Life in the Gang: Family, Friends, and Violence* (Cambridge, Cambridge University Press, 1997) ch 1.

[27] Decker and van Winkle, n 26, 31.

[28] GD Curry and SH Decker, *Confronting Gangs: Crime and Community* (Los Angeles, CA, Roxbury, 1998).

[29] FM Thrasher, *The Gang: A Study of 1,313 gangs in Chicago* (Chicago, University of Chicago Press, 1927).

[30] ibid; Decker and van Winkle, n 26, ch 1.

[31] SH Decker, T Bynum and D Weisel, 'A Tale of Two Cities: Gangs as Organized Crime Groups' (1998) 15 *Justice Quarterly* 395.

[32] eg see Dáil Debates, vol 515, col 1355 (7 March 2000) per Mr Gregory, Mr O'Donoghue and Mr Higgins; Dáil Debates, vol 519, col 657 (17 May 2000) per Mr Howlin, Dáil Debates, vol 519, col 658 (17 May 2000) per Minister for Justice, Mr O'Donoghue; and Dáil Debates, vol 629, col 1667ff, col 1672 per Mr Costello and col 1674 per Mr O'Keeffe (14 December 2006); Dáil Debates, vol 681 col 373 (29 April 2009) per Minister of State at the Department of Foreign Affairs, Mr Power.

[33] See, eg 'London Riots: Dead Man Mark Duggan was a Known Gangster who Lived by the Gun', *The Telegraph*, 8 August 2011; '"Card Game" Money is Seized', *The Herald*, 8 December 2011.

in Ireland 'known to the Gardaí'.[34] Given its rhetorical power, reference by the media to 'gangland' crime is not surprising;[35] what is more noteworthy is the seepage of this phrase into official policy discourse. A previous and particularly proactive Minister for Justice in Ireland noted that the widely-used term 'gangland killing' does not map onto police classifications;[36] nevertheless he adopted and used such an expression in discussing and justifying legislative development.[37] This is echoed in parliamentary debates in the UK,[38] and various governmental reports in the UK and Ireland have adopted the suspect, morally loaded and indefinable term 'gangland'.[39]

As well as being distinct from 'gang' crime, it is arguable that organised crime may also be distinguished from 'white collar' crime. This descriptor was coined by Sutherland, and denotes the 'criminal behavior of business and professional men' who are 'respectable or at least respected', where such acts occur in the course of their business or profession.[40] White collar crime is an 'abuse of a legitimate occupational role which is regulated by law',[41] and thus it appears that the status or position of the actor involved demarcates this from organised crime. However, as Ruggiero has argued, differentiating between legitimate and illegitimate businesses is difficult; corporate, white collar and organised crime are linked inextricably and cannot be analysed separately.[42] Indeed, the potential provision of illegal services and the facilitation of criminality by lawyers and accountants illustrates that there is no clear-cut boundary between white collar crime and organised crime. To this end, Woodiwiss calls for a re-focus not on 'crime bosses' as currently construed, but on government officials and professional interests in the

---

[34] In *People (DPP) v Allen* [2003] 4 IR 295, 297 the trial judge excluded evidence that could influence the jury 'to believe that the accused was, in the well known phrase, known to the Gardaí and therefore, by inference, that he had a criminal record'.

[35] See, eg 'Manchester Launches Gangland Manhunt after Prison Van Raid', *The Independent*, 19 July 2011; '"Gangland Killing" Near London Funeral', *The Guardian*, 3 November 2011; 'Police Elite Targeting Gangland Criminals', *STV*, 23 June 2010; also see www.glasgowgangland.com.

[36] Dáil Debates, vol 518, col 388 (13 April 2000) per Minister for Justice, Mr McDowell.

[37] Dáil Debates, vol 629, col 1677 (14 December 2006) per Minister for Justice, Mr McDowell; Department of Justice, Equality and Law Reform Press Release, 'McDowell Publishes Draft Legislation to Counter Gangland Crime', 19 December 2006.

[38] HC Deb 4 December 2002, vol 395, col 1004; HL Deb 29 January 2003, vol 398, col GC191; HL Deb 26 October 2009, vol 713, col 1018. Scottish Parliament, Thursday 8 March 2007 (S2F-2773); Scottish Parliament, Thursday 14 January 2010 (S3F-2128).

[39] See, eg Houses of the Oireachtas Joint Committee on Justice, Equality, Defence and Women's Rights, *Report on a Review of the Criminal Justice System* (Office of the Houses of the Oireachtas, Dublin, 2004); HM Inspectorate of Constabulary, *Guns, Community and Police HMIC Thematic Inspection into the Criminal Use of Firearms* (HM Inspectorate of Constabulary, London, 2004).

[40] E Sutherland, 'White-Collar Criminality' (1940) 5 *American Sociological Review* 1, 1–2, see also D Nelken (ed), *White Collar Crime* (Aldershot, Dartmouth Pub Co, 1994).

[41] H Croall, *White Collar Crime: Criminal Justice and Criminology* (Buckingham, Open University Press, 1992) 9; H Croall, *Understanding White Collar Crime* (Buckingham, Open University Press, 2001) 6.

[42] V Ruggiero, *Organized and Corporate Crime in Europe: Offers that Can't be Refused* (Aldershot, Dartmouth, 1996); J Lea, *Crime and Modernity* (London, Sage, 2002) 144–46.

context of research on organised crime.[43] Despite conceptual and definitional ambiguity, and certain irrefutable or potential overlap in terms of actors and activities, here it is suggested that organised crime ultimately may be distinguished from white collar crime by virtue of the use or threat of violence that underpins the provision of illegal goods or services.[44]

Thus, some common themes have been established in this definitional analysis: organised crime may be conceived as distinct from terrorism, gang crime and white collar crime, though there may be overlap both in terms of the participants and the relevant criminal acts. In addition, organised crime entails a level of systematic provision of illegal goods or services by a group, which may avail of corrupt linkage and usually uses or threatens violence. Nevertheless, it may be necessary to take a case-by-case approach in delineating what is meant by organised crime(s). Reuter sees as artificial a dichotomous division between organised and non-organised crime and the actors involved,[45] and to this end Hagan proposes a continuum conceptualisation of organised crime, in which the question is asked, 'To what extent does this group and/or its operations resemble crime?'.[46] This underlines the ambiguity and contested nature of the concept of organised crime, and the difficulty in determining which acts and actors fall within its scope.

Drawing on the above scholarship to a greater and lesser extent, an attempt has been made across the UK and Ireland to define organised crime for both public policy purposes and legal ends. In searching for a political and a legal definition of organised crime in the UK and Ireland, policy makers have had to be cognisant of the fact that there is little evidence that criminal groups in these jurisdictions possess a hierarchical structure. In truth, it can be argued that much of what is conceived of as organised crime in the UK and Ireland is in fact 'disorganized',[47] or comprises groups assembled on a relatively short-term basis for specific projects from a broader pool of professional criminals in a particular region.[48] This poses problems in terms of determining the extent of the phenomenon as well as the tactics required to address such groups. Whereas the prosecution and punishment of the leadership of Mafia groups, as well as lower ranking 'soldiers' proved effective in New York, for example,[49] the more nebulous nature and floating arrangements of modern organised crime groups pose difficulties in terms of effective State responses.

Organised crime does not exercise a systematic influence over the legal economy or the political system in Ireland or the UK,[50] and as Levi notes, highly organised

---

[43] M Woodiwiss, *Gangster Capitalism: The United States and the Globalization of Organized Crime* (London, Constable, 2005).

[44] See Wright, n 25, 63.

[45] P Reuter, *Disorganized Crime – The Economics of the Visible Hand* (Cambridge, MA, MIT Press, 1983).

[46] Hagan, 'The Organized Crime Continuum', n 6, 52.

[47] Reuter, n 45.

[48] Levi, n 12, 604.

[49] See J Jacobs with C Panarella and J Worthington, *Busting the Mob United States v Cosa Nostra* (New York, New York University Press, 1994).

[50] Paoli and Fijnaut, n 6, 312.

crime is unlikely to flourish where it is hard to develop corrupt alliances between criminal justice officials, politicians and supplies of illegal commodities.[51] At one time, in both Italy and the United States Mafia groups co-existed with and co-opted the activity of State institutions, meeting community approbation and in some instances addressing unmet needs relating to governance and the provision of security or operating as alternative modes of justice.[52] This provision of quasi-governmental functions requires the 'delegitimisation' of such groups,[53] and this pattern has more parallels with the role of paramilitaries in Northern Ireland than the type of organised crime in the UK and Ireland. There is no indication of organised criminals controlling elections, nor of political alliances protecting such actors. Nevertheless, there appears to be evidence that some criminal groups have corrupted local business structures, if not policy-making organs, and that they may stymie the administration of justice by means of subtle or other threats to witnesses.[54] Overall, there is no endemic threat to the rule of law in Ireland and the UK, and there is no evidence of the systematic intimidation or corruption of the judiciary or the prosecution, such as those that crippled the attempt to address organised crime in parts of the United States in the early twentieth century.[55]

No statutory definition of organised crime exists in the United Kingdom or Ireland. Rather, entities like the Home Office, the Serious Organised Crime Agency and the Northern Ireland Office adopt the definition of organised crime from the National Criminal Intelligence Service as 'those involved, normally working with others, in continuing serious criminal activities for substantial profit, whether based in the UK or elsewhere'.[56] The Home Office states that

> [o]rganised crime involves individuals, normally working with others, with the capacity and capability to commit serious crime on a continuing basis, which includes elements of planning, control and coordination, and benefits those involved. The motivation is often, but not always, financial gain.[57]

So, organised crime in this context refers to people (the 'who'), although they need to be involved in certain types of acts (the 'what'). The Home Office has admitted that a 'spectrum of organisation' exists for criminal groups, and echoes Hagan's continuum model by stating that 'no clear cut-off point' exists for determining whether any group should be categorised as being involved in organised crime,[58] and that many organised criminal groups are loose networks of criminals

---

[51] M Levi, 'Policing Fraud and Organised Crime' in T Newburn (ed), *Handbook of Policing* (2nd edn) (Cullompton, Willan, 2008) 522.

[52] See J Landesco, *Organized Crime in Chicago* (Chicago, University of Chicago Press, 1968) ch VIII.

[53] R Goldstock, *Organised Crime in Northern Ireland: A Report for the Secretary of State* (Belfast, Northern Ireland Office, 2004) 6; Paoli, n 9, 212.

[54] Europol, *OCTA 2009: EU Organised Crime Threat Assessment* (Netherlands, European Police Office, 2009) para 5.6.

[55] See Landesco, n 52.

[56] Home Office, n 2, para 1.1; www.soca.gov.uk/threats/organised-crime-groups.

[57] Home Office, *Local to Global: Reducing the Risk from Organised Crime* (London, Home Office, 2011) 5.

[58] Home Office, n 2, para 1.1.

who come together for the duration of a particular criminal activity.[59] The Department of Justice in Ireland states that organised crime is 'an element of criminal activity carried out by criminal organisations that have as their main purpose the commission of one or more serious offences in order to obtain, directly or indirectly, financial or other material benefits', and thereby implicitly follows Finckenauer.[60] Thus, the participation of a criminal organisation is crucial to the understanding of organised crime in Ireland. Violence or its threat is not a prerequisite in England, Wales, Northern Ireland or Ireland, although as the Northern Ireland Office notes,[61] often it can be involved. Neither is there any mention of corruption, nor of an absence or otherwise of ideology.

Strictly speaking, organised crime is not defined in a statutory sense in Scotland – rather 'serious organised crime' is, in the Criminal Justice and Licensing (Scotland) Act 2010.[62] This is crime involving two or more persons acting together for the principal purpose of committing or conspiring to commit a serious offence or a series of such, where 'serious offence' means an indictable offence committed with the intention of obtaining a material benefit, or an act or threat of violence made with the intention of obtaining such benefit in future.[63] This expansive definition echoes that put forward in a 2009 Scottish Government policy document, although there serious organised crime needed to involve 'control, planning and use of specialist resources'.[64]

Overall, whether the definition of organised crime is a policy one or legally constructed, the approach across the UK and Ireland is to employ a broad descriptor encompassing a range of actions and agents. These definitions are both over- and under-inclusive, by being so loosely defined as to cover the acts of a mere two people such as in Scotland, while concurrently omitting certain corporate crimes. Taken as a whole, the common threads are the gravity of the offences, the group nature of perpetration, and the motivating notion of profit or benefit.

III. The Extent of the Problem

In spite of the adoption of the term 'organised crime' in policy documents across the UK and Ireland and in legislation in Scotland, one might believe that the evident

---

[59] Home Office, *Extending Our Reach: A Comprehensive Approach to Tackling Serious Organised Crime* (London, Home Office, 2009) 7.

[60] www.inis.gov.ie/en/JELR/Pages/Organised_crime.

[61] www.octf.gov.uk/Organised-Crime-in-Northern-Ireland.aspx.

[62] Stelfox refers to the seriousness of organised crime in speaking of the 'lower levels of organised crime', which denotes activity which would normally be investigated at the local or force level, due to the criminal histories of those involved, the perceived seriousness of the offences and their scale and geographical impact. P Stelfox, 'Policing Lower Levels of Organised Crime in England and Wales' (1998) 37 *The Howard Journal of Criminal Justice* 393, 394.

[63] s 28(3).

[64] Scottish Government, *Letting Our Communities Flourish: A Strategy for Tackling Serious Organised Crime in Scotland* (Edinburgh, Scottish Government, 2009) para 6.

difficulties in description and definition lead to an inescapable problem in determining its level. Yet, definitional ambiguities and complications have not inhibited statements about the extent of the problem;[65] this is called a 'double track' approach by Paoli and Fijnaut, whereby the scale and threat of organised crime is emphasised while simultaneously loose and minimal definitions with no or few strict criteria in terms of number of members and group structure are adopted.[66] Due to these definitional problems, organised crime 'threat assessments' are carried out annually in the UK and EU[67] and have been depicted as 'expressionistic'.[68] Nevertheless, Europol, for example, did not shirk in speaking of the presence in Ireland and the UK of organised crime groups who can and intend to use systematic violence or intimidation against local societies to ensure non-occasional compliance or avoid interferences or at least to interfere with law enforcement and judicial processes by means of corruptive influence or violence/intimidation.[69]

The Serious Organised Crime Agency emphasises that the overall threat to the UK from organised crime is high, and that the economic and social costs of organised crime, including the costs of combating it, are 'upwards of GBP 20 billion a year'.[70] The Home Office estimates the cost to be between 20–40 billion, and that there are approximately 6,000 organised crime groups targeting the UK involving an estimated 38,000 individuals.[71] This is despite the fact that to date no-one has been able to pinpoint exactly what is or is not organised crime. In the face of the inherent methodological flaws of threat assessments, the Scottish Government estimates that there are a minimum of 350 serious organised crime groups operating in Scotland,[72] and the Serious Organised Crime Group Mapping Project presented 'objective evidence' that 367 serious organised crime groups, comprising precisely 4,066 individuals, were operating in Scotland.[73] In contrast, and in a remarkably candid exchange, a previous Minister for Justice in Ireland admitted that while two categories of organised crime groups could be identified in the jurisdiction (one of which comprises well-established and tightly structured groups involved in transnational crimes, the other with less cohesive group structures involved in domestic criminality), it is not possible to provide 'an accurate and definitive number' of the various groups operating there because of their fluid nature.[74]

---

[65] See Levi, n 12, 601.

[66] Paoli and Fijnaut, n 6, 312.

[67] See Serious Organised Crime Agency, *The United Kingdom Threat Assessment of Serious Organised Crime 2009/10* (London, Serious Organised Crime Agency, 2010) key judgments, para 1.

[68] PC van Duyne and M van Dijck, 'Assessing Organised Crime: The Sad State of an Impossible Art' in F Bovenkerk and M Levi, *The Organized Crime Community: Essays in Honor of Alan A Block* (New York, Springer, 2006) ch 7, 102. See Hamilton-Smith and Mackenzie, n 6.

[69] Europol, n 54.

[70] Serious and Organised Crime Agency, *Suspicious Activity Reports Regime Annual Report 2010* (London, Serious and Organised Crime Agency, 2010) para 1.

[71] Home Office, n 57, 9.

[72] Scottish Government, n 62, para 7; also Scottish Serious Organised Crime Group, *Preliminary Findings on the Scale and Extent of Serious Organised Crime in Scotland* (Edinburgh, Scottish Government, 2009) 3.

[73] Scottish Government, n 64, para 34.

[74] Dáil Debates, vol 635, col 820 (4 April 2007) (Written Answers: Crime Levels).

Any estimation of the numbers of organised crime groups in Northern Ireland becomes complicated by virtue of the involvement of paramilitary groups, including the Irish National Liberation Army (INLA), the Real Irish Republican Army (RIRA), the Provisional Irish Republican Army (PIRA), and the Ulster Defence Association (UDA), in organised crime, such as drug smuggling and extortion.[75] A link between terrorist organisations and organised crime has been noted in official documents,[76] with persons previously involved in terrorism now using local and international networks to further criminal aims. Former subversives are seen to become involved in armed robbery for personal gain, as 'criminal entrepreneurs'[77] or 'criminal diversifiers'[78] who will engage in any activity if the potential profit is sufficiently high; their knowledge about weaponry may be disseminated to other criminal groups, or they may be involved in the supply of weapons.[79] Whereas once certain areas of criminality were the preserve of paramilitary groups or required 'approval' from such groups, other crime groups can also now operate in these areas.[80] The presence of paramilitaries compounds the problem of organised crime,[81] and blurs the margins of the concept and the extent of the threat posed.

In spite of difficulties in quantifying the number of actors and groups and costs of organised crime, the political account is of a grave and worsening problem. As Levi says, there is a 'social' definition of organised crime: namely, a set of people whom the State wishes us to regard as 'really dangerous' to its essential integrity.[82] This is not to diminish the real harm or pernicious effects caused by organised criminality, but to call attention to the contestable definition on which assessments are based, and alterations to legal norms adopted.

[75] Independent Monitoring Commission, *Eighth Report of the Independent Monitoring Commission* and *Tenth Report of the Independent Monitoring Commission* (London, The Stationery Office, 2006); Independent Monitoring Commission, *First Report of the Independent Monitoring Commission* (London, The Stationery Office, 2004).

[76] An Garda Síochána and Police Service of Northern Ireland, *A Cross Border Organised Crime Assessment 2008* (Belfast and Dublin, Northern Ireland Office and Department of Justice, 2008) 6; Organised Crime Task Force, *2011 Annual Report and Threat Assessment Organised Crime in Northern Ireland* (Belfast, Northern Ireland Office, 2011) 16.

[77] Select Committee on Northern Ireland Affairs, *Eighth Report: The Illegal Drugs Trade and Drug Culture in Northern Ireland* (London, The Stationery Office, 2003) para 64.

[78] N Dorn and N South, 'Drug Markets and Law Enforcement' (1990) 30 *British Journal of Criminology* 171, 177.

[79] Select Committee on Northern Ireland Affairs, *Organised Crime in Northern Ireland* (London, The Stationery Office, 2006) ch 2, paras 11–23; Select Committee 2003, n 77, para 65.

[80] An Garda Síochána and Police Service of Northern Ireland, n 76, 6.

[81] Independent Monitoring Commission, *Tenth Report of the Independent Monitoring Commission* (London, The Stationery Office, 2006) 4.4.

[82] M Levi, 'Perspectives on "Organised Crime": An Overview' (1998) 37 *Howard Journal of Criminal Justice* 335.

IV. Criminalising Organised Crime

Akin to Van Duyne's observation in the European context, the present organised crime situation in Ireland and the UK is marked by much 'political excitement'.[83] Labels have an emotive effect, and so the use of this terminology may garner support for the measures introduced to counter such crime.[84] The 'emotional kick' imparted by the terms justifies increased resources and powers for State bodies,[85] and so the adoption of these phrases may be a political stratagem which ensures the 'ratcheting-up' of State powers to combat the threat of such criminality. Beyond this, such political excitement has been translated into legislative action in Scotland and Ireland with the criminalisation of offences centring on organised crime as a concept or enterprise itself, rather than on any predicate offences as such, as outlined later in this chapter.

In Scotland the aforementioned term 'serious organised crime' is central to a number of new crimes, namely, involvement in, direction of, and failure to report serious organised crime, and other offences may be aggravated by connection with serious organised crime. The Criminal Justice and Licensing Act 2010 makes it an offence to agree with at least one other person to become involved in serious organised crime,[86] punishable on indictment by up to 10 years in prison. Thus organised crime in Scotland may involve just two people. The definition encompasses agreeing to do something, which may not itself be illegal, if the person knows, suspects, or ought reasonably to have known or suspected, that so acting will enable or further the commission of serious organised crime. In addition, any offence is aggravated by a connection with serious organised crime if the person was motivated by the objective of committing or conspiring to commit serious organised crime.[87] Furthermore, directing serious organised crime is now a substantive offence.[88] This involves directing, inciting, persuading or enabling a person to commit a serious offence or an offence connected to serious organised crime, or directing one person to direct another to so act. This is to take account of the often complex hierarchies and structures of organised crime groups. It is irrelevant if the person directed so acts. Furthermore, it is an offence to fail to report one's knowledge or suspicion to a police constable that another person is involved in or directs serious organised crime.[89] That knowledge or suspicion must have originated from information obtained in the course of the person's profession or employment, or as a result of a close personal relationship if the

---

[83] Van Duyne, n 5, 346.
[84] A Ashworth, *Human Rights, Serious Crime, and Criminal Procedure* (London, Sweet & Maxwell, 2002) 107.
[85] M Levi, 'The Organization of Serious Crimes' in M Maguire, R Morgan and R Reiner (eds), *The Oxford Handbook of Criminology* (3rd edn) (Oxford, Oxford University Press, 2002) 894.
[86] Criminal Justice and Licensing Act 2010, s 28.
[87] Criminal Justice and Licensing Act 2012, s 29.
[88] Criminal Justice and Licensing Act 2010, s 30.
[89] Criminal Justice and Licensing Act 2010, s 31.

person has materially benefited from the other's commission of serious organised crime. Framing the offence to require material benefit seeks to mitigate the potential harshness on family members or partners of persons suspected of involvement in serious organised crime who may become aware of matters inadvertently, but who have not benefited from the profits as such. Nonetheless, family and partners in fact often benefit by being provided with food, housing, through to luxury items such as expensive cars, and so there is an onus on them to report knowledge or suspicion regarding other family members to the police.

Scotland is the only one of the comparator jurisdictions to define 'serious organised crime', that is, the noun of 'crime', and, as has been described, has based on this a number of substantive statutory measures criminalising organised crime as an enterprise rather than separate predicate offences. In contrast to this, an attempt has been made in Ireland to define the groups that are involved in such criminality, the 'who', as Finckenauer would advocate.[90] Ireland has sought to define a 'criminal organisation', and it is this concept rather than the action that forms the basis for legislation that essentially criminalises organised crime. A 'criminal organisation' was defined in Ireland for the first time by the Criminal Justice Act 2006 but this has been replaced by the Criminal Justice (Amendment) Act 2009. According to section 3 of the 2009 Act a criminal organisation is a structured group, however organised, that has as its main purpose or activity the commission or facilitation of a serious offence, which is that for which a person may be imprisoned for at least four years. A structured group comprises at least three persons and cannot be randomly formed for the immediate commission of a single offence, and the involvement in the group by two or more of those persons must be with a view to their acting in concert. For the avoidance of doubt, the Irish legislation emphasises that a structured group may exist despite not having formal rules or membership, any hierarchical or leadership structure, or continuity of involvement by persons in the group. This seeks to address the ephemeral and flexible nature of criminal groups in Ireland, as in the UK. The Irish approach draws on the United Nations' definition of an 'organized criminal group' and the definition of 'criminal organisation' in the European Union Council Framework Decision.[91] A previous iteration of the European Union definition referred to the possibility of such offences improperly influencing the operation of public authorities[92] but this is no longer included.

Directing the activities of a criminal organisation is an offence in Ireland.[93] This has a clear predecessor in section 6 of the Offences Against the State (Amendment) Act 1998 which contains the offence of directing an unlawful organisation, a concept which will be returned to later, but which includes paramilitary entities like

---

[90]   Finckenauer, n 16, 75.

[91]   UN Convention Against Transnational Organised Crime, GA Res 25, annex I, UN GAOR, 55th Sess, Supp no 49, at 44, UN Doc A/45/49 (vol I) (2001) Art 2; Council Framework Decision 2008/841/JHA of 24 October 2008 on the fight against organised crime.

[92]   Council of Europe Joint Action on Making it a Criminal Offence to Participate in a Criminal Organisation in the Member States of the European Union, (1) 98/733/JHA of 21 December 1998.

[93]   Criminal Justice Act 2006, s 71A (as amended).

the Irish Republican Army (IRA). A person who controls, supervises, instructs, guides, or requests the activities of a criminal organisation (wherever carried on and regardless of their legality) is guilty of an offence punishable by up to life imprisonment. It is an offence for a person to contribute to or facilitate any legal or illegal activity either intending to or being reckless as to whether this could enhance the ability of a criminal organisation or its members to commit a serious offence anywhere.[94] There is no need to prove knowledge on the part of the defendant of the specific nature of any offence but he needs to know of the existence of the criminal organisation. Intention or recklessness can be presumed unless rebutted if the person possessed certain items like a balaclava, boiler suit or other means of disguise or impersonation, including any article of Garda uniform or equipment, any firearm, drugs, plan of buildings, etc.

Furthermore, a person who commits a serious offence for the benefit of, at the direction of, or in association with a criminal organisation is guilty of an offence punishable by a fine or imprisonment for up to 15 years or both.[95] In essence this means that the term of imprisonment which may be imposed under this section may be a more severe penalty than would be imposed on a person who commits the same offence individually, without any link to a criminal organisation. It is not necessary for the prosecution to prove that the person knew anyone in the criminal organisation.[96] The Act does not specify whether the person needs to know he is committing an offence for the benefit of a criminal organisation, although such a subjective element was read into the equivalent measure in Canada.[97] It remains to be seen whether the Irish courts replicate this approach.

Although a criminal organisation is defined in Irish law, such organisations are not criminalised per se. Indeed, no jurisdiction in the United Kingdom or Ireland has criminalised membership of any organised crime group. In other words, the mere existence of or membership of a criminal organisation is not illegal, in contrast to the proscription in the UK of groups involved in terrorism,[98] and in Ireland of organisations which engage in or promote treason, the non-payment of taxes, the illegal alteration of the Constitution, or the maintenance of an unconstitutional armed force.[99] Membership of any unlawful organisation is an offence in the UK and Ireland,[100] although it is a defence to show lack of knowledge that the organisation was unlawful or to show dissociation once the person became so aware of its nature. Arguably, this is due to the fact that in contrast to the loose and transitory nature of many organised crime groups, the IRA and other

[94] Criminal Justice Act 2006, s 72 (as amended).
[95] s 73.
[96] s 73(2).
[97] See *R v Accused No 1* [2005] BCSC 1727 [49]–[55].
[98] Terrorism Act 2000, pt 2. The Home Office maintains a list of organisations proscribed under the Terrorism Act 2000. Of these, two organisations are proscribed under powers introduced in the Terrorism Act 2006. Fourteen organisations in Northern Ireland are proscribed under previous legislation: see www.homeoffice.gov.uk/publications/counter-terrorism/proscribed-terror-groups/proscribed-groups?view=Binary.
[99] Offences Against the State Act 1939, s 18.
[100] Terrorism Act 2000, s 11 and Offences Against the State Act 1939, s 21.

proscribed organisations usually are organised hierarchically with various strata of superiors.[101]

In summary, Scotland has defined serious organised crime and Ireland a criminal organisation, and the relevant laws are based on these concepts. Rather than legislating against organised crime per se, in England and Wales Part 2 of the Serious Crime Act 2007 creates the inchoate offences of encouraging and assisting crime,[102] but these are not directly linked to organised crime like the measures elsewhere in the comparator jurisdictions.

Problems with the Legislation

Comparable criticisms may be ventured regarding both the Scottish and Irish approaches, concerning the definitions' breadth and lack of specificity, the need for such measures, and the likelihood of their effectiveness in addressing this type of criminality and criminal actors.

The principal concern about these provisions is their scope and the concomitant possibility of over-zealous use. The definition of serious organised crime in Scotland appears unduly general and far-reaching, encompassing as it does a mere two people acting together to commit a serious offence. When the Criminal Justice and Licensing (Scotland) Bill was being debated, a Stage 2 amendment sought to narrow the potential scope of the offences by providing that serious organised crime must involve crime that 'would reasonably be regarded as being both serious and organised'.[103] Despite the logic of this suggestion, it was rejected on the basis that apparently minor or trivial activities 'often form part of a more insidious picture'.[104] Moreover, the offence of failing to report serious organised crime is also problematic in terms of its reach. While it would be preferable for people to report suspicions regarding serious organised crime to the police, the imposition of a criminal sanction for not doing so is questionable both in terms of fairness and effectiveness.[105] Furthermore, it was suggested that the definition would be improved by limiting material benefit to a direct share in the proceeds of crime.[106] This would tighten the definition further and preclude unfair prosecution of family members and partners who may benefit from serious organised crime but are not complicit. In response, the argument was made that flexibility is crucial to deal adequately with such criminality and that rather than narrowing the definition reliance would be placed on the discretion of the police and the

---

[101]   eg the IRA is governed by the IRA Army Council, and is headed by the IRA Chief of Staff.

[102]   s 59 abolishes the common law offence of inciting the commission of another offence.

[103]   Criminal Justice and Licensing (Scotland) Bill, 3rd Marshalled List of Amendments for Stage 2, Amendment 345 per Robert Brown MSP.

[104]   Scottish Parliament Justice Committee, Official Report 12th meeting 2010, Session 3, 13 April 2010, col 2883.

[105]   See Scottish Parliament Justice Committee, 18th Report, 2009 (Session 3) Stage 1 Report on the Criminal Justice and Licensing (Scotland) Bill, para 275.

[106]   ibid, para 263 per Sir Gerald Gordon.

prosecution authorities 'to report and prosecute such offending appropriately'.[107] Relying on these agents of the State is dubious and is contingent on responsible and restrained application of these powers. This may undermine the perceived legitimacy of the law.

Similarly, the definition in Ireland may be questioned in terms of its scope, although an attempt was made to narrow it during parliamentary debate. When initially proposed in the Criminal Justice Bill 2004, the definition of a 'criminal organisation' did not include an explanation of 'structured group'. The absence of such an aspect formed the basis of the ruling of the Supreme Court of British Columbia in *R v Accused No 1* where a provision in the Canadian Criminal Code, which prohibits a person who is part of a criminal organisation from instructing another person to commit an offence for that organisation, was found to be in violation of the Canadian Charter of Rights and Freedoms.[108] The Court held that the definition of criminal organisation in the legislation was so fluid that an individual could not determine with certainty whether he was part of such a group. A criminal organisation was defined as a group, however organised, that is composed of three or more persons and which has as one of its main purposes or activities the facilitation or commission of one or more serious offences that, if committed, would likely result in material benefit by the group or by any member. Holmes J criticised the lack of statutory guidance as to the meaning of 'group, however organized', and noted that there was no requirement that those who constitute the 'group' share a crime-related or any common objective.[109] Forestalling any similar challenge in Ireland, the 2004 Bill was amended and the legislative approach now defines a structured group as comprising at least three persons and which cannot be formed randomly for the immediate commission of a single offence, and the involvement in the group by two or more of those persons must be with a view to their acting in concert. While inclusion of the definition of structured group is to be welcomed, it is still not clear whether a person can determine readily whether or not he is part of a criminal organisation. Moreover, the definition is sufficiently expansive to include a person who is a member of a criminal organisation but may not be involved 'with a view to acting in concert' as long as two other members of the group are.

A further problematic aspect of the Irish legislation is the change to evidential rules that is associated with these offences. The opinion of any member (or former member) of the Garda Síochána who appears to the Court to possess the appropriate expertise is admissible in relation to the existence of a particular criminal organisation.[110] This will not go to the guilt or otherwise of a defendant but will help to establish the existence of a particular criminal organisation. In forming his opinion, that expert may take into account any previous convictions for arrestable offences of persons believed by that expert to be part of the particular organisation. Moreover,

---

[107] Scottish Parliament Justice Committee 2010, n 104, col 2883.
[108] s 467.13; *R v Accused No 1*, n 97.
[109] *R v Accused No 1*, n 97, [85].
[110] Criminal Justice Act 2006, s 71B (as inserted by the Criminal Justice (Amendment) Act 2009).

as is explored more thoroughly in chapter five, trials for the aforementioned offences relating to criminal organisations are to be held in the non-jury Special Criminal Court, on the basis that the ordinary courts are deemed to be inadequate to secure the effective administration of justice and the preservation of public peace and order.[111] This section as enacted ceases to operate 12 months following the passing of the Act unless continued by a resolution passed by each House of the Oireachtas,[112] and such a resolution has been made annually since then.[113]

In addition to ambiguities regarding the parameters of these measures, it is questionable whether they are necessary, given the existing ability to prosecute under the common law offence of conspiracy. This point was raised while the relevant Acts were being debated,[114] and the Law Commission in England and Wales has noted similarly that the freestanding offence of conspiracy, such as conspiracy to import controlled drugs, plays an important part in the armoury of prosecutors.[115] Nevertheless, the Irish Minister for Justice at the time of enactment emphasised that Ireland had no choice but to legislate in this manner due to the United Nations Convention Against Transnational Organised Crime and the Joint Action of the European Union.[116] Both the UK and Ireland signed the UN Convention in 2001 and ratified it in 2006 and 2010 respectively: nevertheless, the UK has not defined in a like manner a 'criminal organisation' nor introduced equivalent provisions.

The dominant justification for the introduction of a separate provision premised on organised crime expressly, apart from conspiracy, is to improve the likelihood of securing a conviction on the basis that involvement in a specific offence needs to be proved for conspiracy.[117] Levi and Smith argued previously that conspiracy law and practice in England and Wales may not be fully effective in combating organised crime given the focus on agreement to engage in conduct which relates to one or a series of closely related crimes: it does not contemplate the activities of a multi-faceted criminal enterprise, strict rules of evidence about acting in concert or association apply, and the requirement to show that each

---

[111] Criminal Justice (Amendment) Act 2009, s 8(1). See ch 5 for further examination of this issue. However, the DPP may direct that a person not be sent forward for trial by the Special Criminal Court on a particular charge.

[112] Criminal Justice (Amendment) Act 2009, s 8(4).

[113] See Iris Oifigiuil, no 54, 9 July 2010, 967; Seanad Debates, vol 208, col 465 (15 June 2011); Dáil Debate, vol 768 (13 June 2012).

[114] See, eg the submissions made to the Scottish Parliament Justice Committee (18th Report paras 229–30); to the Committee on Justice, Equality, Defence and Women's Rights (29th Dáil), *Review of Criminal Justice System: Presentations* (Dublin, 8 December 2003) per the DPP, James Hamilton; Irish Human Rights Commission, *Observations on Additional Proposals for Amendments to the Criminal Justice Bill 2004* (Irish Human Rights Commission, Dublin, 2006) paras 1.2.3–1.2.4.

[115] The Law Commission, *Conspiracy and Attempts: A Consultation Paper* (London, The Law Commission, 2007) para 2.34.

[116] Committee on Justice, Equality, Defence and Women's Rights, Criminal Justice Bill 2004: Committee Stage (Resumed) (10 May 2006).

[117] See the comments of the Director General of the SCDEA and the Lord Advocate: Scottish Parliament Justice Committee. Official Report, 9 June 2009, col 2062 (also referred to at Scottish Parliament Justice Committee, 18th Report, n 105, para 232).

defendant in a single conspiracy indictment has to be shown to be party to the same agreement.[118]

In Scotland, 'a criminal conspiracy arises when two or more persons agree to render one another assistance in doing an act, whether as an end or as a means to an end, which would be criminal if done by a single individual'.[119] In contrast, a person can be involved in serious organised crime even without committing another offence if he knows or ought to know that this act will enable the commission of serious organised crime. Certainly, the statutory provision in the 2010 Act seems easier to satisfy. In Ireland conspiracy comprises two or more parties agreeing to commit an unlawful action.[120] Thus, the statutory offence under section 72 of the Criminal Justice Act 2006, of contributing to an activity that enhances the ability of a criminal organisation or its members to commit a serious offence, is narrower than common law conspiracy as it only relates to crimes punishable by four years or more, rather than unlawful conduct. However, section 72 clearly applies to activities abroad, whereas there is no Irish jurisprudence on an agreement formed in this country to commit a crime elsewhere.

The measures in Ireland can be compared to aspects of the Racketeer Influenced and Corrupt Organizations Act, or RICO,[121] which forms the core of counter-organised crime measures at the United States federal level. RICO introduced various procedural changes and civil measures which seek to address organised crime at the group level rather than solely targeting the individuals involved for alleged specified offences.[122] In other words, undermining or destroying the group at the core of such criminality is the objective of RICO. Whether the analogous approach will be effective in Ireland is unclear. As Levi and Smith state, there is an inevitable time lag between a law coming into force and investigation and prosecution in complex cases, thus it is hard to appraise the use and effectiveness of the legislation.[123] Nonetheless, since enactment in 2009 six persons have been charged with participating in organised crime[124] and two persons pleaded guilty to membership of a criminal organisation,[125] after originally being charged with directing a criminal organisation. There have been no other convictions. The first conviction under the Criminal Justice and Licensing (Scotland) Act 2010 concerned the

---

[118] M Levi and A Smith, *A Comparative Analysis of Organised Crime Conspiracy Legislation and Practice and their Relevance to England and Wales* (London, Home Office, 2002).

[119] *HMA v Wilson, Latta and Rooney* (unreported, 1968) per Lord Justice-Clerk Grant.

[120] Ireland uses the definition in *R v Jones* (1832) 110 ER 485.

[121] Title IX of the Organized Crime Control Act of 1970, Pub L 91-452, 84 Stat 922.

[122] The RICO legislation's aim is to penalise persons who engage in a 'pattern of racketeering activity' or 'collection of an unlawful debt' that has a specified relationship to an 'enterprise'. It is a crime to invest the proceeds of a pattern of racketeering or collection of an unlawful debt in an enterprise which affects interstate commerce (s 1962(a)), to acquire or maintaining an interest in an enterprise through a pattern of racketeering activity or collection of an unlawful debt (s 1962(b)), to conduct the affairs of an enterprise through a pattern of racketeering activity or collection of an unlawful debt (s 1962(c)), or to conspire to commit any of these offences (s 1962(d)).

[123] Levi and Smith, n 118, 6.

[124] Dáil Debates (WA), vol 754 (7 February 2012).

[125] 'Brothers Jailed Under Gang Laws', *Irish Times*, 11 June 2012.

offence of drug trafficking that was aggravated by connection with serious organised crime.[126]

The Irish Minister for Justice at the time of introduction of the relevant legislation conceded that proving these organised offences will be difficult but expressed his preference to have such laws on the statute book even 'if successful prosecutions are comparatively rare'.[127] Similarly, the Cabinet Secretary in Scotland emphasised that the Scottish Act sends the message that society takes organised crime extremely seriously.[128] Thus, the introduction of such measures serves a useful expressive end, by conveying legislative and societal opprobrium towards organised criminality. This expressive function of the criminal law, both in terms of what is criminalised and the use of the criminal sanction, is stressed by Garland.[129] Allied to this is the politicisation of law and order, and the engendering of a perpetual sense of crisis which warrants new measures.[130] In a bid to mollify a concerned public, the State denounces organised crime in a cathartic criminalisation notwithstanding the questionable effect of these measures: the fact that legislative action is being taken is seen as gratifying of itself.[131]

V. What are Organised Crimes?

As this chapter has outlined, there are ineluctable difficulties in defining organised crime, in determining the true extent of the problem in terms of the groups involved, and ultimately in criminalising it as an offence in itself. Alongside this is an even more fluid interpretation of the term comprising a range of crimes which necessitate planning, entail a considerable degree of complexity, the involvement of a number of parties, and are motivated by profit. Such acts are regarded as 'organised crimes' in a popular and rhetorical sense. There is no closed class of such organised crimes, but a representative list could include drug trafficking, money laundering, people smuggling, fraud, armed robbery, counterfeiting, and extortion, as these concern the provision of illegal goods or services, or the commission of acts which meet a given level of gravity, and generally are carried out

---

[126] s 29. See Scottish Crime and Drug Enforcement Agency (SCDEA) Press Release, 'Drug Courier Jailed Under Serious Organised Crime Legislation', 14 May 2012.

[127] Minister for Justice, 'Criminal Justice Bill 2004: Ministerial Presentation to the Joint Committee on Justice, Equality, Defence and Women's Rights', vol 95, 7 September 2005. It was argued that a more effective means of tackling organised crime would be to regard the element of organisation in the commission of a crime as an exacerbating factor at sentencing. Irish Human Rights Commission, 'Oral Submissions', Joint Committee on Justice, Equality, Defence and Women's Rights, 2 December 2003, 24–25 per W Binchy.

[128] Scottish Parliament Justice Committee, *Official Report*, 23 June 2009, cols 2195–96; (also referred to at Scottish Parliament Justice Committee, 18th Report, n 105, para 234).

[129] D Garland, *The Culture of Control* (Oxford, Oxford University Press, 2001) 8ff. See ch 3.

[130] ibid, 19–20.

[131] ibid, 133.

by a number of people working in a coordinated manner. The UK Proceeds of Crime Act 2002 includes a list of 'criminal lifestyle' offences, namely 'areas of criminal conduct associated with professional criminals, organised crime and racketeering',[132] including drug trafficking, counterfeiting, arms trafficking, trafficking for the purposes of sexual exploitation and money laundering. Such offences are deemed to speak to the person's longer-term behaviour. Though ostensibly less problematic than defining and criminalising organised crime itself, by labelling offences in such a broad manner, any act of drug trafficking, for example, is deemed to constitute organised crime, and thus to warrant a robust reaction. This section explores a number of these substantive offences in turn.

The trafficking, supply, sale and manufacture of drugs have long been criminalised in the UK and Ireland, and, as examined in chapter six, attract increasingly punitive sentences.[133] Drug trafficking is seen by Europol as a major aspect of organised crime in the north-west of Europe,[134] and this area is regarded as a principal coordination centre for drug distribution.[135] As well as drugs' importation and export, fuel, guns, tobacco, counterfeit goods, rare animals and people are trafficked into and out of the UK and Ireland. Fuel smuggling is a type of fraud which is a particular issue in both jurisdictions in Ireland because of the land border and the difference in rates of duty and the currency exchange rate.[136] On this point, the House of Commons Northern Ireland Affairs Committee has emphasised the effect that a common regime for fuel duty in Northern Ireland and the Republic would have on organised crime,[137] as this would decrease 'racketeering potential'.[138] In addition, the laundering and subsequent sale of fuels which are sold for use other than in cars is a problem in Northern Ireland.[139] Contraband and counterfeit tobacco is smuggled into the UK and Ireland from Europe and Asia,[140] and some degree of alcohol smuggling occurs also.[141] This is seen more and more as an attractive alternative to the trafficking of illicit drugs because of its lower penalties yet large profits.[142]

---

[132] See Explanatory Notes to the Proceeds of Crime Act 2002.

[133] Misuse of Drugs Act 1971; Misuse of Drugs Act 1977.

[134] Europol, *OCTA 2009*, n 54, 28.

[135] Europol, *OCTA 2011: EU Organised Crime Threat Assessment* (Netherlands, European Police Office, 2011) 6.

[136] House of Commons Northern Ireland Affairs Committee, *Organised Crime in Northern Ireland Vol I* (Third Report of Session 2005–06) (London, The Stationery Office, 2006) 10.

[137] ibid, 35.

[138] Goldstock, n 53, para 3.7.

[139] An Garda Síochána and Police Service of Northern Ireland, n 76, 94. For example, in 2011, 15 large-scale fuel laundering plants with the capacity to produce over 90 million litres of illicit fuel were dismantled. Also see Organised Crime Task Force, n 76, 8.

[140] HM Revenue and Customs, *New Responses to New Challenges: Reinforcing the Tackling Tobacco Smuggling Strategy* (London, The Stationery Office, 2006).

[141] An Garda Síochána and Police Service of Northern Ireland, n 76, 6.

[142] Europol, *OCTA 2011*, n 135, 24. Also see An Garda Síochána and Police Service of Northern Ireland, n 76, 15.

The UK has 'a considerable pull factor for legal and illegal forms of immigration'.[143] Organised immigration crime is a growing issue,[144] and this involves both consensual smuggling and people trafficking, where the victims are controlled and exploited once at their destination. It is now a specific offence in the UK and Ireland to assist unlawful immigration,[145] and to traffic people for exploitation,[146] whether for sexual exploitation[147] or otherwise.[148] Trafficked women and children in particular may be exploited as prostitutes by organised crime groups, who may also maintain and run brothels as part of their illegal enterprise.[149]

Organised crime often involves intellectual property crimes of counterfeiting and piracy, through the imitation of certain brand-named clothes or drugs, or the illegal replication of films, music and other recorded content.[150] Counterfeit currency may also be produced.[151] Moreover, various types of fraud may be carried out, such as identity theft whereby someone's personal information like a name and credit card details are appropriated, often involving interception of information on the internet. Other credit card fraud may involve the use of a card reader or camera which records the card details secretly to permit subsequent use.[152] Tax fraud may involve the failure to pay taxes and duties, and value-added tax (VAT) fraud involves the use of a combination of hijacked and missing trader VAT numbers to obtain goods VAT-free in one jurisdiction and then sell them on in another jurisdiction.[153]

A further quintessential act of organised crime groups is extortion, or the demanding of 'protection money' through racketeering; this is a widespread problem in parts of the United States.[154] While not deemed to be a major issue in Ireland,[155] extortion is a concern in Northern Ireland, affecting small to medium

---

[143] Europol, *OCTA 2009*, n 54, 29.

[144] Serious and Organised Crime Agency, n 70, 40.

[145] See the Immigration Act 1971 (as amended by the UK Borders Act 2007).

[146] Asylum and Immigration (Treatment of Claimants etc) Act 2004, s 4 as amended and the Criminal Law (Human Trafficking Act) 2008, s 4. See UN Protocol to Prevent, Suppress and Punish Trafficking in Persons, Especially Women and Children, Supplementing the UN Convention Against Transnational Organized Crime, Art 3.

[147] Sexual Offences Act 2003, ss 57 and 58 as amended, Criminal Law (Human Trafficking Act) 2008, s 5.

[148] These acts are 'lifestyle offences' for the purposes of the Proceeds of Crime Act 2002. See above n 132.

[149] House of Commons Home Affairs Committee, *The Trade in Human Beings: Human Trafficking in the UK*, Sixth Report of Session 2008–09 vol I (London, The Stationery Office, 2009).

[150] This is in breach of the Copyright, Designs and Patents Act 1988 and the Trade Marks Act 1994 in the UK and the Intellectual Property (Miscellaneous Provisions) Act 1998 and Copyright and Related Rights Act 2000 in Ireland.

[151] See the Forgery and Counterfeiting Act 1981 and the Criminal Justice (Theft and Fraud Offences) Act 2001 (Ireland).

[152] Europol, *OCTA 2011*, n 135, 23.

[153] An Garda Síochána and Police Service of Northern Ireland, n 76, 11.

[154] See R Goldstock, M Marcus, T Thacher and J Jacobs, *Corruption and Racketeering in the New York City Construction Industry: Final Report* (New York, NYU Press, 1990); J Jacobs and F Anechiarico, 'Blacklisting Public Contractors as an Anti-Corruption and Racketeering Strategy' (1992) 11 *Criminal Justice Ethics* 64.

[155] Transcrime, *Study on Extortion Racketeering the Need for an Instrument to Combat Activities of Organised Crime: Final Report* (Milan, Transcrime, 2008) 135.

sized businesses like shops and construction companies,[156] though it is difficult to determine if this is the preserve of organised crime groups or paramilitary organisations or a combination. Extortion is not commonplace in the UK although there is some evidence of its perpetration in certain communities.[157]

As in the case of organised crime groups in the north-east of the United States that were involved in the disposal of rubbish and illegal dumping,[158] cross-border criminality in Ireland avails of the difference in the cost of landfill to make a profit by transporting and disposing of waste.[159] A significant quantity of household and commercial waste which originated in Ireland and illegally moved to the North is 'repatriated' every year.[160] Furthermore, this type of criminality is evident across the UK. Such environmental crimes may be prosecuted by the Environment Agencies across the UK and Ireland.[161]

The potential involvement of organised crime groups in the provision of private security is a live issue all over the UK and Ireland. This may permit the selling of drugs to occur in certain premises without sanction, or it may be linked to cases of extortion.[162] In fact, it is a specific and enduring problem in Northern Ireland due to the links between certain private security providers and paramilitary groups.[163] The private security industry in Northern Ireland was once regulated by the Terrorism Act 2000 which required the Secretary of State to be satisfied that a proscribed organisation would not benefit from the granting of a licence. Now one system exists across the UK, with the Security Industry Authority regulating the granting of licences for such roles as door supervision, security guarding, and the transportation of cash and valuables in transit.[164] Its equivalent in Ireland is the Private Security Authority.

Firearms offences are often carried out by members of organised crime groups or are linked to organised criminality, though this is not necessarily the case. Such offences range from the possession and use of firearms, their importation, through to gun homicides. Armed robberies may be carried out by criminal organisations,

---

[156] House of Commons Northern Ireland Affairs Committee, n 136, 31 and 35; Transcrime, n 155, 241.

[157] N Tilley, M Hopkins, A Edwards and J Burrows, *Business Views of Organised Crime: Key Implications Research Report 10* (London, Home Office, 2008) 38–40.

[158] D Rebovich, *Dangerous Ground: The World of Hazardous Waste Crime* (New Jersey, Transaction Publishing, 1992); A Szasz, 'Corporations, Organized Crime, and the Disposal of Hazardous Waste: An Examination of the Making of a Criminogenic Regulatory Structure' (1986) 24 *Criminology* 1.

[159] An Garda Síochána and Police Service of Northern Ireland, n 76, 8.

[160] Organised Crime Task Force, n 76, 9.

[161] The Environment Agency, the Scottish Environment Protection Agency and the Environmental Protection Agency (Ireland). See the Environmental Protection Act 1990; the Waste and Contaminated Land (Northern Ireland) Order 1997 and the Environmental Protection Agency Act 1992 (Ireland).

[162] See S Morris, *Clubs, Drugs and Doormen,* Crime Detection and Prevention Series Paper 86 (London, Home Office, 1998).

[163] Independent Monitoring Commission, *Fifth Report of the Independent Monitoring Commission* (London, The Stationery Office, 2005). See Northern Ireland Office, *Proposals to Regulate the Private Security Industry in Northern Ireland: Final Regulatory Impact Assessment* (Belfast, Northern Ireland Office, 2006).

[164] See *Anderson v The Security Industry Authority* (Dumbarton Sheriff Court, 8 March 2011).

involving 'hold-ups' of businesses, banks and post offices, cash in transit attacks, ATM thefts, and so-called 'bunker attacks' which occur as the courier enters the area behind an ATM. The effort to safeguard against armed robberies by 'target hardening' financial institutions through the use of closed-circuit television (CCTV), time-locked safes and sophisticated alarm systems has rendered staff more vulnerable, as may be seen in 'tiger kidnappings' in which money is sought through the kidnapping of an individual employee of the business or his family.[165] Despite sensationalist media coverage,[166] figures for such kidnappings remain very low across the UK and Ireland.[167] More broadly, and as is the case regarding drug crime, firearms offences increasingly attract presumptive minimum sentences due to political and popular concern. Notably, a sizeable percentage of homicides in Ireland are carried out with firearms, far greater than the proportion in England, Wales and Scotland,[168] and this may involve persons involved in organised crime.

Once profits have been made from all these types of such criminality, there is a need to mask these earnings and present them as legitimate, and this typically is done through laundering. Money laundering consists of acquiring, using and possessing criminal property, or concealing, disguising, converting, transferring or removing criminal property, or facilitating someone else's acquisition of criminal property.[169] This may involve the participation of or facilitation by witting and unwitting bankers, lawyers and accountants.[170] Despite the prevalence of money laundering and its centrality to the perpetration and maintenance of organised crime, the number of prosecutions and convictions remains low in Ireland, but is rising in the UK.[171]

Despite these examples, certain types of organised crimes have not taken root within the comparator jurisdictions, in contrast to the situation in the US and Italy, for example. There is little evidence in the UK and Ireland of the incursion of organised crime groups into government, or into unions as occurred in the US

---

[165]   R Matthews, *Armed Robbery* (Cullompton, Willan Publishing, 2002) 51–52.

[166]   eg 'How Can Gardaí Tame the Tiger Kidnappings?', *Sunday Business Post*, 28 December 2008.

[167]   See Dáil Debates, vol 676, col 905 (3 March 2009).

[168]   See L Campbell, 'Responding to Gun Crime in Ireland' (2010) 50 *British Journal of Criminology* 414, 415; K Smith (ed), S Osborne, I Lau and A Britton, *Homicides, Firearm Offences and Intimate Violence 2010/11: Supplementary Volume 2 to Crime in England and Wales 2010/11* (London, The Stationery Office, 2012) 15; Scottish Government, *Recorded Crimes and Offences Involving Firearms, Scotland, 2010–11* (Edinburgh, Scottish Government, 2011) table 2.

[169]   Proceeds of Crime Act 2002, pt 7 (POCA). The POCA consolidated pre-existing money laundering offences following an observation concerning the low numbers of money laundering prosecutions in England and Wales: see Performance and Innovation Unit, *Recovering the Proceeds of Crime* (London, The Stationery Office, 2000). For the Irish measures see Criminal Justice Act 1994, s 31 (as amended).

[170]   See, eg M Levi, H Nelen and F Lankhorst, 'Lawyers as Crime Facilitators in Europe: An introduction and Overview' (2005) 42 *Crime, Law and Social Change* 117.

[171]   Financial Action Task Force, *Third Mutual Evaluation/Detailed Assessment Report Anti-Money Laundering and Combating the Financing of Terrorism: Ireland* (Paris, Financial Action Task Force, 2006); Financial Action Task Force, *Third Mutual Evaluation/Detailed Assessment Report Anti-Money Laundering and Combating the Financing of Terrorism: United Kingdom of Great Britain and Northern Ireland* (Paris, Financial Action Task Force, 2007).

through the exploitation of unions, or labour racketeering as it is known.[172] While the UK Organised Crime Threat Assessment has spoken of the corruption of officials and criminal justice agents this was not substantiated by reference to case law or specific instances.[173] Furthermore, there is considerable historical evidence of political corruption in Ireland, but not by organised crime groups as conceived of by policy makers.[174]

Flaws exist with all types of criminal statistics:[175] nonetheless, it is easier to measure the numbers and rates of recorded type of crime, as is done in by the Organised Crime Task Force in Northern Ireland,[176] rather than attempt to determine the number of criminal groups. Official domestic and international reports note the perpetration of various types of 'organised crimes', which, generally speaking, require preparation and the involvement of a number of parties, and are driven by the incentive of profit. Nonetheless, rates of these crimes are not necessarily increasing, and media portrayal may overstate the problem.

VI. New State Agencies

Notwithstanding the sketchy estimation of the extent of the problem of organised crime, the political and legal responses in the UK and Ireland involve not only an increase in police powers (such as those concerning detention and interrogation which are explored in chapter four) but also the development and expansion of State agencies, some of which comprise staff from multiple bodies, and are vested with specific capabilities. Many of these bodies' mandates focus on addressing organised crime. As well as regional and national police forces, there are numerous agencies involved in attending to the threat of organised crime, such as the Serious Organised Crime Agency (SOCA), HM Revenue and Customs, and the Border Agency in the UK, the Revenue Commissioners and the Criminal Assets Bureau (CAB) in Ireland, in addition to less obvious ones such as the Social Security Agency and the Environment Agency.

A shift from the traditional mode of policing due to the changing nature of serious and organised crime was first evident in England and Wales with the statutory establishment in 1997 of the National Criminal Intelligence Service (NCIS) and the National Crime Squad (NCS), which supplemented the work of police forces and were seminal in terms of addressing organised crime at the national

---

[172] J Jacobs, *Mobsters, Unions, and Feds* (New York, New York University Press, 2007).

[173] Serious Organised Crime Agency, n 67, 6.

[174] See the Tribunals of Inquiry (Evidence) Acts 1921–2004 and the associated reports such as Mahon J, *Final Report of the Tribunal of Inquiry into Certain Planning Matters and Payments* (Dublin, Stationery Office, 2012) and Moriarty J, *Report of the Tribunal of Inquiry into Certain Payments to Politicians and Related Matters* (Dublin, Stationery Office, 2006).

[175] See W Chambliss, 'The Politics of Crime Statistics' in C Sumner (ed), *Blackwell Companion to Criminology* (Oxford, Blackwell, 2007) 452–70.

[176] Organised Crime Task Force, n 76.

level. The NCIS gathered, stored and analysed information for criminal intelligence and disseminated this to police forces in the UK, to the NCS and other law
enforcement agencies.[177] In conjunction with this, the NCS had the function of
'prevent[ing] and detect[ing] serious crime which is of relevance to more than
one police area in England and Wales'.[178] The NCS also supported and cooperated
with the NCIS and law enforcement agencies in the UK and abroad, and could
institute criminal proceedings.[179] As Harfield notes, this was a significant departure from the norm of locally delivered policing in the UK.[180]

When the UK-wide National Criminal Intelligence Service and the National
Crime Squad in England and Wales were still in operation, specific bodies were
established in both the UK and Ireland to exercise powers relating to civil asset
forfeiture and the taxation of criminal profits specifically.[181] In Ireland, the
Criminal Assets Bureau Act 1996 established the Criminal Assets Bureau (CAB)
with the objectives of identifying assets which derive or are suspected to derive
from criminal activity, the taking of action to deprive persons of such assets, and
the carrying out of investigations in relation to such proceedings.[182] Moreover,
CAB's functions are the taking of all necessary action to confiscate, freeze or seize
assets deriving or suspected of deriving from criminal activity,[183] to ensure that
the proceeds of (suspected) criminal activity are taxed,[184] to investigate and determine any claim for benefit by any person engaged in criminal activity[185] and to
investigate and determine any benefit claim when social welfare officers may be
subject to intimidation.[186] CAB represents a hybrid of State agencies and authorities, including members of the Garda Síochána, officials of the Revenue
Commissioners and of the Department of Social, Community and Family
Affairs.[187] Such persons retain the powers or duties that accrue from their primary
roles in carrying out CAB business.[188]

Drawing on the Irish model to a large extent, and following the recommenda-
tions of the Home Office and the Attorney General,[189] the Assets Recovery Agency
(ARA) was introduced in the UK by Part 1 of the Proceeds of Crime Act 2002.
ARA was established to disrupt 'organised crime', through confiscation, civil

---

[177] Police Act 1997, pt I.
[178] Police Act 1997, pt II.
[179] Police Act 1997, s 48(3).
[180] C Harfield, 'The Organization of "Organized Crime Policing" and its International Context'
(2008) 8 *Criminology Pand Criminal Justice* 483, 493.
[181] See ch 7.
[182] Criminal Assets Bureau Act 1996, s 4.
[183] s 5(1)(a).
[184] s 5(1)(b).
[185] s 5(1)(c). While s 5(1)(b) refers to criminal activity or suspected criminal activity, the word 'suspected' is absent in s 5(1)(c).
[186] s 5(1)(d).
[187] s 8(1). The Chief Bureau Officer is a member of the Garda Síochána holding the rank of Chief
Superintendent (s 7(6)).
[188] s 8(8).
[189] Home Office Working Group on Confiscation, *Third Report: Criminal Assets* (London, Home
Office, 1998) para 5.7; HL Deb 25 March 2002, vol 633, col 59.

recovery and taxation of criminal assets; however, it was not successful in its attempt to become self-financing, and recovered only a fraction of its expenditure.[190] Furthermore, only a small proportion of the bodies that could refer cases for investigation to the Agency actually did so, and basic failures of management were identified in a review of its operation.[191] Indeed, while the multi-agency aspect seems to have benefited the CAB, it was problematic for ARA and its predecessor the NCIS.[192] To remedy this, section 1 of the Serious Organised Crime and Police Act 2005 established the Serious Organised Crime Agency (SOCA).[193] SOCA replaced ARA, as well as the National Criminal Intelligence Service and the National Crime Squad. The Serious Crime Act 2007 transferred ARA's civil recovery functions to SOCA, the Director of Public Prosecutions, the Director of Revenue and Customs Prosecutions, the Director of the Serious Fraud Office and the Director of Public Prosecutions for Northern Ireland.

Given the bodies it replaced, SOCA has a range of functions: namely, preventing, detecting and reducing serious organised crime and mitigating its consequences, as well as gathering, storing, analysing and disseminating information to police forces and law enforcement agencies relevant to the prevention, detection, investigation or prosecution of offences, or the reduction of crime.[194] SOCA may institute criminal proceedings in England and Wales or Northern Ireland and may act, if requested, in support of any activities of a police force or agency.[195] For example, SOCA works with the Criminal Taxes Unit at HM Revenue and Customs to identify and pursue cases which involve the potential taxation of criminal profits.[196] The Home Office has announced the proposed abolition of SOCA through the Crime and Courts Bill 2012–13, and the establishment in 2013 of the National Crime Agency (NCA) which will address organised, as well as financial and economic, crime.[197]

Moreover, the Organised Crime Division at the Crown Prosecution Service deals exclusively with cases investigated by SOCA, while individual police forces in the UK have specific sub-divisions, like the Serious and Organised Crime Command of the Metropolitan Police. Furthermore, the Strategic Centre for Organised Crime in the Home Office publishes reports and strategy documents on the issue.

Such specific agencies are mirrored in Scotland: the Scottish Drug Enforcement Agency was established in 2001, and has since been renamed as the Scottish Crime

---

[190] House of Commons Committee of Public Accounts, *Assets Recovery Agency Fiftieth Report of Session 2006–07* (London, The Stationery Office, 2007) 5. By the end of 2006, ARA had recovered assets amounting to only £23 million against expenditure of £65 million.

[191] ibid, 6–9.

[192] Harfield, n 180, 494–95.

[193] See the recommendations of the Home Office in *Policing: Building Safer Communities Together* (London, Home Office, 2003).

[194] ss 2 and 3.

[195] s 5(2).

[196] See ch 8.

[197] www.homeoffice.gov.uk/publications/crime/organised-crime-strategy.

and Drug Enforcement Agency (SCDEA) and placed on a statutory footing.[198] The SCDEA has the primary role of preventing and detecting serious organised crime in Scotland, through the gathering and analysis of information and intelligence and through intervention.[199] SOCA works with the SCDEA, and before the creation of the former a Sewel Motion was issued regarding SOCA, though this was passed very narrowly.[200] Despite this falling within the purview of the Scottish Parliament, permitting Westminster to legislate on this matter ensured that the role and operation of SOCA agents in Scotland was clarified and came into force at the same time as SOCA was created.[201] Subsequently created in Scotland, the SCDEA has discrete divisions, such as the Scottish Money Laundering Unit and the Scottish Intelligence and Co-ordination Unit, while each Scottish police force has a specialist financial investigation unit.[202] In order to carry out the functions of the Scottish Ministers with regards to seizing assets the Civil Recovery Unit (CRU) was formed, consisting of solicitors, seconded police and customs officers, and forensic accountants. The CRU has responsibility for processing civil recovery actions in the Court of Session, overseeing all cash seizure cases and applying for forfeiture of seized cash. In addition, a specialist unit has been created in the Crown Office and Procurator Fiscal Service (COPFS) to tackle serious organised crime and in particular to deal with the money laundering provisions of the Proceeds of Crime Act 2002. Moreover, a Serious Organised Crime Taskforce was established in Scotland in 2007 and is chaired by the Cabinet Secretary for Justice, with membership including the Lord Advocate; the Association of Chief Police Officers in Scotland, SCDEA, HMRC and SOCA. The Taskforce develops and publishes strategic plans and documents for tackling serious organised crime.[203]

As well as the crucial role that SOCA plays in Northern Ireland, the Police Service of Northern Ireland (PSNI) has a Crime Operations Department with a dedicated Organised Crime Branch.[204] There is also an Organised Crime Task Force that sets priorities relating to organised crime in Northern Ireland but, like its equivalent in Scotland, it does not play an operational role. In addition, to deal with particular types of organised crime, there is a PSNI Extortion Unit, and a cross-border fuel enforcement group, comprising HMRC, the PSNI, SOCA, the Northern Ireland Office, the Irish Revenue Commissioners and CAB. Similarly, in Ireland there is now a full time specialist Organised Crime Unit in the Gardaí,

[198] Police, Public Order and Criminal Justice (Scotland) Act 2006.

[199] Police, Public Order and Criminal Justice (Scotland) Act 2006, pt 1 ch 1.

[200] Scottish Parliament Official Report, 2 February 2005, col 14143ff. A 'Sewel motion' allows the UK Parliament to legislate on a matter usually within the competence of the Scottish legislature (see ch 1).

[201] eg s 22 provides that SOCA agents operating in Scotland are subject to the direction of the Lord Advocate and Procurators Fiscal as regards the investigation and prosecution of crime.

[202] HM Inspectorate of Constabulary for Scotland (HMICS) and the Inspectorate of Prosecution in Scotland (IPS), *Joint Thematic Report on The Proceeds of Crime Act 2002* (2009, web only publication) www.scotland.gov.uk/Resource/Doc/925/0088557.pdf.

[203] Scottish Government, n 64.

[204] See Government Response to R Goldstock, *Organised Crime in Northern Ireland: A Report for the Secretary of State* (Belfast, Northern Ireland Office, 2004) 33.

which works with the Garda National Drugs Unit and other units, as well as the National Bureau of Criminal Investigation. There is a specific assets seizing section in the Office of the Director of Public Prosecutions.

Finally, in addition to specific policing and prosecution units, other agencies and entities like HMRC, the Serious Fraud Office, the UK Border Agency, the Irish Revenue Commissioners, the Social Security Agency and the Environment Agency play an increasingly central and critical role in the context of detecting and policing organised crime, given the diverse nature of the acts perpetrated. Internationally, the UK and Ireland are members of the Camden Asset Recovery Inter-Agency Network (CARIN) which is an informal network which seeks to improve cooperation and information sharing regarding the recovery of the proceeds of crime. Furthermore, agencies in the comparator jurisdictions liaise with Interpol and the Anti-Organized Crime and Law Enforcement Unit within the United Nations Office on Drugs and Crime which assist law enforcement agencies and officers involved in addressing organised crime. These relationships have an operational dimension, and the international bodies provide support to strategic national bodies, develop empirical accounts of regional and global trends, and identify appropriate reactions.

VII. Conclusion

It has been said that organised crime is what people so label.[205] That is, organised crime may be defined differently depending on how the term will be employed, whether that is for historical analysis, for sociological research, in determining the scope of an investigative agency or when drafting a criminal statute. For van Duyne and van Dijck the term 'organised crime' should be seen as 'a phrase for exciting conversations and political discourse and policy making (with all its risks of rhetorical use and abuse)'.[206] Some legislators in the UK and Ireland admit that defining organised crime is difficult:

> Organised crime is a short-hand phrase that can cover a multitude. But we should not forget that what is at its heart is people coming together for criminal ends who aren't prepared to live by the rules and who will set at nought the rights of others.[207]

Despite epistemological and definitional defects, the extent to which such terminology is embedded in popular and political culture, and its centrality and salience in official documents and legislative and popular debate, suggests that its use for scholars, and specifically in this project on the legal reactions to the phenomenon, is

[205] K Von Lampe, 'Not a Process of Enlightenment: The Conceptual History of Organized Crime in Germany and the United States of America' (2001) 1 *Forum on Crime and Society* 99, 113.
[206] Van Duyne and van Dijck, n 68, 102.
[207] 'Speech by Minister for Justice Mr Dermot Ahern' (8th Annual Organised Crime Cross Border Seminar, Belfast, 4 October 2010).

appropriate. Settling on a coherent and all encompassing definition might not be necessary as long as the State views it as a 'distinct crime category'.[208]

What is deeply problematic, however, is the entrenchment of such definitions in the legal sphere, given the breadth of criminal liability, the duplication of the criminal law and the dubious use of such law to express social disapproval notwithstanding likely ineffectiveness. Moreover, the proliferation of agencies and the creation of further bureaucracies are predicated on the perceived threat. Abandoning the term in a political sense is not feasible, but the recent legal developments in Scotland and Ireland are rather more pernicious. As will be explored in more detail in later chapters, what is needed to address systematic, violent and profiteering serious crime on a large scale is not necessarily more law, but rather increased resources for police investigations, and a careful revision of certain procedural rules and protection (such as surveillance laws in terms of the permitted use of wiretaps). Crucially, all this must be underpinned by a more muted and measured tone of political discourse.

---

[208] 'Discussing Definitions of Organised Crime: Word Play in Academic and Political Discourse' 1 *HUMSEC Journal* 83. See C Hamilton, 'Organised Criminals as "Agents of Obligation": The Case of Ireland' (2010) *European Journal on Criminal Policy and Research* 1.

3

The Theoretical Framework: Tensions in Criminal Justice

I. Introduction

Attempts to address organised crime bring inherent tensions in the criminal justice system into sharp relief. Policies and laws must seek to reconcile as best they may the coexisting and sometimes competing demands of crime control and human rights, and the need to protect the public from crime and to maintain security while also safeguarding civil liberties. No overarching coherent or single trend in respect of the legal reactions to organised crime across the UK and Ireland is identifiable in this regard, given that policies extend and develop over decades, and are affected by changes of administration with differing ideologies and interests. Nonetheless, as this chapter explores, some cross-cutting themes may be discerned, mirroring common trends in criminal justice debate and policy more broadly: public protection and community interests seem to be elevated over individual rights; there is an increasing aversion towards risk; extraordinary measures are integrated into the criminal justice system and thereby normalised; and third parties are co-opted into the policing and prevention of organised crime. The dialogue between the different arms of the State is also critical in the development of law and practice in this area, with the judicial branch often tempering the more punitive and consequentialist tendencies of legislators and policy makers. This chapter provides an outline of these ideas, to provide a basis for the contextualised doctrinal analysis undertaken in subsequent chapters.

Notions of due process and fairness to the individual throughout the criminal trial are predicated on the power disparity between the State and the citizen and on the conventional desire to avoid, to the greatest extent practicable, the conviction and punishment of the innocent,[1] notwithstanding that these rationales may

---

[1] In *R v Hobson* [1823] 1 Lew CC 261 Holroyd J declared that 'it is a maxim of English law that ten guilty men should escape rather than that one innocent man should suffer', while Hale claimed that 'it is better five guilty persons should escape unpunished, than one innocent person should die' (M Hale, *Historia Placitorum Coronae/The History of the Pleas of the Crown* (London, Professional Books, 1971) 289). Fortescue argued that 'one would much rather that twenty guilty persons should escape the punishment of death, than that one innocent person should be condemned, and suffer capitally'. J Fortescue, *De Laudibus Legum Angliæ* (London, 1775) 92. Allen contends that the ratio adopted is not without significance, for if it is extended indefinitely, justice will break down. CK Allen, *Legal Duties*

compromise the pursuit of truth.[2] However, political rhetoric often portrays just-ice and procedure as incompatible,[3] with rules of criminal procedure considered to be 'unreasonably technical obstacles'.[4] The tenor of some public debate in relation to organised crime in particular encapsulates the view of human rights protections as mere inconveniences to be overcome, rather than vital safeguards, given the nature, extent and gravity of this type of crime.

II. Competing Demands in the Criminal Process

Herbert Packer's work on two paradigms of the criminal process is valuable in illuminating the legislative and policy changes introduced in the UK and Ireland in addressing organised crime.[5] While, as is explored below, his dichotomous depiction may be criticised for its polarity, it nonetheless provides a useful frame-work on which to base an analysis of shifts in the criminal justice process.

In *The Limits of the Criminal Sanction*, Packer presents the crime control and the due process models as abstract representations of the two value systems which vie for superiority in the criminal process.[6]   The crime control model views the suppression of criminal conduct as the process's most significant function.[7] Efficiency, speed and finality are of primary importance: therefore the criminal process should not involve 'ceremonious rituals' that delay the progress of a case but rather should resemble 'an assembly-line conveyor belt down which moves an endless stream of cases'.[8] The screening carried out by the police and prosecutors is seen as a reliable indicator of probable guilt, and expert, administrative mecha-nisms of fact-finding are more reliable and efficacious than subsequent formal adjudication.[9] In contrast, the due process model resembles an obstacle course hindering the progress of the accused.[10] While accepting that the repression of crime is desirable in a societal sense, this model highlights the possibility of error

---

and Other Essays in Jurisprudence (Oxford, Clarendon, 1931) 286–87. Similarly, Ashworth argues that '[i]f the maxim is really meant to say something about the balance of the criminal justice system, the ratio it expresses cannot be a matter of indifference'. A Ashworth, 'Concepts of Criminal Justice' [1979] *Crim LR* 412, 417.

[2] A Ashworth, 'Crime, Community and Creeping Consequentialism' [1996] *Crim LR* 220, 221; Royal Commission on Criminal Justice, *Report of the Royal Commission on Criminal Justice* (Dissenting Report) (London, HMSO, 1993) 235 per M Zander.

[3] C Fennell, *Crime and Crisis in Ireland: Justice by Illusion?* (Cork, Cork University Press, 1993) 5.

[4] G Dession, 'The Technique of Public Order: Evolving Concepts of Criminal Law (1995) 5 *Buffalo Law Review* 22, 40. Also R Summers, 'Evaluating and Improving Legal Processes – A Plea for "Process Values"' (1974) 60 *Cornell Law Review* 1, 42.

[5] H Packer, *The Limits of the Criminal Sanction* (California, Stanford University Press, 1968).

[6] ibid, 153.

[7] ibid, 158.

[8] ibid, 159.

[9] ibid, 160–62.

[10] ibid, 164.

in informal adjudicative fact-finding. The aim of the criminal process is as much to protect the factually innocent as it is to convict the factually guilty: therefore, formal, adjudicative and adversarial fact-finding is fundamental, and reliability is of greater consequence than efficiency. Moreover, given that power is susceptible to abuse, a diminution in the efficiency of the criminal process is regarded as acceptable in order to prevent oppression of the individual.[11] Furthermore, even if the facts indicate that the person is likely to be guilty, he is not deemed to be so if there has been a failure to uphold or adhere to certain rules designed to protect him and to preserve the integrity of the process.[12] Although this may preclude the attainment of individual justice in a particular case, it serves the ends of social justice and the protection of due process values.[13]

Packer's models, as interpretive devices, assist in considering whether the demands of crime control are superseding the strictures of due process in dealing with organised crime. Nonetheless, Packer's relatively simple dichotomy belies the range of demands at play in the criminal process and may misrepresent the very idea of due process. One could argue that due process and crime control are not comparable in a conceptual sense, given that crime control is the overarching aim of criminal justice, whereas the due process model provides procedures that regulate and temper that objective.[14] Due process cannot be the animating force of the criminal process seeing as the latter's concern and objective is to detect, address and punish crime, rather than protecting the individual from public officials.[15] In other words, due process is not a goal in itself and only acquires meaning in the context of the pursuit of other goals, such as crime control.[16] To this end, a reconstruction of Packer's models has been proposed, so as to articulate that crime control is the underlying purpose of the system, the pursuit of which is qualified by respect for due process.[17]

Moreover, the titles or descriptions of Packer's models also may be contested. It has been suggested that the crime control model should be renamed the efficiency model, given that crime control may refer to both the goal of the system and a set of values underpinning that goal;[18] that they should be renamed the truth model and the justice model respectively, given the central emphasis in each approach;[19]

---

[11] ibid, 166.

[12] ibid, 167.

[13] AS Goldstein, 'Reflections on Two Models: Inquisitorial Themes in American Criminal Procedure' (1974) 26 *Stanford Law Review* 1009, 1149.

[14] ibid, 1016.

[15] MR Damaška, 'Evidentiary Barriers to Conviction and Two Models of Criminal Procedure: A Comparative Study' (1973) 121 *University of Pennsylvania Law Review* 506, 575.

[16] D Smith, 'Case Construction and the Goals of Criminal Process' (1997) 37 *British Journal of Criminology* 319, 335–36.

[17] A Ashworth and M Redmayne, *The Criminal Process* (4th edn) (Oxford, Oxford University Press, 2010) 40. Ashworth and Remayne also note that Packer's models do not incorporate victim-related matters.

[18] P Duff, 'Crime Control, Due Process and "The Case for the Prosecution"' (1998) 38 *British Journal of Criminology* 611, 614.

[19] Bottoms and McClean propose a third model of the criminal process, the 'liberal bureaucratic model'. AE Bottoms and JD McClean, *Defendants in the Criminal Process* (London, Routledge and

or that a third 'liberal bureaucratic model' should be introduced.[20] Indeed, the very use of the term 'model' has been challenged, and its replacement by 'ideal type', which may be weak or strong, recommended.[21]

Despite these valid claims, Packer's models neatly isolate oppositional ideologies in the criminal process. As Henham notes, Packer's approach is deficient theoretically but a heuristically valuable tool.[22] While the fundamental goal of any criminal justice system is the control of crime,[23] the challenge for legislators and policy makers is to determine how to reconcile this legitimate aim with the concomitant need to protect the individual in the criminal process. The friction identified by Packer essentially seems to be between security and human rights,[24] where the former is conceived of as embodying the rights and interests of the community and the law-abiding majority only, whereas the latter pertain to the rights of suspects and criminals, rather than any person who potentially could be investigated for or accused of a crime.

Another interpretive approach is to see the underlying rationales in contemporary criminal justice as embodying the precepts of deontologism and utilitarianism, which map roughly onto Packer's notions of due process and crime control respectively. Deontologism is concerned with duties and rights, and it centres on the primacy of the individual, so may be seen as the animating force behind the due process model. For deontologists, what is morally right cannot be defined in terms of whether something maximises goodness in the world, and the end cannot justify the means; in other words, even the most commendable goal should not be attained in an unjust manner.[25] This implies that the prevention, repression and punishment of crime at all costs cannot validate the attrition of important individual liberties.

Kegan Paul, 1976) 228–31. The liberal bureaucratic model retains the due process model's concern for formal adjudicative processes and the protection of individual liberty, but disapproves of the restriction on quantitative output and so adopts a more pragmatic approach on certain issues.

[20] ibid, 228–31. The liberal bureaucratic model retains the due process model's concern for formal adjudicative processes and the protection of individual liberty, but disapproves of the restriction on quantitative output and so adopts a more pragmatic approach.

[21] S Macdonald, 'Constructing a Framework for Criminal Justice Research: Learning from Packer's Mistakes' (2008) 11 *New Criminal Law Review* 257.

[22] R Henham, 'Human Rights, Due Process and Sentencing' (1998) 38 *British Journal of Criminology* 592, 593.

[23] M McConville, A Sanders and R Leng, 'Descriptive or Critical Sociology: The Choice is Yours' (1997) 37 *British Journal of Criminology* 347, 355. Accepting that the fundamental goal of criminal justice is crime control does not necessitate acceptance of the crime control model. In the pursuit of crime control, a criminal justice system may reflect crime control values, due process values or a mixture of both. ibid, 356.

[24] L Zedner, *Security* (London, Routledge, 2009); A Ashworth, *Human Rights, Serious Crime, and Criminal Procedure* (London, Sweet & Maxwell, 2002) 42–43; S Greer, 'Miscarriages of Criminal Justice Reconsidered' (1994) 57 *MLR* 58, 60; B Hudson, *Justice in the Risk Society* (London, Sage, 2003) 42.

[25] LW Beck (ed), I Kant, *The Foundations of the Metaphysics of Morals* (New Jersey, Prentice Hall, 1989) 39; I Kant, *The Metaphysical Elements of Justice* (Indianapolis, Bobbs-Merrill, 1965) xx. Hudson, n 24, xi.

One version of a deontological theory of rights classifies an individual right as a 'political trump' which may not be denied by appeal to a collective goal[26] and which derives its strength from its ability to withstand competition.[27] Although some rights may be compromised or eroded, the State may not defend an act solely on the ground that it is likely to produce a benefit to the community, because to do this would make the claim of a right pointless.[28] Thus, if an individual has a fundamental right to something, he must be able to invoke it to resist the claims of general welfare, even if other persons are inconvenienced while it is exercised.[29] In the context of the criminal justice system, deontologism would require the protection of due process rights, notwithstanding that their exercise may, on occasion, stymie crime control.

In contrast to deontologism, utilitarianism advocates the promotion of the greatest good for the largest number of people,[30] and thus may map onto the crime control model. For Bentham, the happiness of the individual is the only end which the legislator ought to consider,[31] while Mill advocated that all decisions should be taken according to the precepts of social utility, given that the determination of a just solution is often arbitrary.[32] In essence, utilitarianism does not necessarily protect the individual against infringements in the name of the good of society as a whole,[33] and each separate person is significant only as the locus of elements of the total aggregate of pleasure or happiness.[34] Although it may be argued that utilitarianism is not inimical to rights given that the recognition of rights may maximise utility, this perspective fails to see rights as independent and stable moral factors.[35] Given that ultimately utilitarianism is committed to the general welfare, rights merely count as factors which may affect this,[36] and thus only if it is expedient to recognise and uphold a right will utilitarianism do so.

While both deontological and utilitarian influences and imperatives may be discerned in the criminal processes in the United Kingdom and Ireland, current legislative trends indicate a strengthening of utilitarian demands with the adoption of measures that are justified by reference to the objectives of crime control. The expansion of powers of surveillance; the reliance on anonymous testimony;

---

[26] R Dworkin, *A Matter of Principle* (Massachusetts, Harvard University Press, 1985) 183; R Dworkin, *Taking Rights Seriously* (London, Duckworth, 1977) xi.

[27] Dworkin, *Taking Rights Seriously*, n 26, 92.

[28] ibid, 191.

[29] D Lyons, 'Utility as a Possible Ground of Rights' (1980) 14 *Nous* 17, 20; J Waldron (ed), *The Theories of Rights* (Oxford, Oxford University Press, 1984) 113.

[30] Frey argues that utilitarianism refers not to a single theory but to a cluster of theories which are variations on a theme. RG Frey (ed), *Utility and Rights* (Oxford, Basil Blackwell Ltd, 1984).

[31] J Bentham, *An Introduction to the Principles of Morals and Legislation* (Oxford, Clarendon Press, 1996) 34.

[32] ibid, 101.

[33] Hudson, n 24, 17.

[34] HLA Hart, 'Between Utility and Rights' in A Ryan (ed), *The Idea of Freedom: Essays in Honour of Isaiah Berlin* (Oxford, Oxford University Press, 1979) 78.

[35] Lyons, n 29, 21.

[36] Lyons, n 29, 30; Dworkin, *Taking Rights Seriously*, n 26, 95.

and the recovery of assets without a criminal conviction: these are but some counter-organised crime measures that privilege the utilitarian pursuit of crime control over deontological considerations of due process.

Linked to utilitarianism, but conceptually distinct, is the notion of pragmatism in criminal justice policy, whereby theory is eschewed, and decisions are made and policies developed on the basis of practical effect rather than any other concerns, such as due process, or deontological principles. The most pronounced examples of pragmatic responses to organised crime are the controlled delivery of illegal goods; undercover policing; the granting of immunity from prosecution or other rewards for cooperating or testifying against former colleagues; and the use of accomplice evidence. While potentially problematic in a rights' sense, in terms of effective investigation and prosecution these measures are valuable in addressing organised crime. Such pragmatism is evident in criminal justice and penal policy in England and Wales in particular since the fall of 'liberal elitism' in the governance of crime: Loader attributes this to the assault on rehabilitation in the 1970s and the rise of 'law and order' politics in the 1980s and 'populist-punitivism' in the early 1990s.[37] In Scotland, where penal welfarism held sway until later, arguably into the early twenty-first century, research was linked more closely to policy development and practice,[38] although much of the relevant legislation pertaining to organised crime did emanate from Westminster.[39] Pragmatism in Ireland is embedded due to the traditional aversion to 'intellectualism' in policy-making generally,[40] the absence of criminal justice and criminology as academic subjects of study until the turn of the twenty-first century, and the historically low rates of public crime, all of which meant that many criminal justice measures were, and remain, *ad hoc* and reactionary.

One cannot directly equate in a conceptual sense various criminal justice developments that may seek to improve crime control, or to increase security in one particular guise, or to further utilitarian objectives, or that are grounded in pragmatic concerns. Nonetheless, their shared commonality is a preference for the expedient detection and resolution of crime over the notions of due process. This is facilitated by characterising the latter as technicalities which pertain to the suspect and offender only, rather than civil liberties vital to and enjoyed by all members of society. Moreover, the tenor and nature of law-making in this area may be explained by the centrality of public protection and risk in political discourse, the perception of a state of emergency, and the need to make adaptations in addressing this type of crime.

---

[37] See I Loader, 'Fall of the "Platonic Guardians": Liberalism, Criminology and Political Responses to Crime in England and Wales' (2006) 46 *British Journal of Criminology* 561, 562ff.

[38] See L McAra, 'Crime, Criminology and Criminal Justice in Scotland' (2008) 5 *European Journal of Criminology* 481.

[39] See ch 1.

[40] M O'Connell, *Right-Wing Ireland? The Rise of Populism in Ireland and Europe* (Dublin, Liffey Press, 2003).

A. Public Protection

The demand for public protection has become a principal theme of criminal justice policy and has led to a diminution in the attention paid to civil liberties more broadly and due process rights specifically.[41] This notion of security from crime is a primary and paramount concern in both political oratory and legal responses to organised crime. Although community safety is a legitimate objective in a criminal justice system, what is most problematic is how the constituent parts of this notion are now constructed: the parameters of the public or community are drawn more narrowly, and there has been a reappraisal of what protection, safety or security consist of and mean.

In both the United Kingdom and Ireland there has been a drive to 'rebalance' the justice system towards the public interest in the detection, prosecution and punishment of crime.[42] This may be described as foregrounding communitarian demands and interests, where communitarianism is an epistemological, moral and political ideology which is focused on the community and places great importance on civil society.[43] The Labour Party, in office in the UK from 1997 until 2010 introduced several criminal justice measures which embodied a certain regressive form of this ideology, such as anti-social behaviour orders, and this was followed, in theory if not in substance or practice, in Ireland and Scotland.[44] The common thread running through the different varieties of communitarianism centres on the obligations owed to society and the need to tie responsibilities to rights.[45] The individualistic nature of a liberal society is rejected, and therefore a reconfiguration of laws and social arrangements is recommended. In contrast to liberalism where the individual is key, here the community's rights may compete with individual rights,[46] and this ascription stems from a desire to protect the community as an entity, in addition to its values and its members.

Shifting the focus from the individual to the community can indeed have many positive results for late-modern societies.[47] In this respect, however, invoking the importance of the community in response to the fear of crime often plays on

---

[41] D Garland, *The Culture of Control* (Oxford, Oxford University Press, 2001) 12.

[42] Home Office, *Rebalancing the Criminal Justice System in Favour of the Law-Abiding Majority: Cutting Crime, Reducing Reoffending and Protecting the Public* (Home Office, London, 2006); Balance in the Criminal Law Review Group, *Final Report of the Balance in the Criminal Law Review Group* (Dublin, Department of Justice, 2007) 3ff; and Dáil Debates, vol 597, col 1276 (15 February 2005) per Minister for Justice, Mr McDowell. For a critique of the notion of balancing see A Ashworth, 'Crime, Community and Creeping Consequentialism' (1996) 43 *Crim LR* 220.

[43] H Tam, *Communitarianism: A New Agenda for Politics and Citizenship* (Basingstoke, Macmillan, 1998) 12; M Walzer, 'The Communitarian Critique of Liberalism' (1990) 18 *Political Theory* 6, 7–9.

[44] Anti-social behaviour orders (ASBOs) were introduced by the Crime and Disorder Act 1998. See Antisocial Behaviour (Scotland) Act 2004; Criminal Justice Act 2006 (Ireland).

[45] Hudson, n 24, 94; A Etzioni, *The Spirit of the Community: Rights, Responsibilities and the Communitarian Agenda* (London, Fontana Press, 1993) 4 and 9.

[46] Hudson, n 24, 82–83.

[47] Hughes argues that insufficient attention is paid to the radical potential of communitarian thinking. G Hughes, 'Communitarianism and Law and Order' (1996) 16 *Critical Social Policy* 17.

defensive reactions[48] and facilitates the introduction and implementation of repressive elements which purport to protect that community. What is (a) 'community' is always contestable, and in the specific context of suspected organised crime and criminals there may be little sympathy for the view of such parties as members of the public with equal entitlements to rights. This may thus facilitate the 'othering' of the suspect, without any finding of criminal guilt,[49] or result in the overly punitive treatment of offenders after conviction. A moral panic is engendered where the 'folk devils', in this instance organised criminals, threaten the safety and security of society.[50] This process of differentiation is evident in political discourse, particularly in Ireland, about those involved in organised and gun crime when compared with 'decent people':[51] 'Anyone who deals in or is in possession of firearms has no place in society',[52] and after a fatal shooting, those responsible were described in political debate as 'animals' who 'have stepped outside the bounds of humanity'.[53] This demarcation between those suspected of a gun-related offence and the rest of the community renders palatable the slow and steady erosion of due process rights, as does the presumption that these robust powers will not be misused or invoked against any 'factually innocent' person.[54]

This type of punitive communitarianism may be criticised on the basis that it sees the interests of the community and those of the suspect as fundamentally at odds. There exists a pervasive assumption that the community's welfare or security is advanced by reducing the rights of defendants and suspects and by intensifying the authority of the agencies involved in the criminal process.[55] This presumes that rights and civil liberties, such as the freedom from prolonged pre-trial detention, the right not to be subject to unjustified surveillance, the right to confront witnesses and to have a jury trial, are of little significance to personal security.[56] People generally regard themselves as likely victims rather than potential suspects,[57] and this results in an underestimation of the need for protective rights to safeguard the interests of the minority who come into contact with agents of the State in the criminal justice system.

In a rhetorical sense, the entitlements of the community often are invoked to justify developments relating to organised crime in Ireland and the UK.[58]

---

[48] Hudson, n 24, 91.

[49] Garland, n 41, 134ff.

[50] S Cohen, *Folk Devils and Moral Panics: The Creation of the Mods and Rockers* (Oxford, Blackwell, 1972).

[51] Seanad Debates, vol 186, col 2088 (26 April 2007).

[52] Dáil Debates, vol 607, col 1531 (18 October 2005).

[53] 'Gardaí Investigate if Murder Linked to Court Case', *Irish Times*, 10 April 2009.

[54] Packer, n 5, 160*ff.*

[55] Ashworth, n 2, 225.

[56] For a similar argument in the context of terrorism laws see L Donohue, 'The Perilous Dialogue' (2009) 97 *California Law Review* 357.

[57] See J Simon, 'Megan's Law: Crime and Democracy in Late Modern America' (2000) *Law and Social Inquiry* 1111.

[58] Department of Justice, Equality and Law Reform, 'A Human Rights Approach to Policing' (Irish Council for Civil Liberties Seminar, 4 March 2003) per Minister of State at the Department of Justice, Equality and Law Reform, Mr O'Dea.

Furthermore, as regards legislative measures, indeterminate and presumptive sentences and other post-conviction orders are the prime examples of the public protection imperative. The danger in presenting and prioritising a particular conception of the public interest in the development of legislation is that due process norms and values like proportionality in sentencing may be disregarded, notwithstanding their significance for the community at large.

Communitarianism can generate a parochial notion of the public interest[59] in which general governing principles such as liberty or equality may be forgotten. While Etzioni argues that communitarians are not majoritarians and do not advocate a utilitarian sacrifice of individual liberties for the greater good,[60] the risk is that the internalisation of such ideas in the political sphere will lead to this very consequence. Moreover, no longer is the State seen as an entity from which we must be protected, rather it is from each other that we must be protected by the State. The right to live in a society with circumscribed police and State powers is a core feature of any late-modern liberal society that purports to support deonto-logical principles, and must not be overshadowed by the desire to restrict crime.

B. Risk

In addition to public protection, a further trend which influences the erosion of the norms of due process in the legal responses to organised crime is the centrality of a discourse of risk, and the aversion towards it within policy development. While risk has always been of concern in the criminal justice system, a new orien-tation towards it has been identified, in which the actuarial probabilistic language of risk is joined to the moral language of blame.[61] Moreover, it seems that risk control rather than management or reduction is now emphasised.[62] In contrast to the latter concepts, both of which accept the inevitability of error and seek to manage and lower risk rather than remove it, risk control aims to prevent the

Dáil Debates, vol 597, col 1276 (15 February 2005) per Minister for Justice, Mr McDowell.
Dáil Debates, vol 465, col 1441 (16 May 1996) per Mr Byrne.
Dáil Debates, vol 444, col 189 (21 June 1994) per Mr Lenihan.

[59] A Crawford, *The Local Governance of Crime: Appeals to Community and Partnerships* (Oxford, Oxford University Press, 1999) 253.

[60] Etzioni, n 45, 255; A Etzioni (ed), *The Essential Communitarian Reader* (Maryland, Rowman and Littlefield, 1998) xiv.

[61] Hudson, n 24, 45 and 51–53. This stems from the seminal work of theorists such as Mary Douglas and Ulrich Beck. See M Douglas and A Wildavsky, *Risk and Culture: An Essay on the Selection of Technical and Environmental Dangers* (Berkeley, University of California Press, 1982), and U Beck, *Risk Society: Towards a New Modernity* (Sheffield, Sheffield Region Centre for Science and Technology, 1992). Shearing argues that a renewed risk emphasis in criminal justice has not led to an abandonment of other ways of thinking, but has moulded them to fit a risk-focused perspective. C Shearing, 'Punishment and the Changing Face of Governance' (2001) 3 *Punishment and Society* 203, 212.

[62] Clear and Cadora contend that risk calculation may be for one of three purposes: risk control, risk management or risk reduction. T Clear and E Cadora, 'Risk and Correctional Practice' in K Stenson and R Sullivan (eds), *Crime, Risk and Justice: The Politics of Crime Control in Liberal Democracies* (Devon, Willan Publishing, 2000) 59.

recurrence of a new crime and to eliminate risk completely.[63] This is usually the preferred approach of politicians as it provides assurances of desirable outcomes, notwithstanding the considerable financial, personal and societal costs that may result from the over-imposition of control.[64] In addition, an actuarial shift in emphasis is evident with offenders being regarded as aggregates rather than individuals.[65] In this respect the focus is less on the responsibility, culpability and treatment of offenders, but rather on techniques to identify, categorise and manage groups according to their dangerousness: 'The task is managerial, not transformative'.[66]

Public protection, as considered previously, represents a key concern of risk-oriented tactics, given that the elimination or prevention of risk to society increasingly appears to displace concern for individual rights and may lead to the overestimation of the likelihood of a particular risk materialising in a bid to protect the majority. Incapacitation, through the use of indeterminate and presumptive sentences, is paradigmatic of a risk logic, given that it seeks to protect the public and does not seek to alter the offender or the social context but merely rearranges the physical distribution of individuals.[67] Moreover, the scheme of presumptive sentences provides a quintessential example of the subsuming of individual characteristics by a standard which applies to offenders as a class. In addition, the concept of the career criminal is a central aspect of the new penology, given that it is agnostic about the causes of crime and is concerned only with the identification of high-risk offenders in order to incapacitate and/or manage them.[68] This notion of a career criminal has gained currency in popular and political discourse on organised crime,[69] (though the reality is more nuanced)[70] and is encapsulated in post-conviction orders which may limit the activities of an offender after release from imprisonment.

The rationale behind the support for risk control lies in the fact that while imprisoning an offender inflicts a largely hidden cost on that individual's liberty, failing to control an offender who then commits further crime imposes costs on

---

[63] ibid.

[64] ibid, 60. Clear and Cadora note that those working in the penal process tend to prefer the other, more realistic, options. In addition to the over-imposition of control, Ashworth remarks that the growing emphasis on risk-assessment and risk-based penal policies tends to underplay the problems of effectively identifying and dealing with risk. A Ashworth, 'Criminal Justice Reform: Principles, Human Rights and Public Protection' (2004) *Crim LR* 516.

[65] M Feeley and J Simon, 'The New Penology: Notes on the Emerging Strategy of Corrections and its Implications' (1992) 30 *Criminology* 449 (hereafter 'The New Penology'); M Feeley and J Simon, 'Actuarial Justice: the Emerging Criminal Law' in D Nelken (ed), *The Futures of Criminology* (Sage, London, 1994) 173–201, 185 (hereafter 'Actuarial Justice').

[66] Feeley and Simon, 'The New Penology', n 65, 452.

[67] ibid, 458–61.

[68] Simon and Feeley, 'Actuarial Justice', n 65, 164–65.

[69] See SOCA Press Release, 'Riches to Rags Fall of a Career Criminal', 14 July 2010; '44 Years for Career Criminals who Planned to Flood the UK with Drugs', 23 April 2010; Dáil Debates, vol 481, col 1368 (21 October 1997) per Minister for Justice, Mr O'Donoghue, and col 1391 per Minister of State at the Department of Justice, Ms Wallace.

[70] M Levi, 'The Organization of Serious Crimes for Gain' in M Maguire, R Morgan and R Reiner (eds), *The Oxford Handbook of Criminology* (5th edn) (Oxford, Oxford University Press, 2012) 607.

the victim and society and compromises the credibility of the justice system.[71] The restriction of the rights of an accused or an offender is tolerated, since preventing the commission of an offence is seen as more important than the adherence to due process demands.

C. A State of Emergency

Another key motivator for the legal reactions to organised crime in which due process norms are subverted or ignored lies in the generation and maintenance of a feeling of crisis. In certain respects, the Irish State and the jurisdictions in the UK view organised crime as portending a state of emergency that merits extra-ordinary legal measures.[72] What is notable, however, are the national divergences in terms of the reactions to this heightened concern. Thus, while there is a shared perception that traditional norms and processes cannot facilitate the effective policing, prosecution and punishment of organised crime, the extent to which and the manner in which this affects the criminal process differs jurisdictionally, due to cultural, historical and legal factors.

The perception in Ireland that organised crime represents a criminal justice crisis beyond that encountered normally might appear to be substantiated by the statistical rise in drugs and some firearms offences, the low detection and prosecution rates for gun homicides in particular, and the incidental deaths of bystanders.[73] Indeed, it is not so much objective crime rates as rates of growth or perceived rates of growth that drive such perceptions. The level of concern is evident in the assertion of the Minister for Justice in 2007 that 'the drug and gun culture . . . poses as significant a threat to the wellbeing of the Irish State and Irish society as the paramilitaries did at any stage of their campaign for a quarter of a century',[74] and reiterated in comments that the increase in 'gangland' killings has been 'enormous' and 'inordinate',[75] that '[l]ife seems to be cheaper',[76] and that the there is a 'serious crisis in criminal justice'.[77] The view that, to all intents and purposes, a state of emergency exists in Ireland is supported by the apparent link between paramilitary actors and the burgeoning 'gun culture':[78] '[g]angland crime constitutes an attack on the State in much

---

[71] Hudson, n 24, 53.

[72] See G Agamben, *State of Exception* (K Attell trans) (Chicago, University of Chicago Press, 2005).

[73] See, eg 'Funeral of Murdered Plumber Held', *Irish Times*, 12 December 2006; 'Murder of Rugby Player "Marks a New Low"', *Irish Times*, 11 November 2008; 'Father Saw Wounded Son Lying on Ground', *Irish Times*, 7 July 2009.

[74] 'Gardaí Investigate Drugs Link in Latest Shootings', *Irish Times*, 25 January 2007.

[75] Dáil Debates, vol 617, col 78 (28 March 2006).

[76] 'Ireland a More Violent Place, Says Garda Chief', *Irish Times*, 12 January 2009.

[77] Dáil Debates, vol 629, col 1672 (14 December 2006) per Mr Costello.

[78] See Dáil Debates, vol 667, col 539 (18 November 2008); Parliamentary Questions (2 October 2008) #69; Dáil Debates, vol 677, col 724 (11 March 2009); Dáil Debates, vol 603, col 1171 (2 June 2005); C McCullagh, *Crime in Ireland* (Cork, Cork University Press, 1996) 37; P Williams, *Evil Empire: John Gilligan, his Gang and the Execution of Journalist Veronica Guerin* (Dublin, Merlin Publishing, 2001).

the same way as the IRA attacked the foundations of the State for many years'.[79] Given that it seems that the existence of subversive crime has contributed, to some extent at least, to organised crime in Ireland, it is logical, although not justifiable, that the State has continued the tradition of using extraordinary measures to deal with this phenomenon.[80]

As a result of this conception of the extent and nature of organised crime, in Ireland some such suspects are arrested and detained, and trials held, under counter-terrorism legislation. Furthermore, extraordinary tactics once used against terrorists have been replicated in legislation that pertains to a broader range of crime, such as prolonged detention and asset forfeiture. Emergencies in Irish legal history prompted by subversion have 'spawned' 'ordinary' criminal justice legislation that poses a great, long-term threat to civil liberties,[81] and this trend has continued unabated in relation to organised crime.

Similarly, measures that were once employed against those suspected of terrorism offences, like reliance on anonymous witness evidence and the holding of non-jury trials, are now being adopted in England, Wales and Northern Ireland against organised criminality. This is not through the use of broadly framed extraordinary legislation, however, but by means of emulation in contemporary legislation. Ostensibly, this situation contrasts with the state of affairs in Scotland, where the absence of such a terrorist legacy, historically and legally speaking, appears in some respects to provide a safeguard against such measures. Nonetheless, this observation is disproven by provisions permitting anonymous witnesses, for example, which although having no precursor in Scotland are now emulated after being introduced in England and Wales.

Defining an emergency is not easy,[82] and clearly demarcating such a state from normalcy may not always be possible.[83] Nonetheless, the paradigmatic understanding is one of a temporary break from the norm due to a particular event or situation.[84] To be sure, an arguable case may be made that organised crime, in particular if trans-national in nature, may sometimes pose a threat to national security.[85] Though the lack of ideology means that the primary impetus for organised crime is monetary profit rather than the usurping of the administration of a State, the incursion of organised crime groups into governance, or the overspill into civil society, may sometimes warrant a temporary declaration of emergency, with the limitations on civil liberties and the deploying of military force that this may entail. However, as outlined in chapter two, organised crime at present poses

[79] Dáil Debates, vol 681, col 373 (29 April 2009) per Peter Power.
[80] See ch 2.
[81] D Walsh, 'The Impact of Anti-Subversive Laws on Police Powers and Practices in Ireland' (1989) 62 *Temple Law Review* 1099, 1101; S Kilcommins and B Vaughan, *Terrorism, Rights and the Rule of Law: Negotiating State Justice in Ireland* (Cullompton, Willan Publishing, 2007) 79ff.
[82] O Gross, 'Once More unto the Breach' (1998) 23 *Yale Journal of International Law* 437.
[83] O Gross, 'Chaos and Rules: Should Responses to Violent Crises always be Constitutional?' (2003) 112 *Yale Law Journal* 1011, 1022.
[84] Gross, n 82, 439–40.
[85] National Security Council, *Strategy to Combat Transnational Organized Crime: Addressing Converging Threats to National Security* (Washington DC, National Security Council, 2011).

little threat to State security in Ireland and the United Kingdom, and in reality the crime concerns seem trivial or disproportionate when compared with the situation elsewhere, such as in certain parts of Mexico.[86] Thus, while the phenomenon of organised crime may in fact sometimes attain such gravity as to warrant extraordinary measures in limited scenarios, such a degree is not evident in Ireland or the UK.

In a constitutional sense such a state of affairs does not exist in Ireland or in the UK as a result of organised crime. There have been no formal declarations under Article 15 of the European Convention on Human Rights which permits derogation from Convention obligations in time of war or other public emergency threatening the life of the nation, to the extent strictly required by the exigencies of the crisis.[87] While comparisons are drawn between the extent and effect of organised crime and the threat of paramilitary crime, in the latter instance such derogations were made explicitly, and though controversial, were predicated on a defined and evident problem.[88] Moreover, there has been no parliamentary declaration under Article 28.3.3° of the Irish Constitution of a national emergency that affects the vital interests of the State.[89]

In the context of organised crime, policy makers in Ireland and the United Kingdom seem to blur the distinction between a very serious social problem and a national emergency,[90] thereby permitting radical measures to be adopted. This is facilitated in Ireland by virtue of the fact that emergency measures have moved from being temporary measures to safeguard or regain the constitutional status quo, to being permanent aspects of the legal system.[91] Although counter-terrorism legislation may be intended to be temporary to allow for later expiration or repeal, in practice it tends to become entrenched permanently[92] and then subsequently applied to a broader range of criminality.[93] In the UK, what were once extraordinary measures, such as anonymous witness evidence or judge-only trials, have been translated into the 'ordinary' criminal justice context. Overall, the adoption and imitation of counter-terrorism measures to deal with organised

---

[86] See V Felbab-Brown, *Calderón's Caldron: Lessons from Mexico's Battle Against Organized Crime and Drug Trafficking in Tijuana, Ciudad Juárez, and Michoacán* (Washington DC, Brookings Institute, 2011). Felbab-Brown notes (at 10) that the Government of Mexico strongly objects to any suggestions that the criminal violence in Mexico in any way resembles insurgency, though it does now refer to some such criminals as terrorists.

[87] See *A v United Kingdom* (2009) 49 EHRR 29, para 173ff.

[88] In *Ireland v United Kingdom* (1979-80) EHRR 25, the parties were agreed, as were the Commission and the Court, that the Art 15 test was satisfied, since terrorism had for a number of years represented 'a particularly far-reaching and acute danger for the territorial integrity of the United Kingdom, the institutions of the six counties and the lives of the province's inhabitants'.

[89] S Kilcommins and B Vaughan, 'Subverting the Rule of Law in Ireland' (2004) 35 *Cambrian Law Review* 55, 57.

[90] Hudson, n 24, 218.

[91] Gross, n 83, 1070–71; Kilcommins and Vaughan, n 81, 73.

[92] See Donohue, n 56, 373.

[93] Hillyard argued that Northern Ireland served as a test-bed for repressive State policies and their subsequent normalisation during the 1970s and 1980s. See P Hillyard, 'The Normalization of Special Powers: From Northern Ireland to Britain' in P Scraton (ed), *Law, Order and the Authoritarian State: Readings in Critical Criminology* (Milton Keynes, Open University Press, 1987).

crime encapsulates the 'normalisation of the extraordinary', namely that what was once unthinkable is made acceptable by perceived necessity and thereby continued, and concomitantly, that increasing 'dosages' are required to deal with each new crisis.[94]

D. Adaptations

Certain measures that address organised crime involve the placing of responsibility for detecting and reporting suspicious behaviour on private parties, and others avoid the criminal justice system altogether by adopting civil tactics. While the former approach does not compromise due process, it reconfigures the nature of the means of dealing with organised crime, and the latter is problematic in a rights' sense. These legal responses may be conceptualised by reference to adaptations in the criminal justice process, and the shifting notion of governance.

In addition to the perception that the nature and level of organised crime in itself is an emergency, it has been argued in a more general sense that there is an enduring crisis in criminal justice.[95] Confidence in the justice system has decreased dramatically, the institutions and practices are no longer seen as adequate, and crucially, the problem is deemed not to relate to implementation but rather to be one of theory failure.[96] This predicament influences all policy decisions, resulting in the formation of 'volatile and ambivalent' measures, which may be classified as either adaptations to reality, or denials of the situation in question.[97] While the latter is embodied in punitive responses such as indeterminate sentences, adaptations to reality may involve the privatisation of justice, the commercialisation of crime control, and the redistribution of responsibility to non-State bodies.[98]

It appears that legislators are faced with a particular difficulty as regards organised crime, given the difficulties in addressing this type of criminality. Various factors contribute to this predicament: detection of organised crime may be difficult; those with criminal power may insulate themselves from detection or prosecution; many typical organised crimes require a degree of public complicity or involvement such as the provision of a market for illicit and trafficked goods; and witnesses may be intimidated or implicated in the actions themselves. Moreover, punishment through imprisonment may not affect the profits that accrue from organised crime and that facilitate and maintain further criminality.

A number of provisions used against organised crime in the UK and Ireland embody adaptations to the reality of late-modern crime control, and may be regarded as 'non-traditional' approaches to controlling organised crime.[99] For

---

[94] Gross, n 83, 1090–92.
[95] Garland, n 41, 105–07.
[96] ibid, 19–20.
[97] ibid.
[98] ibid, 123–27.
[99] M Levi, 'Policing Fraud and Organised Crime' in T Newburn (ed), *Handbook of Policing* (2nd edn) (Cullompton, Willan, 2008) 527–28.

example, the comparator States enlist help from civil society and private actors in money laundering investigations. This diversified approach recruits external bodies and agents in the investigation of crime by assigning responsibility for reporting evidence of unlawful acts to third parties and expands the partnership base so as to facilitate more readily the successful detection and investigation of crime.[100] Responsibilising banks and other third parties in the context of money laundering depicts the changing notion of governmentality, whereby the State is developing a form of rule which involves 'the enlistment of others . . . and the creation of new forms of co-operative action'.[101] Here, the role of the State is redefined as a partner or facilitator, 'steering and regulating rather than rowing and providing'.[102] This is embodied in the devolution of responsibility which does not conflict with due process rights per se, but alters the traditional criminal justice paradigm in which the focus is on the individual and the State to one which co-opts third party assistance.

In another adaptive measure, the comparator States introduced laws to allow the recovery and taxation of criminal assets,[103] necessitated by the perceived ability of powerful criminals to escape detention and prosecution by delegating responsibility for the implementation of criminal acts to lower-level offenders, while still benefiting from the profits of crime themselves. Asset recovery, which operates under the civil burden of proof, mitigates the difficulty in convicting an organised criminal. When traditional approaches were seen as inefficacious, the UK and Ireland altered their response to include this novel strategy which bypasses due process through its situation in the civil realm.

III. The Judiciary and Due Process–Dialogue Between the Arms of the State

A shift in values towards an ethos prioritising utilitarian demands of crime control, security, public protection and risk avoidance over rights is evidenced in many legal developments pertaining to organised criminality, such as the use of accomplice evidence, prolonged detention periods, non-jury trials, and civil asset recovery. Nonetheless, the judiciary sometimes provides a bulwark against these predominantly statutory trends.[104] Packer argues that while the validating authority of the crime control model ultimately is legislative and proximately administrative, the due process model's validating authority is judicial, which requires an appeal to

---

[100] While this may be classified as an adaptive measure, it should also be remembered that the provisions in the UK and Ireland are introduced to comply with the EU Council Directives. See ch 4.

[101] Garland, n 41, 125.

[102] N Rose, 'Government and Control' (2000) 40 *British Journal of Criminology* 321, 323–24.

[103] See ch 6.

[104] For a similar argument in the context of counter-terrorism measures see D Cole, 'Judging the Next Emergency: Judicial Review and Individual Rights in Times of Crisis' (2003) 101 *Michigan Law Review* 2565 and F de Londras, *Detention in the War on Terror: Can Human Rights Fight Back?* (Cambridge, Cambridge University Press, 2011).

the Constitution.[105] Though one may dispute his terminology regarding these two models, it does indeed appear that due process is of declining relevance to the legislature in devising law in this area, while the judiciary, in interpreting the Constitution and the European Convention on Human Rights (ECHR), remains the principal guardian of due process values.

The tension between crime control and security on the one hand and procedural protections on the other has been stressed by the courts. In Ireland, it has been emphasised that '[t]he detection of crime and the conviction of guilty persons . . . cannot . . . outweigh the unambiguously expressed constitutional obligation "as far as practicable to defend and vindicate the personal rights of the citizen"'.[106] Similarly, Simon Brown LJ in *International Transport Roth GmbH* v *Secretary of State for the Home Department* emphasised that 'the court's role under the . . . [Human Rights] Act is as the guardian of human rights. It cannot abdicate this responsibility'.[107]

The significance placed by the courts on due process norms was particularly evident in the dialogue between the House of Lords acting in its judicial capacity and the UK Government regarding counter-terrorism measures. Though not directly pertinent to the means of addressing organised crime, it demonstrates how the actions of the court are often animated by a different rationale to the legislature. The ability to detain foreign terrorism suspects without charge on the direction of the Secretary of State under Part 4 of the Anti-terrorism, Crime and Security Act 2001 was repealed following *A(FC)* v *Secretary of State for the Home Department*,[108] while the subsequently introduced scheme of control orders under the Prevention of Terrorism Act 2005 has been similarly reined in by the courts.[109]

In a more general criminal law sense, robust protection of the right of access to a lawyer in detention was provided by the decision in *Cadder v HMA*[110] where the UK Supreme Court overturned Scottish jurisprudence which had upheld six-hour detention without access to a solicitor.[111] This again demonstrates the magnitude of protective measures in the eyes of the judiciary, and prompted an immediate reaction by the Scottish legislature.[112]

In the specific context of organised crime, and as will be explored in more detail later in this book, both domestic and European courts have sometimes resisted the erosion of certain rights brought about by legislative amendments or have at

---

[105] Packer, n 5, 173.

[106] *People (DPP) v Kenny* [1990] 2 IR 110.

[107] *International Transport Roth GmbH v Secretary of State for the Home Department* [2003] QB 728, [27].

[108] *A(FC) v Secretary of State for the Home Department* [2004] UKHL 56.

[109] *Secretary of State for the Home Department v JJ* [2008] 1 AC 385; *Secretary of State for the Home Department v GG* [2009] EWHC 142; *CA v Secretary of State for the Home Department* [2010] EWHC 2278; *Secretary of State for the Home Department v AP* [2010] UKSC 2; *Secretary of State for the Home Department v Saadi* [2009] EWHC 3390.

[110] *Cadder v HMA* [2010] UKSC 43.

[111] Criminal Procedure (Scotland) Act 1995, s 14, *cf McLean v HMA* [2009] HCJAC 97.

[112] See Criminal Procedure (Legal Assistance, Detention and Appeals) (Scotland) Act 2010.

least mitigated the extent of their application. For example, the European Court of Human Rights often reins in surveillance practices, such as in *Malone v United Kingdom* which required the enactment of clearer legislation in the UK.[113] The House of Lords struck down the use of anonymous witness evidence in *R v Davis*, with the legislature reacting within weeks to remedy the situation with the Criminal Evidence (Witness Anonymity) Act 2008.[114] Moreover, in the context of sentencing the courts subvert the more punitive tendencies of Parliament, with the Irish courts circumventing the application of presumptive sentences, and the Scottish courts rarely imposing orders for life-long restriction.[115]

For parliaments across the UK and Ireland, the protection of the public is valorised increasingly, and risk is to the fore in legislative debate and development. . One reason for this is that law and order has been politicised,[116] and legal reactions to organised crime, which usually take the form of legislation enacted by Parliament, are not immune to political demands and pressures. Crime policy is no longer a bipartisan matter entrusted to professional expertise, as was once the case (at least in the UK, if not in Ireland). The opinions of political bodies and of the general public appear to carry more weight than research findings of professional groups; while public opinion used to serve sporadically as a brake on policy measures, it is now a privileged source to which legislators defer. Crime control measures, encapsulated in sound-bite statements, are announced in political settings such as party conventions. Moreover, there has been a dramatic convergence of policy proposals of all the major political parties in the UK and Ireland, none of which wishes to be seen as 'soft on crime'.

Crime and its control were not important electoral or political issues for most of the twentieth century, until the 1960s in the United States, the mid-1970s in the United Kingdom,[117] and later again in the 1990s in Ireland. It subsequently became a central concern, and the approach to criminal justice arguably became more punitive. Like the UK, Ireland experienced a dramatic increase in crime in the final quarter of the twentieth century, although it began from a lower level and occurred at a later stage. Crime rates in the US and the UK stabilised in the early 1990s, and this pattern was repeated in Ireland after a delay of several years .[118] According to Garland, the policies introduced in the US and the UK developed from a new collective experience of crime and insecurity, constructed by the social and cultural characteristics of late-modernity,[119] and a similar argument can made be made in relation to Ireland. These extra-political factors make robust policies attractive to electorates, and may generate a pronounced fear of crime. Lawmakers

---

[113] *Malone v United Kingdom* Series A no 95 (1985) 7 EHRR 14. See ch 4.
[114] *R v Davis; R v Ellis* [2006] EWCA Crim 1155, [2008] UKHL 36, [2008] 1 AC 1128. See ch 5.
[115] See ch 6.
[116] Garland, n 41, 13–14.
[117] ibid, 145.
[118] S Kilcommins, I O'Donnell, E O'Sullivan and B Vaughan, *Crime, Punishment and the Search for Order in Ireland* (Dublin, Institute of Public Administration, 2004) 90.
[119] ibid, 139.

tap into this public concern and cultivate political capital from an ability, perceived or otherwise, to address such problems.

While the reliability of opinion polls is questionable, the introduction of a swathe of measures to deal with organised crime in Ireland drew on, and was influenced by, considerable reported public concern. In the mid-1990s in Ireland there was a substantial increase in the percentage of people seriously worried about crime, and this was galvanised by the murders of Garda Jerry McCabe and of investigative journalist Veronica Guerin in 1996, leading to 49 per cent of people viewing crime as the most critical issue facing the Government.[120] Concern about crime remained at high levels into the twenty-first century.[121] Moreover, a great deal of the legislation developed in relation to organised criminality was created by a particularly pro-active Minister for Justice, Michael McDowell, who sat in office from 2002–07. He may be regarded as a policy 'entrepreneur'[122] who tapped into public and political concern about a worsening category of crime in Ireland, and who confronted what he believed to be lenient courts in the sentencing of such offences. Nonetheless, by 2006, only 12 per cent of respondents said that crime reduction was their top priority in deciding how to vote.[123] Since then, more robust legislation has been introduced, though no Minister has attained or courted the level of media coverage Michael McDowell garnered. Furthermore, the global recession and the country's economic situation at the time of writing have supplanted crime as primary concern for the public in terms of voting in Ireland.[124]

In the UK, various Home Secretaries have acted as 'entrepreneurs'[125] or 'policy champions'[126] in terms of constructing and pushing through Parliament uncompromising policies reacting to organised criminality. Michael Howard, as Conservative Home Secretary from 1993 until 1997, was renowned for robust legislative developments relating to crime in general, and for pithy and punitive sound-bites, like 'prison works'. The subsequent decade of Labour Home Secretaries maintained both such rhetoric and legislative action, with David Blunkett (2001–04) particularly exercised about organised crime. Most recently the Conservative Home Secretary Theresa May has continued to emphasise this type of criminality, and more broadly wants to abolish the Human Rights Act

[120]   *Survey for Sunday Independent by IMS* (code: 6S-308) 4 July 1996, Q8.
[121]   In 2001, 40% described crime and law and order as one of the three issues that would most influence their vote in the next general election. *Irish Times/MRBI Opinion Poll*, reported in, 'Health to be Key Issue in Next Election, Poll Shows', *Irish Times*, 5 June 2001.
[122]   D Pozen, 'We Are All Entrepreneurs Now' (2008) 43 *Wake Forest Law Review* 283, 283.
[123]   *Irish Times/TNS MRBI Opinion Poll*, reported in, 'Alternative Government the Preference by Margin of 4 per cent', *Irish Times*, 20 May 2006.
[124]   Crime has slipped from the top priority in Ireland, with the Government, the political system and employment being what the public would most like to change. Ipsos MRBI Social Poll, *August 2010* www.ipsosmrbi.com/governance-is-the-number-one-issue.html Only 2% of the population mentioned the reduction of crime as the single most important thing.
[125]   H Becker, *Outsiders: Studies in the Sociology of Deviance* (New York, Free Press, 1963) 147–63.
[126]   N Roberts and P King, 'Policy Entrepreneurs: Their Activity Structure and Function in the Policy Process' (1991) 1 *Journal of Public Administration Research and Theory* 147.

1998 which will have significant implications for crime control, given that the aim is precisely to reduce due process.[127]

This political action was matched by public concern, and both may be seen as contributing to a 'feedback loop' whereby politicians react to perceived popular worry, and consequently add to such fear of crime. In 2006 there were indications that many Britons were concerned about crime, with 42 per cent finding it to be one of the most worrying issues facing Great Britain.[128] Crime rose to become a primary concern of 47 per cent in 2008, but this slipped to 23 per cent in 2011.[129] As regards typical organised crimes in particular, in 2006 39 per cent of people in Great Britain worried about becoming a victim of armed violence.[130] Similarly, a Home Office report from 2009 indicated that almost 70 per cent of the survey respondents agreed that the harm caused by organised crime is extremely serious or very serious, while 67 per cent of respondents thought there was more organised crime when the interviews were conducted in 2006 than there had been two years previously.[131] This is in contrast to the situation in Northern Ireland where 66 per cent felt that organised crime generated a minimal level of harm in the local area, while seven per cent felt it resulted in a great level of harm,[132] and 66 per cent believed the level of harm caused by organised crime in the local area had stayed stable.[133] As well as popular concern, there is dissatisfaction regarding official reaction, in a broad sense as well as in terms of sentencing rules: 82 per cent in Great Britain somewhat or strongly disagreed that from 2002–07 the Government did enough to address the rise in gun crime, while 88 per cent would somewhat or strongly support an increase in the minimum penalty of five years for possessing an illegal firearm.[134] Furthermore, 79 per cent felt that sentencing for organised crimes was too lenient or much too lenient.[135]

---

[127] See Home Office Press Release, 'New National Crime Fighting Agency to Transform the Fight Against Serious and Organised Crime', 8 June 2011, available at www.homeoffice.gov.uk/media-centre/press-releases/national-crime-agency and 'Home Secretary: Scrap the Human Rights Act', *The Telegraph*, 1 October 2011.

[128] Ipsos MORI, 'Britons Most Worried by Crime – and Government is Least Trusted to Deal with it' (London, International Social Trends Unit, 6 November 2006).

[129] See Ipsos MORI, 'Crime Tops Latest Issues Index' (London, Ipsos MORI, 26 August 2008), available at www.ipsos-mori.com/researchpublications/researcharchive/poll.aspx?oItemId=2272 and Economist/Ipsos MORI, *Issues Index October 2011* (London, Economist/Ipsos MORI, 2011), available at www.ipsos-mori.com/Assets/Docs/Polls/Oct11issuestopline.PDF (68% were most concerned about the economy).

[130] Ipsos MORI, 'Almost One in Three People Affected by Gun Crime' (London, Ipsos MORI, 19 June 2006).

[131] K Bullock, R Chowdhury and P Hollings, *Public Concerns about Organised Crime* (London, Home Office Research, Development and Statistics Directorate, 2009) 7.

[132] R Freel and S Toner, *Perceptions of Policing, Justice and Organised Crime: Findings from the 2009/10 Northern Ireland Crime Survey* (Research and Statistical Bulletin 3/2010) (Belfast, Northern Ireland Civil Service Statistics and Research Branch, 2010) table A15.

[133] ibid, table A16.

[134] YouGov, *Gun and Knife Crime* (London, YouGov, 2007) available at today.yougov.co.uk/sites/today.yougov.co.uk/files/YG-Archives-lif-policyex-gunknife-071109.pdf.

[135] ibid, 8, table 2.

A significant number of Scots are equally exercised about crime, with 39 per cent feeling it to be one of the most worrying issues facing the country.[136] Furthermore, relevant Ministers have been pro-active in devising policies and laws in relation to organised crime specifically. Cathy Jamieson, the Labour Minister for Justice in Scotland from 2003–07, placed the Scottish Drug Enforcement Agency on a statutory footing, and pledged the enactment of a Serious and Organised Crime Bill prior to elections in 2007. Since the election of the Scottish National Party in 2007, the Cabinet Secretary for Justice Kenny MacAskill has continued to legislate against organised criminality, via the Criminal Justice and Licensing (Scotland) Act 2010 for example.

In one respect, and relatively speaking, there appears to have been a general decrease in public anxiety about crime because of the global and local recession and this may lead legislators to move away from viewing crime as a driving force in governance and the generation of political capital.[137] Indeed, the recession may also affect the nature of the reactions to organised crime, with more emphasis on third party responsibility as outlined above so as to lessen the immediate impact on the public purse. Nonetheless, concern about organised crime remains to the fore in public and political discourse. This may lead to expressive and punitive modes of action in an attempt to re-establish public confidence. Acting out in this way may provide relief and catharsis, given that it denounces the crime and reassures the public; the fact that 'something is being done' is seen as satisfactory in and of itself.[138]

Legislatures across the UK and Ireland demonstrate a predilection for robust and pragmatic reactions to organised crime that prioritise public protection, and this is often bolstered and legitimated by considerable public concern. However, the capacity of the judiciary and of constitutional or quasi-constitutional documents to counterbalance the results-oriented objectives of the legislature should not be underestimated. The judiciary generally acts according to different commitments and values to those of the legislature; due process ideals, concern for individual rights, and institutional independence under the separation of powers doctrine allow the courts to curb the punitive tendencies of the legislature.

While this resistance by the courts to some incursions on individual rights and liberties demonstrates a degree of friction between the judiciary and policy makers, *imprimatur* has also been given by both domestic and European courts to contentious measures like civil asset recovery.[139] This confounds a straightforward characterisation of the judiciary as process-oriented and rights-enforcing in decision making vis-à-vis the demands of crime control. Thus, although a muscular judiciary holds the capability to stem a punitive trend in terms of policymaking, it

---

[136] Ipsos MORI (2008), n 128, table 2.

[137] Though the recession may result in a decrease in anxiety about crime, some research suggests that a recession contributes to a growth in criminality (eg S Box, *Recession, Crime and Punishment* (Macmillan, London, 1987)).

[138] Garland, n 41, 133.

[139] See ch 7.

is by no means certain that it will oppose legislative changes in relation to organised crime, notwithstanding arguably harsh effects on human rights.

IV. Conclusion

The legal reactions to organised crime in the UK and Ireland embody the ineluctable conflict between crime control or security on the one hand and human rights on the other, with the shift towards the former being driven by manifold penological trends: the imperative of public protection, the avoidance of risk, the normalisation of extraordinary measures and the adaptations to the limitations of traditional criminal justice measures. While the responsibilisation of third parties does not undermine due process norms necessarily, it encapsulates the contradictory elements at play in criminal justice policy whereby certain tasks are delegated to external bodies while the State retains and exerts significant power in other respects. The impetus for such initiatives and laws derives from pragmatic legislatures that are sometimes very responsive, and often overly sensitive, to perceived public opinion, while the judiciary to some extent provides a counterpoint to this.

As Garland cautions, short-term movements in criminal justice should not be mistaken for structural change.[140] While radical measures have been introduced in the UK and Ireland in the context of organised crime which enhance the powers of State and alter the criminal justice system to a considerable extent, many core values and norms remain unchanged. Although rights of the individual, like the right to silence and to a jury trial, have been eroded to a certain degree, fundamental notions on which the criminal process is premised, such as the right to a fair trial, to the presumption of innocence, and to legal representation, remain secure and, on occasion have been strengthened. Moreover, in the context of this comparative work, there is the risk of imposing false homogeneity. The degree to which the reactions to organised crime substantiate certain theoretical insights differs from jurisdiction to jurisdiction, due to cultural, historical and political factors. This is made evident in the doctrinal analysis in subsequent chapters.

The 'controversial aspects of the rules of criminal procedure' which protect the accused to the detriment of police efficiency are justified most persuasively by emphasising the moral principles that underpin and define the liberal system of law.[141] Rather than focusing solely on the imperatives of crime control or on utilitarian gains, the underlying premises on which the UK and Irish systems are

---

[140]   Garland, n 41, 21–22. It has been noted that he fails to observe his own warning: L Zedner, 'Dangers of Dystopias in Penal Theory' (2002) 22 *Oxford Journal of Legal Studies* 341, 343; I Loader and R Sparks, 'For an Historical Sociology of Crime Policy in England and Wales Since 1968' (2004) 7 *Critical Review of International Social and Political Philosophy* 5, 15.

[141]   Dworkin, *Taking Rights Seriously,* n 26, 2.

based must be examined, before encroachments are made on fundamental rights and liberties. While convenience and justice are often not on speaking terms,[142] as we shall see, adherence to traditional liberal legal precepts will ensure the protection of individual rights and liberties notwithstanding the threat posed by organised crime.

---

[142] *General Medical Council v Spackman* [1943] AC 627, 638 per Lord Atkins.

4

Investigating Organised Crime: Altering the Pre-trial Process

I. Introduction

At the initial stage of the criminal process, the State and its agencies are seen to face significant, and sometimes intractable, problems in the detection of organised criminality and the investigation of suspected individuals. The dominant political narrative presents the State as circumscribed unduly by the strictures of the law, and, more specifically, by procedural rules and protections, usually developed and delineated by the courts. The safeguards that accrue to the accused at the pre-trial stage of criminal process, so as to compensate for the imbalance of power between the State and the individual defendant,[1] are viewed as curbing the abilities of the police to conduct speedy and effective investigations, especially given the nature of organised criminality. Conventional investigative measures are deemed to be futile in the face of suspected organised criminals, who adopt sophisticated approaches towards perpetrating and then concealing their criminality. Organised criminals are becoming more technologically advanced, and are able to employ the services of agents like banks or lawyers to facilitate and conceal illegal actions and launder illegitimate earnings, thereby precluding or at least hindering detection in the first instance. In addition to such perceived limitations in terms of detecting crime, there exists a belief that even if the police identify a person as possibly responsible for an act related to organised crime, he may exploit his procedural rights and thereby thwart the investigation's progress by refusing to cooperate and by staying silent. Furthermore, standard detention periods are regarded as too short to facilitate effective and fruitful interviews of suspected organised criminals. While these observations may indeed be true, the degree to which standard protections should be altered to remedy them is debatable, and generally is determined by the priority one gives to due process or crime control.

The traditional weighting of the criminal process favours the individual accused over the State, and so it seems that the latter faces considerable barriers to successful investigations and ultimately prosecutions in the context of systematic organised

---

[1] In *Wardius v Oregon* 412 US 470 (1973) 480 per Douglas J, the US Supreme Court spoke of 'the awesome power of indictment and the virtually limitless resources of government investigators'.

crime. Moreover, the impression of the accused party as a vulnerable individual faced with the might of the State is regarded increasingly as naïve, given the power and resources of many alleged organised criminals. Overall, the existing rights-based framework which safeguards the individual at the pre-trial stage of the criminal process is regarded more and more as an anachronism which fails to acknowledge the dangers posed by organised crime and the extent of the strength and influence of those involved. This belief has underpinned and justified the introduction of a range of measures which augment the crime control capacities of the State, and in doing so arguably impinge on the rights of the individual. In other words, the legislative drive has been away from the due process model as envisaged by Packer,[2] to a pre-trial process which is more pragmatic and uncompromising, and which involves more administrative decisions and less judicial intervention.

To be sure, the investigation of organised crime may be stymied by the means and methods of organised crime groups. Individuals involved may be careful in ensuring an absence of written records, or may rely on corrupt or unwitting third parties to hide any relevant documents. Moreover, much organised crime does not involve a victim as such, and, as a result, the gathering of evidence may prove problematic. For example, in a conspiracy of willing participants without a victim, the only way of obtaining evidence is for a State agent to be a participant (such as an undercover agent or an informant), to 'turn' a participant so he gives evidence against former colleagues through the granting of certain benefits, or to overhear or record any communication or agreement by electronic surveillance. Furthermore, members of organised crime groups may be more seasoned than other accused persons who are not acting on behalf of a criminal enterprise in terms of resisting traditional interview techniques, or they may be fearful of retaliation from other participants and therefore unwilling to answer any police questions. Arguably, this may require an alteration to the length of detention and to the ability to draw inferences from their silence.

This chapter seeks to determine the extent of State powers at the pre-trial stage of the criminal process, when the police investigate crime and establish a prima facie case against a suspect, and in doing so it challenges the presumption that the State is hampered in a legal sense in the investigation of organised criminality. Across the UK and Ireland, a series of legislative developments have formalised and expanded State capacities in this respect, prompted by the nature and practices of organised crime groups. While the logic underpinning these changes is understandable, the inroads made on due process rights are difficult to justify in many instances. The entry and search of premises of a third party who is not the focus of an investigation is now permitted, and certain information in the possession of private bodies must be reported to State agencies. Moreover, extensive surveillance may be carried out, such as through the monitoring of persons' movements, the interception of communications, and by means of undercover policing. Critically, much of this may be approved internally by the relevant

---

[2] H Packer, *The Limits of the Criminal Sanction* (California, Stanford University Press, 1968). See ch 3.

investigating agency rather than requiring judicial authorisation. Detention periods have been extended, and inferences may be drawn from silence. Though some of these amendments do not apply to organised crime solely, nonetheless their introduction was justified by reference to serious and organised crime and they are very valuable in addressing such criminality.

Some of these measures are necessitated by EU Directives and other international obligations, while in the domestic context revisions of protective norms and procedures often emulate counter-terrorism strategies which were employed originally against paramilitary organisations. Overall, these investigative approaches steadily extend the boundaries of crime control measures in seeking to improve the ability of the State to detect and investigate organised crime, albeit within the parameters of the European Convention on Human Rights (ECHR), common law norms and in Ireland also the Constitution. Radical new measures weaken traditional safeguards in the criminal process, regrettably often without sufficient debate, and their introduction challenges the perception that the State is limited in legal powers. Moreover, thorough empirical or conceptual consideration is all too often lacking in this regard, and intuition seems to guide criminal justice policy rather than measured analysis. This is compounded by the marked convergence of political parties, giving rise to a significant lack of opposition to proposed provisions in criminal justice legislation.

The prioritising of expedient investigations and ultimately public protection in this context threatens to obscure the importance of individual liberties. While these objectives are clear and reasonable, their attainment compromises core precepts of due process. These limitations on the rights of the accused suggest that the fabric of the criminal justice realm is being modified slowly yet in a fundamental sense, in a bid to augment the capabilities of the State in targeting organised crime across the UK and Ireland.

II. Access and Disclosure Orders

Participants in organised crime are likely to be vigilant in ensuring the absence of any paper trail or documentary evidence of criminality. If such written texts exist, they may be located elsewhere, rather than being held by the participant himself or in his dwelling or property. Moreover, records of transactions or property deeds that may implicate an individual in organised crime may be filed or stored by professionals such as lawyers and bankers. Third parties like this may act knowingly as 'facilitators'[3] of organised crime or may well be unaware of the content or nature of incriminating documents, data and material.

---

[3] See M Levi, H Nelen and F Lankhorst, 'Lawyers as Crime Facilitators in Europe: An Introduction and Overview' (2005) 42 *Crime, Law & Social Change* 117.

To address this possibility, legislation has broadened the range of people whose property may be searched in the course of a criminal investigation by providing for access orders and disclosure orders, thereby extending the traditional policing tactic of searching and seizing the property of suspected individuals. Agents of the State now may enter and search premises and material of a person who is not the immediate focus of an investigation, so as to enhance the likelihood of gathering useful evidence. In other words, a focus of investigative action may be a third party who is not regarded as being culpable, but who may have certain materials or documents in his possession that relate to a suspected offence or individual. Otherwise, it would be essentially impossible for the police or investigating agency to gather evidence which is not held by the suspect himself, or in his property. This has serious ramifications for the right to privacy, as it extends significantly the extent to which the State may encroach on the lives of unsuspected individuals. To offset this, if such an approach is to be used, there must be reasonable grounds for believing that the material is likely to be of substantial value to the investigation, and that production or access is in the public interest.[4] Moreover, privileged material is excluded.[5] Nonetheless, the risk in such an approach is that the individual's right to privacy is subsumed by the broader and more nebulous interest in detecting and investigating crime.

Under the Proceeds of Crime Act 2002, one of the primary pieces of counter-organised crime legislation in the UK, production and access orders may be granted ex parte by a Crown Court judge or a sheriff in Scotland.[6] Such orders may be granted if a person specified in the application is subject to a confiscation investigation and is reasonably suspected to have benefited from his criminal conduct, or is reasonably suspected to have committed a money laundering offence, or if the property specified in the application is subject to a civil recovery investigation and is reasonably suspected to be recoverable or associated property.[7] A person mentioned in the application must appear to be in possession or control of the material but there is no requirement that he be the person who is under investigation; in other words this may be an unsuspected (and indeed unsuspecting) third party.

As well as orders compelling the production of or access to material or property, disclosure of information from third parties may be required under the UK Proceeds of Crime Act 2002, though not in relation to money laundering investigations. In England, Wales and Northern Ireland a disclosure order may be made by a Crown Court judge for confiscation investigations or by a High Court judge for civil recovery investigations on application by the Director of the Serious

---

[4] Proceeds of Crime Act 2002, s 346(4) (UK); Criminal Justice Act 1994, s 63(4) (Ireland).
[5] Proceeds of Crime Act 2002, s 348.
[6] Proceeds of Crime Act 2002, Pt 8, chs 2 and 3: ss 345 and 347 (England, Wales and Northern Ireland), s 380 (Scotland). Production orders may be issued for detained cash investigations also. Proceeds of Crime Act 2002, s 341(3)(3A) (as inserted by the Serious Crime Act 2007).
[7] Proceeds of Crime Act 2002, ss 345 and 346. See chs 6 and 7 for an analysis of confiscation and civil recovery respectively.

Organised Crime Agency (SOCA), and this requires any person who is considered to have relevant and substantially valuable information to answer questions or provide certain information or documents.[8] In Scotland, the application is to the High Court of Justiciary by the Lord Advocate in the case of a confiscation investigation, and by the Scottish Ministers to the Court of Session for a civil recovery investigation.[9] There must be reasonable grounds for suspecting that the person referred to in the application has benefited from his criminal conduct, or that the property specified is recoverable, but he need not be the person to whom the order is made. Again, this means that the person whose property is being confiscated or recovered and the person ordered to disclose information may be different individuals. Given the gravity of compelling someone to speak, the UK legislation provides that a statement made in response to a disclosure order may not be used in evidence against that person in criminal proceedings,[10] other than in confiscation proceedings, or in perjury proceedings. This takes account of ECHR jurisprudence in *Saunders v UK* where the right of the accused not to incriminate himself under Article 6(1) of the ECHR was deemed to have been breached by the reliance at trial on statements which were obtained compulsorily.[11] So, the protection of due process norms deriving from European case law has limited the extent of domestic legislation in the UK relating to the investigation of serious and organised crime, by providing a buffer against the use of potentially incriminating evidence.

In addition to these third party disclosure orders, in the UK a disclosure notice may be issued by a police constable, a designated member of SOCA or an officer of Revenue and Customs requiring 'any person' to answer relevant questions, or produce certain information or documents, if it appears to the investigating authority that there are reasonable grounds for suspecting the commission of a 'lifestyle' offence[12] under Schedules 2 and 4 of the Proceeds of Crime Act 2002 or a false accounting offence, and that a person has relevant and substantially valuable information.[13] That is to say, a Crown Court judge or High Court judge is not involved as the judiciary is in relation to disclosure orders for confiscation or civil recovery investigations. This means that an internal administrative order may in essence force a person to answer certain questions or produce material. Where a disclosure notice is issued, an authorised person may take copies of documents provided and may require the person producing them to offer an explanation.[14]

---

[8] Proceeds of Crime Act 2002, s 357.
[9] Proceeds of Crime Act 2002, s 391.
[10] Proceeds of Crime Act 2002, s 360.
[11] *Saunders v UK* (1997) 23 EHRR 313. However, in *O'Halloran and Francis v UK* (2008) 46 EHRR 21 the European Court held that a requirement under road traffic legislation to identify the driver of a speeding vehicle was regulatory in nature and was a limited compulsion with adequate safeguards; so, the right to silence or the privilege against self-incrimination was not found to have been breached.
[12] Lifestyle offences include drug trafficking, counterfeiting, arms trafficking, trafficking for the purposes of sexual exploitation and money laundering.
[13] Serious Organised Crime and Police Act 2005, s 62.
[14] Serious Organised Crime and Police Act 2005, s 63.

Privileged information is excluded, although a lawyer may be required to provide the name and address of a client.[15] Furthermore, a statement made or document provided in response to such a disclosure notice may not be used in evidence against the discloser in criminal proceedings unless he is being prosecuted for perjury or attempting to pervert the course of justice, or if he makes a statement in proceedings for another offence which is inconsistent with the original statement.[16] Failure to comply with a disclosure notice or production order is an offence, as is making a false or misleading statement.[17]

In Ireland a District judge may order material to be made available by third parties to the police for the purpose of investigating a drug trafficking or money laundering offence,[18] two quintessential organised crimes. Moreover, an order may be issued by a District judge to make material available, either by producing it or granting access to it, in the context of a Criminal Assets Bureau investigation relating to civil recovery of assets.[19] It is an offence to disclose information which may prejudice the production of material:[20] this is a 'tipping off' offence, which seeks to prevent and punish disclosures which might lead to material being relocated or destroyed. In contrast to the UK, in Ireland there is no internal granting of such orders. Moreover, in Ireland any material obtained under this provision may be retained as evidence for subsequent proceedings.[21] Although this may seem to contravene the right not to incriminate oneself, the European Court of Human Rights has stated explicitly that this right concerns the will of the accused to remain silent, rather than applying to material 'which has an existence independent of the will of the suspect such as . . . documents acquired pursuant to a warrant'.[22] In other words, the reliance on such material, though obtained through compulsory powers, is not in breach of Article 6. This demonstrates how the Irish legislation carefully navigates the limits of due process protections to ensure the most expansive yet legally permissible means of investigating organised crime.

In the UK and Ireland the law relating to search warrants has also been extended to offset the evasion or confounding of disclosure notices which may limit the effectiveness of an investigation into organised crime groups. In the UK, instead of a disclosure notice, a justice of the peace or a sheriff may issue a warrant to an investigating authority (but not to SOCA): if satisfied that particular documents

---

[15] Serious Organised Crime and Police Act 2005, s 64.

[16] Serious Organised Crime and Police Act 2005, s 65.

[17] Serious Organised Crime and Police Act 2005, s 67.

[18] Criminal Justice Act 1994, s 63 (as amended). Section 39 of the Criminal Justice (Terrorist Offences) Act 2005 extends this to encompass the offence of financing terrorism. An order granting access to or production of material may also be issued under s 52 of the Criminal Justice (Theft and Fraud Offences) Act 2001 in the context of any offence under the Act which is punishable by at least five years imprisonment.

[19] Proceeds of Crime Act 1996, s 14A (as inserted by the Proceeds of Crime (Amendment) Act 2005). See ch 7.

[20] Proceeds of Crime Act 1996, s 14B. This provision is modelled on the offence of prejudicing an investigation contained in s 58 of the Criminal Justice Act 1994. See text accompanying n 38.

[21] Proceeds of Crime Act 1996, s 14A(7).

[22] *Saunders v UK*, n 11, para 69.

are on certain premises and that a person has been required by a disclosure notice to produce them but has not done so; or if it is not practicable to give a disclosure notice; or if giving a disclosure notice might prejudice seriously the investigation of specific offences such as drug trafficking, money laundering, and arms trafficking.[23] Similarly, in the UK and Ireland, a search and seizure warrant may be issued: if a production order made in relation to material has not been complied with; if it is not practicable to communicate with any person against whom the production order could be made or who would grant entry to the premises; or if the investigation might be seriously prejudiced unless an appropriate person is able to secure immediate access to the material.[24]

Whereas a warrant permits the search of premises, a production or access order is narrower and more specific given that the officers are not authorised to search through records or property in an attempt to find something relevant or of use. Thus, State agents may prefer to apply for and use a warrant rather than a production or access order, on the basis that once a member of an organised crime group becomes aware of the issuing of a production or access order, he may reorganise or relocate the relevant documents or property, precluding their subsequent discovery by police or another investigating authority. Nonetheless, in *R (Barclay) v Lord Chancellor and Secretary of State for Justice*, the Queen's Bench Divisional Court stated that using search warrants rather than a production order against a firm of solicitors was not necessary, given solicitors' duty not to dispose of relevant material.[25] In this application for judicial review there was thus no basis for the police conclusion that a production order might have caused serious prejudice to the investigation. So, the courts in England and Wales have emphasised a preference for the more limited production order rather than the expansive search warrant, imposing a limit on State power in this context.

In addition to physical access to material or property, an order may be issued to financial institutions specifically, regarding information in their possession. This is significant in the context of suspected money laundering or other financial crime, and to investigate suspicious transactions that may relate to illicit markets or other illegal behaviour. A judge or sheriff may, on an application made to him by an appropriate officer,[26] require a financial institution to provide information about any customer or account holder who is the subject of a confiscation or a money laundering investigation, or if property that he holds is subject to a civil

---

[23] Serious Organised Crime and Police Act 2005, s 66.

[24] Proceeds of Crime Act 2002, ss 352 and 353 (England, Wales and Northern Ireland); ss 387 and 388 (Scotland); Criminal Justice Act 1994, s 64 (Ireland).

[25] *R (Barclay and Others) v Lord Chancellor and Secretary of State for Justice and Others, The Times*, 21 November 2008 (QB).

[26] An appropriate person regarding confiscation and money laundering investigations may be an accredited financial investigator, a constable or a customs officer, and in relation to confiscation and recovery investigations may be the Director of SOCA (Proceeds of Crime Act 2002, s 378). In Scotland an appropriate person means the procurator fiscal in relation to a confiscation investigation or a money laundering investigation, and the Scottish Ministers in relation to a civil recovery investigation (Proceeds of Crime Act 2002, s 412).

recovery investigation.[27] An 'account monitoring order' lasting for 90 days may also be made, which entails the provision of transaction details and records relating to a suspected account.[28] Such statements made by or records disclosed by a financial institution may not be used in evidence against that institution in criminal proceedings.[29] Likewise, in Ireland, a senior Garda may apply ex parte to the High Court for an 'account information order' and/or an 'account monitoring order' from financial institutions in the State or an EU Member State.[30] The order will be granted if the Gardaí are investigating whether a specific person has committed an offence or is in possession of assets deriving from criminal conduct and the institution concerned may have relevant information and it is in the public interest to grant the order. In Ireland, a higher court is involved than in the UK, and a more limited range of agents may apply, indicating a more cautious and due process-oriented approach that may constrain the use of this crime control mechanism. Nevertheless, the Irish provision applies to any criminal investigation, rather than the scheme in the UK which concerns investigations regarding confiscation, money laundering and civil recovery only.

The expansion of police powers of search and the requirement of disclosure when it applies to third parties, whether that is individuals, entities or institutions, is a novel development, compared to the norm of judicially approved search warrants in criminal investigations. This is an archetypal adaptation on the part of the UK and Ireland in an attempt to improve the efficacy of criminal investigations by extending the net of State intervention. Despite the invasion of privacy when third parties are brought within the scope of criminal investigations, such an approach is justified by reference to the nature of organised crime, and the possibility of crucial evidence otherwise being concealed. Access and disclosure orders encapsulate the favouring of crime control over due process, insofar as encroachments are made on the liberty of unsuspected individuals to investigate and ascertain the possible criminality of others. In particular, disclosure orders, which do not involve judicial oversight, embody the drive for effective and resolute reactions to organised crime, by permitting administrative authorisation rather than necessitating independent court approval.

III. Suspicious Activity Reports

In addition to access and disclosure orders which apply to third parties, the fact-finding capacity of the State regarding organised crime has been enhanced further by the recruitment of external bodies in the investigation of crime and the obligation to report evidence of unlawful acts, in particular in the context of money

---

[27] Proceeds of Crime Act 2002, ss 363 and 397.
[28] Proceeds of Crime Act 2002, ss 370 and 404.
[29] Proceeds of Crime Act 2002, ss 367 and 401.
[30] Criminal Justice (Mutual Assistance) Act 2008, s 13.

laundering. Non-State and private entities, such as banks and building societies, now are involved in gathering information through the duty to make 'suspicious activity reports' (SARs), thereby improving the likelihood of a successful investigation and prosecution,[31] as otherwise it would be very difficult to discover and gather evidence on much financial crime and laundering of money. SARs provide details of bank accounts, transactions, addresses and assets that are of use to law enforcement in detecting and investigating organised crime. Moreover, SARs provide intelligence about risky or problematic individuals and businesses, and the vulnerabilities of certain sectors. The value of SARs to the State cannot be understated: the Serious Organised Crime Agency describes the scheme as a 'vital weapon in the UK's armoury'.[32]

Such measures in the UK and Ireland have been shaped by EU Directives on money laundering: the first Directive in 1991 which required the criminalisation of money laundering of drugs offences also necessitated the reporting of suspicious transactions, inter alia; the second in 2001 extended the money laundering provisions to all crimes, and the third in 2007 addressed terrorist financing also and enhanced the customer 'due diligence' regime.[33] Moreover, the international Financial Action Task Force (FATF), established in 1989 by the Organisation for Economic Cooperation and Development to counter money laundering, recommended that each member country should establish a Financial Intelligence Unit (FIU) to receive, analyse and disseminate SARs and other relevant information.[34]

It is an offence in the UK and Ireland for someone in the course of a business in the regulated sector (which includes banks, building societies, bureaux de change, accountants and lawyers)[35] to fail to disclose knowledge or suspicion (or reasonable grounds for such) that another person is engaged in money laundering.[36] Disclosure of this information is by means of SARs submitted to the Financial Intelligence Unit in the UK, and to the Garda Síochána and the Revenue Commissioners in Ireland.[37] Such information may be used in an investigation

---

[31] M Levi and M Maguire, 'Reducing and Preventing Organised Crime: An Evidence-Based Critique' (2004) 41 *Crime, Law & Social Change* 397, 419ff.

[32] www.soca.gov.uk/about-soca/the-uk-financial-intelligence-unit/frequently-asked-questions-faqs.

[33] Directive 2005/60/EC of the European Parliament and of the Council of 26 October 2005 on the prevention of the use of the financial system for the purpose of money laundering and terrorist financing [2005] OJ L309/15; Directive 2001/97/EC of the European Parliament and of the Council of 4 December 2001 amending Council Directive 91/308/EEC on prevention of the use of the financial system for the purpose of money laundering, [2001] OJ L344/76, and Council Directive 91/308/EEC of 10 June 1991 on prevention of the use of the financial system for the purpose of money laundering [1991] OJ L166/77.

[34] Financial Action Task Force, *40 Recommendations*, www.fatf-gafi.org/document/28/0,3746 ,en_32250379_32236920_33658140_1_1_1_1,00.html Recommendation 26. FATF comprises 34 member jurisdictions (including various European jurisdictions, Australia, Canada, China, India, Japan, and the US) as well as the European Commission and the Gulf Cooperation Council.

[35] Proceeds of Crime Act 2002, sch 9.

[36] Proceeds of Crime Act 2002, s 330; Criminal Justice (Money Laundering and Terrorist Financing) Act 2010.

[37] Proceeds of Crime Act 2002, s 330(5); Terrorist Act 2000, Pt 3; Criminal Justice (Money Laundering and Terrorist Financing) Act 2010, ch 4 (Ireland).

into money laundering offences. Moreover, a body is prohibited from warning or 'tipping off' its client that he is under investigation or that a SAR is being made.[38] However, it is not an offence if disclosure occurs within an undertaking or group, including to a professional legal adviser, or between institutions or legal advisers, or if disclosure is to a supervisory authority.[39]

Designated professional bodies, the Bank of England, the Comptroller and Auditor General, and the Gambling Commission must inform SOCA of knowledge or suspicion that a person is or has engaged in money laundering or terrorist financing,[40] to ensure dissemination of necessary information between State agencies. The introduction of this measure was prompted by the lack of information sharing that seemed to stymie the work of the Asset Recovery Agency, SOCA's predecessor.[41] There does not appear to be an equivalent requirement in the Irish legislation, although the ability to share information is evident in the Criminal Justice Act 1994, which facilitates the supply of information by Revenue Commissioners to the Gardaí.[42] If the Revenue Commissioners in Ireland have reasonable grounds for suspecting that a person may have profited from an unlawful source or activity and for believing that information is of value to an investigation, access shall be granted to the information to a Garda not below the rank of Chief Superintendent or to the head of the Criminal Assets Bureau.[43] However, the key differentiating factor between this measure and those involving designated bodies is that in the latter cases the bodies are not State agencies but still are compelled to reveal information to the Gardaí.

The Third Money Laundering Directive was implemented in the UK by means of the Money Laundering Regulations 2007 and in Ireland by the Criminal Justice (Money Laundering and Terrorist Financing) Act 2010.[44] These Acts impose 'customer due diligence' requirements on any entity or body that: establishes a business relationship or carries out an occasional transaction with a customer; suspects money laundering or terrorist financing; or doubts the veracity or adequacy of identification or verification information.[45] 'Customer due diligence' means identifying the customer (and if relevant, the beneficial owner) and verifying his identity based on an independent and reliable source and obtaining information on the purpose and intended nature of his relationship with the financial institution.[46] On-going

---

[38] Proceeds of Crime Act 2002, ss 333A(1) and (3) as inserted by the Terrorism Act 2000 and Proceeds of Crime Act 2002 (Amendment) Regulations 2007; Criminal Justice (Money Laundering and Terrorist Financing) Act 2010, ch 5 (Ireland).

[39] Proceeds of Crime Act 2002, ss 333(B)–(D) as amended.

[40] Money Laundering Regulations 2007, reg 49(1).

[41] See ch 2 and ch 7.

[42] s 63A as inserted by the Disclosure of Certain Information for Taxation and Other Purposes Act 1996.

[43] s 63A(2).

[44] Directive 2005/60/EC of the European Parliament and of the Council of 26 October 2005 on the prevention of the use of the financial system for the purpose of money laundering and terrorist financing [2005] OJ L309/15.

[45] Proceeds of Crime Act 2002, Pt 2; Criminal Justice (Money Laundering and Terrorist Financing) Act 2010, ch 3.

[46] Money Laundering Regulations 2007, reg 5.

monitoring of a business relationship is also required, entailing scrutiny of trans-actions and the maintenance of up-to-date documents and information.[47] The implementing legislation also provides for 'enhanced customer due diligence' and on-going monitoring in the case of persons who are deemed to be of higher risk, such as those who have not been identified in person to the body or entity, and for politically exposed persons who perform or performed in the previous year a prom-inent public function.[48] Policies and procedures in this respect must be established, and training of employees undertaken relating to the law on money laundering and terrorist financing; and in how to recognise and deal with transactions and other activities which may be related to money laundering or terrorist financing.[49] Failure to adhere to any of these provisions could result in a civil penalty or criminal conviction of the entity or body.[50]

In the UK and Ireland, a body like a financial institution, an auditor, an accoun-tant, or a legal professional, may be required to provide information to an officer if requested under this legislation.[51] In the UK no evidence or question relating to such a statement may be adduced in criminal proceedings by the prosecution unless the person himself does this,[52] whereas in Ireland, such a body or person is not required to answer questions if this might tend to incriminate him.[53] Again, this ensures compliance with ECHR case law.[54] In addition, a search warrant may be issued: if entry without warrant was obstructed; if a request for information is not complied with or if there is reasonable belief that it would not be complied with; or if there is reasonable belief that the information would be removed or destroyed and that there is on the premises specified in the warrant recorded information which has been required to be produced. Entry and inspection of property is permitted without a warrant where an officer has reasonable cause to believe that any premises (other than a dwelling) is being used by a relevant per-son in connection with his business or professional activities and if the informa-tion sought reasonably is required in connection with the exercise of functions under the Third Directive.[55] No emergency or evidence regarding the need for expediency is required, such as the likelihood of records being moved before a warrant could be granted. This is a remarkably broad provision which permits significant State intervention without judicial oversight, again encapsulating a shift towards a crime control model of criminal justice.

---

[47] Money Laundering Regulations 2007, reg 8.
[48] Money Laundering Regulations 2007, reg 14.
[49] Money Laundering Regulations 2007, regs 20 and 21.
[50] Money Laundering Regulations 2007, regs 42 and 45.
[51] Money Laundering Regulations 2007, reg 37; Criminal Justice (Money Laundering and Terrorist Financing) Act 2010, ss 67–68.
[52] Money Laundering Regulations 2007, reg 37(9).
[53] Criminal Justice (Money Laundering and Terrorist Financing) Act 2010, s 81.
[54] See n 11.
[55] Money Laundering Regulations 2007, reg 38; Criminal Justice (Money Laundering and Terrorist Financing) Act 2010, s 75. See n 44.

SOCA and the Home Office have expressed concerns about the 'underuse' of suspicious activity reports in the UK as a source of intelligence.[56] Though this may be true from the crime control perspective of the State, from a liberal due process vantage the picture is more nuanced. Currently approximately 240,000 such reports are made in the UK every year,[57] with around 14,500 per year in Ireland.[58] The involvement of non-state bodies in the detection of criminality, although onerous on the relevant individuals and agencies, does not appear to impinge unduly on protective rights. However, the extensive power of entry granted under the Regulations is problematic in its elevation of crime control over other imperatives.

The enforced diffusion of investigative powers to encompass external and private bodies signifies a shift away from liberal norms of limited intervention to widen the reach of crime control. Moreover, the adoption of such a diversified approach may be seen as a quintessential adaptive response to the problem of organised crime. In fact, these domestic laws have been driven by supra-national requirements rather than depicting adaptive State reactions. So, while this responsibilisation is in contrast to previous methods of policing in the UK and Ireland, it is not the paradigmatic adaption envisaged by Garland, given that the Nation States in Europe have little latitude in terms of adoption of these measures.[59] Nonetheless, it appears that the same rationales described by Garland may stimulate the development of policy at a supra-national level, in a bid to use novel means to deal with the problem of organised crime.

IV. Surveillance

Surveillance is of critical importance in the investigation of organised crime, in determining the extent and pattern of criminal behaviour, and in the gathering of evidence to construct a case against a suspect; thus it has been described as one of the most important legal weapons deployed in the United States against Mafia groups and families.[60] Though such tactics could be useful in relation to all types of criminality, the nature of organised crime and the complexity of investigations and building cases against participants in organised crime groups and illicit

---

[56] See Home Office, *Asset Recovery Action Plan, A Consultation Document* (London, Home Office, 2007) 12, referring to S Lander, *Review of the Suspicious Activity Reports System (The SARs Review)* (London, Serious Organised Crime Agency, 2006).

[57] Serious Organised Crime Agency, *Suspicious Activity Reports Regime Annual Report 2011* (London, Serious Organised Crime Agency, 2011) 10.

[58] US Department of State Bureau for International Narcotics and Law Enforcement Affairs, *Money Laundering and Financial Crimes Country Database* (Washington DC, US Department of State, 2011) 174.

[59] D Garland, *The Culture of Control* (Oxford, Oxford University Press, 2001) 19–20.

[60] J Jacobs (with C Panarella and J Worthington), *Busting the Mob: United States v Cosa Nostra* (New York, New York University Press, 1994) 8.

markers means that surveillance is particularly helpful in this context.[61] Surveillance in its various guises provides intelligence and evidence of criminal activity, and regarding the workings and structure of organised crime groups. This is especially important where there may be no victim, such as where all the participants are willing or complicit; where victims may be intimidated or threatened; or where existing evidence is inconclusive and needs to be corroborated. Moreover, the prospect of surveillance, which would lead ultimately to detection and further investigation, may serve a deterrence function, insofar as anything could, in relation to the actions of organised crime groups. Conversely, the discovery or revealing of a surveillance device or an undercover agent could jeopardise a specific investigation or compromise certain policing techniques in future, and so the decision regarding the initiation of surveillance is not taken lightly from an operational perspective.

As Goldstock notes, continuous conspiratorial criminal activity necessitates regular communication, and the more complex the hierarchy and the more insulated the higher layers of individuals are from the actual commission of crime, the more likely it is for commands, consultations and reports between participants to be communicated electronically.[62] Evidence regarding the content of these is provided most dependably by surveillance through an intercept, or by a recording by a person or device that is present at the time, or through a co-conspirator who decides later to cooperate with the authorities. The benefit of surveillance when compared with the latter is its reliability, when compared with human testimony that may be ambiguous or grounded on memories that fade over time.

The relevant UK legislation states that 'surveillance' includes monitoring, observing or listening to persons, their movements, conversations or their other activities or communications whether with a device or otherwise, and the recording of anything so monitored or observed.[63] While observation of suspects has long been a standard practice of law enforcement, technology has facilitated more systematic and invasive approaches. These are now regulated more strictly in Europe, largely because of the jurisprudence of the European Court of Human Rights on Article 8, though not prohibited absolutely. According to this Article, everyone has the right to respect for his private and family life, his home and his correspondence, and any interference must be 'in accordance with the law' and

> necessary in a democratic society in the interests of national security, public safety or the economic well-being of the country, for the prevention of disorder or crime, for the protection of health or morals, or for the protection of the rights and freedoms of others.

---

[61] See Home Office, *Extending Our Reach: A Comprehensive Approach to Tackling Organised Crime* (London, The Stationery Office, 2009) 36; Scottish Government, *Letting Our Communities Flourish: A Strategy for Tackling Serious Organised Crime in Scotland* (Edinburgh, Scottish Government, 2009) para 36.

[62] R Goldstock, *Organised Crime in Northern Ireland: A Report for the Secretary of State* (Belfast, Northern Ireland Office, 2004) para 5.3.

[63] Regulation of Investigatory Powers Act 2000, s 48 (2).

A person's private life is interfered with when the security services systematically collect and retain data on him[64] but this may be permissible and compliant with human rights if necessary for the prevention of disorder or crime.

Similarly, although there is no explicit reference to privacy in the Irish Constitution the Supreme Court has recognised an unenumerated right to privacy in Article 40.3.1 which protects the 'personal rights of citizens'. The unenumerated constitutional right to marital privacy was upheld in *McGee v Attorney-General* where it was stressed that 'the right to privacy is universally recognised and accepted with possibly the rarest of exceptions',[65] and the right to individual privacy was considered in *Norris v Attorney-General* and *Kennedy and Arnold v Ireland*.[66] In the latter, the Supreme Court stressed that

> [t]he right to privacy is one of the fundamental personal rights of the citizen which flow from the Christian and democratic nature of the State. . . . The nature of the right to privacy is such that it must ensure the dignity and freedom of the individual in a democratic society.

So, by definition, surveillance compromises this right to privacy but some limitations are permissible in terms of human rights in both the domestic and European legal contexts. Navigating the balance between the drive to control crime and the individual's rights is a fraught matter, and one which involves a lively dynamic between the legislatures and national and international courts.

As well as physical surveillance of a suspected person or a particular location, law enforcement agencies use electronic equipment like cameras and microphones and other communication interception devices to gather intelligence or evidence about suspected organised criminality. There are many forms that such surveillance can take: it may be by means of image recordings that may be viewed simultaneously or later; telephone calls or emails that may be intercepted (wire or phone tapping); telephone or internet data not related to the content of a communication that may be monitored; a microphone or other listening device that may be placed in a given location to allow the conversations to be heard through a receiver elsewhere (bugging), or the movements of a vehicle or person that may be followed and recorded through the use of global position systems (tracking). Each of these tactics raises concerns regarding the right to privacy and the nature of State intervention in the lives of its citizens.

---

[64] See *Amann v Switzerland* (2000) 30 EHRR 843.

[65] *McGee v Attorney-General* [1974] IR 284.

[66] *Norris v Attorney-General* [1984] IR 36; *Kennedy and Arnold v Ireland* [1987] IR 587.

A. Intrusive and Directed Surveillance

The relevant UK legislation, the Regulation of Investigatory Powers Act 2000,[67] distinguishes between 'intrusive' and 'directed' surveillance, which differ arguably in terms of their impact on the private lives of individuals. Therefore, the authorisation requirements also vary. Intrusive surveillance is covert surveillance (ie the subjects are unaware of its being carried out) of a residence or private vehicle and involves a surveillance device or the presence of an individual on the premises or in the vehicle.[68] Surveillance is not intrusive if carried out by a device which provides information about a vehicle's location,[69] nor if carried out by a device in relation to anything taking place in a residence or private vehicle where the device is not present there, unless the device is such that it consistently provides information of the same quality and detail as might be expected to be obtained from a device actually present.[70]

Essentially, intrusive surveillance usually involves the placing of bugs, cameras or agents in private places,[71] so that officers can overhear or view otherwise confidential and potentially incriminating communications. This may be an investigative necessity or priority so as to gather direct evidence about particular suspected criminality, or the methodologies of criminal groups, their hierarchy and workings. Intrusive surveillance may be authorised by the Secretary of State or a senior authorising officer,[72] and, except in urgent cases, must be approved by a Surveillance Commissioner,[73] who holds or held high judicial office.[74] The Secretary of State or senior authorising officer may permit surveillance only if he believes that it is necessary in the interests of national security or the economic

---

[67] In relation to surveillance in Scotland, the Regulation of Investigatory Powers (Scotland) Act 2000 is the appropriate legislation: for surveillance that starts or mainly takes place outside Scotland or is for purposes reserved to the UK Government, such as national security or economic well-being, the Regulation of Investigatory Powers Act 2000 applies. A 'Sewel motion' was passed regarding the Regulation of Investigatory Powers Bill permitting the UK Parliament to legislate on a matter usually within the competence of the Scottish legislature (see ch 1). The justification for this was that while much of the Bill concerned reserved matters, the boundary between reserved and devolved matters was difficult to determine as regards certain other elements in the Act, and thus for purposes of speed and robustness it was felt that legislation should be enacted which applied to the UK as a whole. Scottish Parliament, *Memorandum: Regulation of Investigatory Powers Bill S1M-733* (9 Feb 2000); Scottish Parliament Official Report, col 1462–79 (6 April 2000).

[68] Regulation of Investigatory Powers Act 2000, s 26(3); Regulation of Investigatory Powers (Scotland) Act 2000, s 1(3).

[69] Regulation of Investigatory Powers Act 2000, s 26(4).

[70] Regulation of Investigatory Powers Act 2000, s 26(5).

[71] This can include consultations between lawyers and clients in detention: *Re McE* [2009] UKHL 15, [2009] 2 WLR 782.

[72] Regulation of Investigatory Powers Act 2000, s 32(6). Senior authorising officers include chief constables of police forces in England, Wales and Scotland; the Commissioner and Assistant Commissioners of the Police of the Metropolis; the Chief and Deputy Chief Constable of the Police Service of Northern Ireland (PSNI); the Director General of the Serious Organised Crime Agency and any designated member of SOCA and any designated senior official of Revenue and Customs.

[73] Regulation of Investigatory Powers Act 2000, Pt IV; Regulation of Investigatory Powers (Scotland) Act 2000, s 14(1); Criminal Justice (Surveillance) Act 2009, s 36.

[74] Police Act 1997, Pt III.

well-being of the United Kingdom or to prevent or detect serious crime,[75] whereas in Scotland a chief constable or the Director General or Deputy Director General of the Scottish Crime and Drug Enforcement Agency may so authorise only if necessary for the purpose of preventing or detecting serious crime.[76] Thus, intrusive surveillance often occurs in the course of an organised crime investigation, and usually will be approved independently, unless in the context of an emergency.

In Ireland, no distinction is made between intrusive and directed surveillance. There a superior Garda officer may apply to a District Court judge for authorisation to monitor, observe, listen to or make a recording of a person or their movements and communications, or of a place or thing using a surveillance device.[77] The Garda officer must have reasonable grounds to believe that surveillance is necessary for an operation or investigation into an arrestable offence,[78] to obtain information or evidence about the offence, to prevent the commission of arrestable offences, or to maintain the security of the State;[79] the surveillance must be proportionate to what is sought to be achieved, and obtaining the information by other means must be considered.[80]

In the UK and Ireland authorisations remain valid for three months and may be renewed (in Ireland this is for another three months at most).[81] As noted, except in urgent cases, any authorisation in the UK must be approved by a Surveillance Commissioner who holds or held judicial office, and in Ireland judicial involvement is required, underlining the cognisance of the legislatures of the invasive nature of this surveillance. In urgent cases in the UK a less senior person may authorise surveillance,[82] whereas in such cases in Ireland judicial consent is not required in contrast to the usual procedure.[83] Such urgent surveillance may last for 72 hours.[84] If intrusive surveillance in the UK requires entry onto private premises such as to plant the device, this must be necessary to prevent or detect serious crime, and be proportionate to its aims.[85] The permission to make such an entry may be granted by a Chief Constable or an equivalent officer. In Ireland an authorisation for surveillance may grant entry to any place whether private or public to start, carry out or withdraw the surveillance.[86]

---

[75] Regulation of Investigatory Powers Act 2000, s 32.

[76] Regulation of Investigatory Powers (Scotland) Act 2000, s 10(2).

[77] Criminal Justice (Surveillance) Act 2009, s 4. Authorisation on the grounds of State security may be granted on application by a superior officer of the Defence Forces, and authorisation may be granted to a superior officer of the Revenue Commissioners to investigate or prevent a revenue offence.

[78] s 2 of the Criminal Justice Act 1997 defines an arrestable offence as an offence for which a person could be punished by imprisonment for five years or more.

[79] Criminal Justice (Surveillance) Act 2009, s 4(1).

[80] Criminal Justice (Surveillance) Act 2009, s 32(4).

[81] Criminal Justice (Surveillance) Act 2009, s 6.

[82] Regulation of Investigatory Powers Act 2000, s 34.

[83] Criminal Justice (Surveillance) Act 2009, s 7.

[84] Regulation of Investigatory Powers Act 2000, s 43; Regulation of Investigatory Powers (Scotland) Act 2000, s 19; Criminal Justice (Surveillance) Act 2009, s 7.

[85] This is governed by a preceding Act, namely the Police Act 1997, Pt 3.

[86] Criminal Justice (Surveillance) Act 2009, s 5(7).

In the UK, 'directed surveillance' is that which is covert but not intrusive and is undertaken for a specific investigation to obtain private information about a person.[87] In other words, directed surveillance involves the secret, undeclared and systematic monitoring of a specific person, but generally in a public place, such as by watching his house or place of work, or following his movements. This may be to gather intelligence of evidence about his behaviour, or his interactions with other suspected members of organised crime groups. Authorisation of directed surveillance is given by an 'authorising officer' of an agency specified in Schedule 1 to the Regulation of Investigatory Powers Act 2000,[88] rather than the Secretary of State or any senior officer and endorsed by a Surveillance Commissioner as is the case with regards to intrusive surveillance. Thus, only intrusive surveillance requires judicial approval of the initial executive direction, based on the understanding that the degree of intrusion and impact on the right to privacy is less, given that the person under surveillance is not being monitored in a private space. This reliance on an internal administrative process is a typical approach of the crime control model, where the impact on the rights of the individual are regarded as not warranting the safeguard of independent court sanction.

Directed surveillance is based on the same grounds of necessity as for intrusive surveillance, and must also be proportionate to its aim.[89] While such surveillance in fact may take place legally without authorisation, authorisation goes some way towards safeguarding the police action from a challenge under Article 8 of the ECHR on the basis that any interference with the right to privacy would be 'in accordance with the law' and 'necessary in a democratic society . . . for the prevention of . . . crime'. Moreover, in *Gilchrist and Quinn v HM Advocate* the Scottish High Court of Justiciary concluded that there is

> no logical basis for assuming . . . that everything done under the invalid authorisation was, by virtue of that invalidity, an infringement of article 8. Whether a particular aspect of the operation involved an infringement of . . . article 8 rights requires to be considered independently of whether there was or was not a valid RIPSA authorisation.[90]

In essence, this underlines the fact that a determination of whether Article 8 is breached is separate to the validity of an authorisation overall, and that an absence of or flaw in the latter does not lead necessarily to the conclusion that the ECHR protection has been compromised unjustifiably.

One particular type of surveillance which may prove difficult to classify and thus regulate is global positioning surveillance (GPS), using satellite technology to facilitate the remote monitoring of persons: this may be at one particular moment,

---

[87] Regulation of Investigatory Powers Act 2000, s 26(2); Regulation of Investigatory Powers (Scotland) Act 2000, s 1(2).

[88] The agencies include the police, SOCA, the Serious Fraud Office, any of the intelligence services, Government departments, any of the armed forces, and HM Revenue and Customs. These may be added to by order of the Secretary of State.

[89] Regulation of Investigatory Powers Act 2000, s 28; Regulation of Investigatory Powers (Scotland) Act 2000, s 6.

[90] *Gilchrist and Quinn v HM Advocate* 2004 ScotHC 53, 2005 1 JC 34 [19].

or for a prolonged period of time.[91] The UK Regulation of Investigatory Powers Act 2000 states explicitly that surveillance is not intrusive if carried out by a device which provides information about a vehicle's location,[92] and the explanatory memo to the Irish Criminal Justice (Surveillance) Act 2009 claims that such a method is 'a less intrusive form of surveillance'. Similarly, the European Court of Human Rights reiterated this view, stating that

> GPS surveillance is by its very nature to be distinguished from other methods of visual or acoustical surveillance which are, as a rule, more susceptible of interfering with a person's right to respect for private life, because they disclose more information on a person's conduct, opinions or feelings.[93]

So, GPS is viewed as relatively innocuous, or at least as less problematic, due to the perception that the substance of the tracking reveals less than other types of surveillance. This is debatable given that GPS can generate substantial quantities of detailed and precise information about a targeted subject for an extended time frame.[94] By regarding GPS in a benign manner, the authorisation requirements are less onerous, thus prioritising the demands of crime control over due process. This misinterprets the extent and depth of GPS tracking, which is a burgeoning form of surveillance, and one of considerable investigative importance, given its ability to reveal patterns of movement and presence at particular places.

Akin to the understanding put forward by the European Court of Human Rights, GPS falls within the definition of directed surveillance in the UK. This means that it need not be approved by a Surveillance Commissioner (who is or was a member of the judiciary) and may last for three months, after which an application for renewal of authorisation may be made.[95] In Ireland, the relevant legislation deals with 'tracking' in a different manner to other surveillance: a member of the Garda Síochána, the Defence Forces or the Revenue Commissioners may monitor the movements of persons, vehicles or things using a tracking device for no more than four months and only if this has been approved by a superior officer on the usual grounds of necessity and proportionality.[96] Such an approval includes the placing and removing of the device itself.[97] Thus, no judicial warrant is required, in contrast to the use of intrusive surveillance in the UK and other modes of surveillance in Ireland. Keeping the approval of GPS monitoring in the administrative realm is a clear representation of the crime control model, where

---

[91] Moreover, unmanned drones may soon be used in police surveillance in the UK; in 2010 SOCA issued a public tender notice requesting 'information-only submissions for covert aerial surveillance services from suppliers of airborne "platforms", including UAV (unmanned aerial vehicles)'. See www.publictenders.net/tender/67952.

[92] Regulation of Investigatory Powers Act 2000, s 26(4); Regulation of Investigatory Powers (Scotland) Act 2000, s 1(4).

[93] *Uzun v Germany* (2011) 53 EHRR 24, para 52.

[94] R McDonald Hutchins, 'Tied Up In *Knotts*? GPS Technology and the Fourth Amendment' (2007–08) 55 *UCLA Law Review* 409.

[95] Regulation of Investigatory Powers Act 2000, s 43.

[96] Criminal Justice (Surveillance) Act 2009, s 8(1).

[97] Criminal Justice (Surveillance) Act 2009, s 8(5).

judicial oversight is circumvented, and the most efficient means of initiating and carrying out this mechanism is adopted.

This absence of judicial involvement does not contravene Article 8, as is evident from *Uzun v Germany*.[98] In that case the applicant had been subject to GPS tracking of a car belonging to S, a presumed accomplice of his, in relation to the criminal investigation of suspected terrorist offences. The European Court of Human Rights found the GPS tracking to be in accordance with law, on the basis that such surveillance could only be ordered against a person suspected of a criminal offence of considerable gravity or, in very limited circumstances, against a third person suspected of being in contact with the accused.[99] Although the prosecution could order a suspect's surveillance via GPS, and so judicial approval was not required, the Court felt that an important safeguard existed by means of the ability of the domestic German criminal courts to exclude unlawfully obtained surveillance evidence and thereby discourage the investigating authorities from collecting evidence by unlawful methods.[100] Though the Court welcomed a subsequent legal amendment to German law that now requires judicial review after one month of GPS tracking, its absence from the scheme applicable to Uzun, and its continued omission from the decision to initiate tracking, was not seen as problematic in terms of Article 8. This emphasis on the power of the exclusionary rule possessed by domestic courts, and the benign interpretation of state power and surveillance, fails to engage with the safeguard that would be provided by judicial oversight of the initial invasion into a person's life by means of GPS. Reliance on the decision of a police officer (or a prosecutor as in *Uzun*) is dubious given the incursion on a person's private life, but is justified by reference to the expedient control of crime. Nevertheless, the European Court concluded that the surveillance was necessary and proportionate on the grounds that the subject was tracked by GPS for a 'relatively short period of time (some three months)', that GPS affected him only when travelling in S's car and so he was not subject to 'total and comprehensive surveillance', and the very serious nature of the suspected offences.[101] In the first instance, the view that police monitoring of one's behaviour for three months as a short period of time is debatable, but indicates that the legislative time frames in the UK and Ireland are ECHR-compliant. Secondly, while it is true that the tracking of Uzun related to his time in his friend's car only, the device could easily have been used more broadly. Thirdly, it is not clear why the gravity of suspected crimes makes it more permissible to encroach on protective rights.

In marked contrast to the approach of the European Court, the US Supreme Court has found that a warrantless use of a GPS to track a private vehicle's movements for 28 days breaches the right against unreasonable search and seizure

---

[98] *Uzun v Germany*, n 93.
[99] ibid, para 70.
[100] ibid, paras 71 and 72.
[101] ibid, para 80.

under the Fourth Amendment to the US Constitution.[102] This may entail judicial oversight before such surveillance is approved. As Sotomayor J emphasised in a concurring judgment,

> GPS monitoring generates a precise, comprehensive record of a person's public movements that reflects a wealth of detail about her familial, political, professional, religious, and sexual associations . . . The Government can store such records and efficiently mine them for information years into the future . . . And because GPS monitoring is cheap in comparison to conventional surveillance techniques and, by design, proceeds surreptitiously, it evades the ordinary checks that constrain abusive law enforcement practices.

This neatly encapsulates the need for judicial approval before the initiation of GPS monitoring. Moreover, as McDonald Hutchins notes, obtaining a warrant for GPS would not be unduly onerous for law enforcement and would ensure a more cautious use of this type of surveillance, which undoubtedly is intrusive by nature, if not by name.[103]

When the Irish Criminal Justice (Surveillance) Bill 2009 was at Second Stage in the Dáil it was noted that

> the changing nature of crime, particularly the growth of organised and ruthless gangs, requires the security response to be stepped up. The threat to society and the integrity and effectiveness of the criminal justice system that is posed by these gangs requires a corresponding robust legal response.[104]

Despite this political rhetoric and the drive to expand powers of surveillance, in fact in Ireland resource implications mean that surveillance is used in carefully selected and targeted cases only, and there appears to be no evidence of any improper use of the Criminal Justice (Surveillance) Act 2009.[105] Similarly, in the UK, the number of intrusive surveillance authorisations remains stable at roughly 390 per year, while more than 300 urgent applications are made, usually in relation to investigations into offences involving drugs or violence and by a small number of forces.[106] On the whole, the Chief Surveillance Commissioner in the UK expressed his belief that there is no systemic misuse of these special provisions.[107] While this may be true, the extent and propriety of surveillance is very hard to gauge, given that it is rarely revealed or discovered by those being monitored.

Intrusive and directed surveillance is a major component in the investigation and prosecution of organised crime, and in many instances is warranted on the basis that otherwise evidence would be almost impossible to gather. Yet, such a crime control mechanism encroaches significantly on the personal life and pri-

---

[102] *US v Jones* 565 US ____ (2012). The approach of the majority in this case has been criticised for focusing on the trespass involved rather than the substance of the surveillance as such.

[103] McDonald Hutchins, n 94, 463.

[104] Dáil Deb, vol 681, col 337 (29 April 2009) per Dermot Ahern.

[105] Feeney J, *Covert Surveillance Report 2009–10* (Dublin, Department of Justice, 2010) 13.

[106] Chief Surveillance Commissioner, *Annual Report of the Chief Surveillance Commissioner to the Prime Minister and to Scottish Ministers for 2010–11* (London, The Stationery Office, 2011) paras 4.5–4.6.

[107] ibid, para 4.6.

vacy of individuals. Moreover, such surveillance, in particular if not assessed and approved by an independent body like a court, holds the potential to alter the nature of governance and the relationship between the State and its citizen by facilitating increased official interference in private personal relations and associations. In this instance, the granting of surveillance by administrative or executive entities indicates the elevation of the pursuit of crime control over due process concerns. Nonetheless, the introduction and use of intrusive and directed surveillance may be regarded as a reasonable reaction to the threat of organised crime if regulated and supervised properly, and if predicated on articulated reasons as approved by a court.

B. Communications Surveillance

In addition to observing and recording people's actions through directed and intrusive surveillance, it is also lawful in certain instances for communications surveillance to take place. This involves either monitoring and intercepting the substance of communications, or logging and accessing data relating to communications, such as the times, patterns, locations and parties involved. Again, while this is admittedly a crucial and valuable dimension of crime control, its broad use has considerable ramifications for due process protections.

i. Interception

Like other means of surveillance, the interception of written or oral communications is used in the investigation and subsequent prosecution of organised criminality, in addition to other serious crimes and terrorism. The physical penetration of the telephone wires once required in this context led to the moniker 'phone tapping', representing the quintessential interception of communication, although interception may apply to electronic, email and postal correspondence also. It is an offence to intercept communications without lawful authority,[108] and the State's capacity to intercept phone calls may be restricted by the right to private and family life under Article 8 of the ECHR and the unenumerated constitutional right to privacy in Ireland.

In the UK a warrant issued by the Secretary of State may authorise or require interception of postal correspondence or telecommunications if necessary in the interests of national security, to prevent or detect serious crime, to safeguard the UK's economic well-being, or to give effect to the provisions of any international mutual assistance agreement, and if this is deemed to be proportionate to the aims of the warrant.[109] The interception of communications is a reserved matter

---

[108] Regulation of Investigatory Powers Act 2000, s 1; in Ireland s 98 of the Postal and Telecommunications Services Act 1983 prohibits the interception of telecommunications messages, unless it is in pursuance of a direction issued by the Minister for Posts and Telegraphs under s 110 of that Act or under another lawful authorisation.

[109] Regulation of Investigatory Powers Act 2000, s 5.

under Schedule 5 to the Scotland Act 1998;[110] however the Scottish Ministers are now permitted to authorise interceptions for the sole purpose of preventing or detecting serious crime.[111] In determining necessity, the extent to which the information reasonably could be obtained by other means must be considered.[112] An application may be made to the Secretary of State (or the Scottish Ministers in cases of serious crime only) by senior officers such as the Director General of SOCA or the Scottish Crime and Drug Enforcement Agency (SCDEA), the Commissioner of Police of the Metropolis; the Chief Constable of the Police Service for Northern Ireland, the Chief Constable of any Scottish police force and the Commissioners for Her Majesty's Revenue and Customs.[113] An interception warrant lasts for three months but may be renewed for up to six months if still necessary.[114] In urgent cases a senior official or a member of the Scottish Administration who is a member of the Senior Civil Service and who is designated by the Scottish Ministers may sign the warrant although the express authorisation of the Secretary of State or Ministers is still required.[115] Such a warrant lasts for five days.

In Ireland, the Minister for Justice may authorise interception after application by the Garda Commissioner for the purpose of criminal investigation or in the interests of State security.[116] Such interception may only be carried out in the investigation of a serious offence where other tactics would fail to produce information showing whether the offence has been committed and where the interception is reasonably expected to be of material assistance in producing evidence.[117]

These tightly framed provisions, which may be applied for by senior officers only, to some extent take account of the drastic incursion that the interception of communications makes on the personal lives of individual citizens, but also the chilling effect it can have on a democratic society. Freedom of expression and of association may be limited if people feel that details regarding their communications and correspondence may be recorded and retained, regardless of the imperative of crime control and investigation. Ultimately, intervention by means of surveillance alters the relationship between the State and its citizens by limiting personal liberty through expansion of State power and oversight. This may transform the nature of governance in a society from one predicated on liberal norms to a model that is more authoritarian in nature. Nonetheless, despite these ramifications, executive rather than judicial approval is required for interception in the UK and Ireland. To ensure adherence to due process values and to protect

---

[110]   See ch 1.

[111]   Scotland Act 1998 (Transfer of Functions to the Scottish Ministers, etc) (No 2) Order 2000.

[112]   Regulation of Investigatory Powers Act 2000, s 5(4).

[113]   Regulation of Investigatory Powers Act 2000, s 6.

[114]   Regulation of Investigatory Powers Act 2000, s 9.

[115]   ibid.

[116]   Interception of Postal Packets and Telecommunications Messages (Regulation) Act 1993, s 2.

[117]   s 4. Similar conditions are outlined in s 5 regarding interceptions carried out in the interests of State security. Section 8 requires a designated judge to monitor the operation of the Act, and a complaints mechanism is provided for in s 9.

individual liberties, interception warrants should be issued by the judiciary rather than a member of the executive, notwithstanding the investigative significance of these tactics in organised crime investigations. Moreover, court authorisation should be required also in the case of directed surveillance that involves invasive oversight (even though it may not fulfil the legislative definition of intrusive).

ii. Communication Records and Traffic Data

Communication records and traffic data assist in investigations and may constitute useful corroborative evidence as they may place a person at a given location or may identify communication traffic between particular parties.[118] The perceived technological nous of organised criminals, the prevalence of mobile telephony and communication by email render such a tactic crucial: the UK's Strategic Defence and Security Review in 2010 asserted that communications data plays a role 'in 95% of all serious organised crime investigations'.[119] Communications data are defined as those necessary to trace and identify the source of a communication, its destination or duration, and not the actual content of phone or internet communications.[120]

The value of such measures for criminal investigations is recognised widely at State level, but the duty on companies and entities to retain communications data in this respect is governed by European-wide legislation. Directive 2006/24/EC was transposed into UK domestic law by the Data Retention (EC Directive) Regulations 2009, which requires communications providers to retain data relating to fixed network and mobile telephony and to internet access and email for a 12 month period.[121] The Directive was implemented in Ireland by the Communications (Retention of Data) Act 2011, requiring communications providers to retain telephone data for two years and internet and email data for one year.[122] Access to data retained in accordance with these Regulations may be obtained only in specific cases, and in circumstances in which disclosure of the data is permitted or required by law.

---

[118] In the trial of Colm Murphy in the Special Criminal Court for the Omagh bombing, evidence concerning telephone records and the traffic between two phones was of significance in corroborating the accused's confession of guilt regarding his part in the conspiracy to plant and detonate the bomb; *DPP v Murphy* (Special Criminal Court, 22 January 2002). However, this conviction was later quashed and a retrial ordered by the Court of Criminal Appeal (*DPP v Murphy* [2005] 2 IR 125), on the grounds that some of the trial court's findings were based on speculation rather than evidence and that the Court failed to assess adequately the credibility of Garda evidence.

[119] HM Government, *Securing Britain in an Age of Uncertainty: The Strategic Defence and Security Review* (London, The Stationery Office, 2010) 44.

[120] Regulation of Investigatory Powers Act 2000, s 21(4); Communications (Retention of Data) Act 2011, s 2 (Ireland).

[121] Directive 2006/24/EC of the European Parliament and of the Council of 15 March 2006 on the retention of data generated or processed in connection with the provision of publicly available electronic communications services or of public communications networks and amending Directive 2002/58/EC [2006] OJL105/54; Data Retention (EC Directive) Regulations 2009, reg 5.

[122] Communications (Retention of Data) Act 2011, s 3(1).

In the UK a designated person[123] may authorise the obtaining or disclosure of communications data held by a postal or telecommunications operator if considered necessary: in the interests of national security, the economic well-being of the UK or public safety; to prevent or detect crime or prevent disorder; to protect public health; to assess or collect a tax, duty or levy; in an emergency, to prevent death or damage to a person's physical or mental health, or for any purpose specified by an order made by the Secretary of State.[124] There is a requirement of proportionality between the authorised conduct and what is sought to be achieved by obtaining the data.[125] This scheme will be replaced by the Communications Data Bill which was published in June 2012, which proposes to extend the scheme to apply to data held by anyone who controls a telecommunications device.

In Ireland, a police officer not below the rank of chief superintendent[126] may request a service provider to disclose data when satisfied they are required for the prevention, detection, investigation or prosecution of a serious offence, the safeguarding of the security of the State, or the saving of human life.[127] Thus, in the UK and Ireland access is permitted without a court order and is not limited to investigations of indictable offences.

These European measures have proved to be controversial;[128] the relevant implementing legislation has been struck down by the German Federal Constitutional Court, for example.[129] Furthermore, Digital Rights Ireland (DRI), a privacy rights watchdog group, demanded the cessation of the collection, storage and accessing of mobile and fixed-line phone data, and in 2010 was granted by the Irish High Court

---

[123] Such designated persons include senior officers in police forces, intelligence forces, SOCA and the Scottish Crime and Drug Enforcement Agency (SCDEA) (see Regulation of Investigatory Powers (Communications Data) Order 2010).

[124] The Regulation of Investigatory Powers Act 2000, Pt 1, ch II, covers the acquisition and disclosure of communications data.

[125] Regulation of Investigatory Powers Act 2000, s 22(5).

[126] Disclosure may be requested by an officer of the Permanent Defence Force not below the rank of colonel where he is satisfied that the data is required to safeguard State security, or by an officer of the Revenue Commissioners when required for the prevention, detection, investigation or prosecution of a revenue offence. This granting of access to Revenue Commissioners as well as to An Garda Síochána and the Defence Forces was criticised by the Data Protection Commissioner (Data Protection Commissioner, *Twenty-first Annual Report of the Data Protection Commissioner 2009* (Dublin, Data Protection Commissioner, 2010) 33).

[127] Communications (Retention of Data) Act 2011, s 6(1). A serious offence is that punishable by imprisonment for a term of five years or more, and offences under ss 11 and 12 of the Criminal Assets Bureau Act 1996, inter alia.

[128] In Case C-301/06 *Ireland v European Parliament and Council of the European Union* [2009] ECR I-00593 Ireland (and Slovakia) challenged the legal basis for the adoption of these provisions, given they were situated under the Community Pillar (governing economic matters) rather than Third Pillar relating to police and judicial cooperation in criminal matters which gave States more latitude (the Pillars have since been abolished by the Lisbon Treaty 2009). Ireland contended that the sole or at least the predominant objective of the Directive is to facilitate the investigation, detection and prosecution of crime, including terrorism, and so it pertained to the Third Pillar. While the Court agreed that this was a component and was indeed referred to, the Directive 'relate[d] predominantly to the functioning of the internal market' (para 85).

[129] See www.bverfg.de/pressemitteilungen/bvg10-011en.html.

the motion for a reference to the European Court of Justice under Article 267 of the Treaty on the Functioning of the European Union.[130] This case is still pending.[131]

The most recent figures from Europe indicate a high use of requests for retained traffic data in the UK, proportionately speaking, when compared with Ireland, with almost 2.5 times more requests per head of population.[132] In the UK, the absence of a constitutional right of privacy may have contributed to a cultural milieu in which police officers feel that this norm can be abrogated without popular disquiet: however the Chief Surveillance Commissioner found no systemic attempts to misuse legislation, notwithstanding occasional and inevitable misjudgments.[133]

In addition, Part III of the Regulation of Investigatory Powers Act 2000 in the UK covers the investigation of electronic data protected by encryption. Section 49 permits members of law enforcement, security and intelligence agencies with appropriate permission[134] to require the disclosure in an understandable format of encrypted information which has come into their possession through lawful seizure, interception, disclosure or otherwise. Disclosure of the information must be necessary in the interests of national security or the UK's economic well-being or to prevent or detect crime; and proportionate. A section 49 notice may require secrecy if the information has come into the possession of the police, Her Majesty's Revenue and Customs or any of the intelligence services is likely to do so, and breach of this secrecy provision is an offence.[135]

While such access to communications data does not reveal its contents, it nonetheless reveals the persons with whom one communicates, and the measures in place apply to all citizens. This is a key example of the primacy that crime control takes over liberal notions of limited State intervention.

C. Cross-border Surveillance

When surveillance is authorised under the Regulation of Investigatory Powers (Scotland) Act 2000, cross-border action may be taken. This permits surveillance to be undertaken anywhere within the UK for a period of up to three weeks at a time.[136]

---

[130] *Digital Rights Ireland Ltd v Minister for Communication* [2010] IEHC 221.

[131] See T Konstadinides, 'Destroying Democracy on the Ground of Defending it? The Data Retention Directive, the Surveillance State and our Constitutional Ecosystem' (2011) *EL Rev* 722.

[132] European Commission, *Final Report from the Commission to the Council and the European Parliament, Evaluation Report on the Data Retention Directive (Directive 2006/24/EC)* (European Commission, Brussels, 2011). In 2008 Ireland made 14,095 requests for retained traffic data, and the UK made 470,222 (table 7) while in 2009 Ireland made 11,283 requests for retained traffic data, and figures for the UK were not provided.

[133] Chief Surveillance Commissioner, n 106, para 4.3.

[134] Regulation of Investigatory Powers Act 2000, Sch 2. Such permission may be granted by a Circuit or District Judge in England and Wales, a sheriff in Scotland or a county court judge in Northern Ireland.

[135] Regulation of Investigatory Powers Act 2000, s 54.

[136] Regulation of Investigatory Powers Act 2000, s 76(2).

In addition, directed and intrusive surveillance which includes surveillance abroad by UK law enforcement may be authorised.[137]

D. Legitimacy and Legality of Surveillance

The European Court of Human Rights has held that the very existence of legislation allowing secret surveillance amounts in itself to an interference with Article 8 of the Convention.[138] Nonetheless, the Court permits surveillance as long as a legal framework is in place which is sufficiently well-defined to give an adequate indication as to the circumstances in which public authorities may use such covert measures.[139] Laws on covert measures of surveillance must be 'particularly precise' given 'this secret and potentially dangerous interference with the right to respect for private life and correspondence'.[140]

Hence phone-tapping and other modes of surveillance have been found to breach Article 8 if the relevant law does not 'indicate with reasonable clarity the scope and manner of exercise of the relevant discretion conferred on the public authorities at the time of the interception'.[141] In fact, the Regulation of Investigatory Powers Act 2000 was enacted to meet criticism from the Strasbourg Court regarding previous incarnations of UK surveillance policy and laws which did not meet such a requirement.[142] In contrast, in *Kennedy v United Kingdom* the European Court approved of the detailed rules in the Regulation of Investigatory Powers Act 2000 and its Codes of Practice,[143] and found the scrutiny of surveillance decisions to be independent and there to be adequate safeguards against arbitrariness. However, as Ashworth observed, this judgment does not affirm the compatibility with Article 8(2) of the ECHR of all the provisions in the Regulation of Investigatory Powers Act 2000 and he further notes that it therefore remains an open question whether the granting of considerable powers to 'designated persons' who are senior police officers, rather than judges, will be held compatible with Article 8(2).[144] The decision in *Uzun v Germany* seems to indicate that judicial oversight for GPS is not required, but this was underpinned by the particular

[137] Regulation of Investigatory Powers Act 2000, s 27(3). See Art 40 of the Schengen Convention (The Schengen acquis – Convention implementing the Schengen Agreement of 14 June 1985 between the Governments of the States of the Benelux Economic Union, the Federal Republic of Germany and the French Republic on the gradual abolition of checks at their common borders [2000] OJ L239/19).
[138] See *Klass and Others v Federal Republic of Germany* Series A no 28 (1979-80) 2 EHRR 214, para 41; *Malone v United Kingdom* Series A no 95 (1985) 7 EHRR 14, para 64; and *Weber and Saravia v Germany* (2008) 46 EHRR SE5, paras 77–79.
[139] *Hewitt and Harman v United Kingdom* (1992) 14 EHRR 657; *Malone,* n 138; *Khan v United Kingdom* (2001) 31 EHRR 45.
[140] *Malone,* n 138, para 67 and *Khan,* n 139, para 26.
[141] *Malone,* n 138, 7; *Kruslin v France* Series A no 176-B (1990) 2 EHRR 547, para 36; *Valenzuela Contreras v Spain* (1998) 28 EHRR 483, para 61; *Khan,* n 139 paras 27–28.
[142] See *Hewitt and Harman,* n 139; *Malone,* n 138, *Khan,* n 139.
[143] *Kennedy v United Kingdom* (2011) 52 EHRR 4.
[144] A Ashworth, 'Case Comment: Secret Surveillance Under Powers in Regulation of Investigatory Powers Act 2000' [2010] *Crim LR* 868, 869.

perspective on the nature and intrusion of GPS, rather than concerning surveillance more broadly.

Communication interception which is not authorised duly under the relevant legislation 'is unlawful, notwithstanding that what emerges from that surveillance is evidence implicating the speaker in criminal activity',[145] and the illegal content of a conversation does not preclude the accused from claiming that interception was illegal.[146] However, the admissibility of unlawful surveillance is no reflection on the content of the information gleaned or revealed and is determined by the domestic law and national courts rather than by the ECHR.[147] The exclusionary rule in Ireland as developed by the courts is remarkably robust in its protection of rights, and this may provide a deterrent towards improper use of surveillance, as was believed by the European Court in *Uzun v Germany*. In Ireland a distinction is made between illegally and unconstitutionally obtained evidence: whereas in the cases of the former, admission is a matter for the trial judge, in the latter instance where evidence has been obtained as a result of a 'deliberate and conscious violation' of the constitutional rights of the accused this evidence is inadmissible, with no discretion for the trial judge to admit such evidence, unless 'extraordinary excusing circumstances' exist.[148] Thus, until recently, if intrusive surveillance breached a constitutional right like the right to privacy,[149] or the inviolability of the dwelling,[150] the evidence would not be admissible absent extraordinary excusing circumstances. However, the Criminal Justice (Surveillance) Act 2009 now provides that error or omission in the authorisation or on the part of the officer shall not render inadmissible information or documents obtained as a result of the surveillance, if the court decides that admission is in the interests of justice and that the error or omission was inadvertent, or if an action was in good faith and the failure was inadvertent.[151] As the Court of Criminal Appeal stated,

[145] *Henderson v HM Advocate* [2005] HCJAC 47, 2005 JC 301 [35].

[146] *People (DPP) v Dillon* [2002] 4 IR 501, 513.

[147] See *Schenk v Switzerland* Series A no 140 (1991) 13 EHRR 242; *Van Mechelen v Netherlands* 25 EHRR 647, para 50, inter alia. See ch 5 for further consideration of the admissibility of surveillance evidence.

[148] *People (AG) v O'Brien* [1965] IR 142, 170; *People (DPP) v Kenny* [1990] 2 IR 110. Extraordinary excusing circumstances include the imminent destruction of vital evidence; the need to rescue a victim in peril; or a search without warrant which was incidental to and contemporaneous with a lawful arrest. See Y Daly, 'Unconstitutionally Obtained Evidence in Ireland: Protectionism, Deterrence and the Winds of Change' (2009) 19 *Irish Criminal Law Journal* 40.

[149] See *Norris v AG* [1984] IR 36.

[150] Art 40.5.

[151] Criminal Justice (Surveillance) Act 2009, s 14(3) and (4). The court, in making its decision, has regard to (i) whether the error or omission concerned was serious or merely technical in nature; (ii) the nature of any right infringed by the obtaining of the information or document concerned; (iii) whether there were circumstances of urgency; (iv) the possible prejudicial effect of the information or document concerned; and (v) the probative value of the information or document concerned. The section does not say shall/must. This amendment follows the criticism of the exclusionary rule in *DPP (Walsh) v Cash* [2007] IEHC 108 per Charleton J, and that of the Balance in the Criminal Law Review Group (*Final Report of the Balance in the Criminal Law Review Group* (Dublin, Department of Justice, 2007) 159). The Supreme Court in *DPP v Cash* [2010] did not alter the current form of the exclusionary rule, holding that it was inapplicable on the facts of this case.

'[t]his is an interesting provision, but it does not shed much light on the position at common law, and has not yet been the subject of authoritative interpretation and application'.[152] It is unclear how the courts will interpret this provision, given its apparent incompatibility with some aspects of existing constitutional case law.

There is no automatic exclusion of improperly obtained evidence in England, Wales and Northern Ireland; such evidence may be excluded under the discretion of the trial judge if its use would result in the trial being unfair.[153] A breach of Article 8 of the ECHR does not render evidence inadmissible but is a factor to be taken into account by a judge in exercising his discretion.[154] Similarly, in Scotland the trial judge has discretion whether to admit such evidence and in doing so must attempt to reconcile the interest of the citizen to be protected from illegal invasions of his liberties with the interest of the State to secure evidence to enable justice to be done.[155] Thus, the law across the UK and Ireland indicates that surveillance evidence may be admitted despite a breach of rights in its implementation. The European Court in *Khan* found that improper use of surveillance breached Article 8 but not Article 6, and thus while the applicant could seek damages for the breach of his right to privacy the evidence did not render the trial unfair and would not be deemed inadmissible automatically.[156] Thus a conviction may rest on evidence obtained through surveillance gathered in an illegitimate or problematic manner. This demonstrates the failure of the European Court to provide a robust procedural buffer against the use of what may be dubious crime control tactics.

To protect due process norms and liberties, and to provide sufficient oversight, the European Court favours a system of external review of the implementation of secret surveillance measures.[157] This appears to be met by the annual review carried out by the Surveillance Commissioner in the UK[158] and by a designated High Court judge in Ireland,[159] though criticisms have been made of the reality of review in the UK.[160] The European Court has also stated that after surveillance is terminated, notification should be made to the persons concerned, as long as this does not jeopardise the purpose of the surveillance.[161] There is no provision in UK or Irish legislation for such notification, and it is difficult to see how this would be workable, given the need to maintain the secrecy of operations and techniques. Rather than insisting on notification after the event, increased judicial involvement before surveillance is

---

[152] *DPP v Mallon* [2011] IECCA 29.
[153] Police and Criminal Evidence Act 1984, s 78(1).
[154] *Abbott and Others v R* [2005] EWCA Crim 2952.
[155] *Lawrie v Muir* 1950 JC 19, 27. See P Duff, 'Admissibility of Improperly Obtained Physical Evidence in the Scottish Criminal Trial: The Search for Principle' (2004) 8 *Edinburgh Law Review* 152.
[156] *Khan*, n 139; *cf* dissent of Loucaides J.
[157] *Klass*, n 138, para 70.
[158] Regulation of Investigatory Powers Act 2000, Pt IV.
[159] Criminal Justice (Surveillance) Act 2009, s 12.
[160] Justice, *Freedom from Suspicion: Surveillance Reform for a Digital Age* (London, Justice, 2011) para 96 *et seq*.
[161] *Klass*, n 138, para 58; *Weber and Saravia*, n 138, para 135.

undertaken is more critical and pressing to protect individual due process rights in the face of the exigencies of effective crime control.

V. Covert Human Intelligence Sources

The use of undercover police officers and informers is becoming more common-place in the investigation of organised criminality (often in conjunction with other means of surveillance),[162] in contrast to the once insubstantial role played by covert policing in certain crime investigations in the UK.[163] Such actors may penetrate criminal groups and relay information about their structure and actions to the authorities, and this infiltration of criminal enterprises is regarded as crucial for effective policing and investigation of organised crime.[164] The term 'covert human intelligence source', or CHIS, encompasses both police agents and civilians, and is defined legislatively as a person who establishes or maintains a relationship with another to obtain or disclose information covertly, or to provide access to any information to another person.[165] This may be for intelligence purposes, or to gather evidence for criminal proceedings, or both.

Much organised crime may involve not a victim as such, or victims may be reluctant to testify, or the evidence gathered may be incomplete or unconvincing. Thus, the benefits that underpin the use of CHIS involve the nature and quality of evidence obtained, especially when this would be otherwise difficult or impossible. Conversely, undercover operations may risk the security of the agents, involve intrusion into personal privacy, may lead to entrapment and an increase in criminal activity, and may compromise the investigation completely if the agent is detected or revealed.

The nature and role of a CHIS is distinguishable from an informant which is essentially anyone who provides any information to the police, regardless of its use, and is in contrast to an informer which 'has certain cloak and dagger connotations'.[166] As Hewitt states, an informer is 'anyone who furtively supplies information

---

[162] A single authorisation may combine two or more different authorisations under Pt II of the Regulation of Investigatory Powers Act 2000, such as for intrusive surveillance and a CHIS: Home Office, *Covert Human Intelligence Sources Code of Practice* (London, The Stationery Office, 2010) para 3.19.

[163] M Levi, 'Covert Policing and Organized Fraud: The English Experience' in C Fijnaut and G Marx, *Undercover: Police Surveillance in Comparative Perspective* (The Hague, Kluwer Law International, 1995) 210.

[164] See Commissioner of An Garda Síochána, *Public Statement by the Commissioner of An Garda Síochána on the Management and Use of Covert Human Intelligence Sources* (Dublin, An Garda Síochána, 2006) 5.

[165] Regulation of Investigatory Powers Act 2000, s 26(8); Regulation of Investigatory Powers (Scotland) Act 2000, s 1(7).

[166] S Greer, 'Towards a Sociological Model of the Police Informant' (1995) 46 *British Journal of Sociology* 509, 510. Cooper and Murphy dispute such an interpretation of the notion of an informant and use the term to refer to someone with access to criminal networks that are relatively impenetrable

to a state security agency'.[167] Moreover, both CHIS and informers differ from a 'supergrass' who, rather than an authorised agent, is an accomplice who later decides to testify against his colleagues, often in return for prosecution leniency.[168] Greer classifies police informers by reference to two main variables, namely the relationship between them and the people upon whom they inform (whether they are 'outsiders' or 'insiders', and whether they are 'single' or 'multiple' event informants), and their relationship with the policing agencies to whom they supply the information.[169] In the context of organised crime investigations, a CHIS is generally an insider (whether an undercover officer or an acquaintance of the suspect(s)), and a 'multiple' event informant.

The use of CHIS has become more structured in the UK and now is regulated and scrutinised strictly.[170] Although a CHIS need not be authorised under the Regulation of Investigatory Powers Act 2000 and its Scottish equivalent, so doing ensures that the operation has lawful approval.[171] In addition, Codes of Practice have been issued, as well as each police force having its own policy and operating procedure.[172] In contrast, in Ireland there is no legislation governing the use of CHIS; rather, internal administrative guidelines are in place akin to the situation in the UK prior to the enactment of the 2000 Act.

In the UK, authorisation of covert human intelligence sources may be issued by various officers such as a superintendent in a police force, the Scottish Crime and Drug Enforcement Agency (SCDEA), HM Revenue and Customs or a Senior Manager in SOCA on application by a member of their own force or agency, and in urgent cases authorisation may be granted by a police inspector or by a Principal Officer in SOCA.[173] Thus, there is no requirement that the Surveillance Commissioner or other judicial agent be involved.[174] Like other modes of surveil-

to the police, who offers information in exchange for real or perceived advantage, and whose assistance to the police raises the need for concealment of his identity: P Cooper and J Murphy, 'Ethical Approaches for Police Officers when Working with Informants in the Development of Criminal Intelligence in the United Kingdom' (1997) 26 *Journal of Social Policy* 1, 2.

[167]   S Hewitt, *Snitch! A History of the Modern Intelligence Informer* (New York, Continuum, 2010) 18.
[168]   See ch 6.
[169]   Greer, n 166.
[170]   Scottish Information Commissioner, Decision Notice, *Mr Stephen Stewart and Chief Constables of Central, Grampian, Lothian and Borders, Strathclyde and Tayside Police* [2009] ScotIC 037_2009 (31 March 2009) *Payments made to police informants and the reasons for payment*, para 20; available at www.bailii.org/cgi-bin/markup.cgi?doc=/scot/cases/ScotIC/2009/037_2009.html&query=chis+and+c overt&method=boolean.
[171]   The Code of Practice, n 162, para 2.11, 'strongly' recommends that a public authority consider an authorisation whenever the use or conduct of a CHIS is likely to engage Art 8 rights.
[172]   The Regulation of Investigatory Powers (Scotland) Act 2000 and the related code apply where the conduct is likely to take place in Scotland unless the authorisation concerns national security or the economic well-being of the UK.
[173]   Regulation of Investigatory Powers (Directed Surveillance and Covert Human Intelligence Sources) Order 2010; Regulation of Investigatory Powers (Prescription of Offices, Ranks and Positions) (Scotland) Orders 2000–11.
[174]   Similarly, in the US undercover operations are not treated as Fourth Amendment searches or seizures which would require advance judicial authorisation and a showing of probable cause. This is in contrast to electronic surveillance. Ultimately, the executive in the US provides oversight of under-

lance, the use of a CHIS must be both necessary and proportionate.[175] An authorisation lasts for 12 months and may be renewed for further such periods, while an urgent approval lasts 72 hours.[176] Authorisations generally frame the CHIS's task in relatively broad terms, so as to ensure new authorisations are not required regularly, but a new one may be needed if the nature of the task changes significantly.[177] Authorisations may be given for the use or conduct of a CHIS both inside and outside the UK but approval for the latter 'can usually only validate them for the purposes of UK law'.[178] Furthermore, a CHIS wearing or carrying a surveillance device does not need a separate authorisation for the device, as long as it is used and kept in his presence.[179] This means that judicial oversight of intrusive surveillance may be circumvented by, for example, the CHIS carrying a sound-recording device in a private home.

Each CHIS has a 'handler', that is a person within the investigating authority with 'day-to-day responsibility for dealing with the source . . . and for the source's security and welfare' and for recording the material supplied by him.[180] There must also be another person within the authority with general oversight of the use made of the source: this is the 'controller'.[181] While authorising officers should not sanction activities where they are the handler of the CHIS or where they are involved in the investigation, this may not always be possible given the small size of certain organisations or in urgent circumstances; nonetheless this should be highlighted in the record of authorisations and the attention of a Commissioner or Inspector should be invited to it.[182]

As noted, there is no legislation in Ireland governing covert human intelligence sources. A Covert Human Intelligence Source System and a Code of Practice for their management and use did not become organisational policy for the Garda Síochána until 2006 following judicial criticism of the handling of informers in a tribunal report inquiring into police corruption in Donegal.[183] The Code of Practice now delineates authorisation, registration, risk assessment and record

cover operations rather than Congress or the judiciary. See J Ross, 'The Place of Covert Policing in Democratic Societies: A Comparative Study of the United States and Germany' (2007) 55 *American Journal of Comparative Law* 493, 512. In the UK, s 38 of the Protection of Freedoms Act 2012 now requires judicial approval for the grant of a CHIS by public authorities.

[175] Regulation of Investigatory Powers Act 2000, s 29. Necessity is determined the same way as in the case of obtaining or disclosure of communications data – see above, n 124. Regulation of Investigatory Powers (Scotland) Act 2000, s 7.

[176] Regulation of Investigatory Powers (Scotland) Act 2000, s 19, Regulation of Investigatory Powers Act 2000, s 43.

[177] Code of Practice, n 162, para 6.2.

[178] ibid, para 4.26.

[179] ibid, para 3.24.

[180] See Regulation of Investigatory Powers Act 2000, s 29(5); Regulation of Investigatory Powers (Scotland) Act 2000, s 7; Code of Practice, n 163, paras 6.7–6.9; Regulation of Investigatory Powers (Scotland) Act 2000 Code of Practice, para 5.26ff.

[181] Code of Practice, n 162, para 6.9.

[182] ibid, para 5.8.

[183] Morris J, *Report of the Tribunal of Inquiry into Certain Gardaí in the Donegal Division: Report on Explosives 'Finds' in Donegal* (Dublin, Government of Ireland, 2004) paras 13.26 and 13.92.

keeping;[184] for example, the authority to recruit, handle and manage CHIS may be given only by the Assistant Commissioner at the Crime and Security Branch of An Garda Síochána.[185] This is far more limited than the scheme in the UK, but still does not include judicial approval. In addition, the Code states that CHIS Handlers and Controllers will be trained to 'approved standards', and the use of CHIS will be subject to 'appropriate reviews'. These terms are not defined anywhere, and embody the opacity of the policing of organised crime in Ireland. The genesis of the Code after a scathing Tribunal report further exemplifies the crisis-driven and *ad hoc* approach to development of policy.

While the Garda Code is claimed to be 'in line with best international practice'[186] the lack of legislation in Ireland is worrying from a due process perspective and is unlikely to be compliant with the requirements of the ECHR. McDermott has noted that this non-statutory, executive action is not 'dissimilar' to the regime which operated in the UK prior to *Malone v UK* where the European Court of Human Rights found that phone tapping was not in accordance with law and that it breached Article 8 due to the fact that the relevant domestic law was obscure and could be interpreted in different ways.[187] Therefore, procedures in Ireland appear to contravene Article 8 given that the expression 'in accordance with the law' in Article 8(2) requires that the measure has 'some basis in domestic law' and 'refers to the quality of this law, demanding that it should be accessible to the person concerned, who must moreover be able to foresee its consequences for him or her, and compatible with the rule of law'.[188]

Regardless of the presence or otherwise of legislation, the use of CHIS may be questionable in both a human rights and logistical sense, given the high risks involved and the need for careful management.[189] Overall, the precepts of due process as interpreted by Packer may be subsumed by the imperatives of crime control. In the first instance, the recruitment of non-police CHIS may be problematic. It is not implausible to think that officers would try to convince certain arrestees to become informants, or to focus on vulnerable or marginal members of criminal networks, perhaps extending to non-criminal sexual partners of offenders.[190] Moreover, there is no judicial involvement or approval of the process by the Surveillance Commissioner. Given that a CHIS wearing or carrying a

---

[184] An Garda Síochána, *Communiqué* (Dublin, An Garda Síochána, 2008) 14 garda.ie/Documents/User/communique%20mar%2008.pdf.

[185] Commissioner of An Garda Síochána, n 164, 5.

[186] An Garda Síochána, *Section 23 Garda Síochána Act 2005 Three-Year Review Report* (Dublin, An Garda Síochána, 2009) 16.

[187] PA McDermott, 'Undercover Investigations and Human Rights', 9th Annual National Prosecutors' Conference (Office of the Director of Public Prosecutions, Dublin, 2008) 4 dppireland.ie/filestore/documents/PAPER_-_Paul_Anthony_McDermott_BL.pdf; see above, n 138.

[188] *Malone*, n 138; *Kruslin*, n 141, para 27; *Huvig v France* Series A no 176-B (1990) 12 EHRR 52, para 26; *Kopp v Switzerland* (1999) 27 EHRR 91, para 55; and *Amann v Switzerland*, n 64, para 50.

[189] See Code of Practice, n 162, para 2.9.

[190] M Maguire, 'Policing by Risks and Targets: Some Dimensions and Implications of Intelligence-led Crime Control' (2000) 9 *Policing and Society* 315, 326.

surveillance device does not need a separate authorisation for the device, the *imprimatur* usually required for intrusive surveillance thus is avoided.[191]

The CHIS may be put at risk by operating for the police in this manner, and the police are required under Article 2 of the ECHR to protect the right to life of the source. As the House of Lords emphasised in *Van Colle v Chief Constable Hertfordshire Police*, Article 2 is breached if 'a real and immediate risk to life is demonstrated and individual agents of the state have reprehensibly failed to exercise the powers available to them for the purpose of protecting life'.[192] This means that if the police become aware that the identity of a CHIS has been revealed and that he may be injured or killed by former associates or colleagues, and nevertheless the police fail to act and he is so injured or killed, then the police have breached Article 2 and civil redress may be obtained.

The remuneration of covert sources and the funding of operations is a further contentious issue. CHIS may be paid or reimbursed in some manner, but this is not delineated statutorily in the UK or Ireland. The Police Service for Northern Ireland (PSNI) has acknowledged explicitly that while the public may not see such payments to individuals who are close to criminal activity as wholly acceptable, CHIS are 'often the most valuable sources of information'.[193] Indeed it has been found that police officers see money as one of the most consistently motivating factors for people becoming and remaining informers.[194] Thus, crime control priorities prevail over public concerns about the legitimacy of the process and regarding possible inducement to provide information. More pragmatically, concerns have been raised about the fact that some CHIS operations may require considerable resources, though it has been asserted also that the use of informants in other instances appears to be relatively inexpensive.[195]

Covert policing requires tacit derogations from the legal system's norms[196] insofar as it may entail police officers skirting close to or even breaching the limits of legality, and may necessitate reliance on parties with dubious records and motivations. This is the paradox of undercover work, whereby an attempt to reduce crime may increase it: good ends are attained by bad means.[197] Ultimately,

---

[191] Code of Practice, n 162, para 3.24. This is akin to the US where the tape-recording of conversations by undercover agents does not count as electronic surveillance and therefore does not require judicial authorisation as Fourth Amendment rights are not engaged. See J Ross, 'Valuing Inside Knowledge: Police Infiltration as a Problem for the Law of Evidence' (2004) 79 *Chicago-Kent Law Review* 1111, 1120.

[192] *Van Colle v Chief Constable Hertfordshire Police* [2008] UKHL 50, [2009] 1 AC 225 [31].

[193] See Police Service of Northern Ireland, Freedom of Information Request no F-2008-04503, *Payment To Informants* and Request no F-2009-01208, *Payments for Covert Human Intelligence Sources (Cont)* 1.

[194] C Dunnighan and C Norris, 'A Risky Business: The Recruitment and Running of Informers by English Police Officers' (1996) 19 *Police Studies* 1.

[195] Cooper and Murphy, n 166, 3.

[196] Ross, n 174, 538.

[197] G Marx, *Undercover* (California, University of California Press, 1988) 319.

reliance on CHIS may compromise the legitimacy of policing,[198] and impinge on due process protections. In this respect Ross speaks of the 'interaction dangers' of undercover policing, where agents participate too actively in the crimes they investigate, or permit or encourage crimes to occur, thereby becoming *agents provocateurs*.[199] Moreover, the nature of covert police or informer work is such that oversight of sources is difficult, and in the UK a number of inquiries are underway regarding inappropriate behaviour and relationships cultivated by undercover agents.[200] Maintaining the legality and acceptability of undercover operations thus turns on the legal or regulatory containment of these risks:[201] whether undercover work is ethical depends on the seriousness of the crimes suspected and committed; the available alternatives to and the decision-making regarding the use of such a tactic; and the reasonableness of suspicion of criminality and of believing that such policing will prevent serious crime from occurring.[202] Ultimately, both a precise legal framework and an ethical culture of policing is required to ensure that due process norms and liberties remain safeguarded in the use of this crime control technique.

A. Encouraging Criminality?

The key danger in the use of CHIS concerns the undercover agents participating in or encouraging criminality: '[i]n many categories of cases it is necessary for the agents to commit acts that, standing by themselves, are criminal'.[203] This may occur in the context of assisting the trafficking of illicit goods, for example. In the United States, informants and undercover agents are shielded from criminal liability by the public authority defence as long as any potentially illegal acts are authorised,[204] but no precise equivalent of such a defence exists in the jurisdictions in the UK and Ireland. Nonetheless, although it is an offence in England, Wales and Northern Ireland intentionally to encourage or assist an offence,[205] a statutory defence of acting reasonably exists, depending on the seriousness of the anticipated offence and any purpose for which or authority by which the person claims to have been acting.[206] Thus, a CHIS, who conspires with or assists a criminal organisation to sell drugs or arms, for example, with the aim of then exposing the criminality, may rely on this defence, as his action arguably permits prosecu-

---

[198] M Innes, 'Professionalizing the Role of the Police Informant: The British Experience' (2000) 9 *Policing and Society* 357.

[199] Ross, n 174, 537.

[200] See www.hmic.gov.uk/news/press/releases-2011/release-002-2011/.

[201] ibid.

[202] Marx, n 197, 315.

[203] *United States v Murphy* 768 F 2d 1518 (7th Cir 1985) 1528–29.

[204] Ross, n 174, 550; see, eg *United States v Achter* 52 F3d 753, 755 (8th Cir 1995).

[205] Serious Crime Act 2007, ss 44–46.

[206] Serious Crime Act 2007, s 50.

tion and prevention of other future crime.[207] In Scotland it is no defence to act in a criminal manner to prevent or stop other offending behaviour.[208] No legislation on point exists in Ireland, and there is little case law; thus the superior courts may turn to the English jurisprudence for guidance. While the common law seemed to view the issue of crime prevention as providing no defence to a charge of conspiracy,[209] the subsequent legislative amendment in the Serious Crime Act 2007 may influence the Irish courts in developing a reasonable defence of acting to prevent crime. Such a defence would strengthen the scheme of CHIS as regards crime control.

B. Entrapment

Moreover, CHIS who are State agents must guard against encouraging criminality on the part of other individuals, such as inducing them to commit offences which they would otherwise have not been likely to commit. If such entrapment occurs, this and the use of any evidence so obtained may breach Article 6.[210] In the United States entrapment is a substantive defence in the federal courts,[211] but this is not the case in the United Kingdom. In England and Wales, remedies in this respect have been developed: the court may stay the relevant criminal proceedings, and may exclude evidence under section 78 of PACE (Police and Criminal Evidence Act 1984).[212] As was expressed in *Looseley*, if the police 'did no more than present the defendant with an unexceptional opportunity to commit a crime' there is no entrapment.[213] The courts in Northern Ireland follow this dictum, though it appears to be interpreted rather broadly, such as occurred in *R v Bellingham* where a planned police operation involved the officer persisting in his request for drugs which resulted in three test purchases of drugs from the defendant.[214] Similarly, there is no substantive defence of entrapment in Scotland; a prosecution based on entrapment is regarded as abuse of court process and should not proceed, rather than entrapment presenting an objection to the admissibility of evidence.[215]

---

[207] The Law Commission *Participating in Crime* (London, The Stationery Office, 2007) (Law Com No 305) para 5.9ff.

[208] *Palazzo v Copeland* 1976 JC 52.

[209] *Yip Chiu-Cheung v R* [1995] 1 AC 111.

[210] See *Teixeira de Castro v Portugal* (1998) 28 EHRR 101; *R v Looseley* [2001] UKHL 53, [2001] 1 WLR 2060 [15]. In the former case the European Court of Human Rights held that the necessary inference from the circumstances was that these officers had 'exercised an influence such as to incite the commission of the offence'.

[211] *Sherman v United States* 356 US 369 (1957) 372.

[212] *Looseley*, n 210, [16]; *cf R v Sang* [1980] AC 402.

[213] *Looseley*, n 210, [23]. See A Ashworth, 'Re-drawing the Boundaries of Entrapment' (2002) *Crim LR* 161, 162–63.

[214] *R v Bellingham* [2003] NICC 2 [22].

[215] *Brown v HM Advocate* 2002 SLT 809; *Jones v HM Advocate* [2009] HCJAC 86, 2010 JC 255; see F Leverick and F Stark, 'How do You Solve a Problem Like Entrapment? *Jones and Doyle v HM Advocate*' (2010) 14 *Edinburgh Law Review* 467.

There is limited case law in Ireland on entrapment, and no reported case relates to suspected organised crime or related offences. The Irish High Court has distinguished between a witness employed by an official body to secure evidence of the commission of an offence, which it is the duty of that body to investigate with a view to prosecution, and that of an accomplice which needs corroboration.[216] One of the few cases which considers the matter is *Syon v Hewitt and McTiernan*, concerning the test purchase of cigarettes by a minor.[217] The High Court found that there is no substantive defence of entrapment arising from the use of the test purchase procedure, but seemed to limit its judgment to the facts. Thus, it is not clear whether *Syon* indicates a broader protection for CHIS in terms of entrapment.

In the European context, it is a violation of Article 6(1) ECHR for the police to '[exercise] an influence such as to incite the commission of the offence'.[218] This is especially problematic if the officers were not authorised to act undercover and were not supervised and basically 'instigated the offence'.[219]

> The use of undercover agents must be restricted and safeguards put in place even in cases concerning the fight against drug trafficking. While the rise in organised crime undoubtedly requires that appropriate measures be taken, the right to a fair administration of justice nevertheless holds such a prominent place . . . that it cannot be sacrificed for the sake of expedience . . . The public interest cannot justify the use of evidence obtained as a result of police incitement.[220]

This embodies the concern of the European Court for notions of due process, notwithstanding the demands of crime control in this instance.

Despite the depth of scholarship on the concept of undercover policing, its legality and the risks it may pose for the parties involved,[221] little is known about the results that such operations yield for criminal investigations.[222] This lack of empirical justification for the use of CHIS undermines their legitimacy, especially given the challenges presented for due process, though it may in fact be the case that quantifying their value is not possible. More fundamentally, statistics regarding the use of CHIS in Ireland are not available publically, whereas in the UK there are usually between 3,000–4,000 CHIS authorised at any given time, with a significant turnover in these figures.[223]

CHIS may be a useful source of intelligence or evidence, and thus a crucial dimension of the State's strategy of investigating organised crime and gathering

---

[216] *Dental Board v O'Callaghan* [1969] IR 181.

[217] *Syon v Hewitt and McTiernan* [2006] IEHC 376.

[218] *Teixeira de Castro*, n 210, [38]. See D Ormerod and A Roberts, 'The Trouble with *Teixera*: Developing a Principled Approach to Entrapment' (2002) *International Journal of Evidence and Proof* 38.

[219] *Teixeira de Castro*, n 210, para 39. This was in contrast to the situation in *Lüdi v Switzerland* (1992) 15 EHRR 173 where judicial approval had been given.

[220] *Teixeira de Castro*, n 210, para 36.

[221] See Ross, n 174 and n 191; Fijnaut and G Marx, n 163; Marx, n 197; AD Macleod, 'Undercover Policing: A Psychiatrist Perspective' (1995) 18 *International Journal of Law and Psychiatry* 239.

[222] EW Kruisbergen, D De Jong and ER Kleemans, 'Undercover Policing: Assumptions and Empirical Evidence' (2011) 51 *British Journal of Criminology* 394.

[223] Chief Surveillance Commissioner, n 106, para 4.9.

the necessary evidence on which to base a prosecution. Nonetheless CHIS may also fail to prevent or may in fact precipitate criminality. In other words, the drive for a more effective means of crime control may paradoxically lead to more crime. Moreover, the situation of CHIS authorisation in the administrative context and the lack of independent judicial oversight is paradigmatic of Packer's crime control model. Ultimately, the more tightly the concept of 'entrapment' is drawn, and the more loosely the 'crime prevention' defence, the greater the potential for de facto instigation rather than prevention of criminality and the imposition of harsh effects in a bid to address organised crime.

VI. Controlled Deliveries

The controlled delivery of drugs or other controlled or illegal materials is a key aspect of organised crime investigations and is relied upon commonly in the UK and Ireland. This is the technique of allowing detected consignments of illicit drugs or other trafficked substances to pass out of, through or into the territory of one or more countries, with the knowledge and under the supervision of the relevant authorities so as to identify persons involved in the offences.[224] The benefit of such a crime control tactic is that it may well reveal powerful actors in a criminal network or syndicate who may otherwise be insulated from detection or prosecution, and may expose international organised crime links and connections. A controlled delivery generally either involves the delivery of discovered illicit material to its originally intended recipient, or the delivery of material by a cooperating witness to a person who intends to resell it to others.[225] In the latter instance the issue of entrapment, as previously explored, may arise.[226] Most controlled deliveries in the UK and Ireland belong to the former category.

There is no specific legislation in the UK concerning controlled deliveries, but HM Revenue and Customs (HMRC), SOCA, and the Association of Chief Police Officers coordinate to manage such deliveries. Controlled deliveries often involve the crossing of borders and jurisdictions by the consignments, and thus an international response is required with cooperation with other police forces and agencies. In Ireland a Memorandum of Understanding and an Operational Protocol exists between the Customs and Excise Service of the Revenue Commissioners, An Garda Síochána and the Naval Service, and this seeks to standardise the controlled deliveries of drugs.[227] In addition, in Ireland the Criminal Justice (Mutual Assistance) Act

---

[224] See Art 2(i) of the UN Convention Against Transnational Organized Crime, GA Res 25, annex I, UN GAOR, 55th Sess, Supp no 49, at 44, UN Doc A/45/49 (vol I) (2001).

[225] S Adamoli, A Di Nicola, EU Savona and P Zoffi, *Organised Crime Around the World* (Helsinki, HEUNI, 1998) 174.

[226] See above, n 212ff.

[227] Dáil WA, vol 655, col 862 (28 May 2008).

2008 governs inter-jurisdictional controlled deliveries.[228] There is no UK equivalent. Under the 2008 Act a request may be made by Ireland to a designated State to allow a delivery to be made to that jurisdiction by specified persons including members of An Garda Síochána and Customs and Excise.[229] Conversely a designated State may make a request for a controlled delivery to be made in Ireland,[230] and specified persons from that other State may be permitted to participate in the operation. The Irish Minister for Justice must be satisfied that there are reasonable grounds for believing that a controlled delivery is in the public interest.[231] If the delivery concerns the importation of illegal drugs, the delivery must be regulated in accordance with the agreed procedures between customs and excise authorities, An Garda Síochána and the Naval Service.[232] Between 2005 and 2008 a total of 73 controlled delivery operations were carried out in Ireland;[233] information on the number of controlled delivery operations in the UK is not collected centrally.[234]

Problematic aspects of controlled deliveries in the UK came to light in a series of cases focusing on the importation of heroin from Pakistan. In such instances 'participating informants' (PIs), who are also couriers for the drug suppliers in question, delivered the heroin to customs officers in Pakistan who then transported it to the UK. The PI travelled to the UK and made the delivery to the purchaser who was arrested and prosecuted based on evidence given against him by the PI. Such controlled importation was criticised robustly by the Court of Appeal in *R v Choudhery* which centred on the non-disclosure of evidential material to the defence.[235] *Choudhery* had been convicted after purchasing heroin imported and supplied by this controlled delivery approach, where informants had been acting on behalf of customs officers with the aim of prosecuting the recipient of the drugs. The Court noted that there appeared to have been a policy of not disclosing details of the operations and the role played by participating informants, not only to the defence, but also to the legal department of HM Revenue and Customs, to the prosecution and trial judges. The Court was careful to emphasise that this was not an assessment of all controlled importations from Pakistan and limited the case to its facts. In *Choudhery* a paradigmatic controlled delivery was described as one where the PI was to play only a minor role and not actively engage in the planning and committing of the crime but to give evidence against the purchaser and the Pakistani Anti-Narcotics Force were to be informed about the identity of the supplier to take such action as they thought fit.[236] Nonetheless, though the Court of Appeal noted that while such an archetypal controlled deliv-

---

[228] Part 6, ch 4 of the Criminal Justice (Mutual Assistance) Act 2008 gives effect to Art 12 of the UN Convention Against Transnational Organized Crime; see n 224.

[229] Criminal Justice (Mutual Assistance) Act 2008, s 89(1).

[230] Criminal Justice (Mutual Assistance) Act 2008, s 90(1).

[231] Criminal Justice (Mutual Assistance) Act 2008, s 90(3).

[232] Criminal Justice (Mutual Assistance) Act 2008, s 90(4).

[233] Dáil WA, vol 655, col 862 (28 May 2008).

[234] See HC WA, vol 440, col 470W (29 November 2005).

[235] *R v Choudhery* [2005] EWCA Crim 1788.

[236] ibid, [46].

ery may exist, it does not 'have the status of a guideline or benchmark against which controlled deliveries should be judged' and the absence in a delivery of a feature of the paradigm is not dispositive of an appeal.[237] These cases are key examples of the Court of Appeal reining in executive power, and they further underline the need for legislation governing this significant and pragmatic crime control mechanism in the detection, prevention and investigation of organised crime.

VII. Detention

In Ireland, there has been an extension of the periods for which the Gardaí may detain and interrogate suspected individuals, in particular those suspected of organised criminality, so as to increase the prospect of effective or fruitful interviewing and gathering of evidence. In contrast, this trend is yet to be replicated in the UK beyond the realms of alleged terrorism offences. The purpose of arrest under the common law was to take the suspect into police custody to charge him with an offence and to bring him before a judge to answer the charge; interrogation and the obtaining of evidence could not be lawful motivating factors for an arrest.[238] Nevertheless, during the 1970s in Ireland the practice developed of questioning an individual between his initial arrest and the time he was brought before a judicial authority.[239] Although the tactic of inviting a person to the station to 'assist the police with their inquiries' was abolished in *People (DPP) v Lynch*,[240] the power to arrest and detain a suspect survived under the Offences Against the State Act 1939 which facilitates detention for up to 72 hours in Ireland.[241] This extraordinary provision, first used in the counter-terrorism context, set a precedent which has endured and been echoed in subsequent Irish legislation.

The generally applicable legislative provision in Ireland permits 24-hour detention, with the requirement for chief superintendent approval after the initial 12

---

[237] *Vernett-Showers and Others v R* [2007] EWCA Crim 1767, 2007 All ER (D) 285 [16].

[238] *People v Shaw* [1982] IR 1, 29–30 per Walsh J.

[239] See Irish Council for Civil Liberties, *Police Interrogation Endangers the Innocent* (Dublin, Irish Council for Civil Liberties, 1993) 18.

[240] *People (DPP) v Lynch* [1982] IR 64. See also *People v Walsh* [1980] IR 294; *People (DPP) v Coffey* [1987] ILRM 727.

[241] Under s 30(3) of the 1939 Act a person may be detained for 24 hours, a period which may be extended by a Garda not below the rank of chief superintendent for a further 24 hours. Section 30(4), as amended by the Offences Against the State (Amendment) Act 1998, permits a Garda not below the rank of superintendent to apply to a District judge to authorise the extension of the detention for another 24 hours. Under s 30(4)(A) the judge may extend the detention only if satisfied that further detention is necessary for the proper investigation of the offence and that the investigation is being conducted diligently and expeditiously. The Committee to Review the Offences Against the State Acts was evenly divided as to whether this section should be repealed. See Committee to Review the Offences Against the State Acts, *Report of the Committee to Review the Offences Against the State Acts, 1939–98 and Related Matters* (Dublin, Stationery Office, 2002) paras 7.38–7.40.

hours.[242] However, 168-hour detention is allowed in the context of quintessential 'organised crimes'. First introduced in relation to drug trafficking,[243] seven day detention is now also permitted for substantive organised crime offences, murder involving the use of a firearm or an explosive, murder of a Garda, prison officer or head of State, possession of a firearm with intent to endanger life, and false imprisonment involving the use of a firearm.[244] Judicial authorisation is needed to extend detention past 48 hours and is again mandated after 120 hours, and the judge must be satisfied that further detention is necessary for the proper investigation of the offence and that the investigation is being conducted diligently and expeditiously.[245] The suspect may make submissions or produce evidence in this respect.[246] The absence of judicial authorisation for seven-day detention in the UK under the Prevention of Terrorism (Temporary Provisions) Act 1984 fell foul of Article 5(3) ECHR in *Brogan and others v UK*,[247] and thus it appears that the Irish measures comply with the ECHR. Although the Court will order the detainee's immediate release if it is not satisfied that detention is justified,[248] the efficacy of this safeguard may be circumvented if the Gardaí claim that divulging the reasons could compromise police intelligence and damage the investigation.[249] The fact that the personal liberty of an individual may be restricted for up to 168 hours represents a fundamental shift in the approach to tackling crime, and elevates crime control over pre-trial liberty, a central concept in the due process model. Overall, prolonged detention augments the powers of the State at the pre-trial stage of the criminal process considerably and has a concomitant impact on the right of the criminal suspect.

In England and Wales, a person may be detained for up to 72 hours under Part IV of the Police and Criminal Evidence Act 1984; detention beyond 60 hours requires approval by a magistrates' court after application by a constable.[250] Although lengthier periods of detention up to 14 days are provided for in the Terrorism Acts 2000 and 2006 which apply to terrorist suspects,[251] this approach has not been emulated in the context of organised crime. Detention periods in Scotland are shorter again: the Criminal Procedure (Scotland) Act 1995 permit-

---

[242] Criminal Justice Act 1984, s 4 (as amended by the Criminal Justice Act 2006).

[243] Criminal Justice (Drug Trafficking) Act 1996, s 2.

[244] Criminal Justice Act 2007, Pt 7 (see ch 2); Criminal Justice Act 2007, s 50 (as amended by the Criminal Justice (Amendment) Act 2009).

[245] Criminal Justice (Drug Trafficking) Act 1996, s 2(2)(g) and (h); Criminal Justice Act 2007, s 50(3)(g) and (h).

[246] Criminal Justice (Drug Trafficking) Act 1996, s 2(3) and Criminal Justice Act s 50(4).

[247] *Brogan and Others v UK* (1989) 11 EHRR 117. Rather than amending the legislation the UK administration derogated from Art 5(3) which provides that '[e]veryone arrested or detained . . . shall be brought promptly before a judge or other officer authorised by law to exercise judicial power'.

[248] Criminal Justice (Drug Trafficking) Act 1996, s 2(4); and Criminal Justice Act 2007, s 50(5).

[249] A Ryan, 'The Criminal Justice (Drug Trafficking) Act 1996: Decline and Fall of the Right to Silence?' (1997) 7 *Irish Criminal Law Journal* 22, 33.

[250] Police and Criminal Evidence Act 1984, ss 43 and 44.

[251] The original period of 28 days was lowered by Pt 4 of the Protection of Freedoms Act 2012 to 14 days.

ted detention for six hours,[252] while the Criminal Procedure (Legal Assistance, Detention and Appeals) (Scotland) Act 2010 amended this to 12 hours.[253] A further 12 hour extension may be granted by a police officer of the rank of inspector or above, who has not been involved in the investigation, if he is satisfied that this is necessary to obtain or preserve evidence and the investigation is being conducted diligently and expeditiously.

Notably there have been no calls in Scotland to extend detention periods to meet the perceived threat of organised crime, in contrast to the shrill demands not only for lengthy investigative periods of detention in Ireland but also for internment (that is detention without trial).[254] A 72-hour detention period has long been permitted in Ireland under counter-terrorism powers,[255] thereby explaining why the extension of detention for other suspected crimes was not deemed too great a leap in the broader control of suspected organised crime. Again, it is striking that rather than dissuading policy makers, the presence and persistence of counter-terrorism measures has made extraordinary tactics rather more palatable and seems to have opened the assortment of available options. The presence of lengthy detention periods in one context facilitates their adoption in another setting, through an archetypal 'normalisation of the extraordinary'.[256]

In essence, the introduction of prolonged detention periods is indicative of a milieu in which the due process rights of the suspect are subsumed by the State's tough stance on crime control, echoing the pattern of extraordinary measures used against terrorist suspects. The utilitarian justifications presented for significant powers of detention, in particular in Ireland, include the need to give State authorities adequate time to gather evidence, given that the investigation may have an international dimension or the suspect may have ingested drugs,[257] to interview suspects and witnesses, and to carry out detailed forensic examinations of crime scenes.[258] When seven-day detention was first introduced in Ireland the Minister for Justice expressed his regret, but claimed that 'it would be far more regrettable if the State did not take all action open to it commensurate with the threat which drug traffickers pose to the community'.[259] Moreover the Gardaí

---

[252] Criminal Procedure (Scotland) Act 1995, s 14.
[253] This Act was introduced in response to *Cadder v HM Advocate* [2010] UKSC 43 to provide legal assistance for persons being questioned by the police. *Cadder* followed the decision of the European Court of Human Rights in *Salduz v Turkey* (2008) 49 EHRR 421 that Art 6(3)(c) was breached by the absence of legal assistance in police custody.
[254] See Dáil Deb, vol 617, col 526 (29 March 2006); vol 668, col 105 (19 November 2008). There is no provision for internment in current UK counter-terrorism legislation, while Pt II of the Offences Against the State (Amendment) Act 1940 is the relevant legislation in Ireland. The European Court held in *Lawless v Ireland (No 3)* Series A no 3 (1979-80) 1 EHRR 15 that internment breached Art 5 but found that Ireland had a valid derogation from these provisions under Art 15.
[255] Offences Against the State Act 1939, s 30.
[256] O Gross, 'Chaos and Rules: Should Responses to Violent Crises Always be Constitutional?' (2003) 112 *Yale Law Journal* 1011, 1090.
[257] Dáil Deb, vol 467, col 2330 (2 July 1996) per Mr O'Donoghue.
[258] Department of Justice, Equality and Law Reform Press Release, 'Criminal Justice Bill Published' (Dublin, Department of Justice, Equality and Law Reform, 2007).
[259] Seanad Deb, vol 151, col 1143 (10 July 2007) per Mr O'Donoghue.

claim that the possibility of lengthy detention has benefited the investigation of drug trafficking offences.[260] No empirical evidence was given to support this contention, and indeed in the first 10 years of its operation not one person was detained for the full 168-hour period.[261] Despite this, a decision was taken to extend 168-hour detention to cover other typical organised crimes, as it would be 'of major benefit in gangland cases'[262] and because 'the existing detention periods are not adequate in these circumstances'.[263]

Notwithstanding the paucity of analysis on the efficacy of seven-day detention, and the fact that no jurisdiction in the UK has adopted such a tactic in the ordinary criminal context (as opposed to in relation to counter-terrorism strategy), it seems that the symbolic effect of the provision is sufficient in itself in Ireland: '[w]e cannot afford at this stage to give the message to drug traffickers that we are softening our approach'.[264] So, the imposition of lengthy detention periods embodies both an instrumental facet, since longer periods of detention are believed to improve the Gardaí's ability to investigate crime, and an expressive element, which demonstrates the Irish State's serious view of certain crimes such as drug trafficking and firearms offences. Given that these powers are rarely if ever used, it seems that the latter element is of more significance. By providing for such a robust response, the Irish Parliament is seeking to appease a concerned public.[265]

VIII. Interrogation

In addition to the intensification of State powers as regards the surveillance and detention of a suspect, the right to silence of the accused throughout interrogation has been eroded incrementally, through the introduction of inference-drawing provisions. Though these developments apply to a broader range of offences than organised crimes only, their introduction was regarded as crucial in the face of suspects who may be professional or career criminals, such as those involved in criminal enterprises and organisations. As the UK's Criminal Law Revision Committee noted in 1972,

> [h]ardened criminals often take advantage of the present rule [precluding the drawing of inferences from silence] to refuse to answer any questions at all, and this may greatly hamper the police and even bring their investigations to a halt. Therefore the abolition of the restriction would help justice.[266]

---

[260] Minister for Justice, 'Submission to the Joint Committee on Justice, Equality, Defence and Women's Rights' (10 December 2002).

[261] ibid; also Minister of State at the Department of Justice, 'Submission to the Joint Committee on Justice, Equality, Defence and Women's Rights' (13 December 2006) vol 629, no 4.

[262] Department of Justice, Equality and Law Reform Press Release, n 258.

[263] Dáil Deb, vol 635, col 1030 (5 April 2007) per Minister for Justice, Mr McDowell.

[264] Minister for Justice, n 261.

[265] Garland, n 59, 133.

[266] Criminal Law Revision Committee on Evidence, *Eleventh Report of the Criminal Law Revision Committee on Evidence* (London, The Stationery Office, 1972) para 30.

The view is that seasoned or hardened suspects may be able to withstand robust police questioning, and so confound the progress of a criminal investigation. In addition, members of organised crime groups may be apprehensive of the possibility of retaliation from fellow members if they divulge details of the group or its acts, and so may be cowed into silence through interrogation.

In Ireland strident opposition to the right to silence has been expressed in Parliament on the ground that 'it does not acknowledge the right of society as being equal to the right of the individual regarding a criminal prosecution'.[267] Moreover, the words of a previous Taoiseach encapsulate the 'zero-sum' thinking that pervades the legal system, in which support for the rights of the accused is seen to impinge on the rights of society: 'The most basic civil liberties issue is the right to life and bodily integrity, to one's personal possessions and one's personal freedom. The arguments for the unrestricted right to silence of an accused . . . are academic by comparison'.[268]

As a result of such sentiments, legislative provisions allowing inferences to be drawn from the silence of the accused have been introduced in England, Wales, Northern Ireland and Ireland.

The right to silence, which may be regarded as overlapping with the right to the presumption of innocence, the right against self-incrimination, and the right to privacy, is a fundamental element of the principle that the prosecution must establish and prove the case against the accused,[269] and a core precept of Packer's due process model. The rationale for the right's existence is to compensate for the imbalance of power and resources that exists between the State and the individual. Furthermore, it is seen as unappealing for the State to place the accused in a position whereby he is likely to be punished whether he answers or remains silent when questioned.[270] Greer claims that the right 'fulfils both a symbolic function in defining the limits of state power vis-à-vis the citizen and offers the innocent subject at least the possibility of protection against wrongful conviction'.[271] The protection it offers to values like personal freedom and dignity is seen to justify the obstacles it poses to police investigation.[272] In addition to this symbolic or ideological reasoning, the right is underpinned by the pragmatic or consequentialist

---

[267] Dáil Deb, vol 444, col 189 (21 June 1994) per Mr Lenihan.

[268] Dáil Deb, vol 467, col 2373 (2 July 1996) per Mr Ahern.

[269] A Ashworth and M Redmayne, *The Criminal Process* (4th edn) (Oxford, Oxford University Press, 2010) 154; D J Galligan, 'The Right to Silence Reconsidered' (1988) 41 *Current Legal Problems* 69, 88.

[270] As Lord Mustill noted in *R v Director of Serious Fraud Office, ex p Smith* [1993] AC 1, 32: 'there is the instinct that it is contrary to fair play to put the accused in a position where he is exposed to punishment whatever he does. If he answers, he may condemn himself out of his own mouth; if he refuses he may be punished for his refusal'.

[271] S Greer, 'The Right to Silence: A Review of the Current Debate' (1990) 53 *MLR* 709, 729.

[272] *Pyneboard Pty Ltd v Trade Practices Commission* (1983) 45 ALR 609. Also see P Arenella, 'Thirteenth Annual Review of Criminal Procedure: United States Supreme Court and Court of Appeals 1982–83: Rethinking the Functions of Criminal Procedure: The Warren and Burger Courts' Competing Ideologies' (1983) 72 *Georgetown Law Journal* 185, 201.

rationale of guarding against unsafe convictions through unsafe and unreliable confessions.[273]

Despite these cogent underlying principles, there is a growing belief in political and popular discourse that the right to silence assists the guilty to evade the full rigours of the law.[274] This is borne out in a comment of the Association of Garda Sergeants and Inspectors in Ireland:

> The present status of the right to silence is an historical relic and harks back to a previous age when suspects were deemed to be of limited intelligence. It is untenable that in serious crimes such as murder and rape, theft or fraud, suspects can refuse to disclose their whereabouts when questioned and courts cannot draw inferences from this.[275]

As the majority of people will never be interrogated in police custody, the right to silence may seem superfluous and useful only to factually guilty persons who wish to conceal evidence of illegal activity.[276] This sentiment has taken legislative form in recent years, with encroachments on the right to silence becoming more commonplace, thereby transforming the balance between the State and the accused, predominantly due to the attempt to tackle organised and systematic criminality.

Inference-Drawing Provisions

Inferences may be drawn from silence in certain instances. These provisions have a broad application, but were prompted by concerns about 'career' and organised criminals. Although the Criminal Law Revision Committee in England and Wales recommended the introduction of such measures in 1972,[277] Ireland was the first of the comparator jurisdictions to legislate in this respect. The Criminal Justice Act 1984 allows inferences to be drawn from the failure or refusal of the accused upon arrest to account for marks, objects or substances when asked to do so by the arresting Garda who reasonably believes that they may be attributable to the person's participation in the offence for which he was arrested.[278] Similarly, inferences may be drawn from the presence of an accused at a particular place if the

---

[273] Indeed, the motivation behind the right to silence has been described as the desire 'to avoid the risk of untrue confessions being obtained from a person while in police custody': *Heaney v Ireland* [1994] 3 IR 593, 604 (Costello J).

[274] P McLaughlin, 'Legal Constraints in Criminal Investigation' (1981) XVI *Irish Jurist* 217, 221. Similarly, Zuckerman rejects the argument that the privilege protects the innocent. AA Zuckerman, *The Principles of Criminal Evidence* (Oxford, Clarendon Press, 1989) 316–17. This view is opposed by D Seidmann and A Stein, 'The Right to Silence Helps the Innocent: A Game-Theoretic Analysis of the Fifth Amendment Privilege' (2000) 114 *Harvard Law Review* 430.

[275] President of the Association of Garda Sergeants and Inspectors, 'Submission to the Joint Committee on Justice, Equality, Defence, and Women's Rights' (8 December 2003).

[276] See R Posner, 'An Economic Approach to the Law of Evidence' (1999) 51 *Stanford Law Review* 1477, 1534.

[277] Criminal Law Revision Committee on Evidence, n 266.

[278] Criminal Justice Act 1984, s 18.

arresting Garda reasonably believes that his presence may be attributable to participation in the commission of an offence.[279]

While failure or refusal may amount to corroboration of other evidence, the suspect shall not be convicted of an offence solely on such an inference, and a court is not obliged to draw inferences.[280] Inferences may now also be drawn in proceedings relating to all arrestable offences from the failure of the accused to mention any fact on which he later relies in his defence, if that fact was one which he could reasonably have been expected to mention when questioned.[281] Again, inferences are corroborative, and only those that appear proper may be drawn. These provisions impose an onerous task on the suspect, who must envisage the particular facts which are likely to be used in his defence. As was noted by the European Court in *Averill v United Kingdom*, there may be legitimate reasons why an innocent person may not be prepared to cooperate with the police in response to questioning, especially before he has had the chance to consult a solicitor.[282]

As noted in chapter two, section 72 of the Criminal Justice Act 2006 created a number of substantive organised crime offences in Ireland, such as participating in or contributing to activity of a criminal organisation to enhance its ability to commit or facilitate a serious offence. Inferences may be drawn from failure to answer any question material to the investigation of such offences although a conviction cannot be predicated solely or mainly on the inference.[283] It is curious that this provision seems to duplicate the power in the Criminal Justice Act 1984 which applies to all arrests for serious offences, although in fact this measure is broader by relating to the failure to answer any question material to the investigation, rather than being related to a mark or presence reasonably believed to be related to the commission of the offence. As well as broadening the powers of the State, this express linking of procedural amendments to substantive offences is a crucial symbolic reaction to organised crime.

The Criminal Evidence (Northern Ireland) Order 1988 mirrored the original Irish legislation, by permitting such inferences as appear proper to be drawn from the accused's failure to mention particular facts when questioned or charged,[284] or from his failure or refusal to account for objects, marks,[285] or his presence at a

---

[279] Criminal Justice Act 1984, s 19. Sections 28 and 29 of the Criminal Justice Act 2007 amend ss 18 and 19 and clarify that the sections apply to the questioning of the accused at any time before he is charged with the offence or when he is being charged with the offence or informed by a Garda that he might be prosecuted for it, and that the Garda in question need not be the arresting Garda. The 2007 Act also makes explicit that inferences may only be drawn if the accused was afforded a reasonable opportunity to consult a solicitor, and the interview is being recorded.

[280] ss 18(1)(c) and 19(1)(d).

[281] Criminal Justice Act 1984, s 19A (as inserted by the Criminal Justice Act 2007). Such a recommendation was made by the Expert Group Appointed to Consider Changes in the Criminal Law which were Recommended in the Garda SMI Report, *Report of the Expert Group Appointed to Consider Changes in the Criminal Law which were Recommended in the Garda SMI Report* (Dublin, Stationery Office, 1998) 31.

[282] *Averill v United Kingdom* (2001) 31 EHRR 839, para 49.

[283] s 72A, as inserted by s 9 of the Criminal Justice (Amendment) Act 2009.

[284] Criminal Evidence (Northern Ireland) Order 1988, s 3.

[285] Criminal Evidence (Northern Ireland) Order 1988, s 5.

particular place.[286] A person shall not be committed for trial, have a case to answer or be convicted of an offence solely on such an inference.[287] In a similar manner, following the 'experiment' in Northern Ireland,[288] the Criminal Justice and Public Order Act 1994 introduced such measures in England and Wales.[289] This was deemed to be necessary, not due to the threat of organised crime per se, but because of the alleged silence of 'the most sophisticated and experienced criminals, not the weak and the vulnerable':[290] 'Is it really in the interests of justice . . . that experienced criminals should be able to refuse to answer all police questions secure in the knowledge that a jury will never hear of it?'.[291] As in Ireland, no adverse inferences may be drawn under the English legislation unless legal advice is offered or made available from the initial stages of interrogation.[292]

In Scotland, there is no legislation governing the drawing of adverse inferences at trial from a suspect's silence during police questioning or charge. The prosecution is not precluded from commenting adversely on an accused's failure to give evidence, but 'such comment is rarely made'.[293] Lord Carloway was asked by the Scottish Government to consider the drawing of adverse inferences from silence, but his Review concluded that there should be no change to the law.[294]

The constitutionality of the Irish provisions was upheld in *Rock v Ireland* where the Supreme Court concluded that the right to the presumption of innocence was not infringed, given that inferences could amount to corroboration only, and that only those that 'appear proper' could be drawn.[295] Similarly, in *Murray v United Kingdom*, the European Court of Human Rights considered the Northern Ireland order and stressed that although a conviction cannot be based solely or mainly on the silence of the accused or on his refusal to answer questions,[296] Article 6 ECHR does not prevent his silence from being taken into account in situations which call clearly for an explanation from him.[297] The Court noted that whether the drawing of adverse inferences breaches Article 6 depends on the circumstances of the case, where inferences may be drawn, the weight attached to the inferences and the degree of compulsion involved. In particular, the European Court stressed the importance of access to legal advice, and the physical presence of a solicitor during police interview, as 'a particularly important safeguard for dispelling any compulsion to speak which may be inherent in the terms of the caution'.[298] This is

[286] Criminal Evidence (Northern Ireland) Order 1988, s 6.
[287] Criminal Evidence (Northern Ireland) Order 1988, s 2(4).
[288] O Gross and F Ní Aoláin, *Law in Times of Crisis: Emergency Powers in Theory and Practice* (Cambridge, Cambridge University Press, 2006) 186.
[289] Criminal Justice and Public Order Act 1994, ss 34, 36 and 37. See *R v Argent* [1997] 2 Cr App R 27.
[290] HL Deb 25 April 1994, col 425, per Lord Rawlinson of Ewell.
[291] *Report of the Working Group on the Right of Silence* (Home Office, London, 1989) 4–5.
[292] Youth Justice and Criminal Evidence Act 1999, s 58.
[293] Lord Carloway, *The Carloway Review: Report and Recommendations* (Edinburgh, 2011) para 3.3.10.
[294] ibid, para 7.5.
[295] *Rock v Ireland* [1997] 3 IR 384.
[296] *Murray v United Kingdom* (1996) 22 EHRR 29, para 47.
[297] As Ashworth and Redmayne note, this indicates a cautious acceptance of the compatibility of such provisions with the Convention: Ashworth and Redmayne, n 269, 104.
[298] *Condron v UK* (2001) 31 EHRR 1, para 60.

a pragmatic approach to this crime control measure, which is seen to be offset by the presence of due process protections.

Research in England and Wales indicates that the provisions have had a marked impact on interviews due to greater candour about evidence between police and legal advisers and 'greater certainty of convictions where silence augments the other available evidence'.[299] Nevertheless respondents to this Home Office study were 'sceptical about the impact of the provisions on 'professional' criminals', suggesting that this amendment may not in fact affect suspected organised criminals, as such.

While the legislatures in parts of the UK and Ireland have extended the power to draw adverse inferences, the courts have firmly delineated limits to this capacity, and in doing so moderated the crime control powers of the State. In *People (DPP) v Finnerty*, the Irish Supreme Court emphasised that unless the right to silence is restricted expressly by statutory provisions which permit the drawing of inferences from the silence of the accused, it must be upheld.[300] Similarly, in England and Wales Lord Bingham in *R v Bowden* advocated a narrow construction of the statutory provisions, on the basis that they restrict common law rights.[301]

IX. Conclusion

This chapter focused on numerous aspects of the pre-trial stage of the criminal process, encompassing the detection and investigation of crime, and the detention and interrogation of the suspect, so as to ascertain the extent of State powers in the context of organised criminality. As was depicted in the preceding doctrinal analysis, elements of the pre-trial aspect of the criminal process across the UK and Ireland are being altered to mitigate the conventional bias in favour of the individual suspect or accused so as to address organised crime more effectively. These changes are precipitated by the nature and methods of organised crime groups and they have considerable value in terms of crime control, however, improving crime control without compromising due process protections is a difficult path to navigate.

The dominant political narrative on the criminal process is that State powers are limited in the investigation of organised crime, and that orthodox procedural protections such as the right to silence and the presumption of innocence, coupled with constitutional safeguards such as the right to privacy and to private property, protect suspected individuals to the detriment of the effective control and investigation of crime. This chapter indicates that this is not always the case, and that the State has increasing powers as is evidenced in the use of search warrants and production orders pertaining to innocent third parties, the reporting

[299] T Bucke, R Street and D Brown, *The Right of Silence: The Impact of the Criminal Justice and Public Order Act 1994* (London, Home Office, 2000) xiii.
[300] *People (DPP) v Finnerty* [1999] 4 IR 364.
[301] *R v Bowden* [1999] 1 WLR 823, 827.

obligations on non-State bodies, the expansion of police powers of surveillance, extended detention periods, and the erosion of the right to silence. These legislative provisions indicate clearly that the balance at the pre-trial stage of the criminal process is not weighted totally in favour of the accused, and that in fact the State is equipped with considerable and adequate legal powers to investigate organised crime. Moreover, while procedural protections may sometimes curb the pursuit of crime control, their importance cannot be overstated and so any abrogation should be done with due care and deliberation.

In Ireland in particular, thorough empirical or conceptual consideration is all too often lacking in this regard, and intuition seems to guide criminal justice policy rather than measured analysis. This is compounded by the marked convergence of political parties across the UK and Ireland which has resulted in a significant lack of opposition to proposed provisions in criminal justice legislation. A number of the legislative measures considered in this chapter indicate a preference on the part of Parliament for the exigencies of crime control over the due process rights of the individual, and represent a move away from traditional liberal norms towards a more utilitarian and result-oriented way of thinking. The overarching rationale for these measures is the imperative of public protection from the threat of organised crime, which eclipses notions of individual liberties. These limitations on the due process rights of the accused suggest that the criminal process is being modified slowly yet in a fundamental sense, in a bid to augment the powers of the State in targeting organised crime. Furthermore, the precursor for many investigative developments lies in counter-terrorism legislation, explaining to an extent Ireland's predilection for and Scotland's avoidance of 'emergency tactics' in addressing organised crime.

The UK Home Office has claimed that 'organised crime investigations rarely affect individuals who are not involved in one way or other in the crime'.[302] Such executive pre-judging of guilt and the benign view of State intervention at the investigation stage of the criminal process belies the inequities and risks that relate to arrest, detention and interrogation. Nonetheless, the courts, both domestic and international, retain a key ability to temper the drift towards a crime control model of the criminal process, by strictly demarcating the extent of State powers and by marking certain rights of the accused as fundamental. So, the situation does not indicate an unmitigated bias in favour of the State, given the existence and survival of important safeguards. The strict limitations on the use of illegally obtained evidence, the impact of the right to privacy in relation to surveillance, and the prohibition on the use of compelled evidence in later criminal trials depict a nuanced picture at the pre-trial stage of the criminal process vis-à-vis the fight against organised criminality. The courts retain a key ability to temper the drift towards a crime control model of the criminal process, by strictly demarcating the extent of State powers and by marking certain rights of the accused as fundamental.

---

[302] Home Office, *One Step Ahead – A 21st Century Strategy to Defeat Organised Crime* (London, Home Office, 2004) para 6.2.

5

Prosecuting Organised Crime: The Criminal Trial

I. Introduction

As was detailed in chapter four, numerous legislative developments have sought to strengthen the investigative powers of the State and its agents as regards organised crime, shifting from the traditional weighting of the pre-trial process in favour of the accused individual to an approach that is more cognisant of the demands of crime control. Beyond this, even if criminality is detected and particular suspects are identified, testimony against organised criminals is very difficult to obtain, and the prevailing political and popular perception is that the odds remain stacked against the State at trial.[1] To address these issues, procedural laws have been changed and protective measures for witnesses and jurors have been introduced, improving the likelihood of prosecution and ultimately conviction for persons linked to organised crime, and to criminal groups and enterprises.

By its nature the State is endowed with substantial resources that facilitate the investigation, detection and prosecution of crime. Consequently, as the norms and structure of the criminal trial developed, certain rights solidified, including the presumption of innocence and the right to silence, both of which aim to establish a degree of parity between the two parties and to protect of the rights of the defendant who was seen as vulnerable by definition. As Stephens remarked:

> If it be asked why an accused person is presumed to be innocent, I think the true answer is, not that the presumption is probably true, but that society in the present day is so much stronger than the individual, and is capable of inflicting so very much more harm on the individual than the individual as a rule can inflict on society, that it can afford to be generous.[2]

The fundamental notion on which the criminal justice process is based is that it is worse to convict an innocent person than to let a guilty individual go free: '[i]n accordance with the values on which our system of law rests, the acquittal

---

[1] See Home Office, *One Step Ahead – A 21st Century Strategy to Defeat Organised Crime* (London, Home Office, 2004) para 6.3.

[2] JF Stephens, *History of the Criminal Law of England*, vol 1 (London, 1883) 354, cited in F McAuley and JP McCutcheon, *Criminal Liability: A Grammar* (Dublin, Round Hall Sweet & Maxwell, 2000) 34.

of the guilty is not of the same order of injustice as the conviction of the innocent'.[3]

The concept of fair procedure in the criminal trial endeavours to establish a position of theoretical equivalence or 'equality of arms' between the State and the accused, and embodies the notion that the accused must enjoy certain safeguards, given the inherent imbalance of power. Therefore, procedures have been introduced which seek to guard against the conviction of the innocent. Article 6 of the European Convention on Human Rights (ECHR) is crucial in this respect, and safeguards, inter alia, the right to an independent and impartial tribunal established by law, the presumption of innocence, and the defence right to examine or have examined witnesses against the accused. In the domestic Irish context, the guarantee in Article 38.1 of Bunreacht na hÉireann that 'no person shall be tried on any criminal charge save in due course of law' implies that every criminal trial shall be 'conducted in accordance with the concept of justice, that the procedures applied shall be fair, and that the person accused will be afforded every opportunity to defend himself'.[4]

In the UK and Ireland, the onus lies on the State to prove beyond a reasonable doubt that the accused is guilty of an offence in accordance with the requirements prescribed by law and the accused is not obliged to establish his innocence,[5] he may maintain silence throughout the course of the proceedings,[6] and he has the right to freedom from self-incrimination,[7] to legal representation,[8] to test the evidence against him,[9] and to trial by jury.[10] This list is not immutable: the extent to which due process rights are preserved and the manner in which they are interpreted may be influenced by the political and popular understanding of the appropriate relationship between the State and the individual, and the common perception of the effectiveness of the criminal justice system. As Galligan commented, '[p]rocedures are themselves deeply rooted in a social context and will reflect the beliefs and understandings prevailing in them'.[11]

While the concept of equality of arms derived from the desire to counterbalance the difference in resources and power between the two parties in the criminal process, the political and media construction of an image of the strong, shrewd and wealthy defendant has brought into question this disparity and the perceived

---

[3] *Fitzgerald v DPP* [2003] 3 IR 247, 258. Similarly, in *Re Winship*, Harlan J emphasised that '[i]n a criminal case . . . we do not view the social disutility of convicting an innocent man as equivalent to the disutility of acquitting someone who is guilty'. *Re Winship* 397 US 358 (1970) 372.

[4] *State (Healy) v Donoghue* [1976] IR 325, 349 per O'Higgins CJ. The Court stated that the phrase 'in due course of law' in Art 38.1 of Bunreacht na hÉireann was equivalent to 'due process of law' in the Fifth Amendment to the US Constitution, as both necessitate fundamental fairness in criminal trials.

[5] *Woolmington v DPP* [1935] AC 462; *Hardy v Ireland* [1994] 2 IR 562.

[6] *R v Director of Serious Fraud Office, ex p Smith* [1993] AC 1.

[7] *Heaney v Ireland* [1996] 1 IR 580.

[8] *State (Healy) v Donoghue*, n 4.

[9] Sir Matthew Hale, *The History of the Common Law of England* (6th edn, 1820) 345–46; *Re Haughey* [1971] IR 217.

[10] Bunreacht na hÉireann, Art 38.5.

[11] DJ Galligan, *Due Process and Fair Procedures: A Study of Administrative Procedures* (Oxford, Clarendon Press, 1996) 20.

need for traditional safeguards as envisaged by the due process model of criminal justice. This attitude is especially pronounced in relation to the suspected organised criminal, who is perceived to have considerable nous and extensive finances such as to place the State and its agents at an intractable disadvantage given the conventional protections for the accused. In particular, the ability of organised criminals and groups to coerce and intimidate witnesses and jurors may lead to a 'paralysis of justice'[12] and so has prompted the amendment of traditional norms and standards of prosecution and trial. Overall, there has been a noticeable shift away from conventional notions of the weak and disadvantaged defendant and this is combined with a view that the powers of the State have been attenuated until now.

Ultimately, it is questionable whether traditional approaches of prosecution and trial practice are effective in relation to organised crime. In this chapter, several legal developments will be examined that demonstrate the realignment of the trial stage of the criminal process in responding to organised crime towards a model that is more pragmatic and oriented towards crime control. While these measures certainly serve to improve the nature and extent of evidence presented and enhance the protection of witnesses and jurors, they have the added consequence of augmenting State powers, thereby compromising the rights of the accused in the drive for public protection and the expedient resolution of organised crime. Changes to procedural law have been made, so that evidence relating to the interception of communications, for example, is now admissible in Ireland though not in the UK, and there has been statutory entrenchment of the use of accomplice evidence and the granting of immunity from prosecution. Such mechanisms are deemed necessary to circumvent the need for witness evidence, given that such people may be threatened, bribed or assaulted. Efforts to protect jurors have led to the use of non-jury trials, replicating extraordinary measures which sought to guard against the threat to jurors from individuals involved in subversive crime. Witnesses are protected from intimidation through devices and processes like the use of screens, voice modulation and, most radically, by testifying anonymously. In addition, the trial of suspected organised criminals often involves testimony from persons on Witness Protection Programmes. The understandable imperative of improving the ability to prosecute and convict individuals of organised crime offences is slowly leading to the erosion of some critical rights which accrue to the defendant in the criminal trial.

II. Procedural Law Changes

A number of changes have been made to the rules of criminal procedure in seeking to ease the prosecution of suspected organised crime, concerning the admissibility

---

[12] J Landesco, *Organized Crime in Chicago* (Chicago, University of Chicago Press, 1968) 22.

of interception evidence and the regulation of accomplice evidence. While the amendments made relating to the former type of evidence do not unduly compromise due process rights, accomplice evidence, though valuable in terms of crime control, is more problematic.

A. The Admissibility of Interception Evidence

As alluded to briefly in chapter four, the UK and Ireland have prohibited the use of certain surveillance evidence in court. Historically in Ireland the practice was not to use any material gained by means of secret surveillance as evidence for legal and operational reasons, and even if a communications intercept was authorised statutorily, the evidence obtained could not be cited in court but rather represented an element of police intelligence.[13] By contrast, in the UK surveillance other than interception material could be admitted and relied upon. The law has now changed in Ireland, but this prohibition on admitting interception evidence remains entrenched in the UK despite calls for reform.

In Ireland, this long-standing exclusion was removed by the Criminal Justice (Surveillance) Act 2009 which expressly permits the admissibility in court of evidence obtained through surveillance.[14] The District Court must authorise any possible disclosure of the existence or otherwise of an application for surveillance or the use of a tracking device, the substance of any surveillance and related information.[15] Such authorisation may not be given if the court is satisfied that it would be likely to create a material risk to State security, to the ability of the State to protect persons from terrorist activity, organised crime and other serious crime, to the maintenance of the integrity, effectiveness and security of the operations of the Gardaí, the Defence Forces or the Revenue Commissioners, or to the ability of the State to protect witnesses. The Act provides no guidance as to the connection between this new admissibility rule and pre-existing rules of evidence, and there is no articulation as to who is applying to use the surveillance evidence and whether the State needs to make the latter arguments to the court.

Intercept evidence remains inadmissible in the UK. There, the Regulation of Investigatory Powers Act 2000 provides that no evidence shall be presented or questions asked in legal proceedings which disclose any contents of an intercepted communication or suggests that interception has or may have occurred, or that it may be about to take place,[16] echoing the previous prohibition in the Interception of Communications Act 1985. Wiretap evidence was held to be admissible in *R v Aujla* on the basis that the intercepts occurred in the Netherlands, although the

---

[13] Criminal Justice (Surveillance) Act 2009, s 2. Interception of Postal Packets and Telecommunications Messages (Regulation) Act 1993, s 12.

[14] Criminal Justice (Surveillance) Act 2009, s 14(1).

[15] Criminal Justice (Surveillance) Act 2009, s 15.

[16] Regulation of Investigatory Powers Act 2000, s 17. Section 18 provides some exceptions to s 17, such as disclosure relating to offences under the Regulation of Investigatory Powers Act 2000.

calls were to England.[17] The Court of Appeal held that the 1985 Act did not pre-clude the use of material obtained by foreign telephone-tapping as evidence.[18] This demonstrates that the prohibition on intercept evidence being used in UK courts is not driven by a rights' oriented reasoning, given the acceptance of admitting such evidence from abroad. In fact, the key aspect of the ban on intercept as evidence concerns the potential revealing of intelligence tactics and the insights and information gleaned therefrom.[19]

There is a perception in the UK (as was previously the case in Ireland) that divulging the fact and process of electronic surveillance and the material so gathered could jeopardise it as a source of intelligence. Moreover, it has been asserted in favour of the inadmissibility of intercept evidence that the whole notion of such evidence is predicated on cooperation with communications service providers, and the bar on intercept as evidence has been described as a critical element in building up the partnership with such companies.[20] Furthermore, the extent to which permitting interceptions as evidence would lead to increase in successful prosecutions has been questioned.[21]

Contra this, the manifold benefits of such surveillance to law enforcement in relation to both the investigation and prosecution of organised crime have been emphasised by academic and practicing commentators,[22] not least because of its reliability, the avoidance of the need for witness testimony, and its ability to establish association beyond parties which may substantiate conspiracy and the existence of an organised crime group/criminal organisation.[23] Without surveillance the testimony of a witness or informant as to the conversations or movements of defendants would be required.[24] The Serious Organised Crime Agency (SOCA) in the UK has expressed the view that interception combined with communications data is 'the single most powerful tool for responding to serious and organised crime' as it involves very low risk of harm to officers, it entails less cost and intrusion than covert entry or surveillance, and it can allow for crime prevention as well as the gathering of evidence.[25] Thus, SOCA observed that most major criminal investigations involve interception,[26] but not, of course, the use of this evidence in court in the UK. Intercept evidence is admitted regularly and to good effect in trials in Australia, Canada, New Zealand, South Africa and the United

---

[17] *R v Aujla* [1998] 2 Cr App Rep 16.

[18] See also *R v P* [2002] 1 AC 146. It appears that such a case has not arisen in the Irish courts.

[19] Privy Council, *Review of Intercept as Evidence: A Report to the Prime Minister and the Home Secretary* (London, The Stationery Office) (Cm 7324, 2008) ch ii, para 46.

[20] ibid, ch 4, 71.

[21] ibid, ch 3, 59.

[22] R Goldstock, *Organised Crime in Northern Ireland: A Report for the Secretary of State* (Belfast, Northern Ireland Office, 2004) para 5.1; Justice, *Intercept Evidence: Lifting the Ban* (London, Justice, 2006); Justice, *Freedom from Suspicion: Surveillance Reform for a Digital Age* (London, Justice, 2011) para 148.

[23] Goldstock, n 22, paras 5.4–5.6.

[24] ibid, para 5.4. See below n 38ff.

[25] Privy Council, n 19, ch 2, para 32.

[26] ibid, ch 2, para 32.

States, though not, until recently, in Ireland.[27] Jacobs has emphasised that electronic eavesdropping figures prominently in almost every organised crime prosecution in the US, and that some organised crime prosecutions are based almost entirely on intercepted conversations.[28] Needless to say, this could not be the case if intercept material were for intelligence purposes only.

The concern that admitting intercept evidence would compromise the gathering of intelligence is allayed by the use of public interest immunity (PII). While generally there is a statutory duty on the prosecution to disclose to the defence all relevant evidence and material,[29] PII may be claimed by the State through the prosecution if disclosure could cause real damage to a public interest, such as revealing the existence or nature of surveillance. Thus, a scheme of PII seeks to balance the competing interests in non-disclosure of sensitive information that may compromise State security or the effectiveness of policing with that of the open and fair administration of justice. This 'derogation from the golden rule of full disclosure' must be the minimum necessary to protect the public interest in the effective investigation and prosecution of serious crime and must never threaten the fairness of the trial.[30] The level of sensitivity involved determines the type of hearing: in type 1 cases, the prosecutor informs the defence of the category of sensitive material, and the defence may make representations at an *inter partes* hearing; in type 2 cases the defence is informed of the immunity application but not of the category of material, the hearing is ex parte and the defendant is represented by special counsel appointed by the court; and for type 3 cases the defence is not notified but his interests again are represented by court-appointed special counsel.[31] The Privy Council *Review of Intercept as Evidence* in 2008 noted that while the prosecution could seek PII to protect against such disclosure, this protection is not absolute.[32] Nonetheless, PII does remedy these concerns about potentially harmful or compromising revelations in court, and ultimately the decision as to whether to rely on certain evidence lies with the prosecution.

The Privy Council Review noted that the interception of communications in the UK becomes more complex in the context of the devolved responsibilities of the Scottish Government, given that although Westminster retains competence over the interception of communications,[33] Scottish Ministers are authorised to sign interception warrants relating to serious organised crime.[34] The Review suggested that intercept should be admissible as evidence in England and Wales,[35] but

[27] ibid, ch 7, para 138.
[28] J Jacobs with C Panarella and J Worthington, *Busting the Mob: United States v Cosa Nostra* (New York, New York University Press, 1994) 9.
[29] Criminal Procedure and Investigations Act 1996, as amended by the Criminal Justice Act 2003.
[30] *R v H and C* [2004] UKHL 3 [18].
[31] *R v Davis, Johnson and Rowe* [1993] 1 WLR 613. Moreover, there is no provision in Irish law regarding the appointment of special counsel to represent the interests of the defendant in cases involving interception or other sensitive material.
[32] Privy Council, n 19, ch 4, para 63.
[33] Scotland Act 1998, Sch 5.
[34] Regulation of Investigatory Powers Act 2000, s 7; Privy Council, n 19, ch IX.
[35] Privy Council, n 19, ch IX.

that no change should be made to the legal regime for interception in Scotland until new legislation was put in place and its potential impact assessed. Since the publication of the Review, the Criminal Justice and Licensing Act 2010 has been introduced in Scotland and provides a PII framework based on the English model, whereby the courts may prevent disclosure of certain information.[36] This seems to mitigate the harm that could occur to investigation without tightly drawn rules of disclosure of sensitive information, and thereby would permit surveillance evidence, as opposed to information or intelligence only, to be used in prosecuting organised crime.

While admitting such intercept evidence would appear to be an effective means of crime control, especially given the difficulties relating to matters of proof of the commission of organised crime, if public interest immunity is claimed then problematic issues may arise regarding the relation between the defendant and special counsel. The interaction between them is very limited, and special counsel are hindered in their representation given the restrictions on instructions that apply once they have viewed the sensitive material. Moreover, counsel might be content for the prosecution not to disclose material which, unknown to the special counsel, might be useful for the defence. So, the special counsel would not necessarily make the best or most appropriate arguments in front of the judge. Ultimately, the relationship with the client lacks the quality of confidence inherent in any ordinary lawyer–client relationship.[37] Indeed, the Court of Appeal was harsh in its assessment of the use of PII regarding intercept evidence from Columbia in *R v Austin*, bemoaning the 'procedural irregularities', like the informality of proceedings and the lack of notes.[38] So, while permitting intercept material to be admitted as evidence ostensibly is an effectual and moderate form of crime control, the implementation of this policy may threaten due process rights.

B. Accomplice Evidence

Persons who are involved in organised crime may be persuaded to give evidence for the prosecution, often in return for certain benefits such as immunity from prosecution or reduced sentences;[39] such a practice is not a new phenomenon and 'partners in crime' have been competent witnesses since the seventeenth century.[40] Members of the Mafia who were willing to break the code of *omerta* and testify against former colleagues played a critical role in the conviction of

---

[36] s 145. This was recommended by Lord Coulsfield in *Review of the Law and Practice of Disclosure in Criminal Proceedings in Scotland* (Edinburgh, Scottish Government, 2007) See P Duff, 'Disclosure of Evidence and Public Interest Immunity'(2007) *Scots Law Times* 63; and 'Disclosure in Scottish Criminal Procedure: Another Step in an Inquisitorial Direction' (2007) *International Journal of Evidence and Proof* 153.
[37] *R v H and C*, n 30, [22].
[38] *R v Austin* [2009] EWCA Crim 1527.
[39] See ch 6 for an analysis of the sentencing of accomplices who testify for the prosecution.
[40] *R v Haddock* [2012] NICC 5.

notorious crime bosses such as John Gotti in the United States.[41] Such persons are referred to in a popular sense as 'turncoats' who have 'flipped', and academically and legally as accomplices, assisting offenders, or collaborators of justice. The latter are people who face criminal charges or have been convicted of taking part in a criminal association or in offences of organised crime, but who agree to cooperate with criminal justice authorities such as through giving testimony about a criminal association or the perpetration of serious crimes.[42] Rather more broadly, the term 'accomplice' may include a person who has neither been convicted nor admitted to the charge, unlike an assisting offender, but who appears to be an associate of the accused.

Accomplice testimony may present issues in terms of credibility and motivation, given that such persons may be willing to inform on past colleagues to avoid punishment, due to ego or self-importance, or because of the likely or perceived benefits.[43] As noted in *R v Turner*,

> [i]t is in the interests of the public that criminals should be brought to justice; and the more serious the crimes the greater is the need for justice to be done. Employing Queen's evidence to accomplish this end is distasteful and has been distasteful for at least 300 years to judges, lawyers and members of the public.[44]

Nonetheless, reliance on such testimony may be unavoidable when there is no other evidence or where it is supportive of other prosecution evidence: it is 'a simple fact that frequently the only persons who qualify as witnesses to serious crime are the criminals themselves'.[45]

A particular type of accomplice, namely the 'supergrass', was used in Northern Ireland in reacting to terrorism[46] and against suspected armed robbers by the Metropolitan Police in London in the 1970s when traditional investigative and information-gathering tactics were seen as ineffective.[47] Such a 'super accomplice witness' differs from an informer or an ordinary accomplice by virtue of the 'extent and nature of the action';[48] the unique contribution of the supergrass was

---

[41] *United States v Locascio and Gotti* 6 F3d 924 (1993); see Jacobs, n 28, 215ff.

[42] Recommendation Rec(2005)9 of the Committee of Ministers to Member States on the protection of witnesses and collaborators of justice I.

[43] See, eg *United States v Shearer* 794 F2d 1545, 1549–50 (11th Cir 1986) where the accomplice was paid to initiate criminality with the expectation of further payment.

[44] *R v Turner* (1975) Cr App R 67, 79.

[45] SS Trott, 'The Use of a Criminal as a Witness' (1996) 47 *Hastings Law Journal* 1381, 1391; see also *R v Lowe* (1978) 66 Cr App R 122, 125.

[46] D Bonner, 'Combating Terrorism: Supergrass Trials in Northern Ireland' (1988) 51 *MLR* 23.

[47] See S Greer, 'Supergrasses and the Legal System in Britain and Northern Ireland' (1986) 102 *LQR* 198, and S Greer, 'The Supergrass System' in A Jennings (ed), *Justice under Fire: The Abuse of Civil Liberties in Northern Ireland* (London, Pluto Press, 1988) 73–103. Supergrass evidence was commonly used in the non-jury Diplock courts in Northern Ireland. See P Hillyard, 'The Normalization of Special Powers: From Northern Ireland to Britain' in P Scraton (ed), *Law, Order and the Authoritarian State: Readings in Critical Criminology* (Milton Keynes, Open University Press, 1987) 300; Amnesty International, *Report of an Amnesty International Mission to Northern Ireland, November 28–December 6, 1977* (London, Amnesty International, 1978).

[48] P Hillyard and J Percy-Smith, 'Converting Terrorists: The Use of Supergrasses in Northern Ireland' (1984) 11 *Journal of Law and Society* 335, 335.

to allow the results of sophisticated police evidence gathering to be presented in court to convict large numbers of organised criminals (or terrorists).[49] As regards the danger of supergrass evidence, in particular in the context of terrorist offences, Lord Hutton noted in *R v Crumley*,[50]

> a supergrass is no ordinary criminal and no ordinary accomplice . . . what is known about the supergrass's character and situation increases the probability that he will be an unreliable witness . . . In this case, as in so many similar cases, we are confronted with a witness who by his own admission was a man of lawless character, a member of an unlawful organisation dedicated to violence and to the principle that the end justifies the means including indiscriminate murder and a person who had wholeheartedly engaged in all the activities of that organisation. He is not just a cornered criminal, who is reluctantly disgorging information to save himself from enduring the penalty of perhaps one moderately serious crime, but he has volunteered a veritable mass of damning information against men whom he alleges to have been his confederates, to whom and with whom he is bound by an oath to further a joint cause which he no doubt regarded as patriotic. His motive may be fear, despair or hope of an enormously improved life for the future, or a mixture of the three: wherever the truth lies, his motive is extremely powerful. It is manifest that the evidence of such a witness must stand up successfully to the sternest criteria before it can be acceptable and become the sole basis for being satisfied beyond reasonable doubt that any accused is guilty of any offence charged against him.

More generally, there is no requirement in the comparator jurisdictions, except in Scotland which is dealt with shortly, that accomplice evidence be corroborated. The common law practice in England, Wales and Northern Ireland of warning the jury about relying on the uncorroborated evidence of an accomplice to convict simply because the witness is an accomplice was abolished and such warnings are now discretionary.[51] Such a warning remains in Ireland.[52] In *The People (Director of Public Prosecutions) v Gilligan* Denham J in the Irish Supreme Court highlighted the danger of acting and relying upon the uncorroborated evidence of an accomplice witness who was a participant in the Witness Protection Programme, namely that the witness may not tell the truth in the hope of receiving benefits.[53] Nevertheless, the Court concluded that there is no rule of law that the uncorroborated evidence of such a person must be rejected, although the trier of fact must be warned that it is dangerous to convict on such evidence alone. Having borne that in mind, if the evidence is so clearly acceptable that the trier of fact is satisfied beyond reasonable doubt of the guilt of the accused to the extent that the danger which is generally inherent in acting on the evidence of a witness in the Programme is not present, then he may rely on the evidence and convict.[54]

---

[49] S Greer, *Supergrasses: A Study in Anti-Terrorist Law Enforcement in Northern Ireland* (New York, Oxford University Press, 1995) 12, n 35.

[50] *R v Crumley* [1986] NI 66.

[51] Criminal Justice and Public Order Act 1994, s 32; Criminal Justice (Northern Ireland) Order 1996, Art 45.

[52] The corroboration warning no longer must be given for victims of sexual offences (Criminal Law (Rape) (Amendment) Act 1990) or child witnesses (Criminal Evidence Act 1992).

[53] *The People (DPP) v Gilligan* [2005] IESC 78, heading 8.5. See below, s VC for analysis of the WPP.

[54] ibid. See L Heffernan, 'The Vagaries of Accomplice Evidence' (2003) *Irish Jurist* 369.

In Scotland, a person cannot be convicted of a crime on the uncorroborated testimony of one witness.[55] This has been described as 'an invaluable safeguard in the practice of our criminal Courts against unjust conviction'.[56] Even so, at one stage the jury in Scotland had to be specifically directed that 'a special scrutiny' must be applied to the evidence of an accomplice or '*socius criminis*', 'over and above the general examination which a jury has to apply to all the material evidence'.[57] This requirement for a special warning was removed in *Docherty v HM Advocate* on the basis that the evidence of any *socius criminis* was not always suspect.[58] However, as was noted in the Carloway Review, Article 6 of the ECHR does not require that evidence be corroborated,[59] and it is likely that the Scottish Government will remove this requirement.[60]

Benefits for Accomplices

Though reliance on accomplice evidence is understandable in a pragmatic and operational sense, it may be problematic when inducements are given or when benefits may accrue to the individual, the most significant of which is that of avoiding prosecution for his own criminality or for certain elements of it, or for no sentence to be imposed. The likelihood of such a benefit being granted and the degree of reward depends on the importance of the case, the value of the information he holds and the relative culpability of the different individuals involved in the alleged crimes. This is a quintessential favouring of crime control over traditional due process norms and principles in the justice system.

The common law in England, Wales and Northern Ireland permitted the giving of undertakings of immunity from prosecution in the public interest to an accused person who 'turned Queen's evidence'. The police could not grant such immunity, and the Director of Public Prosecutions was to exercise this power 'most sparingly'.[61] Now, Chapter 2 of the Serious Organised Crime and Police Act 2005 (as amended) governs the granting of certain privileges to offenders who are involved in assisting investigations and prosecutions in England, Wales and Northern Ireland.[62] An 'immunity notice', precluding the taking of proceedings for a described offence, may be given by the DPP or other specified prosecutor[63] to a particular individual if he thinks it appropriate for the purposes of the inves-

---

[55] *Morton v HM Advocate* 1938 JC 50, 52.

[56] ibid, 55.

[57] *HM Advocate v Murdoch* 1955 SLT notes 57.

[58] *Docherty v HM Advocate* 1987 JC 81.

[59] Lord Carloway, *The Carloway Review: Report and Recommendations* (Edinburgh, 2011) 3.1.6 .

[60] See P Duff, 'The Requirement for Corroboration in Scottish Criminal Cases: One Argument Against Retention' [2012] *Crim LR* 513.

[61] *R v Turner*, n 44, 68.

[62] See ch 6 for a consideration of sentence reductions.

[63] Serious Organised Crime and Police Act 2005, s 71(4). This includes the Director of Revenue and Customs Prosecutions, the Director of the Serious Fraud Office, the Director of Public Prosecutions for Northern Ireland; and a prosecutor designated for the purposes of this section by the aforementioned prosecutors.

tigation or prosecution of any offence.[64] Furthermore, a specified prosecutor may grant an individual a 'restricted use undertaking' as to the use of evidence in criminal proceedings or under recovery proceedings under Part 5 of the Proceeds of Crime Act 2002.[65] This guarantees that certain information of any description will not be used against the person in any proceedings to which this section applies. Failure on the part of the witness to comply with any conditions results in the notice ceasing to have effect.[66] Moreover, immunity does not preclude prosecution of an individual for perjury. These are important safeguards in seeking to ensure that the witness does not exploit the arrangements to his advantage.

These statutory measures require full admission by the 'assisting offender' of his criminality and are predicated on his involvement in a formalised process. So, the individual must divulge his previous acts, in accordance with the statutory framework. Such a structure seeks to avoid the problems related to the previous scheme of 'private' arrangements between the police and the criminal.[67] There is no requirement that prior to making the agreement the assisting offender should have legal representation, but the Crown Prosecution Service indicates that clearly this is preferable in the interests of justice, and so before signing any agreement he will be advised by the investigator of the right to seek independent legal advice.[68]

Originally, under the common law in Scotland, if a decision had been taken not to prosecute and the Crown Office and Procurator Fiscal Service (COPFS) conveyed this to the accused, this was an irrevocable renunciation by the Crown of the right to prosecute.[69] Moreover, the Crown could agree not to move for sentence in return for certain evidence, such as occurred in *Dickson v HM Advocate*.[70] There F had pleaded guilty and had been convicted of drug supply but was not sentenced, as she had given detailed incriminating evidence in respect of the other co-accused. The Court held that while it was necessary for the trial judge to direct the jury specifically to take particular care in assessing the credibility and reliability of her evidence which incriminated the accused, directing the jury that the arrangement constituted an inducement to give false evidence would have usurped the jury's function.[71] The jury needed to consider not whether F had been offered an inducement but rather 'the more delicate question', correctly identified for them by the trial judge, of whether the arrangement had to be viewed as such an inducement as to question the credibility and reliability of her evidence.[72] Now, the Police, Public Order and Criminal Justice (Scotland) Act 2006 places these

---

[64] Serious Organised Crime and Police Act 2005, s 71(7). An immunity notice must not be given in relation to an offence under s 188 of the Enterprise Act 2002 (cartel offences).

[65] Serious Organised Crime and Police Act 2005, s 72. See ch 7 for an analysis of recovery proceedings.

[66] Serious Organised Crime and Police Act 2005, ss 71(3) and 72(4).

[67] *R v P and Blackburn* [2007] EWCA Crim 2290, [2008] 2 Cr App R (S) 5 [27].

[68] Crown Prosecution Service, *Guidance Notes* www.cps.gov.uk/legal/s_to_u/socpa_agreements_-_practical_note_for_defence_advocates/#a01.

[69] *Thom v HM Advocate* 1976 JC 48.

[70] *Dickson v HM Advocate* 2004 SLT 843.

[71] ibid, para 14.

[72] ibid, para 17.

powers on a statutory footing. A prosecutor (this is not defined in the Act) may grant a 'conditional immunity notice' if this is appropriate for the purposes of the investigation or prosecution of any offence.[73] The COPFS has noted that the consent of the Lord Advocate or the Advocate General is required in this respect.[74] As in the other jurisdictions in the UK, breach of the conditions specified in the immunity notice results in the issue of a 'cessation notice' meaning the offer as such is rescinded.

While there is no equivalent legislation in Ireland, the Guidelines for Prosecutors state that '[i]n some circumstances it may be prudent to grant concessions to people who have participated in alleged offences, in order to have their evidence available against others'.[75] These 'concessions' may be granted by the Director of Public Prosecutions only and include indemnity against prosecution or an acceptance of a plea of guilty to fewer charges or a lesser charge than might otherwise have been proceeded with, or an agreement to deal with the case in a summary manner.

The Irish Courts have provided further guidance: as the Court of Criminal Appeal noted in *Director of Public Prosecutions v Gilligan*, if a witness were to give particular evidence in return for a specific sum of money from the Gardaí or the prosecution, that evidence would be inadmissible.[76] The Irish Supreme Court emphasised that to ensure the evidence's reliability it is vital that the benefits to be offered to witnesses are delineated strictly, in addition to an outline of the manner in which negotiations are to take place.[77] In that case, the Supreme Court acknowledged that elements of Garda procedures in this respect compromised the evidence of some witnesses, but concluded that this did not undermine the overall process.[78] Moreover, in *People (DPP) v Ward* the trial judge accepted the testimony of a former accomplice of the accused,[79] concerning the murder of journalist Veronica Guerin. The accomplice, Bowden, received a written undertaking from the Irish DPP that he would not be prosecuted for Guerin's murder and was given a modest prison sentence having pleaded guilty to major drugs and arms crimes, in addition to certain privileges while in prison.[80] Although conceding that such advantages could increase the risk of Bowden altering his story so as to meet the expectations of the prosecution and the Gardaí, the trial court was satisfied that his testimony was sound, on the grounds that Bowden knew that it was

---

[73] Police, Public Order and Criminal Justice (Scotland) Act 2006, s 97.

[74] Crown Office and Procurator Fiscal Service, *Disclosure Manual: A Guide to the Disclosure of Evidence in Criminal Proceedings and Fatal Accident Inquiries* (9th edn) (COPFS, Edinburgh, 2011) 30.3.1.

[75] Office of the Director of Public Prosecutions, *Guidelines for Prosecutors* (Dublin, Office of the Director of Public Prosecutions, 2007) 14.4–14.6.

[76] *DPP v Gilligan* (Court of Criminal Appeal, 8 August 2003) 10.

[77] ibid, 12.

[78] ibid. The court noted that the failure of the Gardaí to keep a record and the returning of monies with no legitimate basis should not have occurred and could be fatal to the evidence in other circumstances.

[79] *The People (DPP) v Ward* (Special Criminal Court, 27 November 1998).

[80] ibid, para 32.

in his best interests to tell the truth to attain these benefits.[81] However the Court of Criminal Appeal overturned Ward's conviction, highlighting that Bowden was an 'inveterate liar', an accomplice in the crime of which Ward was accused, and a recipient of considerable benefits.[82] This approach of the appellate court seems preferable to that of the trial court, given that it recognises the danger of accepting the evidence of an individual to whom significant advantages accrued, and who was revealed to be mendacious.

The irony is that the more involved a person is in criminality or the greater his influence in a criminal organisation, the more information he may have, thus the more valuable he is to the prosecution and so the more likely he is to receive a favourable 'deal'.[83] While granting immunity is a pragmatic crime control response to the need to gather sufficient evidence to convict certain parties suspected of involvement in organised crime, it may compromise the attainment of justice as perceived by the due process paradigm insofar as the accomplices themselves may elude conviction or punishment. This is a measure to be used with care, given that persons higher in criminal hierarchies may avoid punishment by cooperating with the authorities in such a way. Certainly, the motivation and trustworthiness of some such witnesses may be dubious, in that they are likely to be 'working off some charges'.[84] One of the few means of mitigating this is to require corroboration (as remains the situation in Scotland at the time of writing) or at least a corroboration warning (as in Ireland). Robust cross-examination concerning the nature and extent of the involvement and the existence of the agreement is a further crucial due process safeguard[85] to ensure the reliability of the accomplice evidence and thus guard against improper conviction.

The use of and reliance upon accomplice evidence appears to be an unavoidable aspect of prosecuting organised crime. Nonetheless, because of the inherent problems outlined above, reliance on accomplice evidence and the grant of immunity should be in limited instances only. Indeed this approach is used rarely in the comparator jurisdictions,[86] and it has been remarked critically that, despite its potential to disrupt organised crime groups, regional police forces in England and Wales and the Serious Organised Crime Agency appear slow to develop this ability.[87] Though such a cautious approach is to be preferred given the ineluctable dangers in admitting and essentially rewarding accomplice evidence, the reluctance to use such measures appears to be prompted by operational rather than due process concerns.

---

[81] ibid, paras 33–34.
[82] *The People (DPP) v Ward* (Court of Criminal Appeal, 22 March 2002) 12.
[83] Jacobs, n 28, 215.
[84] *US v Medina-Reyes* 877 F Supp 468, 473 (1995).
[85] See below, s VA regarding cross-examination.
[86] From 2006–11, the approximate figures from the Crown Prosecution Service indicate that 7 immunity notices and 11 'restricted use undertakings' were granted. HC Deb 7 July 2011, col 1305W (Solicitor General).
[87] J de Grazia and K Hyland, 'Mainstreaming the Use of Assisting Offenders: How to Make SOCPA 2005, s 73 and s 74 Work' [2011] *Crim LR* 358.

III. Threats to Jurors and Witnesses

Across the UK and Ireland, victims, witnesses and jurors fear intimidation or reprisal from organised crime participants and groups.[88] Intimidation may range from threats to the witness, his family or property, through to physical violence or even homicide. This is essentially the 'neutralisation' of law enforcement, as without such lay involvement and testimony convictions would become impossible.[89] Moreover, the involvement of a coerced or anxious juror may compromise the quality of the trial of fact: 'a frightened juror is a bad juror'.[90]

By its nature, it is difficult to determine the extent of intimidation, although reasonable efforts have been made across the UK, if not in Ireland.[91] While intimidation is not uncommon and certainly is a grave problem in particular locations,[92] other empirical research shows that the percentage of intimidated victims who believed the aggression was to prevent them from giving evidence to the police or in court was in single figures.[93] To date, there is no empirical data available in Ireland.[94] Regardless of the extent of the problem generally, it is perceived that there are three different tiers in this respect: a small core of endangered individuals who need high level protection such as that offered by Witness Protection Programmes, a middle ring of victims and witnesses who have suffered non-life threatening intimidation, and an outer layer of the general public who are fearful of possible harassment and so would not come forward with evidence to the police.[95]

The phenomenon of juror and witness intimidation has prompted the amendment of key elements of the criminal trial in the UK and Ireland, in a bid to reconcile the needs and interests of the victim, witnesses and citizens on the jury with those of the defendant. For example, discrete statutory offences of threatening witnesses and jurors have been introduced. It is a distinct offence to intimidate a witness or juror with the intention of obstructing the investigation or the course of justice,[96] and in Ireland this provision covers a member of such a per-

---

[88] See, eg House of Commons Northern Ireland Affairs Committee, *Organised Crime in Northern Ireland*, vol 1 (Third Report of Session 2005–06) (London, The Stationery Office, 2006) 29–30, para 85.

[89] AK Cohen, 'The Concept of Criminal Organisation' (1977) 17 *British Journal of Criminology* 97, 106.

[90] Lord Diplock, *Report of the Commission to Consider Legal Procedures to Deal with Terrorist Activities in Northern Ireland* (Cmnd 5185, 1972) (London, Her Majesty's Stationery Office) para 36.

[91] N Fyfe and H McKay, *Making it Safe to Speak? A Study of Witness Intimidation and Protection in Strathclyde* (Edinburgh, The Scottish Office, 1998); R Tarling, L Dowds and T Budd, *Victim and Witness Intimidation: Findings from the British Crime Survey* (London, Home Office, 2000); R Elliott, 'Vulnerable and Intimidated Witnesses: A Review of the Literature' in Home Office, *Speaking Up for Justice* (London, Home Office, 1998).

[92] W Maynard, *Witness Intimidation: Strategies for Prevention* (London, Home Office, 1994) 4.

[93] Tarling *et al*, n 91.

[94] A State Prosecutor claimed that 1 in 10 criminal cases could not be successfully prosecuted in Limerick in 2004 because of intimidation: see 'Why this Hitman Holds the Key to Beating Crime', *Sunday Times*, 20 November 2005.

[95] Maynard n 92, 1.

[96] s 41. Proof that an individual threatened the witness or his family member is sufficient evidence that the act was committed with the requisite intention (s 41(3)).

son's family.[97] It is also an offence in England, Wales and Northern Ireland to harm a witness intentionally if the actor knows or believes that the person has been a witness and the act is done or threatened because of that knowledge or belief. This applies once proceedings commence and ends one year after they are concluded.[98]

Moreover, specific alterations have been made to the jury trial and to rules regarding the information available about jurors, as well as to the presentation and admissibility of witness evidence. As in relation to other legal developments, a tension exists in this context between the demands of crime control and the precepts of due process, given that improving the likelihood of successful prosecution may impinge on the rights of the accused. However, the dynamic between jurors and/or witnesses on the one hand and the accused on the other is not a zero-sum relationship, and so it is conceivable that protective measures may safeguard the former without necessarily affecting the latter in a problematic fashion. Achieving this balance in legal doctrine and then in practice is more difficult.

IV. Threats to Jurors

In seeking to address possible intimidation and perversion of the course of justice, measures have been introduced which pertain to the jury specifically.

A. Restricting the Right to Trial by Jury

The trial of suspected organised criminals may pose a danger to jurors who could be intimidated or otherwise coerced in their decision-making as to the facts of a case. Such concern has led to the holding of trials without juries in Ireland, and now also in England, Wales and Northern Ireland. This has repercussions for the right to equality, may involve the stigmatisation of the accused persons, and may affect the quality of the criminal trial itself. In addition, the agent or arm of the State responsible for the decision regarding the mode of trial is significant. In Ireland, non-jury trials of organised crime occurs either on the order of the Director of Public Prosecutions or automatically when the suspected act falls within the scope of counter-terrorism legislation. In contrast, in England, Wales and Northern Ireland, non-jury trials are held only after a court order and when specific criteria have been satisfied.

---

[97] Criminal Justice Act 1999, s 41 (Ireland). Criminal Justice and Public Order Act 1994, s 51 applies to criminal proceedings in England and Wales, while s 39 of the Criminal Justice and Police Act 2001 applies to all proceedings in England, Wales and Northern Ireland.
[98] Criminal Justice and Police Act 2001, s 40. Though there is no specific offence in Scotland the common law crime of assault (*Smart v HM Advocate* 1975 JC 30) and the legislative crime of committing threatening or abusive behaviour would apply (Criminal Justice and Licensing Scotland Act 2010, s 38).

Although not required by the European Convention on Human Rights, trial by jury is seen as a fundamental element of adversarial criminal justice: it has been described as bringing a democratic element to the justice system and therefore should not be interfered with unduly.[99] In the UK and Ireland, trial by jury holds a sanctified position, in theory at least, despite the small proportion of criminal cases that actually are heard before a jury.[100] The rationale behind this was articulated by Henchy J in *People (DPP) v O'Shea*, where he said that the import accorded to the concept in Ireland in particular derived from memories of

> politically appointed and Executive-oriented judges, of the suspension of jury trial in times of popular revolt, of the substitution . . . of summary trial or detention without trial, of cat-and-mouse releases from such detention, of packed juries and sometimes corrupt judges and prosecutors.[101]

Accordingly, the best way to prevent wrongful conviction was

> to allow [the individual] to 'put himself upon his country', that is to say, to allow him to be tried for that offence by a fair, impartial and representative jury, sitting in a court presided over by an impartial and independent judge appointed under the Constitution, who would see that all the requirements for a fair and proper jury trial would be observed.[102]

The jury trial, long regarded as an essential facet of liberal adversarial criminal justice systems, nonetheless was circumscribed all across the island of Ireland as a result of the threat posed by terrorism, thereby providing a precursor for a similar approach in relation to organised crime. This is a paradigmatic example of the seepage of emergency powers into a wider context. The history of paramilitarism and the concomitant threats to the security of the State were instrumental in shaping the Irish Constitution, and ensured the inclusion of extraordinary measures to protect the State. Various constitutional provisions guard State security from subversive activity: any law 'expressed to be for the purpose of securing the public safety and the preservation of the State in time of war or armed rebellion' enjoys constitutional immunity; special non-jury courts are authorised to hear cases when the ordinary courts are deemed to be inadequate to secure the administration of justice and the preservation of public peace and order;[103] and at a time of armed conflict, the Houses of Parliament may declare that a national emergency exists which affects the vital interests of the State, thereby facilitating

---

[99] De Tocqueville noted that juries 'spread respect for the courts' decisions and for the idea of rights throughout the classes'. A De Tocqueville, *Democracy in America* (New York, Doubleday, 1969) 274. Similarly, Devlin claimed that the jury trial 'gives protection against harsh and oppressive laws' (P Devlin, *Trial by Jury* (London, Stevens, 1966) 160) and is 'the lamp that shows freedom lives' (ibid 164).

[100] See P Darbyshire, 'The Lamp that Shows that Freedom Lives – is it Worth the Candle?' [1991] *Crim LR* 740.

[101] *The People (DPP) v O'Shea* [1982] IR 384, 342.

[102] ibid.

[103] Art 38.3.

restrictions on constitutional rights and liberties.[104] A resolution declaring a state of emergency was made in 1939 and lasted until 1946 (although it was not formally rescinded until 1976), and another was made in 1976 until it was rescinded in 1995 following the IRA ceasefire.[105]

The jury trial, although guaranteed expressly in the Irish Constitution,[106] may be restricted by the establishment of 'special' courts where the ordinary courts are deemed to be inadequate.[107] Part V of the Offences Against the State Act 1939, which governs the establishment of such special courts, comes into operation when the Government proclaims that the ordinary courts are inadequate to secure the effective administration of justice and the preservation of public peace and order.[108] This executive power was upheld as constitutional in *Kavanagh v Ireland*.[109] The necessary proclamations under Part V, which do not require any explanation on the part of the Irish Government, have been made for the periods 1939–46, 1961–62, and 1972 to date,[110] and such a declaration can be annulled only by a resolution of the Dáil or when the Government declares that Part V is no longer in force.[111] There are two means by which a non-jury trial may be held, one of which is class-based, while the other is risk-based and premised on prosecutorial discretion. In the first scenario, persons charged with 'scheduled offences' generally are tried before this non-jury court.[112] Secondly, the Irish DPP may also request that a person charged with a non-scheduled offence be tried there on the basis that he believes that the ordinary courts are inadequate to secure the administration of justice and the preservation of public peace and order.[113] As will be

---

[104] Art 28.3.3°.

[105] See S Kilcommins and B Vaughan, 'Subverting the Rule of Law in Ireland' (2004) 35 *Cambrian Law Review* 55, 57.

[106] Art 38.5.

[107] Art 38.3.

[108] s 35. The enactment of this Act, which forms the cornerstone of the legislative protection of State security in Ireland, was precipitated by the paramilitary activity of the Irish Republican Army (IRA) in the late 1930s. It is composed of five parts, the first four of which are permanently in force. Part I concerns interpretation and other general matters; Pt II concerns, inter alia, offences against the State such as the usurpation of government or the President, unauthorised military exercises, and the possession of treasonable and seditious documents; Pt III deals with membership of unlawful organisations; and Pt IV concerns miscellaneous matters, including the prohibition of meetings in the vicinity of the Oireachtas, search warrants, and the re-capture of escaped prisoners.

[109] *Kavanagh v Ireland* [1996] 1 IR 348, 354.

[110] Committee to Review the Offences Against the State Acts 1939–98 and Related Matters, *Report of the Committee to Review the Offences Against the State Acts 1939–98 and Related Matters* (Dublin, Stationery Office, 2002) para 9.8.

[111] s 35(4) and (5).

[112] A list of offences is 'scheduled' under the 1939 Act and are dealt with by extraordinary measures. An equivalent approach is evident in the Northern Ireland (Emergency Provisions) Act 1973 (and its subsequent replacements).

[113] s 46 of the Offences Against the State Act 1939 applies to non-scheduled summary and indictable offences where an individual is charged in the District Court; s 47 provides for the direct charge and trial of an individual before the Special Criminal Court for non-scheduled offences; and s 48 permits the transferral of a trial on indictment to the Special Criminal Court where the accused has been returned for trial to the Central Criminal Court or the Circuit Court. These sections require the written certification of the DPP.

explored below, this request must be upheld – in other words, the judges have limited ability to interfere with this direction.

In Northern Ireland non-jury trials on indictment of scheduled offences have been heard in the 'Diplock Courts' since the Emergency Provisions Act 1973. This piece of legislation was introduced in an attempt by the UK Government to deal with juror intimidation by paramilitary organisations as well as perverse acquittals along religious or sectarian lines.[114] The 1973 Act was replaced by Part 7 of the Terrorism Act 2000 which continued the trial of scheduled offences without a jury unless the Attorney-General for Northern Ireland exercises his discretion and directs that a case is to be tried before a jury on the basis that it is not related to the emergency situation in Northern Ireland. The Diplock Courts were abolished in 2007 under the security normalisation in Northern Ireland, and the Justice and Security (Northern Ireland) Act 2007 now permits trials on indictment without a jury where the DPP for Northern Ireland issues a certificate if he suspects that certain conditions are met, such as a link to a proscribed organisation or political or religious hostility, and that in view of this there is a risk that the administration of justice might be impaired if the trial were conducted with a jury.[115] This is a risk-based approach rather than one predicated on scheduled offences, and applies to suspected subversive or terrorist offences rather than serious and organised crime that is not motivated by sectarianism or ideology. The legislation was also due to expire on 31 July 2011, but was extended for a two-year period.[116]

i. Using Non-jury Trials for 'Ordinary' Crime

Drawing on the example of the Irish Special Criminal Court and the Northern Irish Diplock Courts established originally to deal with the threat of subversive activity, non-jury trials are used increasingly for 'ordinary' crime, especially organised crime. In Ireland this seems to be premised on the view that organised criminality in fact is not 'ordinary' crime and thus merits measures akin to those used against suspected terrorists. Despite the significance of the jury trial as articulated by numerous judges and commentators, there is 'a tendency to think that, if anything goes wrong or is thought likely to go wrong with the criminal process, the first thing to do is to get rid of the jury'.[117] Notably, such an approach has not been countenanced seriously in Scotland, nor in the United States because of the

---

[114] See S Greer and A White, 'A Return To Trial By Jury' in A Jennings (ed), *Justice Under Fire: The Abuse of Civil Liberties in Northern Ireland* (London, Pluto Press, 1988) 58; S Greer and A White, 'Restoring Jury Trial to Terrorist Offences in Northern Ireland' in M Findlay and P Duff (eds), *The Jury Under Attack* (London, Butterworths, 1988) 186. J Jackson, K Quinn and T O'Malley, 'The Jury System in Contemporary Ireland: In the Shadow of a Troubled Past' (1999) 62 *Law and Contemporary Problems* 203.

[115] Justice and Security (Northern Ireland) Act 2007, s 1.

[116] The Justice and Security (Northern Ireland) Act 2007 (Extension of Duration of Non-Jury Trial Provisions) Order 2011.

[117] P Devlin, 'Foreword' in S Greer and A White, *Abolishing the Diplock Courts: The Case for Restoring Jury Trial to Scheduled Offences in Northern Ireland* (London, Cobden Trust, 1986).

US Constitution and related jurisprudence,[118] another useful common law comparator. It appears that the precedent set by the emergency situation across the island of Ireland has broadened the range of possible options when dealing with the threat of organised crime to jurors and other individuals involved in the criminal process rather than sensitising law makers to the potential harm to individual rights.

The primary rationale for restricting or removing the jury trial is juror intimidation: the Irish Government justified the re-introduction of the Special Criminal Court in 1972 on the basis that juries were likely to be threatened by paramilitaries,[119] and that non-jury courts continue to be used other than in the counter-terrorism context on the basis that juries in the trial of organised criminals will be subject to threats or intimidation.[120] As Walsh J noted in *The People (DPP) v Quilligan*:

> There could well be a grave situation in dealing with ordinary gangsterism or well-financed and well-organised large scale drug dealing, or other situations where it might be believed or established that juries were for some corrupt reason, or by virtue of threats, or of illegal interference, being prevented from doing justice.[121]

Similarly, in *Kavanagh v Ireland*, Keane J stated that persons engaged in non-subversive crime could be tried before a special court rather than by a jury where there appeared to be a significant risk of intimidation or corruption of the jury.[122] Moreover, the Committee to Review the Offences Against the State Acts asserted that juries in Ireland are 'distinctly uncomfortable' in cases involving organised crime and that attempts have been made to tamper with juries in high-profile criminal trials in the ordinary courts.[123] Likewise, the House of Commons Northern Ireland Affairs Committee expressed its view that non-jury trials for appropriate offences in Northern Ireland are 'essential' and that only by maintaining them would many witnesses feel able to give evidence against organised crime gangs.[124] How the abolition of the jury assists or safeguards witnesses is dubious, but the Committee's view is yet further official support for the maintenance of extraordinary measures to counter the threat of organised crime.

In Ireland, non-jury trials for suspected organised crimes may be held if the suspected offence is included in the Schedule to the Offences Against the State Act 1939, or if there is a perceived risk of intimidation and the Irish DPP directs such

---

[118] See Art 3 of the US Constitution, and the Sixth and Fourteenth Amendments.

[119] See the submission of the Irish Government in *Eccles, McPhillips and McShane v Ireland* App no 12839/87 (ECtHR, 9 December 1988) as referred to in Irish Council for Civil Liberties, *ICCL Submission to the Committee to Review the Offences Against the State Acts, 1939–98, and Related Matters* (Dublin, ICCL, 2002).

[120] This is notwithstanding the opinion of the UN Human Rights Committee in 1993 that it did not consider that 'the continued existence of that court is justified in the present circumstances'. UNHRC, Report of the Human Rights Committee, Official Records of the General Assembly, 48th Session, Supplement no 40, 1993 (A/48/40) Pt 1, 125–28.

[121] *The People (DPP) v Quilligan* [1986] IR 495, 509.

[122] *Kavanagh*, n 109, 364.

[123] Committee to Review the Offences Against the State Acts, n 110, paras 9.33 and 9.36.

[124] House of Commons Northern Ireland Affairs Committee, n 88, 67 para 222.

a trial. As regards the first class-based approach, the Schedule to the 1939 Act includes not only offences against the Irish State such as sedition, usurpation of the functions of government and the obstruction of government, but also most offences under the Firearms Acts 1925–2006.[125] In addition, certain organised crime offences have recently been added to this schedule. Substantive offences under Part 7 of the Criminal Justice Act 2006 (directing the activities of a criminal organisation, participating in or contributing to certain activities of a criminal organisation, and committing a serious offence for a criminal organisation) have been declared as scheduled offences where the ordinary courts are deemed automatically to be inadequate to secure the effective administration of justice and the preservation of public peace and order.[126] According to the terms of the Criminal Justice (Amendment) Act 2009 this declaration lasts for 12 months. The provision was renewed again in June 2011 despite the fact that not a single case has yet been brought before the Special Criminal Court using these powers,[127] although this is likely to be a function of the length of time it takes to investigate and construct such cases which may well be complicated.

The second means by which a non-jury trial may be held in Ireland centres on the risk of intimidation and is premised on prosecutorial discretion. The Irish Supreme Court has stressed that Part V of the 1939 Act, which governs the establishment of the Special Criminal Court, is not concerned solely with subversive activities but rather applies to the adequacy of the ordinary courts,[128] thereby explaining the DPP's ability to direct that organised crime and other offences be tried there. Cases which have been heard in the Special Criminal Court in recent years with no subversive or paramilitary dimension include kidnapping,[129] the murder of journalist Veronica Guerin,[130] and a charge of receiving a stolen caravan and its contents.[131]

Similarly, in England, Wales and Northern Ireland non-jury trials may be held, but in contrast to Ireland the model is a risk-based decision determined by the courts. The Criminal Justice Act 2003 provides, inter alia, a legislative framework for trials on indictment to be held without a jury where there is a danger of jury tampering,[132] and since 2006 non-jury trials have been heard where such a danger

---

[125] An equivalent approach is evident in the Northern Ireland (Emergency Provisions) Act 1973 (and its subsequent replacements).

[126] Criminal Justice (Amendment) Act 2009, s 8.

[127] See Seanad Debates, vol 216 (20 June 2012).

[128] *The People (DPP) v Quilligan*, n 121.

[129] *DPP v Kavanagh* (Court of Criminal Appeal, 18 May 1999).

[130] See *The People (DPP) v Ward* (Special Criminal Court, 27 November 1998); *The People (DPP) v Meehan* (Special Criminal Court, 29 July 1999).

[131] See Irish Council for Civil Liberties, *Background Paper on the 30th Anniversary of the Establishment of the Special Criminal Court* (Dublin, ICCL, 2002).

[132] Criminal Justice Act 2003, ss 43 and 44. Section 50 of the Criminal Justice Act 2003 provides that Pt 7 applies to Northern Ireland except for trials of scheduled offences which shall be conducted by the court without a jury under s 75 of the Terrorism Act 2000.

exists.[133] The Home Secretary at the time of enactment, David Blunkett, emphasised the need to protect jurors from organised criminals,[134] and rather more pragmatically, the cost of protecting jurors was also noted in Parliament.[135]

For a non-jury trial to be held, evidence must be presented of a real and present danger that jury tampering would take place, and it must be established that despite any reasonable preventative steps, including police protection, there is so substantial a likelihood that tampering would occur that the interests of justice necessitate a non-jury trial. The Court of Appeal in *R v Twomey* emphasised that both conditions must be satisfied.[136] The legislation provides some examples of cases where there may be evidence of a real and present danger of jury tampering, including retrials where the previous jury was discharged due to tampering, where the defendant has been involved in previous criminal proceedings where jury tampering has taken place, or where there has been intimidation, or attempted intimidation, of any person who is likely to be a witness in the trial. However, as was noted in *R v Mackle*, the fact that jury tampering had taken place in the past does not establish the existence of a real and present danger that it would recur and does not create a presumption in favour of trial without a jury, although it is relevant in assessing whether it was likely to happen again.[137] Furthermore, evidence which might demonstrate that there was a real and present danger that the right to jury trial would be abused by jury tampering is not limited to evidence which would be admissible at the defendant's trial.[138] In considering whether reasonable preventative steps might address the danger of jury tampering, their feasibility, cost and anticipated duration are relevant, as are any logistical difficulties to which they might give rise, whether they might affect unfavourably the way in which the jury approached its task, and their likely impact on the ordinary lives of the jurors.[139]

---

[133] Criminal Justice Act 2003 (Commencement No 13 and Transitional Provision) Order 2006 and Criminal Justice Act 2003 (Commencement No 15) Order 2006. The 2003 Act also provided for non-jury trials in cases of serious or complex fraud, where the complexity or length of the trial (or both) must be likely to make the trial so burdensome to a jury that the interests of justice require serious consideration to be given to a non-jury trial. Approval was to be required of the Lord Chief Justice or a judge nominated by him. The enactment and implementation of these provisions proved to be controversial, with substantial opposition from the House of Lords in its parliamentary capacity when the Criminal Justice Bill was being debated. All the sections providing for non-jury trial on indictment were rejected by the House of Lords, and in an attempt to ensure the passage of the Bill the Home Secretary David Blunkett inserted an amendment stating that the approval of both Houses of Parliament would be required before the sections on fraud could be brought into force (s 330(5)(b)). An attempt in the Fraud (Trials without a Jury) Bill 2006–07 to remove the requirement of approval of the two Houses was blocked again in the Lords (HL Deb 20 March 2007, vol 690, col 1201) and the fraud provisions were never enacted. Section 113 of the Protection of Freedoms Act 2012 removed this provision from the 2003 Act.
[134] HC Deb 19 May 2003, vol 405, col 740.
[135] HL Deb 19 November 2003, vol 654, col 1963, Baroness Scotland of Asthal.
[136] *R v Twomey* [2009] EWCA Crim 1035, [2010] 1 WLR 630 [18].
[137] *R v Mackle* [2007] NICA 37, [2008] NI 183.
[138] *Twomey*, n 136, [18].
[139] ibid, [19]; *R v Mackle* [2008] NI 183 [28].

During a trial, a jury may be discharged and the trial continued without one, if the judge is satisfied that jury tampering has taken place, and that to continue without a jury would be fair to the defendant.[140] This occurred in the Crown Court in Northern Ireland in *R v Clarke and McStravick*, involving a 'soi-disant "tiger kidnapping" scenario',[141] where an employee of a security transportation company and his family were kidnapped and he was forced to hand over cash from his employer. Alternatively the judge may terminate the trial and may order that any new trial must be conducted without a jury. The Court in *Twomey* noted that 'save in unusual circumstances, the judge faced with this problem [of tampering] should order not only the discharge of the jury but that he should continue the trial'.[142] Taylor claims that this is based not on efficiency and convenience but on the notion that no advantage should accrue to those involved in jury tampering from terminating a trial rather than proceeding to verdict.[143] As will be explored below, this may raise problems in relation to inadmissible evidence and the quality of decision-making. However, in certain rare and extreme instances, such as in *R v S*, where the judge had been involved in numerous other trials involving the appellant, the judge should not have ordered that the trial continue without the jury due to the realistic possibility of objective perception of judicial bias.[144]

ii. Non-jury Trials and Human Rights

Despite the long standing convention of jury trials for criminal cases, it does not constitute a right as such in the UK, and the right to a fair trial under Article 6 of the ECHR does not guarantee a right to trial by jury. As the Court of Appeal stated in *Twomey*

> [i]t . . . does not follow from the hallowed principle of trial by jury that trial by judge alone, when ordered, would be unfair or improperly prejudicial to the defendant. The trial would take place before an independent tribunal and, as it seems to us, for the purposes of article 6 of the European Convention for the Protection of Human Rights and Fundamental Freedoms, it is irrelevant whether the tribunal is judge and jury or judge alone.[145]

Furthermore, while the right is guaranteed in the Irish Constitution, it may be abrogated in certain circumstances.[146] Notwithstanding the compliance of non-jury trials with Article 6, various problematic issues arise in the context of selective holding such trials, concerning the right to equality, the role of the judge as both arbiter of law and fact, and the 'gate keeper' regarding the mode of trial.

---

[140] *Twomey*, n 136, [46].
[141] *R v Clarke and McStravick* [2010] NICC 7.
[142] *Twomey*, n 136, [20].
[143] N Taylor, 'Case Comment *R v S*: Judge Alone – Jury Discharged because of Jury Tampering' [2010] *Crim LR* 643.
[144] *R v S* [2009] EWCA Crim 2377.
[145] *Twomey*, n 136, [18].
[146] Art 38.

Non-jury trials arguably breach the right to equality under Article 40.1 of the Irish Constitution, given that only certain criminal cases are referred by the DPP to the non-jury court. (It is more difficult to contend a breach of Article 14 of the ECHR which precludes discrimination in the enjoyment of Convention rights, rather than constituting a 'free-standing' right as such).[147] The matter of equality was circumvented in *Kavanagh v Ireland* where the Supreme Court held that as the determination of the adequacy of the ordinary courts was political in nature, such a decision should be regulated in the political rather than the judicial sphere,[148] and the argument that equality was breached was dismissed subsequently in *Byrne and Dempsey v Government of Ireland.*[149] Hamilton J grounded his decision on the fact that the Irish DPP is authorised directly by statute to issue such a certificate and thereby to make a distinction between citizens while a Government proclamation under section 35 of the Offences Against the State Act 1939 is in force.[150] These judgments are resolutely formalistic and fail to engage with the crux of the issue, namely the differential treatment of those accused of a crime. In this instance, the domestic courts have not served as a bulwark against the crime control inclinations of Parliament. When Kavanagh petitioned the United Nations Human Rights Committee (UNHRC), it criticised the ability of the legislature to specify by statute which serious offences were to come within the Special Criminal Court's jurisdiction, and to permit other offences to be so tried at the discretion of the DPP.[151] Ireland was deemed not to have established that the decision to try Kavanagh before the Special Criminal Court was based upon reasonable and objective grounds, and, accordingly, the UNHRC found that his right to equality under Article 26 of the International Covenant on Civil and Political Rights (ICCPR) had been violated.[152] Nevertheless, when Kavanagh sought to have this decision applied in the Irish courts, the ICCPR was held not to form part of domestic law as Ireland had not incorporated it,[153] and thus the substance of the decision was again circumvented.

A further contentious issue pertaining to the erosion of the right to trial by jury lies in the fact that judges in these cases must act as arbiters of both fact and law. In their study of Diplock trials in Northern Ireland Jackson and Doran found that the defendant suffers an 'adversarial deficit' in non-jury trials through the fact that lay triers of fact can afford to take a more wide-ranging view of the merits of the prosecution case than any professional tribunal and that a professional

---

[147]   See A Baker, 'The Enjoyment of Rights and Freedoms: A New Conception of the "Ambit" under Article 14 ECHR' (2006) 69 *MLR* 714.

[148]   *Kavanagh*, n 109, 354.

[149]   *Byrne and Dempsey v Government of Ireland* (Supreme Court, 11 March 1999).

[150]   See n 106.

[151]   *Kavanagh v Ireland*, Communication no 819/1998, UN Doc CCPR/C/71/D/819/1998 (2001) para 10.2.

[152]   International Covenant on Civil and Political Rights, GA res 2200A (XXI), UN Doc A/6316 (1966).

[153]   *Kavanagh v Governor of Mountjoy Prison* [2002] 2 ILRM 81. Ireland has a dualist system, which requires international measures to be enacted into domestic law.

approach necessitates a certain case-hardening in the sense that it demands that a colder, unemotional attitude is taken towards the evidence.[154]

Non-jury trials pose particular problems in the context of inadmissible evidence, when the judges may be required to exclude from their minds incriminating material which cannot be relied on in court. As Finlay CJ revealed in *The People (DPP) v Conroy*, '[e]xperience as a judge indicates that even as a trained lawyer there is a very significant difficulty in excluding from one's mind [such] evidence'.[155] In opposition to this, in *DPP v Special Criminal Court* Carney J asserted that while the members of the Special Criminal Court may be exposed to prejudicial material when examining sensitive information, judges are capable of dealing with the case fairly and in accordance with the law.[156] Moreover, as previously noted, in England, Wales and Northern Ireland evidence regarding the danger of jury-tampering is not limited to evidence which would be admissible at the criminal trial,[157] and the same judge that discharges a jury should continue the trial.[158] It is questionable whether a judge may cast inadmissible material from his mind so as to ensure that his final determination is not prejudiced by such evidence: it is unreasonable to expect any person 'to "unbite" the apple of knowledge'.[159] This is particularly pertinent in the context of accomplice warnings when the judge is also arbiter of fact.[160] As Hillyard noted, when one person decides on the issue, as in England, Wales and Northern Ireland, this 'becomes an unrealistic cerebral activity of one person'.[161]

The trial court's position as arbiter of fact and law may be mitigated by the fact it must provide a written judgment of the decisions, outlining the reasoning in relation to both aspects of its role.[162] In *Gilligan* the Court of Criminal Appeal noted that if the trial had been heard before a jury rather than before the Special Criminal Court, it, as the appeal court, would not have known how the jury reached its verdict or what witnesses it considered to be credible.[163] Although this seems ironic and indicates a potential disadvantage of jury trials,[164] it does not justify the abrogation of the right to equality of the accused without his consent.

---

[154] J Jackson and S Doran, *Judge without Jury: Diplock Trials in the Adversary System* (Oxford, Clarendon Press, 195) 293; also see J Jackson, 'Modes of Trial: Shifting the Balance towards the Professional Judge' [2002] *Crim LR* 260.

[155] *The People (DPP) v Conroy* [1986] IR 460, 472.

[156] *DPP v Special Criminal Court* [1999] 1 IR 60.

[157] *Twomey*, n 136, [18].

[158] *Twomey*, n 136, [20].

[159] M Damaška, 'Free Proof and its Detractors' (1995) 43 *American Journal of Comparative Law* 343, 352.

[160] Greer and White in Findlay and Duff, n 114, 177; T Gifford, *Supergrasses: The Use of Accomplice Evidence in Northern Ireland* (London, The Cobden Trust, 1984). See above, IIB Accomplice Evidence.

[161] Hillyard and Percy-Smith, n 48, 350.

[162] Criminal Justice Act 2003, s 48; Justice and Security (Northern Ireland) Act 2007, s 5.

[163] *DPP v Gilligan* (Court of Criminal Appeal, 8 August 2003) 18–19. See also Ward, n 130, 20.

[164] *cf Taxquet v Belgium* [2010] ECHR 1806; P Roberts, 'Does Article 6 of the European Convention on Human Rights Require Reasoned Verdicts in Criminal Trials?' (2011) 11 *Human Rights Law Review* 213.

The situation in Ireland is especially contentious as regards the decision concerning the form of trial. In Ireland, scheduled offences are tried automatically without a jury, while the decision to have a non-jury trial is otherwise taken by the Director of Public Prosecutions. In contrast, in England, Wales and Northern Ireland it is the Lord Chief Justice or a judge nominated by him who decides whether a non-jury trial is appropriate. The certification power of the Irish DPP, which permits her to deny the accused his right to a jury trial in the context of non-scheduled offences, is not reviewable judicially in the absence of *mala fides*,[165] meaning that the DPP's reasons are not revealed and so cannot be challenged. As the UNHRC remarked, judicial review is 'effectively restricted to the most exceptional and virtually undemonstrable circumstances'.[166]

The Irish Supreme Court pronounced that many factors could provide the basis for the opinion of the DPP, such as 'a general state of unrest within the State, the identity and associates of the accused, the nature of the crime alleged or the apparent motive for it'.[167] In *Savage v Director of Public Prosecutions*, Finlay P concluded that it would be a 'security impossibility' if the DPP was required to reveal in court the facts on which her opinion was based.[168] This could be resolved by the adoption of the approach advocated in *Murphy* v *Dublin Corporation* where the Supreme Court concluded that evidence concerning security information in respect of which executive privilege is claimed may be examined *in camera* by the courts prior to a ruling on its admissibility.[169] In England, Wales and Northern Ireland evidence substantiating the possibility of jury tampering may be disclosed only under the public interest immunity (PII) scheme such as in *R v Twomey*.[170] In Ireland when deciding whether to disclose material the prosecutor must also have regard to any other issues of the public interest that might arise. In such cases, however, the defence should be informed that material has been withheld and as to why a non-jury trial is necessary on such grounds so as to enable the accused to seek a court ruling on the matter.[171] Moreover, in England, Wales and Northern Ireland the parties to a preparatory hearing at which an application to hold a non-jury trial is to be determined are given an opportunity to make representations with respect to the application,[172] a safeguard which is not replicated in Ireland.

In addition, the decision of the Irish legislature to 'schedule' certain offences precludes any intervention by the courts regarding the form of trial, as the decision is

---

[165] *Savage and Owen v DPP* [1982] ILRM 385; *State (McCormack) v Curran* [1987] ILRM 225; *H v Director of Public Prosecutions* [1994] 2 IR 589, 596.

[166] *Kavanagh v Ireland*, n 151, [10.2].

[167] *Re Article 26 and the Criminal Law Jurisdiction Bill* [1977] IR 129, 151.

[168] *Savage and Owen v DPP* [1982] ILRM 385, 389; *cf* S Pye, 'Judicial Review of Discretionary Powers under Part V of the Offences Against the State Act 1939' (1985) 3 *Irish Law Times* 65, 67; R Byrne, 'Judicial Reviewability of a Prosecutorial Discretion' [1981] XVI *Irish Jurist* 86, 90–91.

[169] *Murphy v Dublin Corporation* [1972] IR 215. *Murphy* was applied in *DPP v Special Criminal Court* [1999] 1 IR 60, where the court held that problems relating to disclosure may be resolved by the trial judge examining the documents in question.

[170] *Twomey*, n 136. See above, n 28ff.

[171] Office of the Director of Public Prosecutions, n 75, para 9.24.

[172] Criminal Justice Act 2003, s 45(3).

solely a political one. Generally speaking, the Irish Supreme Court has been oriented strongly towards the demands of due process in its interpretation of the Constitution in the context of criminal law, notwithstanding that this may compromise the control of crime in certain instances. The scheduling of offences and the judiciary's deference in relation to the broad application of counter-terrorism legislation means that the courts have no determinative function regarding the holding of non-jury trials. The erosion of a constitutional right is governed by prosecutorial discretion and legislative action, neatly encapsulating the crime control model of justice. In this scenario the location of the trial of organised crimes in a special court constructed in an emergency situation plays to populist and sensationalist rhetoric but permits the contemporary compromising of a core legal principle on a questionable basis.

In reacting to organised crime, standards of criminal procedure in the UK and Ireland have been altered significantly so as to ease the prosecution and conviction of accused persons, thereby augmenting the crime control capabilities of the State. A normalisation process has occurred in which extraordinary measures first introduced to deal with subversive crime have been adopted in the wider criminal justice sphere,[173] through use of broadly framed counter-terrorism legislation in Ireland and imitation in contemporary measures in England, Wales and Northern Ireland. In particular, the use in Ireland of the Special Criminal Court and the DPP's referral power in the context of organised crime represent 'disquieting evidence of the "seepage" of emergency legislation in to the ordinary law of the State',[174] and this has been emulated everywhere in the UK except Scotland. While such exceptional methods should be used only for a limited time in order to address the concrete specifications of that crisis and to restore regular or constitutional order,[175] the limitation of the jury trial in the context of organised crime breaches this tenet, by permitting radical measures to remain in the standard legal realm on tenuous grounds. This retention of the jury trial for all serious cases in Scotland may be due to the absence of a terrorist problem, and the concomitant lack of familiarity of legislators with extraordinary measures.[176] Moreover, in Scotland the jury comprises 15 people, and an 8 to 7 majority is sufficient, meaning that a conviction is less likely to be obstructed by the intimidation of one or more jurors.

It may be argued that the threat posed to juries in cases involving organised crime is such that non-jury trials are crucial for the protection of citizens and for

[173] Kilcommins and Vaughan, n 105, 56.

[174] G Hogan and C Walker, *Political Violence and the Law in Ireland* (Manchester, Manchester University Press, 1989) 239.

[175] See J McCormick, 'The Dilemmas of Dictatorship: Carl Schmitt and Constitutional Emergency Powers' (1997) 10 *Canadian Journal of Law and Jurisprudence* 163; Kilcommins and Vaughan, n 105, 73.

[176] Juries in the rest of the UK and in Ireland comprise 12 people. Section 13 of the Criminal Justice Act 1967 removed the requirement of unanimity in jury verdicts in England and Wales, so a majority of 10 is now sufficient. The impetus for this included the prevention of acquittal based on the intimidation of a juror. Also see the Criminal Procedure (Majority Verdicts) Act (Northern Ireland) 1971 and the Criminal Justice Act 1984 in Ireland which permit a majority verdict of 10 to 2.

the successful prosecution and conviction of such criminals. Essentially, while security may be enhanced while a jury trial is on-going, when the trial ends the organised crime group may exact retribution or revenge. Thus, doing away with the jury completely may appear the only legitimate and effective reaction to possible juror intimidation. While it may appear that the threat posed by organised criminals to the jury trial jeopardises the justice system itself, the phenomenon of juror intimidation should be seen as a serious social problem rather than a profound crisis which has the potential to subvert the operation of State organs. In other words, less radical responses such as anonymity, which will be examined below, should be adopted rather than omitting a key component that generally is available to defendants in criminal trials for serious offences. As previously noted in chapter three, often in both rhetoric and practice there is an elision of the distinction between social problem and national emergency, and this is exemplified by the use of non-jury trials.[177] Organised crime in the UK and Ireland has not infiltrated the arms of government nor does it seem likely to compromise the pursuit of justice in a systematic way, and therefore it is questionable whether the complete attrition of the traditional right to a jury trial is warranted for certain defendants. Indeed, without the scheme provided for in Ireland in the Offences Against the State Act 1939, it is questionable whether legislation would have been enacted to dispense with jury trials for those suspected of organised criminality.[178] As the Special Criminal Court is now seen as a normal feature of the Irish criminal justice system, there is little political or popular pressure to dispense with it,[179] and the same approach is now entrenched in England, Wales and Northern Ireland.

B. Alternative Protections for Jurors

Other measures, which may safeguard juries from threats in suspected organised crime cases, include limiting the right to inspect the jury list, anonymising the jury and transporting jurors from another district. These may mitigate the threats to individuals and the challenges to effective crime control that juror intimidation poses, while remaining cognisant of the rights of the defendant.

One feasible option would be to limit the existing right to inspect the panel from which the jurors will be drawn.[180] The right to inspect is predicated on transparency regarding potential jurors but, to be sure, the potential for intimidation exists in this regard, given that the names of the jurors chosen could be matched

---

[177] B Hudson, *Justice in the Risk Society* (London, Sage, 2003) 218.

[178] Committee to Review the Offences Against the State Acts, 'Views and Recommendations of the Hon Mr Justice Hederman', n 110, para 9.93.

[179] G Hogan and C Walker, *Political Violence and the Law in Ireland* (Manchester, Manchester University Press, 1989) 238–39. Indeed, the previous Minister for Justice announced in 2004 that a second special court would be established to expedite trials, although this did not occur. Department of Justice, Equality and Law Reform Press Release, 'Minister Announces Establishment of Second Special Criminal Court' (Dublin, Department of Justice, Equality and Law Reform, 2004).

[180] Juries Act 1974, s 5 (England and Wales); Juries Act 1976, s 16 (Ireland).

with the initial panel list to find their addresses.[181] The Irish Court of Criminal Appeal emphasised that the list of the jury panel should be returned once its usefulness has been exhausted; this was deemed to be 'in the interest of the due administration of justice as it serves to prevent jury intimidation'.[182] This comment is perhaps an optimistic view, in that a copy of the list could easily be made in the interim, thereby permitting the retention of any necessary details to make a connection between the jury members and the initial panel. Rather, the right to inspect could be abolished without compromising the integrity of the jury trial itself, thereby safeguarding both the members and the institution of the jury, without compromising the rights of the defendant.

The right to inspect the jury list has been abolished in Northern Ireland, but this has not occurred in the rest of the UK or in Ireland. Schedule 2 of the Northern Ireland Act 2007 removes this right, and places restrictions on the disclosure of juror information by court, electoral and police officers as well as by jurors themselves.[183] In *Re McParland* the applicants challenged the compatibility of these provisions with Article 6 of the ECHR which protects the right to a fair trial, claiming a breach of the right to peremptory challenge of jurors and the right to be informed of the jurors' identity.[184] As the Northern Ireland High Court of Justice noted, neither such right is protected by Article 6 expressly, nor is trial by jury necessary for a fair hearing of a criminal charge.[185] The Court conceded that if one knows nothing about a juror, one cannot know anything about the reasons why she might be unsuitable to serve as a member of that particular jury trying the defendant.[186] Nevertheless, it felt that 'the value of knowing the name and address of a potential juror must not be overstated' and that preserving the integrity of the trial process required anonymisation which would provide considerable reassurance to potential jurors and diminish the risk of intimidation.[187] It concluded that the applicants' claim, that the right to a fair trial under Article 6 of the ECHR was compromised, neglected the safeguards that a properly regulated trial provides.[188]

In addition, and more radically, jurors could be anonymised, such as has occurred in limited instances in the United States in the trial of suspected organised criminals.[189] In *United States v Gotti*, for example, the jurors were referred to by number only, were housed in a secret location, and their telephone calls, mail and visits were monitored. The names of the jurors were not revealed to State and

---

[181] See M Coen, 'Elephants in the Room: The Law Reform Commission's Consultation Paper on Jury Service – Part II' (2010) 20 *Irish Criminal Law Journal* 98.

[182] *DPP v Ward* [2011] IECCA 31.

[183] Juries (Northern Ireland) Order 1996, SI 1996/1141 (NI 6), Art 26A (as inserted by s 10 of the Northern Ireland Act 2007).

[184] *Re McParland* [2008] NIQB 1.

[185] ibid, [48].

[186] ibid, [41].

[187] ibid, [42] and [43].

[188] ibid, [44].

[189] See, eg *United States v Barnes* 604 F 2d 121 (2nd Cir 1979), cert den 446 US 907 (1980) and *United States v Nicodemo Scarfo aka 'The Little Guy'* 850 F2d 1015 (1988).

defence counsel, to the defendants, nor to the trial judge. Such juror anonymity may protect the members of the jury, may assure its and their privacy, and ensure impartiality,[190] as well as enhancing the participation of citizens in jury service, the quality of jury deliberations, and ultimately the fairness of criminal verdicts.[191] These matters are seen as of particular importance in the prosecution of suspected organised crimes and members of organised crime groups. Nonetheless, the same problems regarding equality arise as in relation to non-jury trials.[192] Furthermore, having anonymous jurors in some instances may only stigmatise and suggest a degree of danger about the individual and possibly lead to bias on the part of the jurors against the defendant.[193]

Alternative, less drastic, and more equitable means of safeguarding the jury would be to hold trials without the jury present in court but rather viewing the proceedings by closed-circuit television, or to transport juries to the court from a distance so that they could not be followed. Goldstock further suggests the possibility of creating a structure that permits citizen participation while minimising the likelihood of juror intimidation through the use of a couple of 'jurors' who would advise the judge as to questions of fact but whose advice would not bind the judge.[194] These seem like moderate and careful proposals that are cognisant of the competing demands and tension in the jury trial.

C. Concluding Comments on Non-jury Trials

Intimidation of jurors and jury-tampering are seen as ineluctable concerns in the prosecution of organised crime, and are dealt with in the most radical way by removing the jury from the process altogether. This approach is used sparingly. As was noted by the English Court of Appeal in *R v J, S and M*, the trial of a serious criminal offence without a jury 'remains and must remain the decision of last resort'.[195] While in that case there was in fact a real and present danger of jury tampering, the Court concluded that the necessary protective measures would not impose an unacceptable burden on the jurors, given that the estimated length of the trial was two weeks, nor would the jury be inhibited from giving the case proper attention if they were properly managed and directed.[196] Similarly, in *KS v R* a 'fairly limited level of jury protection' was deemed to be sufficient to outweigh

---

[190] *United States v Barnes*, para 68; *Nicodemo Scarfo aka 'The Little Guy'*. See A Abramovsky, 'Juror Safety: The Presumption of Innocence and Meaningful Voir Dire in Federal Criminal Prosecutions – Are They Endangered Species?' (1981) 50 *Fordham Law Review* 1.

[191] NJ King, 'Nameless Justice: The Case for the Routine Use of Anonymous Juries in Criminal Trials' (1996) 49 *Vanderbilt Law Review* 123.

[192] See above, n 150.

[193] B Rastgoufard, 'Pay Attention to that Green Curtain: Anonymity and the Courts' (2003) 53 *Case Western Reserve Law Review* 1009, 1012.

[194] R Goldstock, *Organised Crime in Northern Ireland: A Report for the Secretary of State* (Belfast, Northern Ireland Office, 2004) para 5.15.

[195] *R v J, S and M* [2010] EWCA Crim 1755 [8].

[196] ibid, [7].

the potential threat of jury tampering.[197] Essentially the courts in England, Wales and Northern Ireland interpret the relevant provisions in the Criminal Justice Act 2003 very strictly, leading to very few cases being heard without a jury.

Moreover, the Irish DPP does not direct the hearing of an inordinate number of cases in the Special Criminal Court. In 2010 there were 16 non-jury trials (including both scheduled and non-scheduled offences); this was an increase from 10 trials in 2009, although the number of accused persons before the Court decreased from 31 to 21.[198] The most common offence was membership of an unlawful organisation, but other suspected crimes tried without a jury included the possession of firearms, ammunition or an explosive substance, false imprisonment and violent disorder,[199] and thus may encompass some typical organised crimes.

The limited use of these provisions does not mitigate the rights' concerns already raised. Nonetheless, given that juror intimidation is a live and real issue, the possibility of sequestration and anonymisation needs to be available in extraordinary circumstances, limited to the small number of cases in which the jurors truly are in danger of being tampered with, and where no alternative protective measures would suffice. It may be argued that the potential threat posed to juries in cases involving organised crime is such that non-jury trials are crucial for their protection and for the successful prosecution and conviction of such criminals. Though security may be enhanced during a jury trial itself, afterwards jurors may be threatened or endangered, and this prospect or fear may alter their decision. Thus, doing away with the jury completely may in fact represent the only legitimate and effective reaction to possible juror intimidation.

The crux of the matter concerning Ireland is its size and population: Ireland has a population of about 4.5 million people, thus rendering the nature of social interaction rather different than in larger jurisdictions. Communities are often close knit, identities may be confirmed readily and people located easily. As Davis claims, there are economies of scale regarding the maintenance of anonymity of the jury,[200] and thus comparing Ireland with jurisdictions such as the United States in this respect may be misconceived.[201] Again, the possibility of transporting juries to the court from a distance to guard against them being followed may not prove practicable in Ireland, given the size of the country. Hence, if these alternatives are not workable or sufficient in Ireland, one may conclude that a scheme permitting non-jury trials is warranted for some suspected organised crime cases, but this must be based on a system resembling the English model. In other words, the decision should rest with the superior courts, rather than with the Director of Public Prosecutions or the legislature through the scheduling of offences.

[197] *KS v R* [2010] EWCA Crim 1756.
[198] Courts Service, *Courts Service Annual Report 2010* (Dublin, Courts Service, 2011) 46.
[199] ibid, 49.
[200] F Davis, *The History and Development of the Special Criminal Court, 1922–2005* (Dublin, Four Courts Press 2007) 151.
[201] Committee to Review the Offences Against the State Acts, 'Views and Recommendations of the Hon Mr Justice Hederman', n 110, para 9.29.

V. Threats to Witnesses

In addition to legal amendments pertaining to the jury, the threats posed to witnesses by organised crime have led to the use across the UK and Ireland of protective measures, the admissibility in court of previous inconsistent evidence, the creation of Witness Protection Programmes, and ultimately has culminated in the use of anonymous witnesses. Negotiating the tension in this respect between crime control and due process is difficult, although as will be outlined, the situation for witnesses can be improved in some instances without compromising due process protections unduly.

A. Special Measures

Certain protections may be provided for intimidated and vulnerable witnesses, not just those involved in cases relating to organised crime. Such special measures include giving evidence in private;[202] before a commissioner;[203] through an intermediary;[204] with a supporter;[205] from behind a screen or by means of a live television link;[206] or by means of a sworn deposition[207] or a recording of evidence made at a time when 'those events were fresh in the person's memory'.[208] This is generally a fact-based eligibility, rather than one based on status, as is the case regarding child witnesses, for example. Originally, a witness would be eligible if the quality of her evidence would be reduced due to fear or distress about testifying, and this may include the accused in Scotland, but not elsewhere.[209] In England and Wales, witnesses in proceedings for specified gun and knife crimes have automatic eligibility, although this may be declined by the witness.[210] In addition, courts in England, Wales or Northern Ireland may prohibit any matter or fact relating to an adult witness from being included in any publication during the lifetime of the witness if it is likely to lead members of the public to identify him as a witness in criminal proceedings.[211]

Measures seeking to protect intimidated and vulnerable witnesses have been challenged on the basis that they undermine and conflict with the right to

---

[202] Youth Justice and Criminal Evidence Act 1999, s 25.

[203] Criminal Procedure (Scotland) Act 1995, s 271I.

[204] Youth Justice and Criminal Evidence Act 1999, s 29; Criminal Evidence Act 1992, s 14 (Ireland).

[205] Criminal Procedure (Scotland) Act 1995, s 271L.

[206] Criminal Justice Act 2003, s 51 and Youth Justice and Criminal Evidence Act 1999, ss 23 and 24; Criminal Procedure (Scotland) Act 1995, ss 271J and 271K; Criminal Evidence Act 1992, s 13 (Ireland).

[207] Criminal Procedure Act 1967, s 4G(3), as inserted by s 9 of the Criminal Justice Act 1999.

[208] Criminal Justice Act 2003, s 137.

[209] Criminal Procedure (Scotland) Act 1995, s 271; Youth Justice and Criminal Evidence Act 1999, s 17(1).

[210] See Youth Justice and Criminal Evidence Act 1999, s 17 and Sch 1A (as amended and inserted by the Coroners and Justice Act 2009).

[211] Youth Justice and Criminal Evidence Act 1999, s 46.

cross-examine or to confrontation, as protected by the ECHR and the Irish Constitution. Article 6(3)(d) of the ECHR guarantees everyone charged with a criminal offence the right to examine or have examined witnesses against him and to obtain the attendance and examination of witnesses on his behalf under the same conditions as witnesses against him, while the Irish Supreme Court has held that a crucial aspect of the constitutional concept of fair procedures is for an accused person 'to hear and test by examination the evidence offered by or on behalf of his accuser'.[212]

Kostovski v Netherlands indicates that special measures such as screens are ECHR-compliant.[213] The European Court noted that

> [i]n principle, all the evidence must be produced in the presence of the accused at a public hearing with a view to adversarial argument. This does not mean, however, that in order to be used as evidence statements of witnesses should always be made at a public hearing in court: to use as evidence such statements obtained at the pre-trial stage is not in itself inconsistent with paragraphs (3)(d) and (1) of Article 6, provided the rights of the defence have been respected. As a rule, these rights require that an accused should be given an adequate and proper opportunity to challenge and question a witness against him, either at the time the witness was making his statement or at some later stage of the proceedings.

Similarly, in Ireland, the giving of evidence by vulnerable witnesses (namely children and alleged victims of sexual or violent offences) by video-link was upheld as constitutional in the High Court in *White v Ireland* and subsequently by the Supreme Court in *Donnelly v Ireland*.[214] Hamilton J in *Donnelly* emphasised that an 'essential component' of the fundamental constitutional right to a fair trial is 'hearing and testing the evidence of his accuser'. The Supreme Court stressed that although there is no specific right of confrontation in Ireland, the central concern of the constitutional requirements of due process and fair procedures is the same, namely to ensure the fairness of the trial of an accused person. This involves the rigorous testing by cross-examination of the evidence against the accused. The Court concluded that giving evidence through video-link did not restrict the rights of the accused, and rejected the contention that a false accuser could lie more easily when not in the physical presence of the accused. The right to a fair trial was deemed to be safeguarded by the cross-examination of the witness, the giving of evidence on oath and the ability of the court and jury to observe both of these.[215] Thus, it appears that special measures like video-links conform to the ECHR and to constitutional law in Ireland.[216]

---

[212] *State (Healy) v Donoghue*, n 4, 335–36.

[213] *Kostovski v Netherlands* (1989) 12 EHRR 434, para 41.

[214] *White v Ireland* [1995] 2 IR 268; *Donnelly v Ireland* [1998] 1 IR 321, 356. See pt III of the Criminal Evidence Act 1992.

[215] *Donnelly v Ireland* [1998] 1 IR 321, 356.

[216] L Hoyano, 'Striking a Balance between the Rights of Defendants and Vulnerable Witnesses: Will Special Measures Directions Contravene Guarantees of a Fair Trial?' [2001] *Crim LR* 948. This is equivalent to the judgment of the majority of the US Supreme Court in *Maryland v Craig* 497 US 836 (1989) which, when considering similarly measures in light of the Confrontation Clause, also concluded that it did not guarantee an absolute right to a face-to-face meeting at trial with the witnesses against them.

Such techniques seem to provide a reasonable means of addressing the problem of witness intimidation while preserving the right to cross-examine or to confront, albeit in an attenuated form. Although cross-examination has been described as 'the greatest legal engine ever invented for the discovery of truth',[217] empirical evidence suggests that witness demeanour is not representative of veracity,[218] and problematic tactics sometimes are employed in cross-examination.[219] Nonetheless, in the adversarial context, cross-examination undeniably is an effective means of challenging and assessing a witness's testimony by looking for 'omission, embroidery, or implausibility'.[220] As Park highlights, a key benefit of cross-examination is that it facilitates such questioning that may commit a lying witness to a story that may be disproven conclusively.[221] The absence of this ability would undoubtedly compromise the reliability of a witness's testimony, but special measures tread a careful ground in seeking to reconcile the accused's Article 6 rights, the witness's interest in safety, and society's interest in dealing with criminality, thereby ensuring that the demands of crime control do not impinge greatly on due process.

B. Previous Inconsistent Evidence

As noted, it is not uncommon for some witnesses to feel apprehension about testifying at trial, and if the statutory requirements are met they may use the various protective measures previously outlined. Such anxiety may occur in relation to suspected organised criminality, particularly regarding acts alleged to have been committed by or on behalf of a criminal organisation. In certain cases, a witness may feel such pressure, trepidation or fear as to alter his previous statements that were provided to agents of the State, leading to an inconsistency between his original words and those uttered at trial. As a result, policy makers have focused on the need to admit such prior statements as evidence as to the facts in them, rather than just speaking to the lack of credibility of the witness's testimony at trial. Notwithstanding contradiction with his testimony at trial, admitting prior statements as evidence of the facts in them has been deemed necessary so as to address adequately organised criminal groups who are believed to intimidate and pressurise potential witnesses.

---

[217] J Wigmore, *Evidence* (Boston, Little, Brown and Company, 1974) 32.

[218] JP Timony, 'Demeanor Credibility' (2000) 49 *Catholic University Law Review* 903, 905; J Blumenthal, 'A Wipe of the Hands, A Lick of the Lips: The Validity of Demeanor Evidence in Assessing Witness Credibility' (1993) 72 *Nebraska Law Review* 1157, 1189; OG Wellbor, 'Demeanor' (1991) 76 *Cornell Law Review* 1075, 1088.

[219] L Ellison, 'The Mosaic Art? Cross-examination and the Vulnerable Witness' (2001) 21 *Legal Studies* 353.

[220] HR Uviller, 'Credence, Character, and the Rules of Evidence: Seeing through the Liar's Tale' (1993) 42 *Duke Law Journal* 776, 782.

[221] R Park, 'Empirical Evaluation of the Hearsay Rule' in P Mirfield and R Smith (eds), *Essays for Colin Tapper* (London, Lexis Nexis, 2003) 101.

At common law, such a previous inconsistent statement cast doubt on the evidence of the witness by impugning his credibility.[222] As Walsh J stated in the Irish Court of Criminal Appeal in *People (AG) v Taylor*:

> It must at all times be made clear to the jury that what the witness said in the written statement is not evidence of the fact referred to but is only evidence on the question of whether or not she has said something else – it is evidence going only to his credibility.[223]

The fact that such prior inconsistent statements could not constitute evidence as to the facts in them posed significant problems for the prosecution, particularly in cases where the evidence against an accused rested solely on an individual recounting his statement.

While this common law rule was amended first in Canada in the 1980s by judicial dictum,[224] statutory amendment has occurred since in many jurisdictions, including England, Wales, Northern Ireland and Ireland. Nonetheless, in Scotland, prior statements remain evidence of the witness's credibility only, not evidence of its facts.[225] Prior statements are admissible only as evidence of any matter stated in it in Scotland if the witness, in the course of giving evidence, indicates that he made the statement and that he adopts it as his evidence.[226]

The Criminal Justice Act 2003 in England and Wales admits a previous inconsistent statement of a person giving oral evidence in criminal proceedings as evidence of the facts in it,[227] as does the Criminal Justice (Evidence) (Northern Ireland) Order 2004.[228] As noted by the English Court of Appeal, one of the reasons for introducing such a measure is

> to deal with the issue of witnesses who are too frightened to admit that their original statement is true. The jury are entitled to look at all of the circumstances and then to decide that in fact the contents of the statement are true and that the witness' denial of the contents can be disregarded.[229]

In Ireland, the equivalent measure, in Part 3 of the Criminal Justice Act 2006, was introduced in response to the collapse of a much publicised murder trial in Limerick in 2003, where six witnesses who had given statements to the Gardaí previously recanted and refused to give evidence against the accused in court, resulting in a direction of *nolle prosequi* by the Director of Public Prosecutions.[230] The Minister for Justice at the time articulated the incensed reaction of policy

---

[222]   Criminal Procedure Act 1865, s 4.

[223]   *The People (AG) v Taylor* [1974] IR 97, 100.

[224]   *R v B (KG)* [1993] 1 SCR 740.

[225]   *Muldoon v Herron* 1970 JC 30.

[226]   Criminal Procedure (Scotland) Act 1995, s 260.

[227]   Criminal Justice Act 2003, s 119.

[228]   Criminal Justice (Evidence) (Northern Ireland) Order 2004, Art 23.

[229]   *R v Gibbons* [2008] EWCA Crim 1574, [2009] Crim LR 197, para 11.

[230]   See Dáil Debates, vol 597, col 1283 (15 February 2005) per Minister for Justice, Mr McDowell. Carney J described the witnesses as suffering from 'collective amnesia'. See 'A Case of Collective Amnesia', *Irish Times*, 8 November 2003; and 'Witness Denies Identifying Accused to Gardaí', *Irish Times*, 4 November 2003.

makers and the media, referring to the challenge the situation represented 'for the Irish State, for the rights of individual citizens and of entire communities, and for the system of criminal justice',[231] and a Circuit Court Judge claimed that society was in danger of descending into a 'state of social chaos and anarchy'.[232]

The essence of these provisions in England, Wales, Northern Ireland and Ireland is to allow previous inconsistent statements to become evidence of the truth of matters contained within them, rather than going towards the credibility of the witness solely. While the Irish measure allows for the admissibility of previous witness statements in criminal cases where the witness refuses to give evidence in court or gives evidence which is inconsistent with the earlier statement,[233] its equivalent in England and Wales appears to have no application if the witness remains completely silent or does not testify.[234] In such situations in Scotland evidence may be given in chief in the form of a prior statement.[235]

In Canada, the jurisdiction held as an exemplar in this respect, prior inconsistent statements are admissible if the statement was made under oath following an explicit warning to the witness as to the existence of severe criminal sanctions for the making of a false statement; it must be video-recorded in its entirety; and the opposing party must be able to cross-examine the witness at trial.[236] In Ireland the prior statement must be voluntary, reliable and made by the witness in circumstances where he understood the need to tell the truth,[237] and when deciding whether the statement is reliable, the court shall have regard to whether it was given on oath or was video-recorded, or if neither, whether other evidence exists in support of its reliability.[238] Moreover, the statement will not be admitted if it is not in the interests of justice to do so or if its admission is unnecessary.[239] Before the enactment of the Criminal Justice Act 2006 in Ireland, the Irish Human Rights Commission recommended that all witness statements admitted under Part 3 should be sworn on oath, video-recorded in their entirety and made in the presence of and after consultation with the witness's legal representative.[240] Regrettably, these proposals were not incorporated into the Act.

The measures admitting a previous inconsistent statement in England, Wales and Northern Ireland are rather more terse; the Court of Appeal noted in *R v Billingham* that it is by no means easy to direct a jury without causing confusion

---

[231] Dáil Debates, vol 573, col 579 (4 November 2003) per Minister for Justice, Mr McDowell.

[232] See 'Judge in Previous Trial Warned of "Anarchy"', *Irish Times*, 5 November 2003.

[233] This measure was first used in May 2007 in the Central Criminal Court in Limerick. See 'Man Acquitted as Jury Hears Contradictory Evidence', *Irish Times*, 3 May 2007.

[234] See D Ormerod, 'Case Comment: Previous Inconsistent Statements: Directing Juries in Relation to Previous Inconsistent Statements in View of Effect and Application of s 119 of the Criminal Justice Act 2003' [2009] *Crim LR* 529, 531.

[235] Criminal Procedure (Scotland) Act 1995, s 271M.

[236] *R v B (KG)* [1993] 1 SCR 740.

[237] Criminal Justice Act 2006, s 16(2).

[238] Criminal Justice Act 2006 s 16(3).

[239] Criminal Justice Act 2006, s 16(4).

[240] Irish Human Rights Commission, *Final Observations on the Criminal Justice Bill 2004* (Dublin, Irish Human Rights Commission, 2004) para 5.3.

about the effect of the provision admitting a previous inconsistent statement as evidence of the facts in it.[241] However, as Ormerod observed, a safeguard exists in the form of the duty requiring the court to stop a jury trial where an out of court statement, on which the case is wholly or partly based, is so unconvincing that conviction would be unsafe.[242]

A further divergence between the model in Ireland and that advocated by the Canadian Supreme Court concerns the cross-examination of the witness whose previous statement is being tendered as evidence. While the Canadian Court imposed a requirement that the opposing party must be able to cross-examine the witness at trial, no equivalent provision exists in Ireland. Admitting an out-of-court witness statement as evidence where the witness refuses to testify seriously undermines the right of the defence to effectively hear and cross-examine the evidence against him, which is fundamental to the adversarial criminal process and the notion of due process.[243] As the Irish Supreme Court has held, and as previously noted, the opportunity to 'hear and test by examination the evidence offered by or on behalf of his accuser' represents a fundamental ingredient in the concept of fair procedures,[244] mirroring the protection in Article 6(3)(d) of the ECHR. Nonetheless, in *Al-Khawaja and Tahery v United Kingdom* the Grand Chamber of the European Court of Human Rights held that hearsay evidence does not prevent a fair trial automatically.[245] The Grand Chamber found that there must be a good reason for the witness's non-attendance, and that Article 6(1) may, but will not be breached automatically, if a conviction is based solely or to a decisive degree on depositions made by a person whom the accused did not cross-examine.[246] Although admission of a hearsay statement which is the sole or decisive evidence against a defendant will not automatically breach Article 6(1) the Court must subject the proceedings to 'the most searching scrutiny', and the dangers of admitting such evidence necessitates counterbalancing factors, such as strong procedural safeguards.[247] Thus, the inability to cross-examine the maker of such a prior inconsistent statement does not necessarily breach the ECHR. This is a considerable dilution of the right to cross-examine in Article 6(3)(d), and a classic elevation of crime control over due process. In addition to limiting the accused's ability to test the evidence, the jury in a criminal trial may be deprived of the opportunity to consider the witness's demeanour.

[241] *R v Billingham* [2009] EWCA Crim 19.
[242] Criminal Justice Act 2003, s 125 – see Ormerod, n 234.
[243] This criticism is not applicable to the model in England, Wales and Northern Ireland which covers contradictory statements only.
[244] *State (Healy) v Donoghue*, n 4, 335–36. See above s VA regarding the screening of witnesses etc.
[245] *Al-Khawaja and Tahery v United Kingdom* [2011] ECHR 2127. Previously the court had found there to be a breach of Art 6(1) read in conjunction with Art 6(3)(d) where use is made in evidence of the statement of a witness who does not appear before the Court because she had died, could not be traced or refused to appear, where it was the sole and decisive evidence (*Al-Khawaja and Tahery v United Kingdom* (2009) 49 EHRR 1). This decision was not followed by the UK Supreme Court in *R v Horncastle* [2009] UKSC 14 which permitted the use of hearsay evidence if sufficiently reliable to be decisive.
[246] *Al-Khawaja and Tahery v United Kingdom* [2011] ECHR 2127, para 119.
[247] ibid, para 147.

An alternative approach to admitting prior inconsistent statements would be to charge an uncooperative witness with the offence of perjury if he lies in court, or with contempt of court if he refuses to attend court or to answer any questions.[248] An uncooperative or hostile witness may also be charged with making a false report or statement to the police.[249] The English courts in particular have taken a robust approach in the past:

> [W]here victims or witnesses to serious crimes refuse to do their duty or succumb to threats or fear of reprisals by refusing to give evidence or answer questions, the result is a failure of law and order; . . . where that occurs it will normally be necessary to impose a custodial sentence of some kind in order to mark the gravity of the matter and to stiffen the resolve of other witnesses or potential witnesses who may be similarly minded to default in their duty.[250]

Nevertheless, any State should be slow to charge a threatened person with perjury or making false statements under oath unless it can guarantee the person's safety. In *C v HM Advocate* the Scottish High Court of Justiciary quashed a sentence for contempt of court and instead admonished the petitioner who was a Crown witness in a murder trial and who had perjured himself by failing to identify an accused as the person about whom he had given evidence.[251] The Scottish High Court felt that the trial judge had failed to consider the wider implications of imposing a sentence which might deter persons in close proximity to the commission of a serious crime from giving information to the police.[252]

Admitting a prior inconsistent statement furthers the ends of crime control through the more ready facilitation of conviction, but may compromise due process norms, above all the right to a fair trial. The circumscription of the right to cross-examine the witness whose statement has changed is a significant erosion of traditional due process safeguards. The crisis-driven approach to policy development in Ireland particularly has lead to the emulation of the Canadian model regarding the admission of prior inconsistent statements, with few of the protections for the accused. On the other hand, targeting the witness himself whose statements differ by means of a prosecution for perjury or contempt of court seems a heavy-handed and misguided way of dealing with coercion or intimidation. To address the problem in what is ostensibly a more protective way, and thereby assist the expedient resolution of organised crime, Witness Protection Programmes have been developed.

---

[248] Perjury Act 1911. Criminal contempt may comprise contempt in the face of the court, scandalising the court, breaches of the *sub judice* rule and other interferences with the administration of justice, such as threatening a witness. See Law Reform Commission, *Report on Contempt of Court* (Dublin, Law Reform Commission, 1994) para 2.7.

[249] Criminal Law Act 1967, s 5(2) (England and Wales); Criminal Law Act (Northern Ireland) 1967, s 5(3); Criminal Law Act 1976, s 12 (Ireland); *Kerr v Hill* 1936 JC 71 (Scotland).

[250] *R v Montgomery* [1995] 2 All ER 28, 33. See DW Elliott, 'Securing the Evidence of Criminal Associates' [1999] *Crim LR* 349, 352.

[251] *C v HM Advocate* [2010] HCJAC 89.

[252] ibid, [15].

C. Witness Protection Programmes

The use of testimony from participants in Witness Protection Programmes (WPP) has been sanctioned in the UK and Ireland and is used in trials for suspected organised crimes, amongst others. The first such programme worldwide was the Federal Witness Security Program in the United States (known as WITSEC), established by the Organised Crime Control Act 1970.[253] In the US this programme first related to organised crime only, and then was expanded to include witnesses to other serious crimes.[254] In the UK, the Metropolitan Police in London and the Royal Ulster Constabulary, now the Police Service for Northern Ireland, have provided protection for witnesses in cases of serious and terrorist crime since the late-1970s.[255] Since then, many more police forces have established specialist units to protect and relocate witnesses.[256] A national English and Welsh scheme was mooted so as to ensure consistency between agencies and to deliver higher standards and savings, and to this end a review was undertaken,[257] but such a national structure has not been enacted. The first witness protection scheme in Scotland was initiated in 1996 by Strathclyde Police, later developing into the national Scottish Witness Protection Unit (SWPU) which in 2003 came within the remit of the Scottish Crime and Drug Enforcement Agency (SCDEA). The SWPU provides a service to all Scottish police forces and law enforcement agencies in cases where witnesses are considered to be under significant threat and it devises plans to deal with each case relating to support, relocation and/or identity change.

Although there is no overarching national WPP in the UK, there is now one relevant piece of legislation: chapter 4 of the Serious Organised Crime and Police Act 2005.[258] A protection provider (that is, a chief officer/constable of a police force, the Director General of SOCA, a Revenue and Customs Commissioner or a person designated by same)[259] may make arrangements to protect a person ordinarily resident in the UK if he considers that the person's safety is at risk due to his being a person described in Schedule 5.[260] Schedule 5 refers, inter alia, to witnesses, jurors, justices

---

[253] See N Fyfe, *Protecting Intimidated Witnesses* (Aldershot, Ashgate, 2001); N Fyfe and J Sheptycki, *Facilitating Witness Cooperation in Organised Crime Cases: An International Review* (London, Home Office Online Report, 2005) iii.

[254] Comprehensive Crime Control Act 1984.

[255] N Fyfe and H McKay, 'Witness Intimidation, Forced Migration and Resettlement: A British Case Study' (2000) 25 *Transactions of the Institute of British Geographers* 77, 79–80.

[256] ibid.

[257] Home Office, n 1, para 6.4.

[258] A Sewel motion was passed in relation to the Serious Organised Crime and Police Bill on the basis that Scottish witnesses at risk are generally relocated elsewhere in the UK, that there is considerable collaboration across the UK, and that failing to extend the provisions to Scotland simultaneously would have the undesirable effect of leading to different laws across the UK. Scottish Executive, *Sewel Memorandum: Serious Organised Crime and Police Bill* (Edinburgh, Scottish Executive, 2004) para 26; SP OR col 14143–65 (2 February 2005).

[259] Serious Organised Crime and Police Act 2005, s 82(5).

[260] Serious Organised Crime and Police Act 2005, s 82(1).

of the peace, prosecutors, holders of an immunity notice or restricted use under-taking,[261] and staff (previous or present) of agencies such as the Revenue and Customs Prosecutions Office, Customs and Excise, SOCA, the Assets Recovery Agency, police and prison officers, or someone who is a family member of such a person or has or had a close personal relationship with such a person. In making such a decision, the protection provider must have regard to the nature and extent of the risk to the person's safety, the cost of the arrangements, the likelihood that the person, and any person associated with him, will be able to adjust to changes in his circumstances, and if the person is or might be a witness in legal proceedings, the nature of these proceedings and the importance of his being a witness.[262] The Act also allows pre-existing witness protection arrangements to be regarded as statutory arrangements, if they comply with the relevant criteria, were in place immediately prior to the statute's enactment, and if the protection provider so agrees within six months of the relevant section coming into force.[263]

Participants in the WPP may need to lie to maintain their new identities, and to construct a false narrative regarding their history and so on. The Serious Organised Crime and Police Act 2005 takes account of this and permits false representations to be made by a protected person who has assumed a new identity, a person associated with him, or a protection provider, if this is made solely to guard the effectiveness of the arrangements made for him.[264] It is an offence to disclose information about protection arrangements if the individual knows or suspects that the information relates to the making of such arrangements.[265] However a person is not guilty of this offence if he was a protected person at the time of dis-closure, if the information related only to arrangements made for his protection and if it was not likely that its disclosure would endanger the safety of any person,[266] or if disclosure was made in similar circumstances but by a third party with agreement from the protected person.[267] It is also an offence to disclose information relating to a person who has assumed a new identity, whether that is by the protected person himself or by a third party.[268] It is a defence that it was not likely that disclosure would endanger anyone's safety, and the protected person agreed to this disclosure.[269] Disclosure is also permitted to safeguard national security or for the purposes of the prevention, detection or investigation of crime.[270] This latter aspect is rather broad and may prove problematic in terms of implementation. Moreover, the Act does not limit this ability to divulge details to prevent or detect crime to official or State bodies.

---

[261] See above, n 63ff.
[262] Serious Organised Crime and Police Act 2005, s 82(4).
[263] Serious Organised Crime and Police Act 2005, s 91.
[264] Serious Organised Crime and Police Act 2005, s 90.
[265] Serious Organised Crime and Police Act 2005, s 86.
[266] Serious Organised Crime and Police Act 2005, s 87(1).
[267] Serious Organised Crime and Police Act 2005, s 87(2).
[268] Serious Organised Crime and Police Act 2005, s 88.
[269] Serious Organised Crime and Police Act 2005, s 89.
[270] Serious Organised Crime and Police Act 2005, ss 87(3) and 89(3).

In Ireland the Witness Protection Programme remains a police-operated system rather than a judicial one, and no legislation exists governing its parameters and procedures. Again, this is a typical illustration of the crime control model, where administrative, *ad hoc* and fluid mechanisms in the criminal justice system are favoured. This state of affairs arguably contravenes the Council of Europe Recommendation which requires an 'adequate legal framework' for WPPs.[271] In the trial of John Gilligan for drug trafficking in which the evidence of numerous people in the WPP was relied upon, the Irish Court of Criminal Appeal commented that the WPP was never actually a programme, was badly thought-out, and lacked clear guidelines concerning what benefits could or could not be offered to the witnesses,[272] and similarly, the Irish Supreme Court noted that the Programme was not well-organised or executed and had deficiencies; nonetheless, and incongruously, this was not deemed to be fatal to its operation or legitimacy.[273] The Programme for Government in 2011 contained a commitment to provide statutory guidelines for the Witness Security Programme although a similar suggestion was opposed previously on the ground that it could be too inflexible and limit people's participation in the WPP.[274] Nonetheless the Witness Protection Programme was acknowledged on a statutory basis in the Criminal Justice Act 1999 which creates an offence of trying to contact a relocated witness without lawful authority.[275] Section 40(3) recognises that witnesses may be relocated or assigned new names or identities on the grounds that they have given evidence in a trial and consequently have moved residence under a programme operated by the Garda Síochána for the protection of witnesses.

According to Garda guidelines, participation in the Irish WPP is available only to witnesses with evidence to offer in relation to serious crimes such as drug trafficking and organised crime, and this evidence must be essential to the prosecution and not available elsewhere.[276] The witness may be an accomplice or associate of the suspect.[277] Moreover, a substantial threat to the safety of the witness must exist,[278] but importantly, a witness may refuse to participate in the Programme, notwithstanding that a threat has been made to his life.[279]

---

[271] Council of Europe Committee of Ministers, Recommendation Rec (2005)9 of the Committee of Ministers to Member States on the protection of witnesses and collaborators of justice, III 24.

[272] *Gilligan*, Court of Criminal Appeal, n 163.

[273] *Gilligan*, Supreme Court, n 53, heading 8.8.

[274] See www.taoiseach.gov.ie/eng/Publications/Publications_2011/Programme_for_Government_2011.pdf and for criticism see Seanad Debates, vol 187, cols 900 and 913 (31 October 2007).

[275] Criminal Justice Act 1999, s 40.

[276] See An Garda Síochána, 'Written Submission by Mr Noel Conroy, Commissioner of an Garda Síochána to the Joint Committee on Justice, Equality, Defence and Women's Rights', 9 December 2003, Appendix 3: HQ Circular no: 31(L)/97; Date: 3 December 1997.

[277] An Garda Síochána Circular, n 276. See above n 41.

[278] An Garda Síochána, *Evaluation of an Garda Síochána Policing Plan 1999* (Dublin, An Garda Síochána, 2000) 25.

[279] eg Owen Treacy, who was the key witness for the State in the trial of the five men for the murder of his uncle Kieran Keane in Limerick in 2003, refused to join the WPP. See 'Keane Witness Refuses to Join Protection Programme', *Irish Times*, 22 December 2003.

Beyond the lack of statutory regulation of the WPP in Ireland, problematic issues arise in relation to such schemes in general, including their failure to address the cause of witness intimidation, the effects of relocation on the witness and family, the method of witness recruitment, the type of people recruited and their motivations, and the preparation of such witnesses for trial.[280]

Much criticism has been made of the exorbitant cost of the WPP in the United States.[281] There are no publicly available figures for the UK: requests for such figures were rejected on the basis that release of such information could compromise investigations, the WPP itself and the safety of individuals involved.[282] Media reports suggest a cost of £22m per annum, though these figures have never been confirmed.[283] In Ireland, the annual cost of the Programme rarely creeps above €1m[284] which is a very small fraction of the criminal justice budget overall.

Although WPPs have been described as 'concerted government supported subterfuge',[285] they constitute a fundamental means of addressing organised crime, and so require sufficient resources, skilled personnel and political will.[286] They represent a key dimension of the crime control reaction to organised crime, without which prosecution of more serious participants may be difficult. Nonetheless, WPP are essentially a situational means of dealing with witness intimidation and may displace rather than address the problem they seek to address, and focus on the minimisation of risk rather than the reasons behind the intimidation.[287] Moreover, one key issue which is often overlooked is the effect on the social and psychological well-being of relocated witnesses and families,[288] given that the success or value of WPPs is usually viewed in terms of the physical security of the witnesses and their participation in the legal process.[289] Participation is far from an appealing prospect for the witnesses: as the Court of Appeal in England and Wales stated, witness relocation is practicable in the rarest of circumstances due to the 'tumultuous' interference with the life of such a witness.[290]

WPPs are a prototypical tactic of the crime control model of criminal justice, embodying a pragmatic response to organised criminality and requiring an adaptation of traditional norms and processes. Despite the value of such programmes

---

[280] Hillyard, n 47, 300.

[281] RJ Lawson, 'Lying, Cheating and Stealing at Government Expense: Striking a Balance between the Public Interest and the Interests of the Public in the Witness Protection Program' (1992) 24 *Arizona State Law Journal* 1429.

[282] Police Service of Northern Ireland, *Freedom of Information Request Number f-2009-00914 Witness Protection Programme*, available at www.psni.police.uk/witness_protection_programme.pdf.

[283] 'The Criminals' New Lives that Cost us Millions', *The Telegraph*, 16 August 2009.

[284] Dáil Debates, WA vol 739 (19 July 2011).

[285] Lawson, n 281, 1455.

[286] F Allum and N Fyfe, 'Developments in State Witness Protection Programmes: The Italian Experience in an International Comparative Perspective' (2008) 2 *Policing* 92, 99.

[287] N Fyfe and J Sheptycki, 'International Trends in the Facilitation of Witness Cooperation in Organized Crime Cases' (2006) 3 *European Journal of Criminology* 319, 333.

[288] Allum and Fyfe, n 288.

[289] Fyfe and Sheptycki, n 287, 334.

[290] *R v Mayers, Glasgow, Costelloe and Bahmanzadeh* [2008] EWCA Crim 2989, [2009] 1 WLR 1915 [9].

in terms of crime control, there exists potential for abuse, and the rights of the accused and moreover of witnesses themselves may be subsumed in the drive for successful prosecutions. This imperative of securing convictions in the face of possible intimidation has led to the introduction and use of methods that are ever more problematic in terms of due process rights.

D. Anonymous Witness Evidence

The most drastic approach in terms of seeking to remedy the problem of witness intimidation, especially in relation to organised crime, is the reliance on totally anonymised witness evidence. This is seen as warranted due to the level and nature of threats to witnesses in certain cases. This tactic is now governed by statute across the UK but has not yet been contemplated in Ireland.

The use of anonymous witness evidence through the common law was permitted by the lower courts in England until challenged in *R v Davis*[291] where the House of Lords overruled the Court of Appeal's support for such a practice. Davis had been convicted on two counts of murder, and the 'unusual feature of the trial'[292] on which his appeal turned concerned the evidence identifying him as the perpetrator. As key witnesses claimed to fear for their lives, the trial judge had made an order specifying certain 'protective measures': these witnesses gave evidence under a pseudonym; their personal details were withheld from the appellant; no question could be asked of them which might lead to their identification; their evidence was given behind a screen, and their voices were distorted. Crucially, without their testimony Davis could not have been convicted of murder.

The Court of Appeal rejected his submissions that these restrictions were contrary to common law and incompatible with the requirements of a fair trial, but certified a point of law to the House of Lords, asking if a conviction could be based solely or to a decisive extent upon the testimony of anonymous witnesses. While the reality and extent of witness intimidation was not disputed by the Law Lords,[293] the protective measures in this instance were found to have so hampered the defence as to render the trial unfair and incompatible with the ECHR.[294] Lord Bingham emphasised the long-established common law principle that a defendant should be confronted by his accusers so he may cross-examine them and challenge their evidence,[295] and found that this was undermined fatally by the totally anonymous evidence and the limitations placed on cross-examination. According to Lord Carswell, the presumption in favour of open justice and confrontation of a defendant by his accuser may be departed from only in a clear case of necessity where there is genuine reluctance and fear to give evidence, and

---

[291] *R v Davis; R v Ellis* [2006] EWCA Crim 1155, [2008] UKHL 36, [2008] 1 AC 1128.
[292] ibid, [2] per Lord Bingham.
[293] ibid, [27].
[294] ibid, [35] and [61].
[295] ibid, [5] and [24].

as a general rule it is unlikely that the trial will be fair if a very substantial degree of anonymising of evidence is permitted where the testimony of the witnesses concerned constitutes the sole or decisive evidence implicating the defendant.[296]

Although this common law right was found to pre-date the ECHR by
centuries,[297] the jurisprudence of the European Court formed a key aspect of the
decision, mirroring as it does the common law position. ECHR case law at the
time provided that while anonymous evidence is not necessarily incompatible
with the Convention, a conviction should not be based solely or to a decisive
extent upon the testimony of anonymous witnesses, even when 'counterbalancing' procedures are in place.[298]

The House of Lords concluded that any further relaxation of the common law
rule of confrontation and cross-examination was a task for Parliament and not
the courts;[299] thus, in response, the Westminster Parliament enacted emergency
legislation that was passed by both Houses in a matter of weeks. So, while the
superior court acted as a buffer of sorts in upholding due process norms in the
face of this radical crime control development, the legislature by virtue of its sovereignty remedied this speedily. The Criminal Evidence (Witness Anonymity) Act
2008 abolished the common law rules relating to anonymous witnesses in
England, Wales and Northern Ireland, and provided a statutory framework for
the making of witness anonymity orders. However, this Act contained a 'sunset'
clause due to the expedited nature of the debate on its provisions, and it was to
expire on 31 December 2009. Chapter 2 of the Coroners and Justice Act 2009
replaced the 2008 Act, and replicated its terms almost exactly.

In England, Wales and Northern Ireland a witness anonymity order may be
made on application by the prosecution or defence by a court[300] permitting certain measures to be taken to prevent disclosure of a witness's identity, such as the
use of a pseudonym, a screen or voice modulation, and by the prohibition of
questions that might lead to identification.[301] The court, however, is not authorised to require the screening or voice modulation of a witness so he cannot be
seen nor his natural voice heard by the judge or the jury (if there is one).

Three conditions must be met for a witness anonymity order to be granted: the
order must be necessary, it must be fair, and it must be in the interests of justice.[302]

[296] ibid, [59] per Lord Carswell.
[297] ibid, [24] per Lord Bingham.
[298] ibid, [75]–[77] per Lord Mance. *Kostovski v Netherlands* Series A no 166 (1989) 12 EHRR 434, para 44; *Doorson v Netherlands* (1996) 22 EHRR 330, para 76; *Van Mechelen v Netherlands* (1997) 25 EHRR 647, paras 55 and 63; *Visser v Netherlands* (ECtHR, 14 February 2002). Such counterbalancing measures in inquisitorial trials have involved the cross-examination of the magistrate who questioned the witnesses prior to trial (*Kostovski*) and the questioning of anonymous witnesses by a magistrate in front of defence counsel (*Doorson*). See *Al-Khawaja and Tahery v United Kingdom*, n 245.
[299] *Davis*, n 291, [27] per Lord Bingham; also [44]–[45] and [98].
[300] Coroners and Justice Act 2009, s 97. The 'Court' is a magistrates' court, the Crown Court or the Criminal Division of the Court of Appeal, a Northern Ireland county court exercising its criminal jurisdiction, the High Court or the Court of Appeal in Northern Ireland.
[301] Coroners and Justice Act 2009, ss 86 and 87.
[302] Coroners and Justice Act 2009, s 88. As was noted in *R v Bowe and Others* [2010] NICC 53, all three must be satisfied.

Firstly, the order must be necessary to protect the safety of the witness or another person, or to prevent serious damage to property or real harm to the public interest. In ascertaining necessity, the court must have regard in particular to any reasonable fear on the part of the witness that if he were to be identified he or another person would suffer death or injury, or that there would be serious damage to property. The Court of Appeal in *R v Mayers* rejected the argument that the defendant need be responsible personally for the threat, and held that the threat may come from any source.[303] So, the danger of intimidation may be generated by third parties such as, but not necessarily, persons associated with or paid by the defendant. The prevention of damage to property seems like a controversial inclusion given that such potential harm is unlikely to be so grave as to overwhelm the right to a fair trial.[304] Nonetheless, the potential for property damage was deemed by Parliament to feed into the decision regarding the anonymisation of witnesses. The latter criterion of harm to the public interest may be interpreted as encompassing the public interest in the investigation and successful prosecution of crime, or in protecting the identity of police informers or undercover agents, notwithstanding that their safety may not be under threat. Despite these potentially expansive aspects of the first condition, their effects are tempered by the second condition that the order must be consistent with a fair trial. Finally, the order must be in the interests of justice, by reason that it is important that the witness should testify and that without the order he would not do so or there would be real harm to the public interest if the witness were to testify without the order.

When deciding whether these conditions are met, the court must have regard to: the general right of a defendant in criminal proceedings to know witnesses' identity; the extent to which the witness's credibility would be relevant when assessing the weight of his evidence; whether the witness's evidence might be the sole or decisive evidence implicating the defendant; whether the witness's evidence could be tested properly without disclosure of his identity; whether there is reason to believe that the witness has a tendency or motive to be dishonest having regard (in particular) to any previous convictions of the witness and to any relationship between the witness and the defendant or any associates of the defendant; and whether protection of the witness by any other means would be reasonably practicable, as well as other matters the court considers relevant.[305] The judge must warn the jury to ensure that the fact that the order was made in relation to the witness does not prejudice the defendant,[306] although the effect of this warning is likely to be questionable as it suggests something dangerous or at least dubious about the individual on trial.

In contrast to the aversion in Scotland to non-jury trials and other radical amendments to criminal procedure relating to organised crime, the Criminal Justice and Licensing Act 2010 emulated developments in the rest of the UK to

---

[303] *R v Mayers*, n 290, [28].
[304] See HL Deb 10 July 2008, vol 703, cols 875–76.
[305] Coroners and Justice Act 2009, s 89.
[306] Coroners and Justice Act 2009, s 90(2).

introduce a statutory framework for witness anonymity orders. The same conditions apply regarding necessity, fairness, and the interests of justice.[307]

Since the enactment of these measures, dicta from the appellate courts in England and Wales express favour for a limited scheme of witness anonymity, based on the threat posed by a certain type of crime. The Court of Appeal has spoken of the 'undiminished' challenge posed to the rule of law 'by gun and weapon carrying individuals or members of gangs of criminals and the legitimate fears which this engenders in the public, particularly where an attack is carried out in public'.[308] Moreover, it has been emphasised that revealing the personal identities of police witnesses, particularly those working undercover, could remove their operational value, diminish the public interest in investigating crime, and compromise their safety.[309] The Court stated that ignorance of the true identity of the officer would usually not disadvantage the defendant as full cross-examination could occur using the names assumed by the witnesses or that by which the defendant knew them. Moreover, if an anonymity order is refused, the prosecution will often be stayed rather than expose the witnesses to the risk of identification.[310]

Neither the Coroners and Justice Act 2009 nor its Scottish equivalent preclude explicitly conviction based on such evidence if sole or decisive. Nevertheless, section 6 of the Human Rights Act 1998 requires the courts in the UK to apply legislation in a manner compliant with ECHR jurisprudence; so, it once seemed unlikely that anonymous witness evidence could ever constitute the sole or decisive evidence against the accused, given the dicta in *Doorson v Netherlands* and *Van Mechelen v Netherlands*, inter alia.[311] In *Mayers* the Court of Appeal noted that where there are a number of anonymous incriminating witnesses, by definition the evidence of one would not provide either the sole or decisive evidence, and that their evidence could prove sufficient to sustain a proper conviction as long as there was no improper collusion and as long as the statutory conditions are met.[312] In other words, the evidence of numerous anonymised witnesses could form the basis of a conviction, notwithstanding the inability to cross-examine in as robust a fashion as usual.

Moreover, and as was previously noted, the Grand Chamber found in *Al-Khawaja and Tahery v United Kingdom* that untested statements of anonymous or absent

---

[307] Criminal Procedure (Scotland) Act 1995, s 271R (as inserted by the Criminal Justice and Licensing Act 2010). This section has no associated Explanatory Notes.

[308] *R v Mayers*, n 290, [27].

[309] *R v Mayers*, n 290, [30]–[34]. See R Costigan and P Thomas, 'Anonymous Witnesses' (2000) 51 *Northern Ireland Legal Quarterly* 326.

[310] *R v Mayers*, n 290, [35].

[311] n 298 above. In *Doorson* two witnesses were examined anonymously in front of an investigating judge, in the presence of defence counsel who was permitted to cross-examine them but not to ask questions which would reveal identity. The Judge was aware of their identities and made a report on their evidence. In *Van Mechelen* anonymous police witnesses were interrogated before an investigating judge who also wrote a detailed report. In this case defence counsel was absent, and the testimony was the sole identifying evidence. While the *Doorson* approach was seen as permissible, the situation in *Van Mechelen* failed to comply with Art 6 of the ECHR .

[312] *R v Mayers*, n 290, [25].

witnesses that are read to the court as evidence and which are the sole or decisive basis for conviction do not automatically breach Article 6(3)(d).[313] In such instances there must be a good reason for the witness's non-attendance,[314] and if the evidence is sole or decisive the proceedings must be rigorously scrutinised.[315] The Grand Chamber found that the sole or decisive rule is not one which should be applied in an inflexible manner,[316] and that sole or decisive evidence is permitted if the witness's fear is attributable to the defendant or person acting on his behalf because 'to allow the defendant to benefit from the fear he has engendered in witnesses would be incompatible with the rights of victims and witnesses'.[317] While the Grand Chamber conceded the difficulties in ascertaining whether a defendant or his associates have threatened or directly induced fear in a witness it concluded that these are not insurmountable.[318] Any such defendant is deemed to have waived his rights to question such witnesses under Article 6(3)(d).[319]

Davis was a principled decision, which recognised the fundamental unfairness of any conviction based on uncorroborated evidence which was not tested by full and frank cross-examination. Ormerod *et al* note that, contra *Mayers*, a number of components to confrontation, namely effective cross-examination, orality and openness, are inhibited by witness anonymity orders.[320] Moreover, while ECHR jurisprudence was once sufficiently careful and cognisant of the accused's rights while still acknowledging the necessity in certain limited instances of permitting anonymous evidence, permitting such evidence even if sole and decisive is a step too far in eroding Article 6(3)(d) in attempts to prosecute organised and other serious crime. This compounds the erosion of due process rights in a bid to improve the crime control mechanisms of the State.

In contrast to the situation in the UK, there is a notable absence from official documents and legislative debate in Ireland of the notion of anonymous witnesses, despite the trend of policy transfer so often visible in criminal justice. This mirrors the aversion in the US to such an approach, despite the serious problem of witness intimidation there, and this appears to derive from the constitutional right to confrontation, as in Ireland.[321] Ultimately, the critical issue concerning the proposed use of anonymous witness evidence in Ireland is the extent to which it would comply with the right to a fair trial, as protected by Article 38.1 of the Irish Constitution: 'no person shall be tried on any criminal charge save in due

---

[313] *Al-Khawaja and Tahery v United Kingdom* (2009), n 245.

[314] ibid, [119].

[315] ibid, [147].

[316] ibid, [146].

[317] ibid, [123].

[318] ibid.

[319] ibid.

[320] D Ormerod, A Choo and R Easter, 'Coroners and Justice Act 2009: the "Witness Anonymity" and "Investigation Anonymity" Provisions' [2010] *Crim LR* 372, 386.

[321] Sixth Amendment to the US Constitution.

course of law'.[322] It thus appears that the presence of a robust protection like this has dissuaded policy makers from even considering such a measure.

Nevertheless, witness anonymity is permitted in Ireland in the context of the Proceeds of Crime Acts 1996–2003, which, as is examined in chapter seven, cannot lead to criminal conviction. Officers from the Criminal Assets Bureau are granted anonymity in all aspects of their work, including court proceedings if there are reasonable grounds in the public interest.[323] It was held in *Criminal Assets Bureau v PS* that 'there is no absolute constitutional bar to the granting of anonymity to witnesses', and anonymity was granted on the basis of police evidence that the defendant was involved in organised crime and that revealing the officer's identity would endanger his safety, because '[o]ne of the traits of organised crime is that they utilise intimidation of witnesses'.[324] In other words, a specific threat to the witness by or on behalf of the particular individual is not required under the Proceeds of Crime Acts in Ireland. However, as is explored further in chapter seven, the Irish Supreme Court has found that the process of asset forfeiture operates in the civil realm, despite its ostensible aim of targeting criminal behaviour,[325] and thus the right to a fair trial, under domestic law and Article 6(3) of the European Convention, is not engaged.

As regards criminal conviction, however, the Irish Supreme Court has stated robustly that detecting crime and convicting guilty persons cannot supersede the constitutional protections of the personal rights of the citizen.[326] This, as previously noted, is in keeping with Packer's view of the due process model's validating authority as judicial.[327] Thus, any leaning of the policy makers towards anonymous witness evidence in criminal proceedings inevitably is tempered by the courts, which generally favour due process and individual rights of the accused. Crucially, the Irish Supreme Court may invalidate legislation under Articles 15.4.2° and 34.3.1° on the ground of unconstitutionality; thus, should the Irish Parliament introduce legislation permitting anonymous witness evidence, the Supreme Court would have the capacity to invalidate it on the basis that it contravenes the constitutional right to a fair trial.[328] Given the absence of debate on the idea of anonymous evidence, it seems unlikely that such a political move would occur, and the constitutional right to cross-examine appears to have set a bulwark in this respect.

---

[322] *State (Healy) v Donoghue* [1976] IR 325, 349. This provision has been found to encompass numerous protective rights, including the right to cross-examine witnesses: *Re Haughey* [1971] IR 217, 261; *State (Healy) v Donoghue*, 335–36.

[323] Criminal Assets Bureau Act 1996, s 10(7).

[324] *Criminal Assets Bureau v PS* [2004] IEHC 351.

[325] *Gilligan v Criminal Assets Bureau* [1998] 3 IR 185.

[326] *The People (DPP) v Kenny* [1990] 2 IR 110, 134.

[327] H Packer, *The Limits of the Criminal Sanction* (California, Stanford University Press, 1968) 173.

[328] This contrasts with s 4 of the Human Rights Act 1998 which merely permits the English courts to make a 'declaration of incompatibility', if satisfied that legislation conflicts with the European Convention on Human Rights.

VI. Conclusion

As can be seen, numerous amendments have been made to the trial of criminal offences in a bid to counter organised crime and the particular and very real threat it sometimes poses to the administration of justice, to witnesses and to jurors. Surveillance evidence is used as testimony in Ireland and should be so permitted in the UK, while accomplice evidence and the associated immunity notices provide an alternative method of evidence-gathering where the secretive nature of criminal gangs renders conventional investigative and prosecutorial approaches less effective. In addition, the threats posed to jurors and witnesses have resulted in the enactment of specific substantive offences, the amendment of the rules of evidence, the anonymisation of juries and witnesses, the use of non-jury trials and the creation of Witness Protection Programmes.

The prosecution of individuals suspected of involvement in organised crime is often hindered by bribery, intimidation, and perjury.[329] The construction of a prosecution case and, beyond this, success at trial is often compromised by a critical lack of evidence, which can be remedied by the amendment of procedural rules and the introduction of protective measures. To this end, considerable changes have been wrought to fundamental principles in the criminal process in the UK and Ireland, such as the right to a jury trial, and the right to cross-examine witnesses. Though these measures protect intimidated witness and jurors, they also improve the likelihood of successful prosecutions of organised criminals. Notwithstanding these understandable aims, the increase in State crime control powers concomitantly impinges on the due process rights of the individual. These amendments to the criminal trial indicate a shift from liberal notions of due process towards the utilitarian demands of the State, driven by the desire to prosecute crime successfully. There has been a move away from traditional norms and safeguards towards a results-oriented approach, often precipitated by once-off controversies or crises. Whether such alterations are justified on the basis of the threat posed by organised criminality is a fundamental and contentious question which merits measured analysis, not the knee-jerk reaction so often evident in the development of policy in this context. Indeed, it is unclear whether any possible increase in the number of guilty verdicts, facilitated by the amendment of standards in the criminal process, warrants tampering with protective devices which guard against unfair trial processes and convictions.

Galligan highlights that while the trial process is addressed to the defendant,[330] it is also, and more significantly, addressed to the community to show that legal standards are to be taken seriously.[331] The upholding of individual rights and strict delineation of the power of the State is important in ensuring the integrity of

---

[329] See Landesco, n 12.
[330] RA Duff, *Punishment, Communication and Community* (Oxford, Oxford University Press, 2000).
[331] Galligan, n 11, 39.

the criminal justice system, and in protecting the public interest in avoiding unfair and unsafe convictions.[332] While the general public may seem to be more concerned with the successful prosecution of the guilty than the punctilios of the law of evidence, this sentiment, in relation to organised crime especially, should not be exploited by politicians in a bid to introduce more repressive measures which neglect due process values and individual liberties, given the wider and fundamental public interest in guarding against dubious convictions.

---

[332] A Ashworth, 'Crime, Community and Creeping Consequentialism' [1996] *Crim LR* 220, 225.

6

Punishing Organised Crime: The Post-Conviction Stage of the Criminal Process

I. Introduction

As has been described in previous chapters, alterations to the pre-trial and trial aspects of the criminal process have been made in an effort to undercut the threat posed by organised criminality, and in doing so the powers of the State have been augmented, often to the detriment of due process protections. These changes have been prompted by the nature of organised crime and the methods adopted by such criminal actors, such as the laundering of assets, the hiding of incriminating documents, and the absence or intimidation of witnesses. Comparable legislative developments may be identified in the post-trial realm, expanding the range of orders available upon conviction so as to prevent and deter organised crime, usually with the added effect of increasing the punitiveness of sentencing.

Across the UK and Ireland, the post-trial stage of the criminal process is being moved from a loose, discretionary and individualised model to a more mechanical and punitive one involving presumptive or minimum sentences, in an attempt to address the problem of organised crime. The development and implementation of such sentences highlight the tension between the legislature and courts in dealing with this particular type of criminality, with the latter often resisting statutory changes in a bid to retain the usual principles of sentencing but also their traditionally held discretion. In addition to such alterations to sentencing policy and practice, there has been a legislative formalisation of the sentence reduction scheme for accomplices who assist the investigation or prosecution of crime, and a range of ancillary measures have been enacted, permitting confiscation and forfeiture of property, and imposing notification and monitoring requirements. All of the measures demonstrate a shift in focus away from the characteristics and circumstances of the offender, evidencing a more pragmatic emphasis on the type of offence and the protection of the public.

II. General Principles of Sentencing

For the last century the judiciary in the UK and Ireland has enjoyed wide discretion in terms of sentencing, but this is constrained increasingly by guidelines and statutory provisions, many of which were prompted by the drive to deal with organised criminality in a more robust fashion. In a general sense, the sentencing of offenders is grounded on numerous principles and purposes. In England and Wales, the purposes of sentencing, to which any court dealing with an offender must have regard, are described statutorily: namely, the punishment of offenders; the reduction of crime including through deterrence; the reform and rehabilitation of offenders; the protection of the public; and the making of reparation by offenders to persons affected by their offences,[1] and a subsequent provision in the relevant Act then refers to the principle of proportionality.[2] There is no statutory delineation of either the purposes or principles of sentencing in the rest of the UK and Ireland,[3] though they also include retribution, deterrence, prevention of crime and rehabilitation.[4] Some general principles have been developed by the Irish courts: each sentence must be formulated with the individual facts of the case in mind[5] and must be proportionate to the gravity of the crime and the circumstances of the perpetrator.[6] As Ashworth noted in relation to the English legislation, these purposes may be in conflict, thereby inviting inconsistency.[7] In other words, as the objectives of sentencing may not be compatible, the particular aims that are prioritised may affect the length and nature of the sentence. Indeed, the statutory measures analysed later in this chapter indicate a favouring of certain objectives and rationales over others, in seeking to react to and punish organised crime vigorously and effectively.

Sentencing courts may also be steered by guidelines which differ in terms of how prescriptive they are. The Court of Appeal in England and Wales has handed down sentencing guidelines for a number of decades, while the Sentencing Advisory Panel was later established to contribute to, but not prescribe, such decisions.[8] Then in 2003 the Sentencing Guidelines Council was established

---

[1] Criminal Justice Act 2003, s 142.

[2] Criminal Justice Act 2003, s 143.

[3] While such details were included in the Criminal Justice and Licensing (Scotland) Bill, ultimately they did not appear in the 2010 Act. Similarly, calls have been made to entrench sentencing principles in statute in Northern Ireland (see Northern Ireland Office, *Consultation on the Review of the Sentencing Framework* (Belfast, Northern Ireland Office, 2005) 6) but this has yet to occur.

[4] See *Dempsey v Parole Board for Scotland* 2004 SLT 1107, 1134; *People (DPP) v MS* [2000] 2 IR 592, 600.

[5] *People (DPP) v Gallagher* (Court of Criminal Appeal, 4 March 1994); *People (DPP) v Sheedy* [2000] 2 IR 184.

[6] *State (Healy) v Donoghue* [1976] IR 325, 353; *Cox v Ireland* [1992] 2 IR 503, 524; *Rock v Ireland* [1997] 3 IR 484, 500.

[7] A Ashworth, *Sentencing and Criminal Justice* (5th edn) (Cambridge, Cambridge University Press, 2010) 101.

[8] Crime and Disorder Act 1998, s 81.

specifically to create guidelines.[9] Since 2010 the Sentencing Council has replaced these two bodies,[10] and every court in England and Wales must now 'follow any sentencing guideline which is relevant to the offender's case'.[11] In Northern Ireland sentencers are assisted by guideline cases from the English Court of Appeal, but these guidelines are deemed to be secondary and may be followed only when they accord with 'local experience'.[12] Moreover, the Northern Ireland Department of Justice is considering the establishment of a Sentencing Guidelines Council for Northern Ireland,[13] and guidelines for the Magistrates' Courts there are now available.[14] Part 1 of the Criminal Justice and Licensing (Scotland) Act 2010 creates a Scottish Sentencing Council which 'is from time to time to prepare, for the approval of the High Court of Justiciary, guidelines relating to the sentencing of offenders'.[15] This provision has not yet been brought into force. Despite calls for sentencing guidelines in Ireland none exist;[16] there are few formal constraints on judicial discretion,[17] and the system in place is described as one of the most unstructured in the common law world.[18] So, while there appears to be a drive for more systematised sentencing practice across the UK and Ireland, the actual implementation of any proposed measures leaves considerable latitude.

In addition to the guidance provided by sentencing principles, purposes and guidelines, the European Convention on Human Rights (ECHR) provides some parameters in terms of the sentencing of offenders. The imposition of a disproportionate sentence may be guarded against by Article 3 of the ECHR which protects the individual against torture and inhuman or degrading treatment or punishment, and Article 5, which safeguards the right to liberty and security.[19]

III. Sentencing Organised Crimes

Within these strictures provided by the constitutional principle of proportionality, various domestic guidelines and the ECHR, Parliaments in the UK and Ireland have sought to increase the punishments for certain quintessential organised

[9] Criminal Justice Act 2003, Pt 12, ch 1.

[10] Coroners and Justice Act 2009, Pt 4, ch1.

[11] Coroners and Justice Act 2009, s 125(a).

[12] *Attorney General's Reference (No 1 of 2008) Gibbons et al* [2008] NICA 41 [44].

[13] Sentencing Working Group, *Monitoring and Developing Sentencing Guidance in Northern Ireland a Report to the Lord Chief Justice from the Sentencing Working Group* (Northern Ireland Office, Belfast, 2010).

[14] See www.jsbni.com/Publications/sentencing-guides-magistrates-court/Pages/default.aspx.

[15] Criminal Justice and Licensing (Scotland) Act 2010, s 3(1). These guidelines may include the principles and purposes of sentencing,

[16] See Working Group on the Jurisdiction of the Courts, *The Criminal Jurisdiction of the Courts* (the Fennelly Report) (Dublin, Courts Service, 2003) 20; Balance in the Criminal Law Review Group, *Final Report of the Balance in the Criminal Law Review Group* (Dublin, Stationery Office, 2007) 227.

[17] T O'Malley, 'Resisting the Temptation of Elegance: Sentencing Discretion Reaffirmed' (1994) 4 *Irish Criminal Law Journal* 1, 3.

[18] T O'Malley, *Sentencing Law and Practice* (Dublin, Round Hall Sweet & Maxwell, 2000) 8.

[19] Ashworth, n 7, 68–69.

crimes, such as drugs and firearms offences, by introducing presumptive minimum sentences. This involves both instrumental and expressive dimensions: lengthier sentences means that imprisoned individuals are removed from society for an extended period of time, they involve more harsh punishment in terms of retribution, they serve as a more robust deterrent in an individual and general sense, as well as communicating moral censure for such acts.

The need for 'effective, proportionate and dissuasive' sentences for serious drugs offences, for example, has been emphasised at the European level,[20] thereby seeking to reconcile the desire for robust, deterrent sentences with the imperative of proportionality in sentencing. While discretionary maximum sentences of life imprisonment have long existed for the sale and supply of proscribed drugs in the UK and Ireland,[21] the drive for more robust sentencing has taken the form of presumptive minimum sentences more recently.

In the UK, drugs are classified into three categories, A, B and C, ostensibly according to the harm they pose,[22] with A being the most harmful and C the least. This categorisation affects the maximum penalties imposed for offences regarding their cultivation, possession and supply. The class of the drug combined with its purity determines the appropriate sentences, which until now have been based on guideline cases issued by the Court of Appeal. In *R v Aranguren* the Court of Appeal held that rather than relying on monetary or street value as a factor in sentencing the importation of Class A drugs, the sentence should relate to the weight of the pure drug imported.[23] Moreover, *R v Mashaollahi* provided that the sentencing court should assume that the opium was 100 per cent pure, but that if evidence indicated otherwise the sentence could be tempered.[24] Street value would be relevant only to cross-check approximate equivalence between Class A drugs. In this instance, 40 kilogrammes of pure opium was deemed to equate in value to 5 kilogrammes of pure heroin.[25] The Sentencing Council's guideline for the sentencing of drug offences came into effect in 2012, and this provides that in assessing harm, quantity is determined by the weight of the product.[26] In the preceding consultation the Council noted that street value is rarely useful as a determinant of seriousness due to its highly variable nature, but rather the role of the offender and the quantity of the drug are key.[27] Thus, the sale of large quantities of drugs on behalf of an organised crime group is regarded as being at the high end in terms of gravity and as warranting a lengthy sentence.[28]

---

[20] Council Framework Decision 2004/757/JHA, 25 October 2004, [2004] OJ L335/8, Art 4.
[21] Misuse of Drugs Act 1971 (UK) and Misuse of Drugs Act 1977 (Ireland).
[22] Misuse of Drugs Act 1971, Sch 2. See Home Office Crime and Drug Strategy Directorate, *Review of the UK's Drugs Classification System – a Public Consultation* (London, Home Office, 2006).
[23] *R v Aranguren and Others* [1995] 16 Cr App R (S) 211; *R v Morris* [2001] 1 Cr App R (S) 297.
[24] *R v Mashaollahi* [2001] 1 Cr App R (S) 330.
[25] SOCA's Project Endorse analyses samples of seized illegal drugs to assess and report on the purity levels and adulteration of heroin, cocaine and amphetamine. See www.soca.gov.uk/threats/drugs/forensic-intelligence.
[26] Sentencing Council, *Drug Offences Definitive Guideline* (London, Sentencing Council, 2012) 4.
[27] ibid, 11.
[28] See *Litwinski v Crown Prosecution Service* [2011] EWCA Crim 727 [39].

Beyond this, legislation requires a court in England, Wales and Scotland to impose a minimum sentence of seven years' imprisonment for a third Class A trafficking offence, except where the court is of the opinion that there are particular circumstances relating to the offence or to the offender which would make it unjust to do so.[29] Such particular circumstances, which are not the same as 'exceptional circumstances', include cases where good progress has been made on a drug treatment and training order,[30] where there was a considerable interval between the previous and present offences,[31] and where the offender was not a commercial dealer.[32] Until 2007 the number of people sentenced under section 110 per annum was in single figures, and this increased to 25 in 2008 and 33 in 2009.[33]

In a similar vein, the Irish Parliament has been proactive in terms of prescribing minimum sentences, and this trend gathered momentum quite quickly from a base of very loose and discretionary sentencing. Now, any person convicted of the possession of drugs with a value of at least €13,000 with intent to supply shall receive a minimum term of 10 years, unless there are exceptional and specific circumstances which would make such a term unjust.[34] Among the matters to which the court may have regard in determining sentence is whether that person pleaded guilty, at what stage and in what circumstances he did so,[35] and whether he materially assisted the investigation.

These provisions indicate clearly policy makers' perspective on the gravity of drug trafficking and the need to respond forcefully.[36] In England, Wales and Scotland, the minimum sentence for a third drug offence may be avoided where particular circumstances would make it unjust to impose the sentence, whereas the term used in Ireland is 'exceptional and specific circumstances'. It appears that this is a narrower exception than that in the UK: nonetheless this has not precluded its widespread application by the Irish courts even though the prescribed sentence has been described as 'clear and definite guidance'[37] which should only be departed from for good reason.[38] While the prescribed minimum

---

[29] Powers of Criminal Courts (Sentencing) Act 2000, s 110; Criminal Procedure (Scotland) Act 1995, s 205B (as inserted by the Crime and Punishment (Scotland) Act 1997).

[30] *R v McDonagh* [2005] EWCA Crim 2742, [2006] 1 Cr App R (S) 111 [11]. DTTOs were introduced by pt IV of the Crime and Disorder Act 1998, since replaced by Pt IV of the Powers of Criminal Courts (Sentencing) Act 2000.

[31] *R v McDonagh*, n 30, [11].

[32] *R v Turner* [2005] EWCA Crim 2363, [2006] 1 Cr App R (S) 95 [15] and [16].

[33] Ministry of Justice, *Annual Statistics 2009, Sentencing Statistics Supplementary Tables* (London, The Stationery Office, 2011) Table 2b: Persons sentenced under the Powers of Criminal Courts (Sentencing) Act 2000, 2000–09.

[34] Misuse of Drugs Act 1977, s 15A (as inserted by the Criminal Justice Act 1999).

[35] However, the Court of Criminal Appeal stressed in *People (DPP) v Dunne* [2003] 4 IR 87 that a trial judge is not obliged to impose a sentence of less than 10 years because of a guilty plea. Furthermore, in *People (DPP) v Ducque* (Court of Criminal Appeal, 15 July 2005) Geoghegan J noted that a plea of guilty on its own, in particular a late plea, could not be taken into account because it would rarely, if ever, constitute an exceptional and specific circumstance.

[36] See *DPP v Henry* (Court of Criminal Appeal, 15 May 2002).

[37] *People (DPP) v Botha* [2004] 2 IR 375, 384 [25].

[38] *People (DPP) v Heffernan* (Court of Criminal Appeal, 10 October 2002).

sentence has been imposed in Ireland in numerous cases due to the sophistication of the drug dealing,[39] the amount of drugs involved,[40] and failure to cooperate with the police,[41] the exceptional circumstances caveat has been used on many occasions,[42] and, sometimes, suspended sentences have been imposed.[43]

Because of this, the popular and political perception in Ireland is that the 10-year sentence is circumvented frequently by lenient judges,[44] who have described the provision as 'a revolutionary alteration superimposed on the conventional principles of sentencing'.[45] The tenor of public debate reached fever pitch and the friction between the courts and the other arms of the State became most fraught after a shooting of a woman in Dublin in 2006, when it was reported that one of the suspects would still have been in prison had he received the presumptive sentence when convicted of drug trafficking in 2000.[46] The Minister for Justice argued that '[t]he executive has produced massive resources in terms of cash and Garda numbers for the force. And the judicial arm of the State as well must play its part in the suppression of gangland violence'.[47]

Thus, an attempt was made subsequently to strengthen this approach to sentencing in Ireland. Now the prosecution need not prove that the defendant had knowledge of the value of the drugs or was reckless in a case concerning the possession of drugs with a value in excess of €13,000.[48] Moreover, the presumptive minimum sentence was extended to cover the importation of drugs of that value;[49] the exceptional circumstances provision is now available only to persons

---

[39] *People (DPP) v Byrne* [2003] 4 IR 423, 429.

[40] *Ducque*, n 35. *DPP v Long* (Court of Criminal Appeal, 7 April 2006); *People (DPP) v Harrison* (Dublin Circuit Criminal Court, 26 May 2006); *People (DPP) v Deering* (Dublin Circuit Criminal Court, 2 February 2006).

[41] *Ducque*, n 35; *People (DPP) v McDonald* (Dublin Circuit Criminal Court, 8 June 2005); *DPP v Costelloe* [2009] IECCA 28.

[42] Indeed, research carried out for the Department of Justice on the application of the sentence under s 15A from November 1999–May 2001 indicates that of the 55 cases studied, the presumptive minimum sentence was imposed in only three cases: P McEvoy, *Research for the Department of Justice on the Criteria Applied by the Courts in Sentencing Under s 15A of the Misuse of Drugs Act 1977 (as amended)* (Dublin, Department of Justice, Equality and Law Reform, 2005) 8. Department of Justice figures reveal that of 80 drug offenders who were on trial in 2005 and were eligible for the s 15A sentence, 10 received the sentence. See 'Nine out of 10 Drug Dealers not Given Mandatory 10-year Jail Term', *Irish Times*, 29 November 2006. See *Botha*, n 37, 382ff; *People (DPP) v Vardacardis* (Court of Criminal Appeal, 20 January 2003); *People (DPP) v Benjamin* (Court of Criminal Appeal, 14 January 2002); *DPP v Malric* [2011] IECCA 99.

[43] *People (DPP) v Alexiou* [2003] 3 IR 513, 523; *People (DPP) v McGinty* [2007] 1 IR 635.

[44] 'Mandatory Drug Offence Terms Rarely Imposed', *Irish Times*, 7 March 2006.

[45] *DPP v Dermody* (Court of Criminal Appeal, 21 December 2006).

[46] 'Mandatory Drug Offence Terms Rarely Imposed', *Irish Times*, 7 March 2006.

[47] See 'McDowell Criticises Bail Law Application', *Irish Times*, 15 December 2006. The Deputy Chief Whip of the Government formally wrote to Finnegan P about the high proportion of drug dealers escaping the 10-year sentence. See 'Courts Pulled up for "Low" Drug Jail Terms', *Irish Independent*, 13 November 2006. The associated 'coolness' in relations between the judiciary and the Minister for Justice culminated in a boycott of a Christmas party held by the Department of Justice by the vast majority of senior judges. See 'Judges Boycott McDowell Reception over Bail Comments', *Irish Times*, 22 December 2006.

[48] Criminal Justice Act 2006, s 82(3).

[49] Misuse of Drugs Act 1977, s 15B.

convicted of a first offence of drug possession or importation;[50] and a mandatory minimum sentence of 10 years was introduced for a second such offence.[51] Nonetheless, the constitutional principle of proportionality in sentencing limits the extent to which the legislature can constrain the sentencing discretion of the courts.

The minimum sentence in Ireland is predicated on the value of the drugs seized, in contrast to the sentence in England, Wales and Scotland which applies when a person commits a Class A trafficking offence for the third time. In Ireland, the presumptive minimum sentence comes into play when the drugs seized are worth at least €13,000, according to the judgement of a member of the Garda Síochána or an officer of Customs and Excise who has knowledge of the unlawful sale or supply of controlled drugs.[52] It appears that there is no objective means of determining the value of the seizure, given that it may vary according to location and demand.[53] Thus there is potential for miscalculation or overestimation of the value of the drugs so as to reach the threshold, and there is no classification or ranking according to the nature and effect of different drugs as in the UK. Nonetheless, the Irish courts scrutinise the means of assessing the value carefully: a conviction was set aside by the Supreme Court in *People (DPP) v Connolly* on the basis that the forensic testing of the drugs did not establish the purity and so there was no reliable evidence that the value threshold had been reached.[54] While the street value was once used in the UK,[55] as noted above, weight and purity is now key. Although using weight as a measure of seriousness is not unproblematic due to the potential to punish 'mules' more than professionals,[56] the Sentencing Council's guideline includes low purity and role in the offence as factors that may mitigate sentence,[57] and this is preferable to the Irish scheme which is contingent on an estimation of street value which is, by definition, variable.

In addition to presumptive sentences for drugs offences, a number of statutory measures across the UK and Ireland provide robust sentences for firearms offences.[58] The perceived leniency of the courts in this regard was recognised by the English Court of Appeal in *R v Avis*: 'some of the sentences imposed for these offences [of possession and use of firearms] in the past . . . have failed to reflect the

---

[50]   s 15(3E) as inserted by Criminal Justice Act 2007, s 33.

[51]   s 15(3F).

[52]   Misuse of Drugs Act 1977, s 15A(3) (as amended by the Criminal Justice Act 1999).

[53]   The difficulty the State may have in determining exactly how to value drugs is illustrated by an example reported in the *Irish Times*. In July 1992, Customs officers seized 55kg of benzyl methyl ketone, a chemical used in the manufacture of amphetamines. Whilst the initial estimate of the haul was put at £4m, a few days later the chemical was valued at approximately £7,000. See 'State Keeps to High Value Assessment of Drugs When Price on Streets is Lower', *Irish Times*, 20 November 1997.

[54]   *People (DPP) v Connolly* [2011] IESC 6.

[55]   *R v Aranguren* (1994) 99 Cr App R 347; *R v Warren and Beeley* [1996] 1 Cr App R 120. For an assessment of street value see *R v Patel* (1987) 9 Cr App R (S) 319.

[56]   J Fleetwood, 'Five Kilos: Penalties and Practice in the International Cocaine Trade' (2011) 51 *British Journal of Criminology* 375.

[57]   Sentencing Council, n 26, 14.

[58]   None of the devolved Parliaments in the UK has competency in relation to firearms, and so the Westminster Parliament legislates on such matters.

seriousness of such offences and the justifiable public concern which they arouse'.[59]

Such public concern is heightened inevitably by the commission and media depiction of certain crimes, resulting in sentencing policy in this respect often being driven by crises. For example, the murder of two young women in the UK in 2003 prompted the amendment of the Firearms Act 1968 to include a minimum sentence of five years for certain offences involving the possession of prohibited weapons or ammunition unless the court is of the opinion that there are exceptional circumstances relating to the offence or to the offender which justify its not doing so.[60] Furthermore, there is no reduction in sentence for a guilty plea in relation to such a charge; as Ashworth notes, this is the only such provision in the UK.[61] In enacting this section,

> Parliament intended, that, for the protection of the public against the dangers arising from the unlawful possession of firearms, considerations of retribution and deterrence should be given greater emphasis, and the personal circumstances of the offender less emphasis, than would normally be the case in sentencing.[62]

This encapsulates the prioritisation of certain principles and aims of sentencing over others, in a drive to address particularly pernicious types of criminality.

As Thomas observes, however, '[l]ike most legislation introduced in haste, s.51A was severely deficient in a number of ways', such as failing to encompass those persons convicted of an offence involving the use (rather than possession) of such a weapon.[63] Subsequent legislation thus extended this minimum sentence provision to cover the possession of a firearm with intent to injure or to cause fear of violence; use of a firearm to resist arrest; carrying a firearm with criminal intent; carrying a firearm in a public place and trespassing in a building with firearm.[64]

Akin to the situation in the UK, presumptive sentences are now imposed in Ireland for firearms offences: 10 years for the possession of a firearm with intent to endanger life or cause serious injury or to enable another person to do so,[65] and for using a firearm while resisting arrest or in the course of an escape;[66] and five years for using a firearm when taking a vehicle without authorisation,[67] for possession of a firearm in suspicious circumstances, and for possession with criminal intent.[68]

[59] *R v Avis* (1998) 1 Cr App R 420, 430.
[60] Firearms Act 1968, s 51A (inserted by the Criminal Justice Act 2003, s 287). See 'Birmingham Shooting Victims Named', *The Guardian,* 3 January 2003.
[61] Ashworth, n 7, 27. See *R v Jordan, Alleyne and Redfern* [2004] EWCA Crim 3291, [2005] 2 Cr App R (S) 44.
[62] *HM Advocate v McGovern* [2007] HCJAC 21, 2007 JC 145 [11].
[63] D Thomas, 'Sentencing: Firearms Act 1968 s 51A – Required Minimum Sentence (Case Comment)' [2011] *Crim LRev* 169, 170.
[64] Violent Crime Reduction Act 2006, s 30; also Firearms (Northern Ireland) Order 2004, Art 70 and Violent Crime Reduction Act 2006, Sch 2.
[65] Criminal Justice Act 2006, s 42.
[66] Criminal Justice Act 2006, s 58(4).
[67] Criminal Justice Act 2006, s 57(4).
[68] Criminal Justice Act 2006, ss 59(4) and 60(4).

In the UK, it is in exceptional circumstances that the firearms sentences need not be imposed, rather than in particular circumstances as is the case regarding drugs offences: '[t]hese cases [of "real exceptional circumstances"] will be rare'.[69] This arguably leaves less leeway for the courts in terms of circumventing the will of the legislature, and the courts usually adhere to the legislative prescription. For example, in *R v McEneaney* the defendant had paranoid schizophrenia and long-standing personality difficulties, and he also claimed that he had merely found the gun and kept it; this combination of factors did not amount to exceptional circumstances.[70] Moreover, in the UK, a plea of guilty does not constitute exceptional circumstances,[71] while the Irish legislation explicitly permits a guilty plea to be so regarded, depending on the stage of the process and the circumstances.[72]

The English Court of Appeal has found exceptional circumstances to exist in limited instances, such as where the person believed the gun was a replica;[73] where he was a paraplegic with many consequential physical disabilities which would make it very difficult for him to cope with a sentence of imprisonment;[74] where the law relating to possession of the particular type of revolver had changed but he was suffering from depression at the time, had originally intended it to be used for sporting purposes and did not possess any ammunition for it;[75] and where he pleaded guilty at the first opportunity, was unaware of the unlawfulness of the replica weapon, had a previously good character and cooperated throughout the procedure.[76] The Irish Court of Criminal Appeal has found that exceptional circumstances include a case where the individual had a low level of involvement in the offence and was pressured into commission through threats to his family.[77] Moreover a number of cases in the UK have considered whether possession of firearms in suspicious circumstances warrants the minimum sentence where the defendant had been given a container by someone else that in fact contained firearms, but it was unclear whether the person was aware of the contents. The English Court of Appeal found that while ignorance is a significant factor in determining whether there are exceptional circumstances, it is not decisive.[78]

In addition to presumptive sentences for first offences, a series of legislative provisions have been introduced in the UK for second serious offences, to remedy the leniency referred to by the English Court of Appeal in *Avis*. Section 2 of the

[69] *R v Jordan,* n 61, para 30.
[70] *R v McEneaney* [2005] ECWA Crim 431.
[71] *R v Jordan,* n 61.
[72] See, eg Criminal Justice Act 2006, s 42(5)(a). Sub-section (5)(a) of each provision includes this statement.
[73] *R v Jordan,* n 61.
[74] *R v Blackall* [2005] EWCA Crim 1128, [2006] 1 Cr App R (S) 22.
[75] *R v Mehmet* [2005] EWCA Crim 2074, [2006] 1 Cr App R (S) 75.
[76] *R v Rehman* [2005] EWCA Crim 2056.
[77] *People (DPP) v Barry* (Court of Criminal Appeal, 23 June 2008); see Law Reform Commission, *Mandatory Sentences* (Dublin, Law Reform Commission, 2011) paras 3.182 and 3.185.
[78] See *R v Havill* [2008] EWCA Crim 2952, [2009] 2 Cr App R (S) 35, 254; *R v Boateng* [2011] EWCA Crim 861, [2011] 2 Cr App R (S) 104 (CA (Crim Div)); DA Thomas, 'Case Comment *R v Boateng (Mary)*: Sentencing – Required Minimum Sentence – Firearms Act 1968, section 51A' [2011] *Crim L Rev* 565.

Crime (Sentences) Act 1997 imposed a 'mandatory sentence' for a second serious offence , including manslaughter, soliciting murder and various firearms offences, unless the court is of the opinion that there are exceptional circumstances relating to either of the offences or to the offender which justify its not doing so. A challenge to this provision under Article 7 of the ECHR which precludes retrospective punishment[79] was rejected in *R v Offen* on the basis that while the imposition of a life sentence was predicated on the individual having been previously convicted he was not being sentenced or having his sentence increased for the first offence.[80]

The Powers of Criminal Courts (Sentencing) Act 2000, as a consolidating Act, replaced this section, and maintained what is truly a presumptive rather than mandatory life sentence for a second serious offence.[81] In this instance exceptional circumstances justified the Court not imposing the life sentence. An exceptional circumstance 'need not be unique, or unprecedented, or very rare; but it cannot be one that is regularly, or routinely, or normally encountered'.[82] Moreover, what constitutes exceptional circumstances is influenced by the context:

> The policy and intention of Parliament was to protect the public against a person who had committed two serious offences. It therefore can be assumed the section was not intended to apply to someone in relation to whom it was established there would be no need for protection in the future. In other words, if the facts showed the statutory assumption was misplaced, then this, in the statutory context, was not the normal situation and in consequence, for the purposes of the section, the position was exceptional.[83]

This was approved subsequently in *R v Drew*.[84]

The precursor for such a punitive measure, which seeks to affect judicial discretion but in fact retains concern for the individual characteristics of the accused, is evident in the notorious 'three strikes' provision in California which imposes an automatic life sentence on persons convicted of a third felony.[85] Despite its political appeal in the UK, the 'two strikes' measure was replaced by indeterminate sentences for public protection (IPPs) through the Criminal Justice Act 2003.[86] A

---

[79] Art 7 provides 'No one shall be held guilty of any criminal offence on account of any act or omission which did not constitute a criminal offence under national or international law at the time when it was committed. Nor shall a heavier penalty be imposed than the one that was applicable at the time the criminal offence was committed'.

[80] *R v Offen* [2001] 1 WLR 253 [90].

[81] Powers of Criminal Courts (Sentencing) Act 2000, s 109 and Criminal Procedure (Scotland) Act 1995, s 205A.

[82] *R v Kelly* [2000] QB 198, 208.

[83] *Offen*, n 80, [79].

[84] *R v Drew* [2003] 1 WLR 1213.

[85] California's 'three strikes' laws were upheld in *Ewing v California* 538 US 11(2003), where a five to four majority of the Supreme Court found that a sentence of 25 years to life for the felony theft of golf clubs did not violate the US Constitution's Eighth Amendment prohibition on cruel and unusual punishments.

[86] Criminal Justice Act 2003, s 225 (as later amended by the Criminal Justice and Immigration Act 2008). See B Hebenton and T Seddon, 'From Dangerousness to Precaution: Managing Sexual and Violent Offenders in an Insecure and Uncertain Age' (2009) 49 *British Journal of Criminology* 343; J Jacobson and M Hough, *Unjust Deserts: Imprisonment for Public Protection* (London, Prison Reform Trust, 2010).

person convicted of a serious specified offence in England and Wales (that is, an offence which carries a maximum punishment of 10 years or more or one that is punishable with life imprisonment but a life sentence was not justified by the seriousness of the offence) and who was assessed as dangerous by the court, could be given an IPP, if he committed a serious offence including possession of a firearm with intent to injure, use of a firearm to resist arrest, carrying a firearm with criminal intent and robbery involving a firearm or imitation firearm.[87] The IPP in turn has now been abolished, and replaced by a life sentence for a second 'listed offence' if the second offence would otherwise attract a sentence of 10 years or more.[88] Listed offences include soliciting murder, wounding with intent to cause grievous bodily harm, and various firearms offences.[89] The court must impose a life sentence unless the circumstances of either of the offences or of the offender make this unjust. Thus, while this has been described as a mandatory sentence, the judge retains discretion, leading to criticism in debate in the House of Lords referring to 'political posturing',[90] and a 'strangely contradictory' provision.[91] Such incoherence in the construction of legislation, and the development of sentencing policy in this piecemeal manner indicate the tenor of political debate on sentencing and the centrality of perception over substance in this regard.

As firearms and drugs policy remains the preserve of the Westminster Parliament, it may appear that London is solely responsible for the drive towards presumptive sentencing across the UK. Nonetheless indeterminate sentences have been reproduced in Scotland. The equivalent measure to the IPP in Scotland is the 'order for lifelong restriction' (OLR).[92] A court may make a risk assessment order where the offence is a violent one or endangers life or where the nature or circumstances of the offence intimate a propensity on the part of the person to commit any such offence.[93] If the risk assessment suggests that the nature or circumstances of the commission of the offence demonstrate a likelihood that the accused could seriously endanger the lives, or physical or psychological wellbeing, of the public, then the court shall make an OLR.[94] Thus, while judicial discretion may appear rather more constrained in Scotland, the court holds the ultimate choice as to whether a risk assessment is needed in the first instance. Despite the emulation of indeterminate sentences, the IPP was used far more in England and Wales than the OLR in Scotland: in March 2011 there were a total of 6,550 IPP prisoners,[95] whereas in March 2010 there were only 30 people subject to

---

[87]   Criminal Justice Act 2003, s 225 (as amended); see Sch 15A for list of offences.

[88]   Criminal Justice Act 2003, s 224A as inserted by ch 5 of the Legal Aid, Sentencing and Punishment of Offenders Act 2012.

[89]   Criminal Justice Act 2003 Sch 15B.

[90]   HL Deb 9 February 2012, vol 735, col 447 per Baroness Mallalieu.

[91]   HL Deb 9 February 2012, vol 735, col 448 per Lord Carlile.

[92]   Criminal Procedure (Scotland) Act 1995, s 210F (introduced by the Criminal Justice (Scotland) Act 2003).

[93]   Criminal Procedure (Scotland) Act 1995, s 210B.

[94]   Criminal Procedure (Scotland) Act 1995, s 210.

[95]   Ministry of Justice, *Provisional Figures Relating to Offenders Serving Indeterminate Sentence of Imprisonment for Public Protection (IPPs)* (London, Ministry of Justice, 2011) table 5.

an OLR in Scotland.[96] It remains to be seen whether the OLR follows the same fate as the IPP.

While not limited to organised crimes, IPPs were imposed on persons involved in armed robberies,[97] robbery and kidnapping,[98] possession of firearms and use of them in resisting arrest,[99] and it is likely that their successor, the 'life sentence' for a second listed offence would have similar applicability.[100] The significance of IPPs in the context of firearms crime was affirmed by the Court of Appeal:

> Criminals who are prepared to deal in such lethal weapons invariably represent a serious public danger, and it cannot be assumed that the danger they represent will have dissipated when the determinate element of their sentences has been completed. We therefore supplement the guidance in *Avis and others* by emphasising that for criminals involved in this level of gun crime along with very lengthy determinate sentences, indeterminate sentences, whether discretionary imprisonment for life or IPP, inevitably arise for consideration.[101]

This case considered the large-scale importation or manufacture, sale, and distribution of guns. The Court noted the anomaly whereby the importation of Class A drugs may attract a discretionary life sentence whereas the maximum sentence for importing firearms (including handguns and machine guns with ammunition) is 10 years' imprisonment.[102] Moreover, there is no equivalent statutory firearms offence to the possession of drugs with intent to supply. While possession of firearms and ammunition with intent to endanger life has a maximum penalty of life imprisonment,[103] specific intent to endanger life or to enable another to do so must be proven.[104]

> We respectfully suggest that the offence of importing firearms, or being in possession of firearms with intent to supply them, whether manufactured by someone else or not, is not less criminally reprehensible than the importation of drugs or possession of drugs with intent to supply them. It is indeed difficult to anticipate many such cases where an imminent risk to life is not an inevitable concomitant of the offence.[105]

The fact that the matter of firearms is reserved to Westminster limits the applicability of Scottish measures to such offenders. The interaction between the maximum sentences prescribed in the Firearms Act 1968 and OLRs was considered by

---

[96] Scottish Government, *Statistical Bulletin: Crime and Justice Series: Criminal Justice Social Work Statistics, 2009–10* (Edinburgh, Scottish Government, 2010) table 25.

[97] *R v Smith* [2011] UKSC 37, [2011] 1 WLR 1795; *R v Knight* [2010] EWCA Crim 237, [2010] 2 Cr App R (S) 84.

[98] *R v Rusha* [2010] EWCA Crim 3231, [2011] 2 Cr App R (S) 20.

[99] *R v McDonald* [2010] EWCA Crim 127, [2010] 2 Cr App R (S) 67.

[100] Criminal Justice Act 2003, s 224A as inserted by ch 5 of the Legal Aid, Sentencing and Punishment of Offenders Act 2012.

[101] *Attorney General's Reference No 43 of 2009: R v Wilkinson and Others* (2009) EWCA Crim 1925, [2010] 1 Cr App R (S) 100.

[102] ibid, [25].

[103] Firearms Act 1968, s 16.

[104] *Attorney General's Reference No 43 of 2009*, n 101, [25].

[105] ibid, [26].

the Scottish High Court of Justiciary which found in a case involving an accused person with a lengthy criminal record that it was outside the legislative competence of the Scottish Parliament to pass legislation which authorised the making of such an order on an offender convicted of a firearms offence, given that this is a matter reserved to the UK Parliament.[106]

There is no equivalent to the IPP or OLR in Ireland, but as in in the UK, 'mandatory' sentences are provided for second offences, including false imprisonment, certain firearms offences, aggravated burglary, drug trafficking, and organised crime offences.[107] When a person has been convicted of such an offence and sentenced to at least five years, and then commits another from the range of relevant offences within seven years (excluding any period of imprisonment) from the date of conviction of the first offence, the minimum term of imprisonment to be imposed is not less than three-quarters of the maximum term of imprisonment for such an offence, or not less than 10 years if the maximum term is life imprisonment.[108] This 'two strikes' law imposes a lesser sentence than in the UK, but applies to a broader range of offences.

A. Aggravating Factors in Sentencing

In addition to presumptive sentences, the maximum sentences for certain firearms offences have been increased in the UK,[109] again reflecting heightened public and political concern about the 'spiralling' rates of such crime[110] and the perceived level of sentencing being imposed by the courts. Moreover, and contrary to the depiction of the courts in some political quarters, the English Court of Appeal has stated that where arms are used in the carrying out of a robbery a consecutive rather than a concurrent sentence (ie for the separate robbery and firearms offences) should be imposed to send a 'clear message to those who commit crimes of this nature' that they would receive an additional sentence.[111] Furthermore, the use of a person aged less than 18 years to take care of a weapon when the offender is an adult is an aggravating factor.[112] In Ireland, the fact that a serious offence was committed as part of, or in furtherance of, the activities of criminal organisation is an aggravating factor at sentencing,[113] and the Court is required to impose a greater sentence than would be imposed in the absence of that factor unless the sentence is one of life imprisonment or there are exceptional circumstances

---

[106] *Henderson v HM Advocate* [2010] HCJAC 107.

[107] Criminal Justice Act 2006, ss 71–73.

[108] Criminal Justice Act 2007, s 25. This provision does not apply to an offence under sub-s (3F) or to a range of firearms offences for which Pt 6 of the Act delineates presumptive sentences. When the Bill was originally drafted this measure applied to persons sentenced to at least 12 months imprisonment on indictment.

[109] Violent Crime Reduction Act 2006, s 41.

[110] HC Deb 5 December, vol 440, col 588 per David Davis.

[111] *R v Greaves and Jaffier* [2003] EWCA Crim 3229 [14].

[112] Violent Crime Reduction Act 2006, s 29(11).

[113] Criminal Justice Act 2006, s 74A (as inserted by the Criminal Justice Amendment Act 2009).

justifying its not doing so.[114] Calls for an equivalent statutory provision in Northern Ireland have been made.[115] Similarly, the Sentencing Guidelines Council in England and Wales has noted that factors indicating higher culpability include offenders operating in groups or gangs, 'professional' offending, commission of the offence for financial gain (where this is not inherent in the offence itself) and a high level of profit from the offence, all of which encapsulate elements of organised criminality.[116]

B. Concluding Remarks

Presumptive minimum sentences indicate a legislative preference for the mechanical application of generalised standards over an individualised approach determined by the judiciary which takes the specific characteristics of the accused into account. This is representative of a favouring of aggregates over personal characteristics and illustrates the affinity of the legislature for facets of the new penology and notions of actuarial justice, in which the offender is classified as a member of a group, rather than as an individual with distinguishable features and circumstances.[117] In particular, mandatory and indeterminate sentences encapsulate the new penology's shift in emphasis towards probability and risk. Furthermore, the imperative of public protection is also identifiable, seeing as the rationale is not the protection of individual liberties but the general reduction of crime so as to safeguard the public.[118] Moreover, the imposition of relatively severe minimum sentences encapsulates Garland's description of the re-emergence of punitive sanctions.[119] Although IPPs and OLRs pertain to a broader range of criminality than just organised crime, their use ramped up the ability of the State to address this specific species of offending through a declaratory statement encapsulating a 'tough on crime' logic.

The justification for the introduction of more punitive measures and for the limitations on judges' discretion is founded on the perceived disconnect between the judiciary on the one hand, and the public and policy makers on the other when it comes to appropriate sentencing levels for organised crime. Research of public attitudes in England and Wales indicates a preference for sentences that were more punitive than current judicial practice (although preferences for medium-scale importation offences were often lenient relative to practice) and

---

[114] This is in line with Council Framework Decision 2004/757/JHA, 25 October 2004, [2004] OJ L335/8, Art 4 .

[115] House of Commons Northern Ireland Affairs Committee, *Organised Crime in Northern Ireland*, vol I (Third Report of Session 2005–06) (London, The Stationery Office, 2006) 59–60.

[116] Sentencing Guidelines Council, *Overarching Principles: Seriousness* (London, Sentencing Guidelines Secretariat, 2004) 6.

[117] M Feeley and J Simon, 'The New Penology: Notes on the Emerging Strategy of Corrections and its Implications' (1992) 30 *Criminology* 449, 449–50.

[118] D Garland, *The Culture of Control* (Oxford, Oxford University Press, 2001) 12.

[119] ibid, 53 and 61.

many of those surveyed saw little value in an individualised approach to the sentencing of drug offences.[120] Such sentiments are bolstered by the perception that the judiciary are detached from the reality of the threat posed by organised crime. As post-trial issues of sentencing are now politically important, public representatives are reluctant to be seen as lenient or soft on crime and so may pit themselves against the judiciary in public discourse.

Sentencing involves a public statement about an offender and his behaviour. In Ireland, the 'unequivocal' message that the original presumptive sentence in the 1999 Act would send to criminals was emphasised in Parliament,[121] as was its capacity to demonstrate society's abhorrence of the trafficking of drugs.[122] Expressive sanctions relieve tension and serve as a cathartic and gratifying moment of unity in the face of crime.[123] By stipulating a minimum sentence, the legislature expresses its disapprobation of those crimes regarded as most pernicious to society. Nonetheless, this may not make a substantial difference in practice. As Ashworth wryly notes, the seven-year sentence in section 110 created the impression that the UK Parliament was taking a firm stand against drug dealers when in fact a higher sentence than this normally would be given to a third-time dealer.[124] Moreover, when the two strikes provision in Ireland was being debated, a sub-section was inserted to provide that the sentence would not be imposed where it would be disproportionate in all the circumstances of the case, so as to safeguard it from constitutional challenge.[125] This encapsulates the political rhetoric about the leniency of sentencing and the judiciary: while the punitive inclinations desires of policy makers are now embodied in legislation, the overarching precept of proportionality must still be respected.

As well as their symbolic significance, presumptive minimum sentences are hoped to have deterrent value in an instrumental sense. Deterrence has long been key to drug sentencing in England and Wales,[126] and it has been emphasised by the Court of Appeal that deterrent and punitive sentences should be imposed whenever a gun was made available for use.[127] In *R v Rehman* the same Court noted that section 51A imposes 'deterrent sentences', that is,

> sentences that pay less attention to the personal circumstances of the offender and focus primarily upon the need for the courts to convey a message that an offender can expect

---

[120] J Jacobson, A Kirby and M Hough, *Public Attitudes to the Sentencing of Drug Offences* (London, Institute for Criminal Policy Research, 2011).

[121] Dáil Debates, vol 503, col 837 (21 April 1999) per Minister for Justice, Mr O'Donoghue. Also Dáil Debates, vol 493, col 883 (1 July 1998) per Minister for Justice, Mr O'Donoghue.

[122] Dáil Debates, vol 503, col 787 (21 April 1999) per Minister for Justice, Mr O'Donoghue.

[123] D Garland, 'The Culture of High Crime Societies: Some Preconditions of Recent "Law and Order" Policies' (2000) 40 *British Journal of Criminology* 347, 350.

[124] Ashworth, n 7, 226.

[125] Before the Irish President, Mary McAleese, signed the Bill into law on 9 May 2007, she convened a meeting of the Council of State to determine if the Bill should be referred to the Supreme Court for its constitutionality to be determined under Art 26 of the Irish Constitution, but decided not to do so. See 'President McAleese Signs Criminal Justice Bill into Law', *Irish Times*, 10 May 2007.

[126] *R v Aramah* (1983) 76 Cr App R 190.

[127] *Attorney General's Reference No 43 of 2009*, n 101, [3].

to be dealt with more severely so as to deter others than he would be were it only his personal wrongdoing which the court had to consider.[128]

Akin to this focus on general deterrence, the 'mandatory sentence' in Ireland was described as providing a 'substantial deterrent' to those convicted of firearms offences.[129]

Organised crimes and associated offences are seen as motivated by profit and as operating along business lines and logic; thus the relevant actors are seen as motivated rationally and as amenable to deterrence through heightening the potential risk of punishment and lowering the rewards of criminal behaviour. Nonetheless, empirical evidence suggests that the conception of presumptive sentences as a means of deterring drugs and firearms crime may be premised on an unduly simplistic understanding of the actor, and may be overly acceptant of the rational choice model of human action. Qualitative studies of gun criminals, in particular, indicate that the decision to commit the act is rarely driven by 'rational' considerations per se: for example, Matthews' interviews with imprisoned armed robbers in England revealed little or no awareness of security measures or amount of money available at the crime scene, or of the possible sentence or likelihood of being caught.[130] Numerous other studies seem to substantiate Hirschi's approach of limiting rational choice to specific criminal events, namely a theory of crimes, rather than propounding a general theory of criminality or involvement, viz a theory of offenders.[131] In other words, the individual's decision to commit crime in a broad sense may not be influenced by rational factors, but his choice as to where and when to commit the act may be governed by such reasoning. Drawing on this, it may be contended that the perpetrator of an armed robbery, say, thinks rationally in the context of the act itself, such as regarding the choice of weapon, the time of day, the location and the number of people involved, but that his ultimate involvement in the crime must be interrogated using more than the rational actor paradigm, thereby questioning the likely deterrence of such sentences.

It is reasonable to suggest that there are differences in individuals' susceptibility to changes in legal threats.[132] Professional and persistent armed robbers were found to be more likely than amateurs or intermediate actors to incorporate elements of rational considerations,[133] suggesting that 'organised criminals' may in

---

[128] *R v Rehman*, n 76, [4].

[129] Department of Justice, Equality and Law Reform Press Release, 'Minister Announces 7% Decrease in Provisional Headline Crime Figures' (Dublin, Department of Justice, Equality and Law Reform, 2004).

[130] R Matthews, *Armed Robbery* (Cullompton, Willan Publishing, 2002) 37.

[131] T Hirschi, 'On the Compatibility of Rational Choice and Social Control Theories of Crime' in DB Cornish and RV Clarke (eds), *The Reasoning Criminal: Rational Choice Perspectives on Offending* (New York, Springer-Verlag, 1986) 105. See SA Morrison and I O'Donnell, 'Armed and Dangerous? The Use of Firearms in Robbery' (1997) 36 *Howard Journal of Criminal Justice* 305; I Piliavin, R Gartner, C Thornton and R Matsueda, 'Crime, Deterrence and Choice' (1986) 51 *American Sociological Review* 101, 115.

[132] M Tonry, 'Learning from the Limitations of Deterrence Research' (2008) 37 *Crime & Justice* 279, 281.

[133] F Feeney, 'Robbers as Decision-Makers' in Cornish and Clarke, n 131, 66.

fact be deterred by more severe sentences. This suggests that presumptive minimum sentences may be effective in addressing organised crime. Nonetheless, while robbers appear to consider rationally the potential rewards of the offence, they put less effort into examining the possible costs,[134] and the risk element of the rational choice model rarely impacts on the decision to commit a crime.[135] Furthermore, individuals who perceive a low risk to themselves will only be marginally, if at all, influenced by more punitive approaches.[136] The crux of the matter may be whether those who have yet to be deterred (by evidence of their continued commission of crime) can be deterred by additional punishment threats.[137] Overall, there is no evidence that the introduction of presumptive sentences has had an effect on crime rates,[138] though such a causal link would be difficult to draw. Regardless of their efficacy, these measures embody the concern of legislators about such criminality and about the perceived leniency of the judiciary who overall are wedded to a different model of sentencing.

It does not follow that the presence of such sentences on the statute book leads to their imposition in practice. Ultimately, the imperatives of deterrence, the incapacitation of criminals and the conveyance of disapproval are tempered by the determining principle of proportionality in sentencing. The 'exceptional circumstances' caveat has permitted the Irish courts in particular to circumvent the punitive intention of the legislature and to withstand the drift towards a crime control model of criminal justice, by ensuring that the personal circumstances of the offender remain central to the sentencing decision. This resistance is less pronounced across the UK, but in a similar fashion OLRs have failed to gain traction in Scotland. Essentially, the fact remains that policy makers are limited in the degree to which they may constrain the judiciary in sentencing practice, notwithstanding public and political sentiment about the appropriate level of punishment for organised crime and the rationales that should animate this dimension of the criminal process.

IV. Reduction of Sentences in Return for Assistance

Contemporaneous to this prescription of punishment for organised crimes has been a formalisation in the UK of the scheme of sentence reduction for offenders who provide evidence or other information to agents of the State.[139] Such an

---

[134] Morrison and O'Donnell, n 131, 178.

[135] Piliavin *et al*, n 131, 115.

[136] G Hales, C Lewis and D Silverstone, *Gun Crime: The Market in and Use of Illegal Firearms* (London, Home Office, 2006) 95.

[137] S Bushway and P Reuter, 'Deterrence, Economics, and the Context of Drug Markets' (2011) 10 *Criminology & Public Policy* 183, 184.

[138] See Law Reform Commission, n 77, para 3.283.

[139] See ch 5 IIB re accomplice evidence.

incentive to cooperation is critical in the context of organised crime,[140] given that intelligence or testimony may otherwise be difficult to obtain, due to the absence of a victim or because of witness intimidation. The secretive nature of organised crime groups means that assistance from participants is extremely valuable, both in terms of intelligence about the workings, structure, membership and methodology of the group, in addition to evidence about specific instances of criminality.

At common law a sentence reduction was granted to offenders who provided information about other criminals, depending on the extent and value of the information, and the police would draft a 'text', setting out the assistance given by the offender, for consideration by the sentencing judge.[141] Now, such a reduction scheme is regulated by the Serious Organised Crime and Police Act 2005.[142] There is no equivalent measure in Ireland, although as noted in chapter five concessions in terms of indemnity against prosecution or an acceptance of a plea of guilty to fewer charges or a lesser charge may be granted by the Irish Director of Public Prosecutions.[143]

The Court of Appeal stressed the benefit of cooperation by organised crime participants to law enforcement and the community as a whole:

> It is to the advantage of law-abiding citizens that criminals should be encouraged to inform upon their criminal colleagues. They know that if they do so they are likely to be the subject of unwelcome attention, to say the least, for the rest of their lives. They know that their days of living by crime are probably at an end. Consequently, an expectation of some substantial mitigation of what would otherwise be the proper sentence is required in order to produce the desired result, namely the information.[144]

Without such credit there is no encouragement for others to come forward.[145] Nevertheless, as Fyfe and Sheptycki observe, this may run the risk of the 'cooperation paradox' whereby those higher in the hierarchy of an organised crime group receive lower sentences than their subordinates by having more information to exchange.[146]

Defendants who plead guilty in the Crown Court in England, Wales or Northern Ireland or in proceedings on indictment in Scotland may receive a reduction in sentence if they have entered a written agreement with a specified prosecutor to

[140] eg a former, high-ranking Cosa Nostra member Philip Leonetti testified against 38 members and associates of the Mafia, in return for which he received a sentence of six years, rather than a 45-year sentence: see www.state.nj.us/sci/pdf/ocbars2.pdf; also J Jacobs and L Gouldin, 'Cosa Nostra: The Final Chapter?' (1999) 25 *Crime and Justice* 129–89.
[141] *R v Lowe* (1978) 66 Cr App R 122; *R v Sinfield* (1981) 3 Cr App R (S) 258. See DA Thomas, 'Case Comment *R v Chaudhury and Others*: Sentencing – Assistance to Prosecuting Authority – Assistance Given after Sentence' [2010] *Crim LR* 246, 248.
[142] This follows the recommendations in Home Office, *One Step Ahead – A 21st Century Strategy to Defeat Organised Crime* (London, Home Office, 2004) 47.
[143] Office of the Director of Public Prosecutions, *Guidelines for Prosecutors* (Dublin, Office of the Director of Public Prosecutions, 2007) paras 14.4–14.6.
[144] *King* (1985) 7 Cr App R (S) 227.
[145] *R v Lowe*, n 141, 125.
[146] N Fyfe and J Sheptycki, 'International Trends in the Facilitation of Witness Cooperation in Organized Crime Cases' (2006) 3 *European Journal of Criminology* 319, 347.

assist the investigator or the prosecutor in relation to any offence.[147] The legislation does not provide directly for the appropriate level of discount,[148] but states that in its determination the court may take into account the extent and nature of the assistance. If a lower sentence is imposed because of cooperation than otherwise would be the case the judge must state so in open court, and also what the greater sentence would have been.[149] Given that the defendant is required to divulge previous criminal activities which may have been unknown to the police and which might not otherwise have been attributed to him, 'sentencing for offences which fall into this category should usually be approached with these realities in mind and . . . should normally lead to the imposition of concurrent sentences'.[150]

An offender may get off 'very lightly' in return for giving evidence against his co-defendants:

> Such a possibility is inherent in the SOCPA regime. It does not provide a good reason for excluding the evidence, though it does reinforce the need to ensure that the jury are properly directed on how to approach the evidence.[151]

In essence, 'the common law, and now statute, has accepted that this is a price worth paying to achieve the overwhelming and recurring public interest that major criminals, in particular, should be caught and prosecuted to conviction'.[152]

While the defendant has earned 'an appropriate reward for the assistance provided to the administration of justice' and there is a need to 'encourage others to do the same', only in the most exceptional cases would the appropriate level of reduction exceed three-quarters of the total sentence which would otherwise be passed, and the normal level is a reduction of between one-half and two-thirds.[153] For example, an application for leave to appeal against the result of a review of sentence which resulted in a reduction of about 25 per cent was dismissed by the Court of Appeal in *R v D* on the basis that while D had provided valuable information and fulfilled the agreement he did not describe his own criminality completely nor give evidence against anyone.[154] Moreover, in *Bevens* the Court of Appeal upheld a reduction of five years on a life sentence with a minimum term of 26 years, on the basis that while B complied with his statutory agreement and thereby made a specific contribution to the successful prosecution of a corrupt police officer, '[h]is level of cooperation was completely calculated: it was very far from full'.[155]

---

[147] Serious Organised Crime and Police Act 2005, s 73; Police, Public Order and Criminal Justice (Scotland) Act 2006, s 91.

[148] *R v P and Blackburn* [2007] EWCA Crim 2290 [37].

[149] Serious Organised Crime and Police Act 2005, s 73(2).

[150] *R v P and Blackburn*, n 148, [40].

[151] *R v Daniels* [2010] EWCA (Crim) 2740 [57]. See A Roberts, 'Case Comment *R v Daniels (John)*: Evidence – Evidence of Co-accused – Co-accused Having Entered into Statutory Agreement to Give Assistance to Authorities' [2011] *Crim LR* 556.

[152] *R v P and Blackburn*, n 148, [22].

[153] ibid, [40].

[154] *R v D* [2010] EWCA Crim 1485 [13].

[155] *R v Bevens* [2009] EWCA Crim 2554 [17].

It has been claimed that the Serious Organised Crime and Police Act 2005 encourages the sentencing of defendants at the time of plea, which results in their obtaining the benefit of the deal based on a mere offer of assistance and before they fulfil their most important commitment under the agreement, namely testifying at trial.[156] However, this may be an unfair criticism of legislation given that some such agreements do not require testimony at trial. Moreover, in certain instances a specified prosecutor has the capacity to refer a case back to the sentencing court for review if the person is still serving his sentence.[157] Such reference may occur when a person receives a discounted sentence due to his written offer to assist but knowingly fails to do so: 'this provides an important safeguard against dishonest manipulation of the process by the defendant'.[158] It could also arise when a person offers to give further assistance according to another written agreement, or when a person who has received a sentence which is not discounted subsequently gives or offers to give assistance.[159] A case so referred must, if possible, be heard by the original sentencing judge.

Prior to the Serious Organised Crime and Police Act 2005 it was noted that 'Queen's Evidence' was underused in serious and organised crime cases[160] and this does not appear to have been altered greatly by the new legislative provisions.[161] Figures from the Crown Prosecution Service indicate that from 2006–11 approximately 114 reductions in sentence were given in return for assistance to the prosecution.[162] Nonetheless, the inclusion on the statute books of this ability to grant sentence discounts is a pragmatic recognition of the fact that, as previously alluded to in chapter five, much eyewitness information or testimony regarding organised crime may be available only from those who are implicated to a degree in criminality themselves. This may suggest that sentence discounts are an unavoidable aspect of addressing organised criminality, but it is problematic for the mitigation of sentences to be predicated on knowledge of and involvement in crime. While this is bona fide individualised sentencing, the danger remains that shrewd or seasoned individuals may circumvent the law and the possibility of lengthy punishment by providing evidence against their (former) associates, but only to a certain, limited and calculated degree. Though the Court of Appeal demonstrated its ability to recognise this in *Bevens* and in *D*, the individuals involved still received a substantial reduction in sentence. Ultimately, reducing sentences in return for assistance appears to undermine, or, at the very least, fails to address the purposes of sentencing, given that does not serve the aim of retribution,

---

[156] J de Grazia and K Hyland, 'Mainstreaming the Use of Assisting Offenders: How to Make SOCPA 2005, s 73 and s 74 Work' [2011] *Crim LR* 358, 365.

[157] Serious Organised Crime and Police Act 2005, s 74; Police, Public Order and Criminal Justice (Scotland) Act 2006, s 92. Section 75A of the Serious Organised Crime and Police Act 2005 allows a s 74 sentencing to take place via live link under s 57E of the Crime and Disorder Act 1998.

[158] *R v P and Blackburn*, n 148, [29].

[159] Serious Organised Crime and Police Act 2005, s 74.

[160] Home Office, n 142, 47.

[161] De Grazia and Hyland, n 156, 358, fn 5.

[162] HC Deb 7 July 2011, col 1305W (Solicitor General).

deterrence, reparation, or rehabilitation. More tenuously, it could be argued that such sentence reduction may improve public safety by increasing the likelihood of prosecution and punishment of another offender, yet this is at the price of punishing adequately the wrongdoing of the assisting offender. In a truly pragmatic manner, both the legislature and the courts in the UK have concluded that this is worthwhile. Ultimately, this is the triumph of crime control over due process.

V. Confiscation of Property upon Conviction

A further critical development in the post-conviction context focuses on the money generated from organised crime. Organised criminals may conceal effectively the wealth they accrue, and therefore the view developed that imprisonment alone could not strike adequately at the capital which facilitates the continuation of criminality and organised crime groups themselves. As Lord Woolf CJ noted in *R v Sekhon*,

> [o]ne of the most successful weapons which can be used to discourage offences that are committed in order to enrich the offenders is to ensure that if the offenders are brought to justice, any profit which they have made from their offending is confiscated.[163]

It was thus deemed 'essential' to have '[e]ffective but fair powers of confiscating the proceeds of crime'.[164] The rationale for the implementation of this measure, which may in some circumstances be 'penal or even . . . draconian', is to '[strip] criminals of the benefits of their crimes'.[165] Moreover, the confiscation of assets of convicted criminals is seen as a powerful deterrent to the commission of further criminal offences.[166] Thus, confiscation may be seen as punitive, as well as preventative and reparative.[167] In this vein, a number of legislative provisions in the UK and Ireland allow for the confiscation and forfeiture of property after an individual has been convicted of certain crimes.[168]

Although drug trafficking in particular was the target when such laws originated, they have now been extended to cover all serious crimes. The first such provision on the UK statute book was section 27 of the Misuse of Drugs Act 1971, echoed in section 30 of the Irish Misuse of Drugs Act 1977, which allowed for the forfeiture and destruction or other disposal of property related to an offence under the Acts for which a person was convicted. However, as the House of Lords

---

[163] *R v Sekhon* [2003] 1WLR 1655, 1658.

[164] *R v Rezvi* [2002] UKHL 1, [2002] 1 All ER 801, [2003] 1 AC 1099 [14].

[165] *R v Smith* [2001] UKHL 68, [2002] 1 All ER 366 [23].

[166] Director of Public Prosecutions, *Annual Report 2008* (Dublin, Office of the Director of Public Prosecutions, 2009) 48.

[167] Ashworth, n 7, 360.

[168] See also the terms of the United Nations, UN Convention Against Illicit Traffic in Narcotic Drugs and Psychotropic Substances 1988 and the Council of Europe, Council of Europe Convention on Laundering, Search, Seizure and Confiscation of the Proceeds from Crime 1990.

noted with 'considerable regret' in *R v Cuthbertson*, this did not facilitate the forfeiture of profits or the sum of criminally accrued gains.[169] Thus, the Hodgson Committee recommended that criminal courts should have the power to order the post-conviction confiscation of the profits of the offence.[170] This prompted the enactment of a number of Acts in the UK which enabled the courts to make orders confiscating drug trafficking profits, either after prosecution request or court decision, when the offender had benefited from drug trafficking.[171] After various amendments,[172] this process was replaced by the Drug Trafficking Act 1994. Operating in parallel to this was a scheme for confiscation in relation to indictable cases other than drug trafficking and specified summary offences, introduced by the Criminal Justice Act 1988, and amended, clarified and enhanced by subsequent legislation.[173] After a critical review of the confiscation provisions by the Cabinet Office Performance and Innovation Unit,[174] the Proceeds of Crime Act 2002 consolidated these two confiscation processes in the UK. The seizure of property upon conviction in Ireland is delineated in the Criminal Justice Act 1994.

A. Restraint Orders

One means of dealing with the money relating to organised crime is to impose a confiscation order after conviction, creating a personal debt due to the State that the offender is obliged to pay from whatever assets are available to him.[175] Before this occurs, assets are usually frozen.

Across the UK and Ireland, the Crown, Sheriff and High Courts may make a restraint order prohibiting any specified person from dealing with realisable property held by him, upon application by a prosecutor, the Director of SOCA, or an accredited financial investigator (a specially trained officer who works in a police service, HMRC or various other public bodies[176]).[177] This order seeks to prevent the dissipation or concealment of assets which may be prompted by a

---

[169] *R v Cuthbertson* [1981] AC 470, 479. See also the comment of the Law Reform Commission, *Report on the Confiscation of the Proceeds of Crime* (Dublin, Law Reform Commission, 1991) 8.

[170] D Hodgson, *Profits of Crime and their Recovery: The Report of a Committee Chaired by Sir Derek Hodgson* (London, Ashgate Publishing Ltd, 1984).

[171] Drug Trafficking Offences Act 1986; Criminal Justice (Scotland) Act 1987; Criminal Justice (Confiscation) (Northern Ireland) Order 1990.

[172] Prevention of Terrorism (Temporary Provisions) Act 1989 and Criminal Justice (International Cooperation) Act 1990.

[173] Criminal Justice Act 1993; Proceeds of Crime Act 1995; Proceeds of Crime (Scotland) Act 1995 and Proceeds of Crime (Northern Ireland) Order 1996. The Criminal Justice (Terrorism and Conspiracy) Act 1998 permits confiscation of monies used in furtherance of an illegal organisation after conviction of membership of such a group.

[174] Cabinet Office Performance and Innovation Unit, *Recovering the Proceeds of Crime* (London, Cabinet Office, 2000).

[175] J Ulph, 'Confiscation Orders, Human Rights, and Penal Measures' [2010] *LQR* 251.

[176] See Proceeds of Crime Act 2002, sch 1, as substituted by the Proceeds of Crime Act 2002 (References to Financial Investigators) (Amendment) Order 2009.

[177] Proceeds of Crime Act 2002, ss 41, 120 and 190; Criminal Justice Act 1994, s 23 (Ireland).

criminal investigation and which could stymie the ultimate aim of confiscating those assets permanently. In essence, restraint orders play a critical role in ensuring that enforcement opportunities for confiscation are maximised.[178]

In the UK, a restraint order may be made if there is reasonable cause to believe that the alleged offender has benefited from his criminal conduct and if a criminal investigation has been started in the particular jurisdiction of the UK, or if an application for reconsideration of the order has been or is likely to be made.[179] The Irish High Court may grant such an order where proceedings have been or are going to be instituted against the defendant for a drug trafficking or other indictable offence but have not been concluded, or where a confiscation order has been made or reasonably is thought to be made.[180] In the UK and Ireland a restraint order may be made ex parte[181] and may be based on hearsay evidence.[182] To ensure the effectiveness of a restraint order, the High Court may order a defendant to swear an affidavit as to the existence and location of assets.[183] The imposition of a condition in the order precluding the use of such information in criminal proceedings was stressed in relation to previous equivalent measures in *Re O*[184] and so there is no self-incrimination involved.[185] In the UK and Ireland a receiver or management administrator may be appointed to manage and control the property;[186] property to which a restraint order applies may be seized to prevent its removal from the jurisdiction;[187] and restraint orders may be enforced abroad.[188]

The prosecutor or any person affected by the restraint order may apply for it to be discharged or varied,[189] and appeal lies to the Court of Appeal and from there to the Supreme Court,[190] or the Court of Session in Scotland, or the Irish High Court.[191] The restraint order must be discharged once the relevant proceedings have started or if investigation is not started within a reasonable time.[192] Funds

---

[178] K Bullock, D Mann, R Street and C Coxon, *Examining Attrition in Confiscating the Proceeds of Crime* (London, Home Office, 2009).

[179] Proceeds of Crime Act 2002, ss 40, 119 and 189.

[180] Criminal Justice Act 1994, s 23(1).

[181] Proceeds of Crime Act 2002, ss 42, 121 and 191; Criminal Justice Act 1994, s 24(4) (Ireland).

[182] Proceeds of Crime Act 2002, s 46. There is nothing regarding the admissibility of hearsay evidence in the parts pertaining to Scotland and Northern Ireland, but given that the proceedings are not criminal in nature the criminal rules of evidence will not apply: see *R v Clipston* [2011] EWCA Crim 446, [2011] 2 Cr App R (S) 101 (CA (Crim Div)).

[183] See E Bell, 'The ECHR and the Proceeds of Crime Legislation' [2000] *Crim LR* 783, 786.

[184] *Re O and Another (Restraint Order: Disclosure of Assets)* [1991] 2 QB 520, 530.

[185] See T Millington and M Sutherland Williams, *The Proceeds of Crime* (3rd edn) (Oxford, Oxford University Press) 47–51. See ch 4, VIII for a consideration of the privilege against self-incrimination in the context of police interrogation.

[186] Proceeds of Crime Act 2002, ss 48, 49, 125 and 196; Criminal Justice Act 1994, s 24(7) (Ireland).

[187] Proceeds of Crime Act 2002, ss 45, 126 and 194; Criminal Justice Act 1994, s 24(9) (Ireland).

[188] Proceeds of Crime Act 2002, ss 74, 141 and 222.

[189] Proceeds of Crime Act 2002, ss 42(3), 122, 181; Criminal Justice Act 1994, s 24(5) and (6) (Ireland).

[190] Proceeds of Crime Act 2002, ss 43 and 44, 181.

[191] Criminal Justice Act 1994, s 24(5) (Ireland).

[192] Proceeds of Crime Act 2002, ss 42(6) and (7), 121(8) and (9), 191(6) and (7); Criminal Justice Act 1994, s 23(3) (Ireland).

under restraint may not be released to the defendant for legal expenses related to the offences in respect of which the restraint order is made; instead public funding for legal expenses is available.[193] This was in reaction to what was perceived to be unnecessary expenditure on legal fees which diminished the restrained assets and as a result the amount which could ultimately be confiscated by the State. This measure has been found not to breach the property right under Article 1 of the First Protocol to the ECHR.[194]

Although a restraint order is temporary and does not take away a person's property permanently, it is nonetheless 'far-reaching' and may be 'draconian' insofar as it may affect his capacity to do business or conduct other private affairs.[195] Moreover, '[t]he Crown's concern to safeguard an accused's property against dissipation or removal abroad must always be weighed against the possibility that the price to be paid will fall upon an innocent man'.[196] To this end, compensation may be paid in both the UK and Ireland if proceedings are not started after investigation or if the person is acquitted or pardoned, and if in the investigation or proceedings there has been a serious default by a police or customs officer or member of the Crown Prosecution Service, the Serious Fraud Office or Inland Revenue, without which the investigation or proceedings would not have continued and as a result of which the property owner suffered a loss.[197] In other words, the ability of the individual to recover losses is limited to cases in which there has been serious default by an investigator of a kind which caused the investigation to continue when otherwise it would not have done. This was criticised roundly in the House of Lords' parliamentary debate where it was proposed that for due process reasons compensation should be paid in cases of negligent default and not just serious default, but this suggestion was rejected.[198]

B. Confiscation Orders

A confiscation order may be imposed after conviction, requiring the offender to pay a prescribed amount to the State.[199] In the UK, such an order may be considered when a person is before the Crown Court or Sheriff Court in Scotland after conviction, when the prosecutor or the Director of SOCA asks the court to proceed, or in England, Wales, or Northern Ireland where the court believes it is appropriate for it to do so.[200] If certain statutory criteria are then satisfied, the

[193] Proceeds of Crime Act 2002, ss 41(4), 120(4) and 190(4).
[194] *APU Ltd v Crown Prosecution Service* [2007] EWCA Crim 3128; *Re S Restraint Order (Release of Assets)* [2005] 1WLR 1338.
[195] *Director of the Serious Fraud Office v A* [2007] EWCA Crim 1927 [4].
[196] *Hughes v Customs and Excise* [2002] EWCA Civ 734, [2003] 1 WLR 177 [60].
[197] Proceeds of Crime Act 2002, ss 72, 139 and 220; Criminal Justice Act 1994, s 65 (Ireland).
[198] HL Deb 13 May 2002, vol 635, col 24 per Lord Kingsland.
[199] Ulph, n 175.
[200] Proceeds of Crime Act 2002, ss 6, 92, 156. Part 2 of the Proceeds of Crime Act 2002 governs the confiscation regime in England and Wales, Pt 3 relates to Scotland (replacing Pt 1 of the Proceeds of Crime (Scotland) Act 1995), and Pt 4 to Northern Ireland.

court has no discretion in terms of imposing a confiscation order.[201] A confiscation order not in excess of £10,000 may also be made by the Magistrates' Courts in England, Wales and Northern Ireland.[202] In Ireland a court must consider imposing a confiscation order where the offender has been convicted on indictment for a drug trafficking offence.[203] In addition, a confiscation order may be made requiring a convicted person who has benefited from an offence other than drug trafficking to pay the value of the property so obtained.[204] This is not a mandatory order, but may be imposed by the court upon application by the Irish DPP.

In the UK, the relevant court must decide, on the balance of probabilities, whether the defendant has a 'criminal lifestyle'.[205] If so, the court must decide whether he has benefited from his general criminal conduct, and if not it must decide whether he has benefited from his particular criminal conduct.[206] A three-part test is laid down regarding the determination of a criminal lifestyle. A defendant has a criminal lifestyle if his offence is a criminal lifestyle offence mentioned in Schedules 2, 4 or 5 of the Proceeds of Crime Act 2002 (including trafficking of drugs, people or arms, money laundering, counterfeiting, and blackmail); or if the offence constitutes conduct forming part of a course of criminal activity; or it is an offence committed over a period of at least six months and the defendant has benefited from that conduct. Conduct forms part of a course of criminal activity if the defendant has benefited from the conduct and in the proceedings he was convicted of three or more other offences from each of which he has benefited, or in the previous six years he was convicted on at least two separate occasions of an offence constituting conduct from which he has benefited.[207] A threshold is imposed: the defendant must have obtained benefit of not less than £5,000 from the offence.[208] The recoverable amount is an amount equal to the defendant's benefit from the conduct concerned, which the court believes is just,[209] and the court must take account of conduct occurring and property obtained up to the time it makes its decision.[210]

---

[201] When the Bill was first created, the Scottish confiscation provisions retained judicial discretion, drawing on the pre-existing law; during the debate members of the Scottish Parliament expressed their view that the measures in Scotland should emulate those in the rest of the UK in being mandatory once certain conditions are satisfied. House of Commons Proceeds of Crime Bill Standing Committee B, 15th sitting (6 December 2001).

[202] Serious Organised Crime and Police Act 2005, s 97.

[203] Criminal Justice Act 1994, s 4 (as amended). As enacted initially, s 4 required the court to consider a confiscation order where the DPP entered an application expressing his suspicion that the accused had benefited from the sale and supply of drugs. However, s 25 of the Criminal Justice Act 1999 amended this provision and imposes a mandatory requirement on the trial court to consider such an order for drug trafficking offences.

[204] Criminal Justice Act 1994, s 9.

[205] Proceeds of Crime Act 2002, ss 6(4); 92(5) and 156(4).

[206] Criminal conduct is that which constitutes an offence in the particular jurisdiction of the UK, or would constitute such an offence if it occurred in that jurisdiction (Proceeds of Crime Act 2002, ss 76, 143 and 224). A person benefits from conduct if he obtains property as a result of or in connection with the conduct (sub-s (4)).

[207] Proceeds of Crime Act 2002, ss 75, 142 and 223.

[208] Proceeds of Crime Act 2002, ss 75(4), 142(3) and 223(4).

[209] Proceeds of Crime Act 2002, ss 7, 93 and 157.

[210] Proceeds of Crime Act 2002, ss 8(2), 94(2) and 158(2).

If the court decides, on the balance of probabilities, that the defendant has a criminal lifestyle it is obliged to make the following assumptions in deciding whether and to what extent he has benefited from his general criminal conduct: it must assume that any property transferred to him at any time within six years prior to the start of proceedings or after the date of conviction was obtained as a result of his general criminal conduct; that any expenditure incurred within six years before initiation of proceedings was met from property obtained as a result of his general criminal conduct, and that for the purpose of valuing any property obtained by the defendant, he obtained it free of any other interests in it.[211] As Ulph notes, first time offenders who commit an offence under the schedules will be treated as having a criminal lifestyle and so any property or income gained in the previous six years is seen as derived from general criminal conduct, and rebutting this may prove difficult.[212] This is a particularly draconian provision. Nonetheless, such an assumption cannot be made if shown to be incorrect by the offender,[213] or if there is a serious risk of injustice.[214]

As noted above, if the person has a criminal lifestyle the court must decide whether he has benefited from his general criminal conduct; and if not it must decide whether he has benefited from his particular criminal conduct.[215] A person benefits from conduct if he obtains property as a result of or in connection with the conduct.[216] The equivalent provision in section 74 of the Criminal Justice Act 1988 was considered in *Crown Prosecution Service v Jennings* where the House of Lords noted that

> the object of the legislation is to deprive the defendant of the product of his crime or its equivalent, not to operate by way of fine. . . . This must ordinarily mean that he has obtained property so as to own it, whether alone or jointly, which will ordinarily connote a power of disposition or control, as where a person directs a payment or conveyance of property to someone else.[217]

As noted obiter in *R v May*, 'D ordinarily obtains property if in law he owns it, whether alone or jointly, which will ordinarily connote a power of disposition or control'.[218] The benefit gained is the total value of the property or advantage obtained, not the defendant's net profit after deduction of expenses or any amounts payable to co-conspirators.[219] A person benefits from conduct if he

---

[211] Proceeds of Crime Act 2002, ss 10, 96 and 160. This includes gifts: *Crown Prosecution Service v Malik* [2003] All ER (D) 33.

[212] Ulph, n 175, 271.

[213] *R v Whittington* [2009] EWCA Crim 1641, [2010] 1 Cr App R (S) 83 (CA (Crim Div)).

[214] Proceeds of Crime Act 2002, ss 10(6), 96(6) and 160(6).

[215] ss 76, 143 and 224 of the Proceeds of Crime Act 2002 provide that criminal conduct is that which constitutes an offence in the particular jurisdiction of the UK, or would constitute such an offence if it occurred in that jurisdiction. Sub-section (2) provides that it is immaterial whether the conduct occurred or property constituting a benefit was obtained before or after the passing of this Act.

[216] Proceeds of Crime Act 2002, ss 76(4), 143(4) and 224(4).

[217] *Crown Prosecution Service v Jennings* [2008] UKHL 29 [13].

[218] *R v May* [2008] UKHL 28.

[219] ibid, endnote para 48(1).

obtains property as a result of or in connection with the conduct.[220] The courts have interpreted this broadly. For example, an importer of goods, who intends not to pay any duty on them, derives a benefit through not paying the required duty, even where the goods are forfeited by HM Customs following importation before their value can be realised by him.[221] Similarly, a person may be deemed to have benefited from property criminally obtained from the true owners if he obtained possession and control of those items only temporarily, and the subsequent seizure of the items by the police did not negate his benefiting from them.[222] While couriers transporting packages of cash do not benefit to the extent of the value of the cash, money launderers who pass the money through bank accounts will so benefit.[223]

If the person is deemed to have benefited the court decides the recoverable amount and makes a confiscation order requiring payment.[224] In other words, once benefit is proven there is no discretion for the court. However, the court does not have to impose an order if it believes that a victim of the conduct has started or intends to start proceedings against the defendant.[225] In the UK, the court may allow the defendant six months to pay the order, and this may be extended to 12 months in exceptional circumstances.[226] Confiscation proceedings themselves may be postponed for up to two years from the date of conviction,[227] in contrast to postponement periods of six months under the Criminal Justice Act 1988 and the Drug Trafficking Act 1994 which gave rise to a large number of decisions in which confiscation orders were quashed on the ground that time limits were not adhered to.[228] Furthermore, when the Director of SOCA gives more evidence to the court it may make a fresh decision in a case where it had not made an order,[229] or it may recalculate the benefit made and issue a new order.[230] The prosecutor, Director of SOCA or Lord Advocate may appeal to the Court of Appeal in respect of the order or if the court decides not to make a confiscation order,[231] and the appellate court may issue, confirm, quash or vary a confiscation order, or direct the court to proceed again.[232] Further appeal lies to the UK Supreme Court from a decision of the Court of Appeal.[233] If a confiscation order is varied or discharged and a person suffers loss as a result of the order, the court

---

[220]   ss 76(4), 143(4) and 224(4).

[221]   *R v Smith* [2001] UKHL 68, [2002] 1 All ER 366.

[222]   *R v Leslie* [2008] NICA 28 [18].

[223]   *R v Allpress* [2009] 2 Cr App R (S) 58.

[224]   Proceeds of Crime Act 2002, ss 6(5), 92(6) and 156(5).

[225]   Proceeds of Crime Act 2002, ss 6(6), 92(7) and 156(6).

[226]   Proceeds of Crime Act 2002, ss 11, 116 and 161.

[227]   Proceeds of Crime Act 2002, ss 14, 99 and 164.

[228]   DA Thomas, '*Revenue and Customs Prosecution Office v Iqbal*: Sentencing – Confiscation Order - Proceeds of Crime Act 2002 (Case Comment)' [2010] *Crim LR* 511.

[229]   Proceeds of Crime Act 2002, ss 20, 104 and 169.

[230]   Proceeds of Crime Act 2002, ss 21, 105,106 and 170. Where there is a new allegation of criminality the criminal burden of proof is used: *R v Briggs Price* [2009] UKHL 19 [43].

[231]   Proceeds of Crime Act 2002, ss 31, 115 and 181.

[232]   Proceeds of Crime Act 2002, ss 32 and 182.

[233]   Proceeds of Crime Act 2002, ss 32 and 183.

may order the payment of such compensation as it believes is just to the applicant by the Lord Chancellor or Lord Advocate.[234]

In Ireland, if the court determines on the civil burden of proof that the person convicted of a drug trafficking offence has benefited from drug trafficking,[235] it must make a confiscation order requiring him to pay the value of the proceeds of the trafficking.[236] That is, a confiscation order is mandatory if the accused has so benefited. If the person has been convicted of an offence other than drug traffick-ing and is deemed to have benefited from that offence, then a confiscation order may also be made.[237] Similar to the UK, there is a statutory assumption that any property received by the respondent in the six years prior to conviction consti-tutes the proceeds of drug trafficking.[238] There is no such assumption in relation to other types of offences.

In the UK, the court must consider confiscation before any other financial orders.[239] Furthermore, property which has been taken into account in deciding the amount of a person's benefit from criminal conduct for the purpose of mak-ing a confiscation order cannot be the subject of a subsequent recovery order.[240] Conversely, the presence of a recovery order or a forfeiture order excludes that property from the calculation of benefit.[241] In other words, the property cannot be counted or recouped by the state twice.

Failure to pay a confiscation order results in imprisonment, as the order is treated as a fine,[242] and the length of imprisonment is determined by the amount payable under the order. In fact, it was noted that the extent to which offenders would be prepared to suffer an additional prison sentence in lieu of payment may have been underestimated.[243] For an amount between £100,000 and £250,000 the default term is three years; for an amount between £250,000 and £1 million it is five years and in excess of £1 million it is 10 years.[244] In Ireland, the term of impris-onment imposed for default of payment is consecutive to any term imposed for

---

[234] Proceeds of Crime Act 2002, ss 73, 140 and 221.

[235] Criminal Justice Act 1994, s 4(6).

[236] In *People (DPP) v Gilligan* (Special Criminal Court, 22 March 2002) O'Donovan J stated that such a determination involved five matters: (i) the cost to the plaintiff of purchasing drugs; (ii) the amount of drugs involved in the plaintiff's drug trafficking activities; (iii) the expense of the shipment, sale and distribution of such drugs; (iv) the consideration received by the plaintiff when disposing of those drugs; and (v) the net profit accruing to the plaintiff as a result of his drug trafficking activities. Although the Supreme Court later held that the Special Criminal Court did not have jurisdiction to impose con-fiscation orders under s 4 of the 1994 Act in *Gilligan v Special Criminal Court* (Supreme Court, 21 December 2005) para 6.3, on the basis that the Special Criminal Court was established for the trial of offences and was so limited, it is useful to see the factors that were considered by the trial court.

[237] Criminal Justice Act 1994, s 9.

[238] Criminal Justice Act 1994, s 5(4)(ii).

[239] Proceeds of Crime Act 2002, s 13.

[240] Proceeds of Crime Act 2002, s 278(9); Criminal Justice Act 1994, s 3(7).

[241] Proceeds of Crime Act 2002, ss 7(4), 93(4) and 157(4).

[242] Proceeds of Crime Act 2002, ss 35, 118 and 185; Criminal Justice Act 1994, s 19.

[243] M Levi and L Osofsky, *Investigating, Seizing and Confiscating the Proceeds of Crime* (London, Home Office Police Department, 1995).

[244] Powers of Criminal Courts (Sentencing) Act 2000; Criminal Procedure (Scotland) Act 1995 and Criminal Justice Act (Northern Ireland) 1945.

the offence itself but is reduced in proportion to any sum recovered under the order.[245] Although the court is not obliged to impose a sentence of imprisonment, it has been argued that the 'emphatic nature of the legislation' means that only in 'the most exceptional cases of hardship' would a court not do so.[246] As the English Court of Appeal noted,

> [t]he court must have particular regard to the purpose of the imposition of a period of imprisonment in default, that is to say to secure payment of the amount that the court has ordered to be paid. This is because the overriding purpose of the legislation is to ensure that those who benefit from such crimes do not retain those benefits. The power to imprison in default is given to ensuring or obtaining as far as possible the co-operation of the defendant in complying with the order. It is to be made clear to him that he has nothing to gain by non-compliance.[247]

C. Forfeiture Orders

In addition to confiscation orders, which require the convicted person to pay a sum equivalent to the proceeds of crime to the State, the State may seize property because of its use in commission of crime through the process of forfeiture. Across the UK and Ireland powers exist to deprive the offender of property used to commit or facilitating the commission of crime.[248] This means the State may remove and retain the 'instrumentality' of crime, which is the object used in the crime or for the purposes of hiding the crime. These mechanisms may operate in conjunction with confiscation, which Alldridge believes is 'unnecessary and unfair'.[249] On the contrary, it is posited that as long as confiscation is predicated on conviction this is not a problematic response to organised and serious crime which is motivated, generated and perpetrated by profit.

D. Challenges to Confiscation

The nature of confiscation and the assumptions permitted in the legislation regarding the origins of property accrued within a certain time frame have been challenged in national and European courts under domestic law and under Articles 6 and 7 and Article 1 of the First Protocol to the ECHR.

As outlined above, the Irish and UK legislation contains assumptions regarding the provenance of property prior to conviction. In the first instance, an equivalent assumption in section 3(2) of the Proceeds of Crime (Scotland) Act 1995 was

---

[245] Criminal Justice Act 1994, s 19(4).
[246] F Murphy and B Galvin, 'Targeting the Financial Wealth of Criminals in Ireland' (1999) 9 *Irish Criminal Law Journal* 133, 142.
[247] *R v Smith* [2009] EWCA Crim 344; see also *R v Qema* [2006] EWCA Crim 2806, and *R v Liscott* [2007] EWCA Crim 1706.
[248] Powers of Criminal Courts (Sentencing) Act 2000, s 143; Proceeds of Crime (Scotland) Act 1995, pt 2; Criminal Justice Act 1994, ss 61–62.
[249] P Alldridge, *Money Laundering Law* (Oxford, Hart Publishing, 2003) 782.

challenged in *McIntosh v Lord Advocate* on the basis that it breached the presumption of innocence protected by Article 6(2) of the ECHR.[250] The Privy Council, overturning the decision of the Scottish High Court of Justiciary, held that that reliance upon such assumptions did not violate Article 6(2) because property could be confiscated only after conviction, and thus the presumption of innocence was not applicable as it applies to persons charged with an offence not those who have already been convicted. So, while confiscation proceedings 'are an extension of the sentencing hearing and, therefore, criminal in nature',[251] there is no bringing of a new charge and the purpose of this procedure is not the conviction or acquittal of the applicant for any other drugs-related offence but rather a decision regarding the level of the confiscation order.[252] The European Court of Human Rights concluded that the 'procedure was analogous to the determination by a court of the amount of a fine or the length of a period of imprisonment to be imposed on a properly convicted offender'.[253] Moreover, the applicant could rebut the assumptions and the court did not need to apply the assumption if there was a serious risk of injustice.[254] The key distinction between these measures and the civil recovery process (which will be considered in chapter seven) is that

> the confiscation proceedings are treated by the European Court of Human Rights as linked to the prior criminal proceedings, but analogous to the process of sentencing rather than establishing a criminal charge, and therefore not normally subject to article 6(2) ... By contrast Part 5 of the 2002 Act is not necessarily linked to criminal proceedings of any kind.[255]

It was further held in *McIntosh* that while the Article 6(1) protection of the right to a fair trial is relevant, it was not breached as the court could make the assumptions only if there was a significant discrepancy between the accused's property and expenditure and the accused's known sources of income.[256] Similarly, in *R v Benjafield* the House of Lords held that the statutory assumptions[257] were no wider than was necessary to achieve the legitimate aim of depriving criminals of the proceeds of criminal conduct and were not disproportionate so as to breach the defendant's rights under Article 6(1).[258] Ulph notes that this shifting of the burden of proof to rebut the assumptions may pose difficulties in terms of the presentation of convincing evidence to demonstrate that the property has a legitimate origin.[259] Nevertheless, this does not seem like an unjustifiable onus on

---

[250] *McIntosh* (2001) SC (PC) 89. Also see *Phillips v UK* (2001) 11 BHRC 280; *R v Briggs-Price* [2009] UKHL 19.

[251] *Clipston v R* (Rev 1) [2011] EWCA Crim 446 [45]; *McIntosh v Lord Advocate* [2001] UKPC D 1R.

[252] *Phillips v UK*, n 250, [34].

[253] ibid.

[254] ibid, [43].

[255] *Serious Organised Crime Agency v Gale* [2010] EWCA Civ 759 [44].

[256] *McIntosh v Lord Advocate*, n 251.

[257] In s 72AA of the Criminal Justice Act 1988 and s 4(3) of the Drug Trafficking Act 1994.

[258] See also *R v Benjafield* [2002] UKHL 2, [2003] 1 AC 1099 [7].

[259] Ulph, n 175, 273.

convicted offenders, given the valid public policy imperatives of the legislation,[260] to recoup illegally obtained property.

Similarly, the Irish High Court has rejected the claim that confiscation and its ancillary provisions constitute a criminal procedure which imposes a penalty.[261] The provisions do not purport to create a criminal charge, nor do they require the court to make a direct finding that the person committed any offence other than that for which he was convicted. The Court relied on case law upholding the constitutionality of the Proceeds of Crime Act 1996[262] to conclude that the making of an order under the Act did not involve the imposition of a penalty or punishment, but rather sought to recover the value of the benefits gained through drug trafficking.[263] The court must determine whether the person benefited from drug trafficking, rather than whether he committed a drug trafficking offence, and the amount to be recovered is limited to the amount of benefit received by the defendant and also by his means, so that he cannot be ordered to make a payment without the means to do so, in contrast to financial penalties imposed for criminal offences which are absolute, irrespective of the defendant's resources. Moreover, the payment of the amount benefited from drug trafficking does not absolve the individual from liability for the offence.[264]

Despite the upholding of the confiscation process as a whole, domestic courts and the ECHR have found that the application of the process has breached Article 6 when there was an unjustifiable delay in the institution of proceedings to imprison someone for failing to satisfy a confiscation order. This is a notable favouring of due process over the precepts of crime control, albeit within the parameters of an otherwise stringent regime. In *Lloyd v Bow Street Magistrates' Court*, the High Court considered whether the right under Article 6(1) to have a criminal charge determined within a reasonable time was violated where delay occurred in the institution or prosecution of proceedings to commit a defendant to prison in default of payment of a sum due under a confiscation order.[265] The Court held that Article 6(1) applied to proceedings to enforce the confiscation order, and rejected the contention that because it was the defendant's continuing duty to satisfy the order, he had no right to have the enforcement proceedings completed within a reasonable time. The High Court stayed the proceedings as an

---

[260]   *Grayson and Barnham v UK* (2009) 48 EHRR 30, para 49.
[261]   *Gilligan v Special Criminal Court* (High Court, 8 November 2002).
[262]   *Murphy v GM* [2001] 4 IR 113; *Gilligan v Criminal Assets Bureau* [1998] 3 IR 185. See ch 7.
[263]   *Gilligan*, n 261.
[264]   ibid. When the constitutionality of confiscation was challenged on appeal in the Irish Supreme Court, the Court determined that the decision concerning the jurisdiction of the Special Criminal Court was sufficient to dispose of the case and so did not consider the issue. *Gilligan v Special Criminal Court*, n 236.
[265]   *Lloyd v Bow Street Magistrates' Court* [2003] EWHC 2294. Lloyd was convicted in 1996 and failed to pay the associated confiscation order within the requisite 12 months. A receiver was appointed in 1999, but did not realise the assets, and in 2001 a summons was issued to enforce the confiscation order by means of a warrant to commit Lloyd to custody for non-payment. The hearing of the summons took place in 2002.

abuse of process, and stressed that the public interest in stripping criminals of the proceeds of their criminal activities is best served

> if those authorities whose task it is to enforce confiscation orders (a) take prompt steps to secure payment by 'civil' procedures and (if those fail) (b) take prompt steps to activate any term of imprisonment in default. The longer the authorities delay, the less likely it is that the offender will still have assets to meet the confiscation order.[266]

Similarly, in *Crowther v United Kingdom* the European Court of Human Rights found Article 6(1) to have been breached by the lapse of more than eight years after the applicant had been charged before enforcement proceedings were concluded: the applicant's duty to pay the sum owing under the confiscation order did not absolve the authorities from ensuring that the proceedings were completed within a reasonable time.[267] In addition to such cases centring on Article 6(1), the imposition of a confiscation order in a certain context has been found by the European Court of Human Rights to breach the presumption of innocence as protected by Article 6(2). The appellant in *Geerings v Netherlands* had been acquitted of most of the charges against him, yet a confiscation order was imposed including the benefit derived from all the offences with which he had been charged, even those of which he had been acquitted.[268] This expression of suspicion was held to breach Article 6(2), given that the confiscation was not predicated on conviction as is usually the case.

Furthermore, it has been claimed that the imposition of a confiscation order amounts to a retrospective penalty contrary to Article 7(1) of the ECHR where the acts took place before the enactment of the relevant legislation. Before dealing with this point, it should be noted that the status of confiscation as a penalty is not contested in the UK and Europe: in *R v Banks* the English Court of Appeal accepted that the confiscation provisions in the Drug Trafficking Act 1994 were penal, and could see 'no reason in principle why two penalties should not be imposed for the same unlawful act', emphasising the 'evils of the international drug trade'.[269] Similarly, the European Court of Human Rights in *Welch v UK* determined that the confiscation order amounted to a penalty.[270] However, returning to the matter of retrospectivity specifically, the European Court in *Welch* agreed with the applicant that the imposition of the confiscation order violated Article 7(1) as it could not have been imposed at the time that he committed the offences for which he was convicted. In reaching this conclusion, the Court emphasised the 'sweeping statutory assumptions': that all property passing through the offender's hands over a six-year period was the fruit of drug trafficking unless he could prove otherwise; the fact that the confiscation order was directed at the proceeds involved in drug dealing and was not limited to profit,

---

[266] ibid, [35].
[267] *Crowther v United Kingdom* App no 53741/00, *The Times*, 1 February 2005, para 29. This case was followed in *Stone v Clerk to the Justices, Plymouth Magistrates' Court* [2007] EWHC 2519 (Admin).
[268] *Geerings v Netherlands* (2008) 46 EHRR 49.
[269] *R v Banks* [1996] EWCA Crim 1655.
[270] *Welch v United Kingdom* (1995) 20 EHRR 247.

and the possibility of imprisonment in default of payment.[271] The retroactive application of a confiscation order breached the ECHR as the applicant faced more far-reaching detriment as a result of the order than that to which he was exposed at the time when he was convicted.[272] The Court stressed that this determination concerned the retrospective application of confiscation only, and did not question the power of confiscation. Since *Welch* the English Court of Appeal has rejected a submission that the imposition of a default sentence for failing to pay a confiscation order amounted to a 'heavier penalty' and therefore was a breach of Article 7, determining that it was simply a means of enforcement.[273]

Finally, challenges to confiscation have been raised under Article 1 of the First Protocol to the ECHR which safeguards the right to private property. This argument relating to previous legislation was rejected in *Phillips v United Kingdom* on the basis that the interference with the right is justified, and was reiterated in *Rezvi*: '[t]he legislation is a precise, fair and proportionate response to the important need to protect the public'.[274]

Thus, while certain aspects of the application of confiscation have fallen foul of the ECHR, the scheme itself has not been challenged. Though the assumptions permitted in the legislation are truly broad, such as the assumption relating to a criminal lifestyle, they are not unduly so, given that conviction on the criminal burden of proof is first required, and given the ability of the individual to rebut these assumptions.

E. Effectiveness of Confiscation

The potential effectiveness of confiscation as a means of addressing organised crime in the UK and Ireland has been stymied in various respects. Some problems with confiscation are difficult to avoid: in the first instance, the failure to convict many high-ranking organised criminals precludes confiscation, and moreover, even if a prosecution is successful, funds may have been spent or dispersed already.[275] In addition to such 'behavioural attrition', 'administrative attrition' may occur through settlement by negotiation and as a result of defence challenges.[276] It is these flaws in confiscation which Kennedy suggests explain the subsequent introduction of civil recovery legislation.[277] Though this may be so in the UK, this observation is not sustainable in Ireland, given that the latter followed the introduction of confiscation by just two years, and so the post-conviction process was still nascent.

[271] ibid, para 34.
[272] ibid, paras 33–36.
[273] *Malik*, n 211, [43].
[274] *Phillips v UK*, n 250; *Rezvi*, n 164, [17].
[275] Levi and Osofsky, n 243.
[276] Bullock *et al*, n 178, 23–24.
[277] A Kennedy, 'Justifying the Civil Recovery of Criminal Proceeds' (2004) 12 *Journal of Financial Crime* 8.

It seems that the true extent of the confiscation powers has not been felt in Ireland, and civil recovery under the Proceeds of Crime Act 1996 has superseded post-conviction orders to a large degree.[278] The civil mechanism of asset recovery has proved more appealing to the authorities than the criminal confiscation scheme, given that the former relies on the civil burden of proof and is not contingent on the conviction of an individual. Nonetheless, every year criminal confiscation and forfeiture orders totalling approximately €1m are made, with between a quarter and half of this being confiscation alone.[279] No figures for restraint orders are available. In England, Wales and Northern Ireland, £27.2m was the subject of restraint orders in 2006–07, £46.8m in 2007–08, £128.8m in 2008–09, £103.7m in 2009–10, £45.8m in 2010–11 and £58.9m in 2011–12, while the figures for confiscation orders were £14.5m, £11.6m, £29.7m, £17.2m and £33.8m and £14m respectively.[280] In Scotland, between £1m and £4m was confiscated annually from 2003 until 2009, in 2010 £16m was confiscated and in 2011 £7m.[281] These figures suggest that the effectiveness of confiscation in the UK has improved somewhat since certain critical reviews.[282] Nonetheless a recent report highlights lost opportunities for the early identification and value assessment of assets, delays, and insufficient cooperation between investigators and prosecutors,[283] though this was disputed by the Crown Prosecution Service.[284] The success of confiscation depends to a great extent on the financial investigator,[285] and calls have been made for a more systematic approach to confiscation investigations.[286] Further remediable issues include the absence of organisational incentive to deal vigorously with confiscation matters and the lack of benefit from

---

[278] See ch 7.

[279] In 2008 53 confiscation and forfeiture orders were made, totalling €1,062,796; in 2009 72 amounting to €1,637,857 and in 2010 59 orders (€821,087). As regards confiscation alone, in 2008 13 orders were made confiscating €279,000; in 2009 19 orders (€495,552); and in 2010 19 orders (€324,749). Office of the Director of Public Prosecutions, *Office of the Director of Public Prosecutions Annual Reports 2007–10* (Dublin, Director of Public Prosecutions, 2008–11) table 12.

[280] Serious Organised Crime Agency, *Annual Report 2008–09* (London, Serious Organised Crime Agency, 2009) 32; Serious Organised Crime Agency, *Annual Report and Accounts 2009–10* (London, Serious Organised Crime Agency, 2009) 20. Serious Organised Crime Agency, *Annual Report and Accounts 2010–11* (London, Serious Organised Crime Agency, 2011) 16; Serious Organised Crime Agency, *Annual Report and Accounts 2011–12* (London, Serious Organised Crime Agency, 2012) 15.

[281] Crown Office and Procurator Fiscal Service News Release, 'Proceeds of Crime Figures Announced for End of 2011–12', 13 May 2012.

[282] Home Office Working Group on Confiscation, *Third Report: Criminal Assets* (London, Home Office, 1998); HM Inspectorate of Constabulary for Scotland, *Making Crime Pay: Confiscation of Criminal Assets in Scotland* (Edinburgh, HM Inspectorate of Constabulary for Scotland, 2000) para 1.4.

[283] HM Crown Prosecution Service Inspectorate, HM Inspectorate of Constabulary and HM Inspectorate of Court Administration, *Joint Thematic Review of Asset Recovery: Restraint and Confiscation Casework* (London, Stationery Office, 2010) 28 and 36.

[284] Crown Prosecution Service Press Statement, 'CPS has Mixed Response to the Joint Thematic Casework Review of Asset Recovery', 25 March 2010, available at www.cps.gov.uk/news/press_statements/cps_statement_on_assets_recovery/index.html.

[285] See n 176.

[286] K Bullock, 'The Confiscation Investigation: Investigating the Financial Benefit Made from Crime' (2010) 4 *Policing* 7.

confiscation efforts at a resource allocation level (ie the confiscating agencies do not share in the assets acquired), the absence of expertise and training, and the cost of enforcement.[287] Asset recovery is seen to remain as a 'minority speciality' amongst the judiciary, and calls have been made for the enshrining as a principle of sentencing the deprivation of criminals of their illicit gains to improve rates of confiscation.[288]

Therefore it seems that, although under-utilised, post-conviction confiscation serves as another valuable facet of the State's powers in the context of punishing, and to an extent preventing, organised crime. The scheme of restraint and confiscation moves beyond the traditional range of custodial sentences to provide a further mechanism with which to address organised criminality and represents the adaptation of the State to both the nature of organised crime which often requires ready capital, and the limitations of imprisonment in addressing this.

VI. Further Ancillary Orders

Beyond confiscation and forfeiture which address the instrumentalities and profits of organised criminality, other post-conviction orders may be imposed. These measures include conditions and requirements that aim to prevent crime and improve the ability of State agencies to monitor offenders upon release.

Across the UK, travel restrictions may be imposed on drug traffickers who have been imprisoned for at least four years, prohibiting them from leaving the UK for at least two years as specified after leaving custody,[289] and breach of the order is an offence.[290] If the court determines that it is not appropriate to make a travel restriction order (TRO), it must state its reasons. The purpose 'is to prevent or reduce the risk of re-offending after the defendant's release from prison', and this is a 'very important public interest'.[291] Nonetheless, a TRO would not be upheld in a case where the individual's involvement in drug trafficking was a 'one-off'.[292] Similarly, in Ireland, any person convicted of drug trafficking who has been imprisoned for at least a year must inform the Gardaí of certain matters, and the period for which notification is required is determined by the length of sentence.[293] Such a person must inform the Gardaí within seven days of conviction of

---

[287] Levi and Osofsky, n 243.

[288] Home Office, *Asset Recovery Action Plan: A Consultation Document* (London, Home Office, 2007) 29.

[289] Criminal Justice and Police Act 2001, s 33.

[290] Criminal Justice and Police Act 2001, s 36.

[291] *R v Mee* [2004] EWCA Crim 629 [8].

[292] *R v Fuller* [2005] EWCA Crim 1029; [2006] 1 Cr App R (S) 8.

[293] Criminal Justice Act 2006, pt 9. The period for which notification is required is 12 years if the sentence imposed was life imprisonment; 7 years if the sentence imposed was one of imprisonment for more than 10 years but not life imprisonment; 5 years if the sentence imposed was between 5 and 10 years imprisonment; 3 years if the sentence imposed was between 1 and 5 years imprisonment; and 1 year if a suspended sentence was imposed. These periods are halved if the individual was younger than

his names or nicknames and home address,[294] and within seven days of being released he must inform the Gardaí of a number of other matters, including using another name and any change of address.[295] Furthermore, he must inform the Gardaí if he intends to leave the State for a continuous period of seven days or more, and after returning from abroad after being away for more than seven days.[296] Failure to adhere to these conditions is a criminal offence.[297]

A further comparable development is the introduction in Ireland of monitoring orders and protection of persons orders.[298] A court may impose a monitoring order on an offender who is convicted on indictment of an offence including murder, false imprisonment, certain firearms offences, drug trafficking, and organised crime offences, and who received a sentence of less than the maximum term of imprisonment for such an offence.[299] The order, which lasts for at most seven years, requires the individual to notify in writing an inspector of the Gardaí of his address, any change in this or any proposed absence for a period of more than seven days. A protection of persons order aims to protect the victim of the offence concerned or any other person from harassment, distress or intimidation caused by the offender.[300] Moreover, a post-release (restriction of certain activities) order may be imposed on a person convicted of an organised crime offence if it is in the public interest to do so.[301] Such an order may impose restrictions or conditions on the offender's movements or activities, or association with others, and may last for seven years at most. It is an offence to fail without reasonable cause to comply with any such order.[302]

In the UK, financial reporting orders (FROs) may be imposed. These have a preventative aim, by facilitating close monitoring of a person's financial affairs. When a person is convicted of a deception offence under the Theft Acts, a lifestyle offence under the Proceeds of Crime Act 2002 (including trafficking of drugs, people or arms, money laundering, counterfeiting, and blackmail), or an offence of bribery, the court may make a financial reporting order in addition to any

18 years at the time of sentencing (s 90(4)). A person who is subject to the maximum notification period may apply to the court after 8 years (or four years in the case of a minor) of being released from prison for an order discharging these obligations on the ground that the interests of the common good are no longer served by his continuing to be subject to them (ss 93(1) and (2)).

[294] Criminal Justice Act 2006, s 92(1).

[295] Criminal Justice Act 2006, s 92.

[296] Criminal Justice Act 2006, s 92(3) and (4).

[297] Criminal Justice Act 2006, s 94.

[298] Criminal Justice Act 2007. The Bill as published originally provided for 'crime prevention orders' which empowered the court to impose 'such conditions as it considered necessary' such as requiring the individual to keep the peace, stopping him from accessing certain places or contacting certain people, and obliging him to notify the Gardaí of a change of address, employment or education.

[299] Criminal Justice Act 2007, s 26(2).

[300] Criminal Justice Act 2007, ss 26(4) and (5).

[301] Criminal Justice Act 2007, s 26A, as inserted by the Criminal Justice (Amendment) Act 2009. Such an offence is one in Pt 7 of the Criminal Justice Act 2006 or an offence specified in Sch 2 that has been committed as part of, or in furtherance of, the activities of a criminal organisation.

[302] For consideration see M Rogan, 'The Innocence Rights of Sentenced Offenders' (2011) 2 *Irish Journal of Legal Studies* 55, 62.

sentence, if satisfied that there is a sufficiently high risk of the person committing another such offence to justify making such an order.[303] This order requires the individual to make reports at specified periods, setting out particulars of his financial affairs; failure to comply or the inclusion of false or misleading information without reasonable excuse is an offence punishable by imprisonment.[304] An FRO made by a Magistrates' or Sheriff Court must not exceed five years, or otherwise, must not exceed 20 years after a sentence of life imprisonment or 15 years for other offences. The person to whom the report is made may disclose the report to appropriate persons to ascertain its accuracy or to prevent, detect, investigate or prosecute criminal offences.[305]

After an obiter statement in *R v Adams* that an FRO was not a penalty but rather a preventative measure,[306] the issue was addressed directly in *R v Wright*.[307] The point was abandoned because the appellant was advised that it was unarguable and the Court felt that this advice was correct.[308] The Court noted that

> an indirect effect of information given under the financial reporting order might turn out to be of some assistance to those who are seeking to enforce a confiscation order. The obvious case in which that might happen is if a prosecution for a money laundering offence followed and revealed into the public domain the existence of assets against which the order could be enforced. There may be other situations in which such indirect effect might occur.[309]

This illustrates how an FRO can assist in the other provisions used against organised crime. Nonetheless, the Court cautioned that 'it ought not to be thought that [an FRO] . . . is routinely to be made without proper thought'.[310] This indicates the careful application of this measure in practice.

In addition, and more broadly, Part 1 of the Serious Crime Act 2007 allows serious crime prevention orders (SCPOs) to be imposed in England, Wales and Northern Ireland. SCPOs contain prohibitions, obligations or other terms that the court see as appropriate to protect the public by preventing or disrupting involvement in serious crime by the person who is subject to the order. These orders may limit or place conditions on working arrangements, associations, communications, the use of premises and travel.[311] SCPOs arguably blur the

---

[303] Serious Organised Crime and Police Act 2005, ss 76–81 (as amended by the Bribery Act 2010 and the Justice Act (Northern Ireland) 2011). A Sewel motion was passed in relation to the Serious Organised Crime and Police Bill on the basis that FROs may be triggered by a mix of reserved and devolved offences, and so legislating at Westminster was most practical. Scottish Executive, *Sewel Memorandum Serious Organised Crime and Police Bill* (Edinburgh, Scottish Executive, 2004) para 22; SP OR col 14143–65 (2 February 2005).

[304] Serious Organised Crime and Police Act 2005, s 79.

[305] Serious Organised Crime and Police Act 2005, s 81.

[306] *R v Adams* [2008] EWCA Crim 914.

[307] *R v Wright* [2008] EWCA Crim 3207.

[308] ibid, [3].

[309] ibid, [10].

[310] ibid, [13].

[311] Serious Crime Act 2007, s 5.

boundary between civil and criminal measures, as they may be imposed by the Crown Courts on a person convicted of a serious criminal offence in the Crown or Magistrates' Court, or by the High Court without conviction, and the burden of proof is the civil one.[312] In the first instance, the Crown Court may impose an SCPO where it has reasonable grounds to believe that this would protect the public by preventing, restricting or disrupting involvement by the subject in serious crime in England, Wales or Northern Ireland. The Court of Appeal in *R v Hancox* stressed that

> [i]t follows that the court, when considering making such an order, is concerned with future risk. There must be a real, or significant, risk (not a bare possibility) that the defendant will commit further serious offences . . . in England and Wales.[313]

The provision of the order must also be proportionate to the risk.[314] Breach of the order anywhere in the UK is an offence.[315]

All of these orders are comparable to the notification obligations imposed on sex offenders.[316] Indeed, as Garland notes, governments are on a 'war footing' with respect to drug trafficking and sex offending,[317] and this may explain why similar approaches are adopted in both contexts. Such a registration obligation for sex offenders was challenged unsuccessfully in *Ibbotson v United Kingdom* where the European Commission of Human Rights held that this was not a penalty within the meaning of Article 7 of the ECHR on the basis that the requirement was not punitive but rather was preventative.[318] When compared to confiscation, notification by sex offenders is less severe and does not involve imprisonment for default.[319] Similarly, in *Enright v Ireland*, the equivalent Irish measure was found not to constitute a penalty[320] and to be a proportionate measure to protect the rights of other citizens.[321] While an indefinite registration requirement was found by the UK Supreme Court in *R v F* to be a disproportionate interference with a person's Article 8 rights,[322] none of the orders pertaining to organised crime lasts a lifetime. Therefore it seems that the imposition of notification and other requirements is not an additional punishment, nor does it constitute a disproportionate response to the issue of drug trafficking or organised crime offences, given that the effects on the rights of the individual in question appear to be minor, though breach may result in a period of imprisonment.

---

[312] See ch 7.
[313] *R v Hancox* [2010] EWCA Crim 102 [9].
[314] ibid, [10].
[315] Serious Organised Crime and Police Act 2005, s 25.
[316] See Sex Offenders Act 2001(Ireland); Sex Offenders Act 2003 (UK). A register of convicted sex offenders was first introduced in the US by the Jacob Wetterling Crimes against Children and Sexually Violent Offender Registration Act 1994 which required all States in the US to implement a sex offenders' register.
[317] Garland, n 118, 172.
[318] *Ibbotson v United Kingdom* (1998) 27 EHRR CD 332.
[319] Ashworth, n 7, 360.
[320] *Enright v Ireland* [2003] 2 IR 321, 337.
[321] ibid, 343.
[322] *R v F* [2010] UKSC 17, [2011] 1 AC 331.

These orders focus on the supervision and control of released drug traffickers and other serious criminals, rather than on rehabilitation or reform. This exemplifies the 'new penology', where the focus is on management of groups rather than the altering of individual behaviour.[323] By monitoring people through such orders, the State seeks to prevent the commission of crime, or if this is not possible, to ease its task in investigation in an adaptive response by ensuring that the police are furnished with sufficient information to track the movements of ex-convicts. Such an approach evinces a growing belief that criminals are not capable of reform, but rather retain the potential to commit further criminal behaviour and so should be surveyed continuously: there is 'no such thing as an ex-offender – only offenders who have been caught before and will strike again'.[324] Or, as SOCA emphasised, '[c]areer criminals regard prison as an interruption – it rarely marks the end of their involvement in organised crime',[325] and, hence, the Agency is 'committed to driving serious organised criminals out of business through lifetime management of offenders'.[326] This again echoes the paradigmatic notion of the career criminal in the new penology.[327]

Post-conviction orders also hold a preventative imperative: they seek to prevent the further commission of crime by the individual in question, and thereby protect other individuals, such as the victim of the offence, from him. This is a further example of a novel approach in tackling organised criminality. Nevertheless, there is great divergence in terms of the application and implementation of these measures. SCPOs and FROs are imposed by the courts in England and Wales, and indeed SOCA proudly publishes details of the orders.[328] In contrast, no statistics regarding the use of any of these post-conviction orders are available in Ireland. This demonstrates acutely the failure to translate rhetoric into practice, and the divergence between the law in the books and the law in action. Critically, Scotland has no such system, indicating that the shift towards such a risk-focused model is by no means inevitable.

---

[323] M Feeley and J Simon, 'The New Penology: Notes on the Emerging Strategy of Corrections and its Implications' (1992) 30 *Criminology* 449, 452.

[324] Garland, n 118, 142.

[325] Serious Organised Crime Agency, 'Details Published to Aid Lifetime Management of Offenders', 10 June 2010, available at www.soca.gov.uk/news/239-ancillary-orders-published-to-aid-lifetime-offender-management.

[326] See Serious Organised Crime Agency, 'Serious Organised Crime Agency Secures First Conviction under New Power', 5 April 2008, available at www.soca.gov.uk/assessPublications/downloads/FRO_press_release.doc.

[327] M Feeley and J Simon, 'Actuarial Justice: the Emerging Criminal Law' in D Nelken (ed), *The Futures of Criminology* (Sage, London, 1994) 173–201, 164–65.

[328] See Serious Organised Crime Agency, 'Publication of Ancillary Orders – January 2012', available at www.soca.gov.uk/about-soca/library/cat_view/82-library.

VII. Conclusion

Various developments in sentencing practice, either prompted by, or used against organised criminality, denote a move away from the traditional model in which sentences were imposed on the basis of the circumstances of the particular offender and the crime, towards a generalised model which is concerned with the classification and features of the particular offence. The introduction and subsequent expansion of the scheme of presumptive sentences typifies the drift towards a mechanical strategy, and while many customary facets of sentencing policy remain intact, ancillary orders represent a significant rowing-back on certain conventional elements of the sentencing framework. There is a growing emphasis on the deterrent power and the expressive elements of punishment, to the neglect of the individual offender and his particular characteristics and circumstances. All of these changes are underpinned by the perception of the organised criminal as motivated by rational concerns, predominantly related to the generation of profit by any means and the maintenance of control over a given illicit market. Thus, presumptive sentences are hoped to deter, confiscation orders engage with the profits and capital that maintains organised crime, while further post-conviction orders seek to prevent further crime through monitoring and notification requirements.

Alterations in the realm of sentencing, and more generally at the post-conviction stage of the criminal process, are indicative of the shift in focus away from the individual towards the crime control-oriented needs of the State. Risk management and the control of offenders, either by incapacitative sentences or through post-conviction orders, have increased in significance. In addition, the expressive element of tactics such as presumptive minimum sentences must not be overlooked, given their ability to convey the disapprobation of policy makers and society in general, while the imposition of confiscation orders exemplifies the adoption of novel and adaptive tactics by the State in a bid to undercut the profits accrued as a result of criminal behaviour. Moreover, the reduction of sentence is a pragmatic means of improving the investigation and prosecution of further crime, despite potentially compromising justice in specific cases and undermining the principles and purposes of sentencing more broadly.

All of this is facilitated and motivated by the increase in parliamentary intervention and action in the post-trial realm, which affects the usual discretion accorded to judges in this context. The delineation of presumptive sentences and the requirement that judges consider post-trial conviction orders demonstrate the growing influence of the legislature in an area which was traditionally the preserve of the courts. Notwithstanding these developments, certain factors ensure that the measures introduced by the legislature remain circumscribed. The judiciary's strident protection of its independence, coupled with the nature of guidelines has allowed the flexible structure of sentencing in Ireland and the UK to be retained, thereby mitigating the more punitive tendencies of the legislature. This capacity of the judiciary to counterbalance the trend towards a crime control model of criminal justice is evident from the widespread application of the exceptional circumstances caveat to presumptive sentences. Thus, while the aforementioned alterations may indicate the parliamentary predilection for more punitive measures, such a tendency is tempered by the courts and by the enduring strength of the traditional structures and principles in place.

7

Beyond the Criminal Realm: Civil Asset Recovery

I. Introduction

Throughout the 1990s, the perception took root in the UK and Ireland that considerable illegitimate wealth was being accrued and enjoyed by organised criminals and that the existing legal frameworks were ineffective in addressing this phenomenon. Measures facilitating the confiscation of a convicted offender's property were already in place at this time, as has been outlined in chapter six; however now property may be seized and retained in the absence of a criminal conviction, fundamentally revising the means used to counter serious and organised crime. The rationale behind this civil procedure lies in the apparent ability of leaders of organised crime gangs to distance themselves from criminal behaviour by delegating responsibility for the implementation of illegal acts, thereby helping to insulate themselves from prosecution. Furthermore, the methods adopted by organised criminals were seen to have become more advanced and impenetrable to law enforcement agencies, thereby necessitating innovative techniques on the part of the State. The Home Affairs Committee noted in 1995 that 'organised crime [is] resourced to an hitherto unimaginable extent' and thus can 'take advantage of a criminal justice system which has evolved to meet the challenges of a lower level of essentially localised crime'.[1] In the words of Garland, the State is thus faced with a 'criminological predicament' and so is required to adapt to the 'new reality' of crime control[2] through the adoption of a 'radically new and thorough approach' which requires evidence only on the civil burden of proof.[3] As was stated in the Irish Parliament, '[i]f traditional methods fail we must devise new ones . . . If we cannot arrest the criminals, why not confiscate [sic] their assets?',[4] while the Attorney-General in England and Wales stated that asset recovery 'is needed to fill an important gap in the law'.[5] The financial motivations of

---

[1] Home Affairs Committee, *Third Report on Organised Crime* (London, The Stationery Office, 1995) 177.

[2] D Garland, *The Culture of Control: Crime and Social Order in Contemporary Society* (Oxford, Oxford University Press, 2001) 105ff.

[3] Seanad Debates, vol 148, col 420 (27 June 1996); *Murphy v GM* (High Court, 4 June 1999) 136.

[4] Dáil Debates, vol 467, col 2435 (2 July 1996).

[5] HL Deb13 May 2002, vol 635, col 71.

organised criminals led to the feeling that 'getting at the money and the profit from organised crime is likely to be a more effective lever than some others'.[6] Such remarks encapsulate the rationale underpinning this adaptive response. As the conventional means of criminal prosecution were deemed to be deficient, a system of civil recovery was devised which eases the burden on the State and facilitates the control of such criminality in a novel way: by pursuing the funds of the leaders of organised crime groups and so stifling future criminality; by removing negative role models; and by generating confidence in a fair and effective criminal justice system.[7]

Countering the typical policy-transfer trend whereby the Irish legislature emulates developments originating in its neighbouring jurisdictions,[8] civil asset recovery in Ireland predated its UK equivalent.[9] In this chapter both local and global templates for civil recovery in Ireland and the UK will be examined. The enacting legislation will be compared, and particular attention paid to key definitional aspects which have proved instrumental in the degree of application and success of these laws. While civil recovery was viewed at its inception as a key mechanism against organised criminality, it has been used more widely and effectively in Ireland than in the UK, and reasons for this will be explored. Challenges that have been posed to asset recovery will be raised, focusing on the privilege against self-incrimination, the right to private property and the nature of the process.

II. The Irish Prototype

In Ireland, support for civil recovery of the proceeds of crime was expressed as far back as 1985 by the Committee of Inquiry into the Penal System and by the Select Committee on Crime, Lawlessness and Vandalism,[10] and the issue was further contemplated in the early-1990s when the Law Reform Commission recommended against its introduction due to the likelihood of successful constitutional challenge.[11] It fell from the political agenda until two murders in 1996 focused the

---

[6] S Lander, 'SOCA: One Year On', 'New Developments in Criminal Justice' seminar series (London, Centre for Crime and Justice Studies, 2007).

[7] Cabinet Office Performance and Innovation Unit, *Recovering the Proceeds of Crime* (London, Cabinet Office, 2000) paras 1.3 and 1.10.

[8] eg anti-social behaviour orders were introduced in England and Wales in the late 1990s in the Crime and Disorder Act 1998 (as amended by the Police Reform Act 2002), and were provided for in a modified form in Ireland in the Criminal Justice Act 2007. For an examination of the concept of policy transfer see T Jones and T Newburn, *Policy Transfer and Criminal Justice* (Maidenhead, Open University Press, 2007).

[9] Whereas in the UK the term 'asset recovery' is used, 'forfeiture' is used in Ireland.

[10] Committee of Inquiry into the Penal System, *Report of the Committee of Inquiry into the Penal System* (Dublin, Stationery Office, 1985); Select Committee on Crime, Lawlessness and Vandalism, *Sixth Report of the Select Committee on Crime, Lawlessness and Vandalism: Confiscation of Assets Illegally Acquired Through Drug Trafficking* (Dublin, Stationery Office, 1985).

[11] Law Reform Commission, *Report on the Confiscation of the Proceeds of Crime* (Dublin, Law Reform Commission. 1991) ch 4, paras 22–23.

attention of the Government on speedy legislative reform. The killings of police officer Jerry McCabe and investigative journalist Veronica Guerin by members of a criminal gang in the summer of 1996 expedited the enactment of three seminal statutes pertaining to civil asset recovery: the Proceeds of Crime Act 1996 (governing the recovery process), the Criminal Assets Bureau Act 1996 (establishing the agency which implements the process), and the Disclosure of Certain Information for Taxation and Other Purposes Act 1996 (permitting the Criminal Assets Bureau to look at information retained by the Revenue Commissioners and other State agencies). These Acts, proposed in a private member's motion by Fianna Fáil (the main opposition party at the time), were enacted within a mere five weeks, and the desire to confront directly wealthy criminals was to the fore in political rhetoric: as one member of the Dáil insisted, if we 'as a community [are] prepared to tolerate the continued unhindered existence in our midst of people who have accumulated vast and unexplained wealth . . . Veronica Guerin died in vain'.[12]

An equivalent mobilising event was absent in the UK, thereby potentially explaining the later introduction of civil recovery there. Although the Home Office recommended such a civil process in 1998, the Government decided on another review resulting in the Cabinet Office's report in 2000[13] before the enactment of the Proceeds of Crime Act 2002.[14] Hence the Irish civil recovery scheme predated the British model by a number of years. A further possible reason for this disparity which confounds the usual trend of policy transfer lies in the fact that in the mid-1980s, a comparable measure was introduced in Ireland to combat subversive crime, such as that perpetrated by the Irish Republican Army (the IRA), which provided significant influence and legitimacy for the present mechanism, rather than, or at least in addition to, the oft-cited historical tradition of forfeiture[15] and the contemporary US approach.[16]

---

[12] Dáil Debates, vol 467, col 2406 (2 July 1996) per John O'Donoghue.

[13] Home Office Working Group on Confiscation, *Third Report: Criminal Assets* (London, Home Office, 1998); Cabinet Office Performance and Innovation Unit, n 7.

[14] The Proceeds of Crime Act 2002 pertains to both reserved and devolved matters. While the Act covers reserved matters such as money laundering, taxation and the misuse of drugs, civil recovery and confiscation are devolved to the Scottish Parliament. Thus, a Sewel motion was passed in relation to the Proceeds of Crime Bill, permitting the Westminster Parliament to legislate for Scotland also, to avoid legal loopholes and to enact comprehensive UK legislation that recognises the nature of criminal activity. See Scottish Executive, *Memorandum: Proceeds of Crime Bill* (Edinburgh, Scottish Executive, 2001); SP OR cols 3248–60 (24 October 2001).

[15] Traditionally, the value of an inanimate object which directly or indirectly caused the accidental death of a King's subject was forfeited to the Crown; forfeiture resulted after conviction for felonies and treason; and admiralty forfeiture occurred after breach of maritime or customs law. For an examination of the history of asset forfeiture see C Greek, 'Drug Control and Asset Seizures: A Review of the History of Forfeiture in England and Colonial America' in T Mieczkowski (ed), *Drugs, Crime and Social Policy* (Boston, Allyn and Bacon, 1992) 109–37. Also see *Calero-Toledo v Pearson Yacht Leasing Co* 416 US 663 (1974) 680ff.

[16] The 'RICO' provision (the Racketeering Influenced Corrupt Organisations, title IX to the Organised Crime Control Act 1970, 18 USC 1961), the most well-known of US forfeiture measures, was cited in the Irish legislature prior to the enactment of the Proceeds of Crime Act 1996. Dáil Debates, vol 467, cols 2372–73 (2 July 1996) per B Ahern; col 2444 per A Shatter; and col 2473 per W O'Dea. See J Gurule, 'Federal Asset Forfeiture Reform Introduction: The Ancient Roots of Modern Forfeiture Law' (1995) 21 *Journal of Legislation* 155.

204 Beyond the Criminal Realm: Civil Asset Recovery

The Offences Against the State (Amendment) Act 1985 was introduced in Ireland to facilitate the civil seizure and forfeiture of property of members of a paramilitary group, thereby providing a workable example for the subsequent 1996 Act with its broader application. That the 1985 Act would establish a frame-work for dealing with future cases of this nature was explicitly recognised in the legislature,[17] where it was described as a 'clear and direct precedent' for the Proceeds of Crime Act 1996.[18] Section 2 of the 1985 Act allowed the Minister for Justice to freeze monies which he believed to be the property of an unlawful organisation[19] and require them to be paid to the High Court, and this action was not dependent on the initiation of criminal proceedings. After six months, the Minister could make an ex parte application to the High Court that the monies be paid to him, but any person claiming to be the owner of the property could also so apply, bearing the burden of proof to establish ownership.[20] The 1985 Act was limited in its lifespan, as it was brought in on a temporary basis and was to operate for a mere three months unless continued in force by Government order (which did not occur). It was used in only one instance and the subject of the order chal-lenged its constitutionality in *Clancy v Ireland*,[21] where in a brief judgment Barrington J concluded that the process amounted to a permissible limitation of property rights in the interests of the common good, and was not in breach of fairness of procedures.[22] He stated that the possibility of compensation and the right to apply to court for determination of ownership ensured constitutional compliance,[23] and the inclusion of these two safeguards in the 1996 Act was later stressed in legislative debate.[24] This decision of the Supreme Court proved pivotal in the introduction, and subsequent judicial approval, of the Irish Proceeds of Crime Act 1996, which in turn influenced the comparable UK measures.

III. The Proceeds of Crime Acts

Many points of commonality may be identified in the civil asset recovery pro-cesses in Ireland and the UK, which are governed by the Proceeds of Crime Act 1996 and the Proceeds of Crime Act 2002 respectively.[25] Civil recovery orders may

---

[17] Dáil Debates, vol 356, col 132 (19 February 1985) per Minister for Justice, M Noonan.

[18] Dáil Debates, vol 467, col 2409 (2 July 1996) per J O'Donoghue. Also see col 2374 per B Ahern and col 2473 per W O'Dea.

[19] s 18 of the Offences Against the State Act 1939 proscribes seditious and subversive organisations, such as the Irish Republican Army (the IRA).

[20] Offences Against the State (Amendment) Act 1985, s 3.

[21] *Clancy v Ireland* [1988] IR 326.

[22] ibid, 336.

[23] ibid.

[24] Dáil Debates, vol 467, col 2409 (2 July 1996) per John O'Donoghue.

[25] For commentary on the different systems see P Alldridge, *Money Laundering Law: Forfeiture, Confiscation, Civil Recovery, Criminal Laundering and Taxation of the Proceeds of Crime* (Oxford, Hart, 2003) 224ff; J Meade, 'Organised Crime, Moral Panic and Law Reform: The Irish Adoption of Civil

be made against property worth at least €13,000 in Ireland and £10,000 in the UK which are deemed to be the proceeds of crime, that is, obtained as a result of or in connection with the commission of an offence,[26] or through unlawful conduct.[27] It is not necessary for proceedings to have been brought for an offence in connection with the property,[28] and property need not be related to a particular crime as this would make the scheme 'useless and unworkable'.[29] In other words, there is no predicate offence. Indeed, the very rationale is to facilitate State recovery of assets where a conviction and thus criminal confiscation is not possible because of circumstances such as lack of evidence or the death of the suspect.[30]

Most significantly, the standard of proof is the civil one[31] which 'enable[s] the lower probative requirements of civil law to be utilised in appropriate cases . . . to effectively deprive such persons of such illicit financial fruits of their labours as can be shown to be proceeds of crime'.[32] However,

> the serious nature of the allegations being made and the serious consequences of such allegations being proved mean that careful and critical consideration has to be given to the evidence for the Court to be satisfied that the allegations have been established.[33]

In the UK, it was stressed in the House of Commons that the possibility of civil recovery could not render the need to prosecute void.[34] A proposed amendment in the House of Lords, precluding civil proceedings after there has been an acquittal or conviction in criminal proceedings in relation to the same conduct[35] so as to prevent civil proceedings becoming a 'second bite of the cherry', was rejected essentially on the basis that this is the precise aim of the civil process.[36] In *Director*

Forfeiture' (2000) 10 *Irish Criminal Law Journal* 11; J Meade, 'The Disguise of Civility: Civil Forfeiture of the Proceeds of Crime and the Presumption of Innocence in Irish Law' (2000) 1 *Hibernian Law Journal* 1; L Campbell, 'Theorising Asset Forfeiture in Ireland' (2007) 71 *Journal of Criminal Law* 441; P McCutcheon and D Walsh, 'Seizure of Criminal Assets: An Overview' (1999) 9 *Irish Criminal Law Journal* 127; S Murphy, 'Tracing the Proceeds of Crime: Legal and Constitutional Implications' (1999) 9 *Irish Criminal Law Journal* 160.

[26] Proceeds of Crime Act 1996, s 1.

[27] Proceeds of Crime Act 2002, s 240(1). The Home Office suggested that this could be amended to include property retained by unlawful conduct, or 'assets obtained by or in connection with unlawful conduct'. Home Office, *Asset Recovery Action Plan: A Consultation Document* (London, Home Office, 2007) para 3.4. Cash may also be recovered by summary procedure in the Magistrates or Sheriff Courts (Proceeds of Crime Act 2002, Pt 5, ch 3) and this pertains to a wide range of criminality.

[28] Proceeds of Crime Act 2002, s 240(2).

[29] *McK v F and H* [2005] IESC 6, [2005] 2 IR 163 [15]; *Director of Assets Recovery Agency v Green* [2005] EWHC 3168 (Admin), [2005] All ER (D) 261 [17]; *Director of the Assets Recovery Agency v Szepietowski* [2007] EWCA Civ 766, [2007] All ER (D) 364 [26].

[30] See Attorney-General, *Attorney-General's Guidance to Prosecuting Bodies on their Asset Recovery Powers under the Proceeds of Crime Act 2002* (London, Attorney-General's Office, 2009) point 5.

[31] Proceeds of Crime Act 1996, s 8(2); Proceeds of Crime Act 2002, s 241(3).

[32] *M v D* [1998] 3 IR 175, 178 per Moriarty J.

[33] *Serious Organised Crime Agency v Pelekanos* [2009] EWHC 2307, referring to *Re D* [2008] 1 WLR 1499 [27] and *R (N) v Mental Health Review Tribunal (Northern Region)* [2006] QB 468.

[34] HC Deb 30 October 2001, vol 373, col 761 per Minister for Police, Courts and Drugs (John Denham); Cabinet Office Performance and Innovation Unit, n 7, para 5.26.

[35] HL Deb 13 May 2002, vol 635, col 75 per Lord Kingsland.

[36] HL Deb 13 May 2002, vol 635, col 77 per Lord Goldsmith.

of the Assets Recovery Agency v Kean Stanley Burnton J emphasised that the respondent's acquittal was not a reason to preclude the Assets Recovery Agency (the relevant agency at the time) from relying on the evidence in question, given that his 'guilt' may be proved on the balance of probabilities.[37] This statement is deeply troubling, given the conflation of the criminal notions of guilt and civil liability. Moreover, the UK Supreme Court, in the first civil recovery case it considered, held that the courts are not precluded from considering evidence that formed the basis of charges abroad, in this instance in Portugal, of which the appellant was acquitted.[38]

In the UK, where a person uses 'recoverable' property (ie that obtained through unlawful conduct)[39] to acquire other property or to make a profit, the latter become recoverable.[40] While the Irish legislation does not refer to property that is bought partially by legitimate means or profits, it seems likely that mixing of illegitimate and legal funds would not prove fatal to the grant of an order, unless it would cause serious hardship to the individual. Therefore assets or property acquired by a combination of legitimate and illegitimate funds may be recovered in the UK and Ireland. The location of the property is also significant. In the UK, property includes all property wherever situated.[41] While property was defined in the Irish Proceeds of Crime Act 1996 as including money and all other property, real or personal, heritable or moveable,[42] section 3 of the Proceeds of Crime (Amendment) Act 2005 clarified this definition to include property which is situated outside the State when the respondent is domiciled, resident or present in Ireland and where any part of the criminal conduct concerned occurs therein.[43] In Ireland, 'criminal conduct' includes any conduct which occurs outside Ireland and which would constitute an offence if it occurred within Ireland, if it constituted an offence under the law of the State concerned, and if, at the time an application for an order is made, any property obtained or received in connection with the conduct is situated in Ireland.[44] A similar dual criminality rule applies in the UK,[45] although this differs for Scotland: the Court of Session may make an order in respect of moveable property wherever situated, but this cannot occur where the person is not domiciled, resident or present in Scotland and the property is

---

[37] *Director of the Assets Recovery Agency v Kean* [2007] All ER (D) 286 [64].

[38] *Gale and Another v Serious Organised Crime Agency* [2011] UKSC 49.

[39] Proceeds of Crime Act 2002, s 304(1).

[40] Proceeds of Crime Act 2002, ss 305 and 307.

[41] Proceeds of Crime Act 2002, s 316 (4).

[42] Proceeds of Crime Act 1996, s 1.

[43] In *McKenna v EH* [2002] 1 IR 72 and *McK v RM (Service outside jurisdiction)* [2003] 3 IR 1 Finnegan P held that the Irish Parliament intended that persons who are resident outside the jurisdiction but hold assets inside the jurisdiction which represent the proceeds of crime should be subject to the Act.

[44] Proceeds of Crime (Amendment) Act 2005, s 3. This provision remedied the judgment in *McK v D (Proceeds of crime outside State)* [2004] 2 IR 470, 488–90 where Fennelly J concluded that the Act of 1996 'clearly has effect only within the boundaries of the State'. This decision itself had overruled *DPP v Hollman* (High Court, 29 July 1999) and *McK v RM,* n 43, where it was held that the Act applied even where the crime was committed abroad.

[45] Proceeds of Crime Act 2002, s 241.

not situated in Scotland, unless the unlawful conduct took place in Scotland.[46] These provisions ensure that an individual who holds property outside the State but whose criminal conduct retains an Irish or British dimension falls within the scope of the civil recovery legislation. This is crucial in dealing with organised criminality and improves the abilities of the State.

The Serious Organised Crime Agency (SOCA), the Serious Fraud Office, the Director of Public Prosecutions for England and Wales, the Scottish Ministers and the Criminal Assets Bureau (CAB) in Ireland may apply to the High Courts or the Court of Session for a number of orders culminating in asset recovery. Essentially, three types of civil orders may be issued in this context: in the UK these are freezing,[47] interim receivership,[48] and recovery orders, and in Ireland interim, interlocutory, and disposal orders.[49] Freezing and interim receivership orders/interim administration orders (IROs/IAOs) in the UK and interim orders in Ireland prevent a specified person from dealing with the property for a limited period, pending the investigation of the case, and they may be issued ex parte.[50] An IRO must be founded on 'a good arguable case',[51] while the Scottish IAO requires *probabilis causa litigandi*[52] that the particular property is or includes recoverable property.[53] In Ireland, an interlocutory order may be applied for instead of an interim order, or within 21 days of the making of the interim order.[54] The High Court must make an interlocutory order[55] if satisfied that the evidence establishes that a person possesses or controls property constituting the proceeds of crime and is of the requisite value, unless this is refuted or if there would be a serious risk of injustice. Such an application is not subject to any statute time bar provisions.[56] Furthermore, section 7 allows a receiver to be appointed by the High

[46] Proceeds of Crime Act 2002, s 286.

[47] These are referred to as '*prohibitory property orders*' in Scotland (Proceeds of Crime Act 2002, s 255A as inserted by the Serious Organised Crime and Police Act 2005).

[48] In Scotland these are called interim administration orders (Proceeds of Crime Act 2002, s 256).

[49] Proceeds of Crime Act 1996, ss 2–4.

[50] Proceeds of Crime Act 2002, s 245A (as inserted by the Serious Organised Crime and Police Act 2005, s 98) and Proceeds of Crime Act 1996, s 2.

[51] In *R (Director of Assets Recovery Agency) v He and Chen* [2004] EWHC 3021 [77]–[79], Collins J rejected the claim that in an application to discharge or vary under s 251(3) the test to be applied was not that of a 'good arguable case'. In *Szepietowski*, n 29, [26], the Court of Appeal stressed that it must be established by a good arguable case that a certain kind of unlawful conduct occurred and that the property was obtained though such unlawful conduct.

[52] Proceeds of Crime Act 2002, s 256.

[53] Proceeds of Crime Act 2002, ss 245A(5) and 246(5).

[54] Proceeds of Crime Act 1996, s 3.

[55] A s 3 order has been held not to be an interlocutory order in the normal sense of the phrase, seeing as the proceedings for a disposal order under s 4 is not the trial of the action (*McK v AF and JF* [2002] 1 IR 242, 256). The interlocutory order is a substantive remedy as it is a free-standing measure which is not ancillary to a s 4 order and there is no obligation on the applicant to apply for a disposal order; ibid, 257. The interlocutory hearing itself constitutes the trial of the issue (*McK v FC* and *McK v MJG* [2001] 4 IR 521, 523), and a s 4 hearing for disposal of the property is not the final trial of the action (*Murphy v GM*, n 3, 154). In *McK v F* and *McK v H*, [6], the Supreme Court held that, despite the 'contextually unusual use of the expression "interlocutory order"' s 3 proceedings are separate from s 4 proceedings.

[56] In *McK v F* and *McK v H*, [17].

Court to manage or take possession of the property which is subject to an interim or interlocutory order.

As originally enacted, the Irish Proceeds of Crime Act 1996 allowed for the making of a disposal order where an interlocutory order had been in force for not less than seven years;[57] now, disposal may occur after a shorter period when an application is made with the consent of the parties.[58] A disposal order deprives the respondent of his rights in the property and transfers the property to the Minister for Finance.[59] In the UK, if the High Court or the Court of Session is satisfied that the property is recoverable it must make a recovery order,[60] and this must be within 12 years of the date on which the cause of action accrued.[61] Recovered property is retained by the Home Office and distributed according to the incentivisation fund.[62] In Scotland, a maximum of £30m in recovered property per year is used by Scottish Ministers and any balance is sent to the UK Treasury,[63] while assets recovered in Northern Ireland are returned to the Home Office, from where 50 per cent is distributed to the agencies involved.[64] This is now done by the Northern Ireland Department of Justice.[65] As will be discussed in more detail below, this encourages agencies to be proactive and robust in the pursuit of civil recovery investigations and actions.

In addition, in the UK, there is a separate procedure for cash amounting to more than £1,000.[66] Cash may be seized by a customs officer or constable, detained and ultimately forfeited after order by the Magistrates Court or Court of Session if it was obtained through unlawful conduct (ie 'recoverable')[67] or is intended by any person for use in unlawful conduct.[68] As noted by the English High Court in *R (Bavi) v Snaresbrook Crown Court*, 'the police do not have to specify what the unlawful conduct alleged is'.[69]

Given that the rules of civil procedure apply in relation to recovery hearings, hearsay evidence is permitted and previous convictions are admissible automatically in Ireland and the UK. In Ireland, opinion evidence from a senior police

---

[57] Proceeds of Crime Act 1996, s 4.

[58] Proceeds of Crime Act 1996, s 4A, as inserted by Proceeds of Crime (Amendment) Act 2005, s 7.

[59] Proceeds of Crime Act 1996, s 4(4).

[60] Proceeds of Crime Act 2002, s 266(1). The respondent in *Director of the Assets Recovery Agency v Prince* [2006] EWHC 1080 (Admin), [2006] All ER (D) 205 [55], could not avail of this section because he had not 'obtained the recoverable property in good faith' and it would not be 'just and equitable' to refrain from making a recovery order given his 'knowledge of the provenance of the funds'.

[61] Proceeds of Crime Act 2002, s 288.

[62] See Comptroller and Auditor General, *Report by the Comptroller and Auditor General, The Assets Recovery Agency* (London, National Audit Office, 2007) para 2.1 and text accompanying n 186.

[63] Scottish Government Press Release, 'Upping the Stakes on Crime-Fighting', 5 May 2010.

[64] Organised Crime Task Force, *2011 Annual Report and Threat Assessment Organised Crime in Northern Ireland* (Belfast, Northern Ireland Office, 2011) 36.

[65] Justice Act (Northern Ireland) 2011, s 94.

[66] This figure had stood at £5,000 but was reduced by the Proceeds of Crime Act 2002 (Recovery of Cash in Summary Proceedings: Minimum Amount) Order 2006.

[67] Proceeds of Crime Act 2002, s 304(1).

[68] Proceeds of Crime Act 2002, Pt 5, ch 3.

[69] *R (Bavi) v Snaresbrook Crown Court* [2008] EWHC 3420 (Admin) [6].

officer or officer of the Revenue Commissioners is admissible in applications for these orders if the High Court is satisfied that there are reasonable grounds for that belief,[70] though significant circumspection and care should be exercised where such evidence alone is proffered.[71] The use of hearsay evidence in this context has been challenged unsuccessfully,[72] and the possibility of cross-examining the officer *viva voce* is seen to ensure that the demands of natural justice are met[73] and to present the possibility of undermining his belief.[74] Such evidence of belief was described merely as creating a prima facie case which may be answered by the defendant if he has a credible explanation as to how he lawfully came into possession or control of the property.[75] A direct precedent for this provision exists in counter-terrorism legislation in the form of section 3(2) of the Offences Against the State (Amendment) Act 1972 which provides that the belief of a member of the Garda Síochána not below the rank of chief superintendent is sufficient evidence on which to grant a conviction for membership of an unlawful organisation,[76] thereby demonstrating the seepage of extraordinary measures and the equating of organised crime with subversive crime in terms of the procedural changes that are permitted.

As regards the investigations preceding civil recovery, in the UK the Crown and Sheriff Courts may grant production orders, orders to grant entry, search and seizure warrants, and disclosure orders ex parte on the application of the investigating agency.[77] Furthermore, customer information orders and account monitoring orders, if granted, require financial institutions to provide such information.[78] In Ireland, search warrants may be issued not only by a District judge but also by a bureau officer who is a member of the Garda Síochána not below the rank of superintendent in circumstances of urgency,[79] and production orders may be granted by the courts.[80] The District Court may direct the respondent to file an affidavit specifying the property he possesses or controls and/or his income and its sources for anytime during the previous 10 years.[81]

In the UK, information held by public bodies such as the Director of Public Prosecutions, the Serious Fraud Office, and the National Crime Squad may be disclosed to the Serious Organised Crime Agency,[82] to the Lord Advocate and to

---

[70] Proceeds of Crime Act 1996, s 8.

[71] *M v D*, n 32, 179; *Gilligan v Criminal Assets Bureau* [1998] 3 IR 185, 243.

[72] *Murphy v GM*, n 3.

[73] *M v D*, n 32, 179.

[74] *McK v McD* [2005] IEHC 205.

[75] *McK v H* [2006] IESC 63.

[76] Dáil Debates, vol 467, col 2409 (2 July 1996) per Mr O'Donoghue. The High Court in *DPP v Hollman*, n 44, emphasised that evidence given in an application under the Proceeds of Crime Act 1996 must be from a person who is chief superintendent at the time of giving evidence and not a former chief superintendent.

[77] Proceeds of Crime Act 2002, ss 345 and 380; 347 and 382; 352; 357 and 391. See ch 4.

[78] Proceeds of Crime Act 2002, ss 363 and 397; 370 and 404.

[79] Proceeds of Crime Act 1996, s 14.

[80] Proceeds of Crime Act, s 14A (as inserted by the Proceeds of Crime (Amendment) Act 2005).

[81] Proceeds of Crime Act, s 9.

[82] Proceeds of Crime Act 2002, s 436 (as amended by the Serious Crime Act 2007 Sch 8, para 132).

Scottish Ministers who bear responsibility for civil recovery in Scotland, and to other persons responsible for civil recovery such as the DPP and the Director of the SFO.[83] The permission of the Commissioners themselves is required for sharing information held by Her Majesty's Revenue and Customs.[84] SOCA may disclose information for the purpose of any criminal or civil recovery investigation whether in the UK or overseas,[85] and the Irish legislation permits cooperation with any police force or any authority outside Ireland which has functions related to the recovery of the proceeds of crime.[86] Furthermore, a Bureau officer may impart information to other Bureau officers, members of the police, the Revenue Commissioners and the Department of Social, Family and Community Affairs to fulfil their respective functions,[87] and may receive and act upon information received from the Bureau.[88] As was observed in *CAB v Craft*, members are not only entitled to exchange information but would be in dereliction of their duty if they failed to do so,[89] and this 'joined-up' way of working was praised explicitly by the English Attorney-General in the House of Lords.[90]

In Ireland, a number of provisions in the Criminal Assets Bureau Act 1996 ensure the protection of officers in the course of CAB work. It is an offence to obstruct,[91] intimidate,[92] or assault[93] an officer or member of the Bureau, or a member of their family. In addition, section 10 provides for the anonymity of CAB officers in all aspects of their work, including court proceedings, although the court must be satisfied that there are reasonable grounds in the public interest before granting anonymity.[94] This provision, which was described as a 'responsible precaution in the circumstances',[95] stresses that reasonable care must be taken to ensure that the identity of any Bureau staff is not revealed, and it is a criminal offence to identify or publish the addresses of non-Garda Bureau officers, staff and their families.[96] It was held in *Criminal Assets Bureau v PS* that the anonymity provision 'operate[s] in special and limited cases within the meaning of the Constitution', and that if, in a particular case, the grant of anonymity resulted in injustice this would not render the section itself unconstitutional, but rather its

---

[83] Proceeds of Crime of Act 2002 (Disclosure of Information) Order 2008.

[84] Proceeds of Crime of Act 2002, s 436(8).

[85] Proceeds of Crime Act 2002, s 438 (as amended by the Serious Crime Act 2007, sch 8, para 134).

[86] Criminal Assets Bureau Act 1996, s 5 (as amended by the Proceeds of Crime (Amendment) Act 2005).

[87] Criminal Assets Bureau Act 1996, s 8(7).

[88] Criminal Assets Bureau Act 1996, s 8(5).

[89] *Criminal Assets Bureau v Craft* [2001] 1 IR 113 (HC) 133.

[90] HL Deb 25 March 2002, vol 633, col 59. CAB's structure and *modus operandi* has been heralded as an example for other jurisdictions, with its multi-agency approach in particular attracting considerable international attention. See Criminal Assets Bureau, *Annual Report 1999* (Dublin, Criminal Assets Bureau, 2000) para 3.2.

[91] Criminal Assets Bureau Act 1996, s 12.

[92] Criminal Assets Bureau Act 1996, s 13.

[93] Criminal Assets Bureau Act 1996, s 15.

[94] Criminal Assets Bureau Act 1996, s 10(7).

[95] Seanad Debates, vol 148, col 1522 (9 October 1996) per Minister for Finance, Mr Quinn.

[96] Criminal Assets Bureau Act 1996, s 11.

operation only.[97] In that case anonymity was granted on the basis of the belief of a Chief Superintendent that the defendant was involved in organised crime, and on the ground that revealing the identity of a CAB officer would endanger his safety, as '[o]ne of the traits of organised crime is that they utilise intimidation of witnesses'.[98] Moreover, Finnegan P noted that the anonymity did not pose an impediment to the presentation of a defence. Similarly, in the UK, the Director of SOCA may allocate pseudonyms to the staff and the courts may accept evidence from such staff.[99]

The Proceeds of Crime Acts provide explicitly for the payment of compensation: in Ireland, the Minister for Finance compensates any loss incurred by the owner where he shows that the property is not the proceeds of crime[100] thereby ensuring that injustice is not perpetrated against meritorious respondents,[101] and in the UK, SOCA reimburses an applicant who has suffered loss as a result of an interim order where the property is not decided by the court to be recoverable.[102] This is a crucial counterpoint to the civil powers accorded to the State in this context, yet notably there is no reported case to date involving the payment of compensation to an individual in Ireland or the UK.[103]

IV. Interaction between Confiscation and Recovery Powers

How the powers of civil recovery and confiscation fit together may influence the success of the former process. In the UK, property is rendered unrecoverable if it is subject to a restraint order,[104] or if it has been taken into account in deciding the amount of a person's benefit from criminal conduct for the purpose of making a confiscation order under Part 2 of the Proceeds of Crime Act 2002.[105] This interaction was considered more deeply in *Singh v Director of the Assets Recovery Agency* where the Court of Appeal examined whether the Assets Recovery Agency could seek to recover assets taken into account in making a confiscation order which had been quashed subsequently.[106] As Latham LJ noted, 'the purpose of section

---

[97] *Criminal Assets Bureau v PS* [2004] IEHC 351.

[98] ibid. For measures introduced to protect intimidated witnesses see ch 5.

[99] Proceeds of Crime Act 2002, s 449. See ch 5 for an analysis of anonymous witness evidence in criminal trials.

[100] Proceeds of Crime Act 1996, s 16.

[101] *M v D*, n 32, 178 per Moriarty J.

[102] Proceeds of Crime Act 2002, s 283.

[103] At least, given that the Freedom of Information regime is not applicable to SOCA (Freedom of Information Act 2000, s 23) or to the Gardaí, and therefore CAB (Freedom of Information Act 1997, s 23), such details could not be found.

[104] Proceeds of Crime Act 2002, s 308(8).

[105] Proceeds of Crime Act 2002, s 308(9).

[106] *Singh v Director of the Assets Recovery Agency* [2005] EWCA Civ 580.

308(9) was clearly to prevent double recovery' and the provisions accord priority to confiscation by ensuring that 'the only mechanism for recovery in relation to property taken into account if a confiscation order has been made is that provided for under the confiscation order'.[107] If criminal proceedings are brought but no confiscation order is made, or if the property is not taken into account in determining benefit for the purpose of a confiscation order, the 2002 Act does not prevent application for a civil recovery order. However, recovery cannot occur when the property in question has been disposed of through forfeiture under section 27 of the Misuse of Drugs Act 1971 or section 43 of the Drug Trafficking Act 1994.[108] Similarly, a post-conviction confiscation or forfeiture order under the Criminal Justice Act 1994 or the Misuse of Drugs Act 1977 in Ireland takes precedence over an existing interim or interlocutory order under the Proceeds of Crime Act 1996.[109]

V. Challenges to Civil Recovery

Various challenges have been posed to civil recovery, insofar as it appeared to extend the boundaries of existing means of dealing with organised criminality; none of these arguments has been accepted by domestic or European courts. The retrospective application of the provisions has been objected to, as has its effect on the right to private property, and the characterisation of the process as civil rather than criminal.

A. Retrospective Punishment

It has been argued in the UK that civil recovery involves the retrospective application of punishment by including allegedly criminal behaviour that took place before the enactment of the relevant legislation. Article 7 of the ECHR prohibits the imposition of a heavier penalty than the one that was applicable at the time the offence was committed. When the Proceeds of Crime Bill was debated in the House of Lords, it was speculated that the process would breach Article 7 if the unlawful conduct had occurred before the passing of the Bill.[110] Though this reiterated the concern of the Joint Committee on Human Rights,[111] Attorney-General Goldsmith refused to amend the provision to cover only proceeds acquired as a result of criminal conduct after the Bill had been enacted, as was advocated by the Lords.[112]

---

[107] ibid, [18].
[108] Proceeds of Crime Act 2002 (Exemptions from Civil Recovery) Order 2003.
[109] Proceeds of Crime Act 1996, s 3(7).
[110] HL Deb 25 March 2002, vol 633, col 23 per Baroness Buscombe.
[111] Joint Committee on Human Rights, *Third Report* (London, The Stationery Office, 2001) para 41.
[112] HL Deb 13 May 2002, vol 635, cols 60–61 per Goldsmith.

For Article 7 to apply, the measure must constitute a penalty within the specific meaning of the ECHR. Courts all over the UK have concurred that no penalty is involved in recovery proceedings, on the basis that the purpose and function is to recover property obtained through unlawful conduct, not to penalise or punish any person who is proved to have engaged in such conduct.[113] This ensured that the Proceeds of Crime Act 2002 can apply to offences committed before it came into force. Nevertheless, it is hard to square this conclusion with the decision in *Welch v UK* that confiscation is a penalty within the meaning of the ECHR despite the contention by the courts that the absence of a criminal conviction distinguished the recovery process from a penalty as such.[114]

B. The Right to Private Property

Recovery's incursion on the right to private property has been challenged in the national and the European contexts. Article 43 of the Irish Constitution protects the right to private property, the exercise of which may be regulated by 'the principles of social justice' and delimited by 'the exigencies of the common good'. In the domestic setting, the Irish courts have approved restrictions imposed on this constitutional right by the Proceeds of Crime Act 1996, having regard to the aims of the legislation and the threat posed by organised crime. In *M v D*, Moriarty J stated that the interference was not an unjust attack, given the public interest inherent in the legislation,[115] and similarly, in *Gilligan* the court accepted that the exigencies of the common good include measures designed to prevent the accumulation and use of assets which derive from criminal activities.[116] McGuinness J stressed that '[t]he right to private ownership cannot hold a place so high in the hierarchy of rights that it protects the position of assets illegally acquired and held'. Furthermore, the Act was found not to attack property rights unjustly, given that the State must first demonstrate that the property is the proceeds of crime and that an order shall not be made if there is a serious risk of injustice.[117]

Similarly, a qualified right to property is protected by Article 1 of the First Protocol of the ECHR. In *Raimondo v Italy* the European Court concluded that the freezing of suspected Mafia assets in Italy was proportionate to its aim and compliant with the right.[118] It recognised the difficulties in dealing adequately with the Mafia with its enormous financial turnover and concluded that confiscation is 'an

---

[113]   *R (Director of the Assets Recovery Agency) v He and Chen* [2004] EWHC 3021; *R (Director of the Assets Recovery Agency) v Ashton* [2006] EWHC 1064 (Admin); *Walsh v Director of the Assets Recovery Agency* [2005] NICA 6 (26 January 2005) *Assets Recovery Agency v Belton* (2006) NICA 2; *Scottish Ministers v McGuffie* (2006) CSOH 34, 2006 SLT 1166.

[114]   *Welch v United Kingdom* (1995) 20 EHRR 247. See ch 6.

[115]   *M v D*, n 32, 184.

[116]   *Gilligan*, n 71, 237.

[117]   ibid.

[118]   *Raimondo v Italy* (1994) 18 EHRR 371.

effective and necessary weapon in the combat against this cancer'.[119] This case was cited in the House of Lords by the English Attorney-General as supporting the proposed Proceeds of Crime Bill,[120] despite the fact that *Raimondo* concerned the temporary confiscation or freezing of property, which was eventually returned to the applicant, and so is not directly on point. Nonetheless, according to the principles of interpretation of the ECHR, the right to property may be affected to the extent that this is proportionate to the aim of the law. This flexibility of the proportionality balancing exercise in light of the threat posed by organised crime suggests that civil recovery does not breach this right.

C. The Nature of the Process

The most fundamental criticism of asset recovery focuses on its construction as a civil scheme which is not bound by the due process constraints of Articles 6(2) and (3) of the ECHR and Article 40.1 of the Irish Constitution. Indeed, the efficacy and appeal of civil recovery lies in the fact that a criminal conviction is not required, that the civil standard of proof is used, and that the individual bears the onus to establish the legitimate origins of the property. While it has been contended by numerous applicants that asset recovery is criminal in nature, this has been roundly rejected by the domestic and European courts. Overall, the judicial reasoning in such cases seems to be informed by a consequentialist fear of undermining the process which is heralded as a vital tool against organised crime, leading to the conclusion that it is not a 'criminal charge' but rather a civil process which does not engage Article 6.

The '*Engel*' test, from ECHR jurisprudence, has been used in many domestic cases to frame the determination of the nature of asset recovery.[121] This test involves the court examining the classification of the issue in national law; the nature of the offence alleged against the individual; and the seriousness of what is at stake or the nature of the penalty to be imposed. In doing so, Irish and UK courts have cited numerous 'indicia' of crimes in rejecting the argument that asset recovery is criminal in nature: crimes are 'offences against the community at large' which attract a punitive sanction and which require *mens rea*; they involve detention, search, charge, bail and the possible imposition of a pecuniary penalty with liability to imprisonment if the penalty is not paid.[122] Criminal proceedings

> involve a formal accusation made on behalf of the state or by a private prosecutor that a defendant has committed a breach of the criminal law, and the state or the private prosecutor has instituted proceedings which may culminate in the conviction and condemnation of the defendant.[123]

---

[119] ibid, para 30. Support for this interpretation may be found in A Kennedy, 'Civil Recovery Proceedings under the Proceeds of Crime Act 2002: the Experience so far' (2006) 9 *Journal of Money Laundering Control* 245.

[120] HL Deb 13 May 2002, vol 635, col 71.

[121] *Engel v Netherlands (No 1)* (1976) 1 EHRR 647, 678–79. Also see *Walsh*, n 113, [19]ff.

[122] *Melling v O'Mathghamhna* [1962] IR 1 (SC).

[123] *Customs and Excise Commissioners v City of London Magistrates Court* [2000] 4 All ER 763, 767.

Applying these criteria, recovery procedures were deemed not to have 'the features of a criminal prosecution'.[124] Thus, the courts have held, using somewhat circular logic, that a procedure is not a criminal process if it does not involve characteristics such as arrest or detention. However, it appears that it is the avoidance of these aspects at the stage of enactment which facilitates the depiction of recovery as civil – in other words, the schemes are designed deliberately so as to meet the 'civil' criteria. For example, while the lack of detention under the Proceeds of Crime Acts may be cited as evidence that the proceedings are not criminal, the initial classification of the process as civil in nature by the legislature has resulted in the fact that an individual may not be detained.

Reliance was also placed on the civil categorisation of forfeiture in circumstances such as tax evasion. In Ireland, proceedings for the forfeiture of goods which had been exported illegally from the State were not seen to constitute a criminal procedure which required the safeguards of Articles 6(2) and (3), despite the need to establish that an individual committed a criminal offence.[125] Similarly, the penalty for failure to make tax returns was found to be a deterrent or incentive and not a criminal sanction, because, besides the provision of a penalty, none of the characteristics of a criminal offence were present.[126] And in the English domestic setting, proceedings concerning the evasion of import duty were not deemed criminal because the usual consequences of a criminal conviction did not flow from them: there was no conviction or finding of guilt; the person condemned was not treated as having a conviction, and he was not subject to any other penalty.[127] This approach was followed subsequently, despite the acknowledged severity of the repercussions for the individual in question.[128] Such jurisprudence is also influenced by European Court of Human Rights decisions, such as *Allgemeine Gold- und Silberscheideanstalt v United Kingdom* where the forfeiture of items of a third party which affected the applicants, subsequent to criminal prosecution, did not render the proceedings a 'criminal charge', and *Air Canada v United Kingdom*, where seizure of an aeroplane and its return on payment of a fine was not a criminal charge, given that the criminal courts were not involved and failure to pay would not result in criminal proceedings.[129] These cases were relied upon in national courts to conclude that 'legislation providing for forfeiture is not necessarily criminal in nature'.[130]

Notwithstanding this weighty line of jurisprudence in the British and European contexts, a number of characteristics indicate that this reasoning is disingenuous

---

[124] *Gilligan*, n 71, 217; *Murphy v GM*, n 3, 147; *Director of the Assets Recovery Agency v Customs and Excise Commissioners and Charrington* [2005] EWCA Civ 334 [17]; *Walsh*, n 113, [23].

[125] *AG v Southern Industrial Trust Limited* (1957) 94 ILTR 161, 167.

[126] *McLoughlin v Tuite* [1989] IR 82.

[127] *Goldsmith v Customs and Excise Commissioners* [2001] EWHC Admin 285.

[128] *R (Mudie) v Dover Magistrates' Court* [2003] EWCA Civ 237; *Gora v Customs and Excise Commissioners* [2003] EWCA Civ 525, [2004] QB 93 [34]–[35].

[129] *Allgemeine Gold- und Silberscheideanstalt v United Kingdom* (1986) 9 EHRR 1; *Air Canada v United Kingdom* (1995) 20 EHRR 150.

[130] *Gilligan*, n 71, 223. *Murphy v GM*, n 3, 153.

and that civil forfeiture ought to be regarded as a criminal process in substance: namely, the centrality of culpability, the promotion of the traditional objectives of punishment, and the power of the relevant agencies.

The courts in Ireland and the UK have viewed the absence of a *mens rea* requirement, amongst other factors, as indicating that forfeiture is civil in nature, because the focus purports to be on the property rather than the person.[131] However, as Bishop observed as long ago as 1858,

> disguise the matter as we may, under whatever form of words, if the intent which the owner of the property carries in his bosom is the gist of the thing on which the forfeiture turns, then the question is one of the criminal law, and forfeiture is a penalty imposed for crime.[132]

Given that allegedly criminal behaviour is at the core of recovery, the intention of the individual seems pivotal. Evidence that the assets were accrued as a result of criminal activity or conduct is required before an order is made, and although the court does not need to establish to the criminal standard of proof that the respondent is responsible for criminal behaviour or for a specific offence, the blameworthiness of the generator of the property remains fundamental to the forfeiture of assets in what is essentially an 'indirect finding of guilt'.[133] Although it may be argued that it is the origin of the assets which is at issue, as exemplified by the cases taken by the Assets Recovery Agency against the estates of alleged drug dealers who have since died,[134] it is still necessary to establish criminality on the part on the original holder of the property, demonstrating that his intention is key.

The presence of what is described in US jurisprudence as an 'innocent owner' defence may substantiate this contention.[135] In Ireland, orders under sections 3 and 4 of the Proceeds of Crime Act 1996 may not be imposed or may be lifted if there is a serious risk of injustice, a caveat which is comparable to an innocent owner defence, for if a person can prove that he was unaware of the criminal origins of property, he may retain the assets and have the order lifted. Moreover, the logic behind the seven-year waiting period before a disposal order could be granted under section 4 (as it originally was enacted)[136] was to ensure that any person who owned property jointly with an individual who was allegedly involved in criminal activity or conduct would have the opportunity to make a claim that

---

[131] See HC Deb 30 October 2001, vol 373, col 761; HL Deb 13 May 2002, vol 635, col 72; also *Green*, n 29, [25]; *Walsh*, n 113, [41].

[132] J Bishop, *Criminal Law* (1858) 703, cited in T Piety, 'Scorched Earth: How the Expansion of Civil Forfeiture Doctrine Has Laid Waste to Due Process' (1991) 45 *University of Miami Law Review* 911, 942.

[133] Liberty, *Proceeds of Crime: Consultation on Draft Legislation* (London, Liberty, 2001) para 7.3.

[134] Kennedy, n 119.

[135] *Austin v United States* 509 US 602 (1993) 618–19.

[136] As originally enacted, s 4 of the Proceeds of Crime Act 1996 allowed for the making of a disposal order where an interlocutory order had been in force for not less than seven years; now, disposal may occur after a shorter period when an application is made with the consent of the parties (s 4A, as inserted by the Proceeds of Crime (Amendment) Act 2005, s 7).

the property was his, rather than belonging to the individual appearing to be the owner. Similarly, in the UK, a bona fide exception exists, in that a recovery order must not be made if it would not be just and equitable to do so, owing to the respondent having obtained the property in good faith and without notice that it was recoverable, and his having taken steps in this regard which he otherwise would not have taken.[137] Also, a victim of theft may apply for an order that the property obtained by unlawful conduct was not recoverable (that is, not obtained through unlawful conduct)[138] prior to it being taken from the owner.[139] This suggests that the focus of the order is not the property, but rather the allegedly culpable individual, thereby refuting the contention that the orders are *in rem*. In other words, guilt appears to be an issue in the context of forfeiture, given that individuals who are perceived to be innocent of organised crime are treated differently to those suspected to be guilty. A comment of the English Attorney-General betrays this sentiment:

> If, in a criminal trial, the prosecution cannot prove that the person before the court is in fact guilty . . . then he is entitled to be acquitted. Yet it is as plain as a pikestaff that his money has been acquired as the proceeds of crime.[140]

So, while *mens rea* need not be established as occurs in conventional criminal trials, and while the focus in a civil recovery hearing is on proving where the assets came from, an inability to prove that their origins lie in innocent or legal behaviour results in a de facto finding of guilt.

The promotion of the aims of punishment further demonstrates that characterising asset recovery as purely civil is inaccurate. Although there are undoubtedly preventative and reparative elements to this mechanism, it also embodies condemnation, retribution and deterrence. Certainly, civil recovery may be viewed as preventative, because it ensures that illegal profits cannot be accumulated and used to corrupt democratic institutions, and stops people becoming bad role models. Another interpretation is that civil recovery seeks to redress an imbalance by seizing assets accrued as a result of criminal activity and therefore is reparative.[141] Civil recovery may also be defended on the basis that it is analogous to a civil suit for the return of illegally obtained property. In the same way that a civil action for misappropriation of property seeks to restore the injured party to the position he was in prior to the commission of the tort, it is arguable that civil recovery also seeks to return the state of affairs to that before the alleged criminal offence. However, this reparative argument is rebutted by the fact that the party bringing the action in this instance is the State, with its vast resources and agents, characteristics which necessitate the existence of counterbalancing due process rights in the criminal context.

[137] Proceeds of Crime Act 2002, s 266(4).
[138] Proceeds of Crime Act 2002, s 304(1).
[139] Proceeds of Crime Act 2002, s 281.
[140] HL Deb 25 June 2002, vol 636, col 1270. This comment was lamented by Lord Lloyd of Berwick: HL Deb 11 July 2002, vol 637, col 844.
[141] *Gilligan*, n 71, 218.

Furthermore, it may be argued that recovery is more than reparative in Ireland given that the legislation does not preclude the taking of assets acquired by a combination of legitimate and illegitimate funds. In other words, the ability in Ireland to recover legitimate property which have been mixed or joined with the proceeds of crime indicates that the process is not simply remedial. In the UK, the mixing of recoverable property with other property is dealt with explicitly in the Proceeds of Crime Act 2002 which provides that the portion of the mixed property which is attributable to the recoverable property represents the property obtained through unlawful conduct.[142] This somewhat circular definition implies that the recoverable section of mixed property may be separated and thereafter thus recovered.[143] This sought to ensure that money laundering efforts on the part of suspected criminals would not render their gains unrecoverable, but also permits the separation of mixed funds. In contrast, no mention is made of 'mixed' property in the Irish legislation, and it seems likely that mixing of funds would not necessarily preclude the granting of an order, unless it would cause a serious risk of injustice.[144] When the issue was raised before a Parliamentary Committee in 2004, the Irish Minister for Justice, Equality and Law Reform, Michael McDowell, responded sardonically that

> [o]ne could not possibly have a system whereby if a person proved that an aunt gave him or her a fiver which was invested in a mansion the person built, it therefore ceased to be the proceeds of crime because a tiny fraction of it was a voluntary gift from an aunt.[145]

Therefore it appears that assets acquired by a combination of legitimate and illegitimate funds may be the subject of a recovery order under the Irish Act, although the issue has not yet been considered by the courts.

In addition, civil recovery fulfils punishment's aims of censure. Criminal sanctions 'take their character as punishment from the condemnation which precedes them and serve as the warrant for their infliction'.[146] 'Blaming' distinguishes criminal from civil measures, with the former connoting 'should not do',[147] and indeed it seems that forfeiture does represent 'an instance of the use of state power to condemn or punish individuals for wrongdoing'.[148] Certainly, moral responsibility and social blame accrues as a result of judicial determination that property represents the proceeds of crime.[149]

---

[142]   Proceeds of Crime Act 2002, s 306(2).

[143]   In *Director of the Assets Recovery Agency v Olupitan* [2007] EWHC 162 (QB), Langley J observed that the Act 'gives no guidance about what "portion" of a mixed property is attributable to recoverable property beyond the language itself used in section 306(2)'.

[144]   Proceeds of Crime Act 1996, ss 3 and 4.

[145]   Minister for Justice, 'Submission to the Select Committee on Justice, Equality, Defence and Women's Rights' vol 37 (Dublin, Select Committee on Justice, Equality, Defence and Women's Rights, 2004).

[146]   HLA Hart, 'The Aims of the Criminal Law' (1958) 23 *Law and Contemporary Problems* 405.

[147]   C Steiker, 'Punishment Theory and the Criminal–Civil Procedural Divide' (1997) 85 *Georgetown Law Journal* 775, 804; A Ashworth, 'Is the Criminal Law a Lost Cause?' (2000) 116 *LQR* 232.

[148]   *Mudie*, n 128, [36].

[149]   M Stahl, 'Asset Forfeiture, Burdens of Proof and the War on Drugs' (1992) 83 *Journal of Criminal Law and Criminology* 274.

In this respect, it has been argued that the presumption of innocence as protected by Article 6(2) is breached where civil recovery follows acquittal on the basis that the State is censuring or at least expressing suspicions about an individual who has not been convicted. As well as pertaining to the trial process, the European Court has held that where a court expresses suspicion about an acquitted individual (rather than opining that he is guilty), such as by refusing compensation to him or by saying that suspicion has not been 'dispelled', the presumption will have been infringed.[150] In this vein, the respondent in *Scottish Ministers v Doig* contended that averments relating to a recovery order that stated he was involved in the supply of controlled drugs breached Article 6(2) ECHR as he had been acquitted of those charges.[151] The Court of Session in Scotland rejected this, stressing that recovery and criminal proceedings are entirely separate, and that the averments did not invite or assert a finding of guilt of a particular offence, but rather contended that the conduct was generally unlawful and this did not offend Article 6(2).[152] Similarly, in the first civil recovery case it considered, the UK Supreme Court held that the courts may consider evidence that formed the basis of charges abroad of which the appellant was acquitted, and that this does not represent an expression of suspicion by the State regarding his guilt such as to breach the presumption of innocence.[153] The European Court has stressed that Article 6(2) seeks to safeguard an acquitted person's reputation from statements or acts that would seem to undermine the acquittal.[154] Viewing these cases in light of the presumption more broadly demonstrates the State's declaration of guilt in a way as to shape public opinion and to prejudge assessment by the criminal courts. What is contentious is the State declaration regarding guilt through the seizing of assets described as the proceeds of crime, that is, obtained through unlawful conduct but without proof beyond reasonable doubt. Asset recovery involves the stigma of a quasi-criminal label, admittedly without imprisonment, but also without the protection of due process norms.

Asset recovery also seems to display deterrent aims and effects, thus fulfilling another of the traditional aims of punishment. While it has been contended that it does not serve as a deterrent because it merely recoups what was not legitimately owned and therefore does not render the individual any worse off than before the criminal conduct,[155] the seizure of alleged criminal earnings arguably is a general deterrent (insofar as anything can be such) as it may remove one of the major incentives to commit unlawful behaviour.[156] Asset recovery may also serve as a specific deterrent to the individual whose property has been seized and

---

[150] *Sekanina v Austria* (1994) 17 EHRR 221, para 29.
[151] *Scottish Ministers v Doig* [2009] CSIH 34, 2009 SC 474.
[152] ibid, [32].
[153] *Gale*, n 38.
[154] *Taliadorou and Stylianou v Cyprus* [2008] ECHR 1088, para 26.
[155] D Fried, 'Rationalizing Criminal Forfeiture' (1988) 79 *Journal of Criminal Law and Criminology* 328, 371–72.
[156] Although one could indeed argue that it instigates further unlawful behaviour in a bid to replace the seized assets.

retained, as is exemplified by this political observation in Ireland: '[c]riminals are on the run as never before. They have gone to ground overseas and elsewhere because their assets are being seized and their ill gotten gains, their motivation for committing crime, are being taken from them'.[157] So, the position of the Government seems inconsistent – in creating such legislation its capacity to deter crime is stressed, yet then its nature as purely reparative is then cited in its defence as a civil process.

Finally, it seems that the link between the police and the asset recovery process in Ireland in particular undermines claims that it is civil in nature. As noted in chapter two, in a structural sense, the Irish Criminal Assets Bureau represents a hybrid of State agencies and authorities, including members of the police, officials of the Revenue Commissioners and of the Department of Social, Community and Family Affairs.[158] CAB has 'not inconsiderable powers of investigation'[159] and may initiate investigations and other actions on its own motion, without need for external referral or recommendation.[160] In addition to the fact that many CAB staff are members of the police force, an officer from each police division is trained as a 'criminal asset profiler' to gather information at a local level and indicate possible foci for the Bureau's work.[161] Furthermore, the nexus between the DPP's office and CAB in Ireland was highlighted in *M v D* by Moriarty J,[162] while in *Gilligan* McGuinness J noted that the evidence given in the case showed 'an even clearer nexus than Moriarty J might have envisaged between the personnel of the Criminal Assets Bureau and the criminal investigation section of the Garda Síochána'.[163] This link with the police and the prosecution service and the implications this has for the nature and perception of the asset recovery process may explain why the UK system was designed so that the non-police civilian Assets Recovery Agency held responsibility for recovery,[164] although this has been altered by the subsequent assumption of this role by SOCA and prosecution authorities, the SFO and Revenue and Customs.[165] This, combined with the fact that asset recovery serves the purpose of criminal punishment, suggests that its depiction as civil is incomplete at best.

If asset recovery were found to be a criminal process, then Article 6(2) and (3) would be engaged, altering the burden of proof, undermining the reliance on hearsay evidence and requiring specificity in the type of criminal behaviour which

---

[157] Dáil Debates, vol 481, col 276 (8 October 1997) per Jim Higgins.

[158] Criminal Assets Bureau Act 1996, s 8(1). The Chief Bureau Officer is a Garda holding the rank of Chief Superintendent (s 7(6)).

[159] *Murphy v Flood*, 1 July 1999 (HC) per McCracken J.

[160] Criminal Assets Bureau Act 1996, s 4.

[161] Dáil Debates, vol 635, col 57 (14 April 2007) per Michael McDowell.

[162] *M v D*, n 32, 181.

[163] *Gilligan*, n 71.

[164] Home Office Working Group on Confiscation, n 13, para 5.7; HL Deb 25 March 2002, vol 633, col 59.

[165] ARA was abolished by the Serious Crime Act 2007, and its civil recovery and other functions transferred to the Serious Organised Crime Agency (SOCA). Serious Crime Act 2007, s 74 and Sch 8.

generated the property.[166] Nevertheless, domestic and international jurisprudence indicates widespread court approval of its characterisation as a civil measure. Thus, in theory at least, civil recovery should represent an effective and useful tool for the State against organised crime. However, its application has been less than consistent in the UK, in marked contrast to the situation in Ireland.

VI. Success of the Civil Process

Despite the common purposes and definitions in the Irish and UK legislation, the former has been far more successful in terms of monies and property recouped. A previous Minister for Justice in Ireland spoke of 'the outstanding performance and success of the Criminal Assets Bureau'[167] evident a mere two years after its introduction, and a Garda Commissioner viewed the Bureau as playing a 'significant role' in the fight against organised crime.[168] The capacity of CAB to generate money for the Irish Exchequer augments its popular and political support:[169] each year millions of euros' worth of property are subject to interim and interlocutory orders, and between €1.4m and €3.5m has been disposed of each year since 2005.[170] In contrast to the situation in the UK outlined earlier in this chapter,[171] CAB's funding is not dependent on the revenue recovered or disposed of, nor does it represent a proportion of the property seized,[172] despite the recommendation of the Select Committee in 1985 that the agency established to examine and trace assets of suspected drug dealers (which took the form of CAB) should eventually be funded from the proceeds of confiscation orders.[173] The 'ring-fencing' of assets 'for those communities who have suffered most at the hands of the drug barons' was also mooted when the Proceeds of Crime (Amendment) Bill 2003 was debated, but rejected by the Irish Government.[174]

In addition to such financial gains, CAB's structure and *modus-operandi* represents a model for other jurisdictions, with its multi-agency approach in particular

---

[166] Alldridge, n 25, 244.

[167] Dáil Debates, vol 497, col 122 (19 November 1998).

[168] Criminal Assets Bureau, *Annual Report 2009* (Dublin, Criminal Assets Bureau, 2010) letter from Fachtna Murphy.

[169] See 'CAB Recovered €16m from Criminals Last Year', *Irish Times*, 26 August 2006; 'CAB Froze More than €6m in Criminal Assets in 2005', *Irish Times*, 24 July 2006.

[170] Criminal Assets Bureau, *Annual Report 2005* (Dublin, Criminal Assets Bureau, 2006) 29; Criminal Assets Bureau, *Annual Report 2006* (Criminal Assets Bureau, 2007) 23; Criminal Assets Bureau, *Annual Report 2007* (Dublin, Criminal Assets Bureau, 2008) 14; Criminal Assets Bureau, *Annual Report 2008* (Dublin, Criminal Assets Bureau, 2009) 16; Criminal Assets Bureau, *Annual Report 2009* (Dublin, Criminal Assets Bureau, 2010) 16; Criminal Assets Bureau, *Annual Report 2010* (Dublin, Criminal Assets Bureau, 2011) 16.

[171] See n 62.

[172] Proceeds of Crime Act 1996, s 19.

[173] Select Committee on Crime, Lawlessness and Vandalism, n 10, para 6.3.

[174] Dáil Debates, vol 572, col 1437ff (21 October 2003) per Fergus O'Dowd; col 1454 per Minister for Defence, Michael Smith.

attracting considerable international attention.[175] This permits the sharing of information more effectively than in the 'multi-disciplinary' UK model.[176] Indeed, a review in Scotland lamented the absence of a clear process for law enforcement agencies to report a case for civil recovery where it is clear that there is insufficient evidence to reach a criminal standard of proof.[177]

While the interaction of many bodies in the Irish recovery context is viewed as a strength, the potential for disjointed effort by a hybrid agency was highlighted by the Home Office in 2004,[178] which noted the 'patchy' application of the Proceeds of Crime Act 2002 powers across England and Wales. The fear regarding ARA's structure and operation seems to have been borne out in the UK, given the low levels of assets recovered by the Agency, its inability to meet self-financing targets and 'basic failures' in management practice.[179] Nevertheless, its Annual Report for 2006/07 records that £57.2m was disrupted by civil recovery actions, while £15.1m was collected in civil recovery cases,[180] not insignificant amounts.

As noted in chapter two, the multi-agency structure proved problematic for the operation of the Assets Recovery Agency and hence it was replaced by the Serious Organised Crime Agency (SOCA).[181] Since the establishment of SOCA, in 2009–10 £22.3m was recovered in the civil process, in recovery settlements and tax settlements, in 2010–11 £2.0m was the subject of civil recovery orders, and consent orders comprised £7.5m, while in 2011–12 the equivalent figures are £11.5m and £2.6m.[182] In addition, cash seizure and forfeiture has been lucrative for the UK: since 2006 between £5m and £13m has been recouped in this manner.[183] As regards Scotland, the Civil Recovery Unit has recovered approximately £1m

---

[175] CAB, *Annual Report 1999* (Dublin, Criminal Assets Bureau, 2000) 5; CAB, *Annual Report* 2008 (Dublin, Criminal Assets Bureau, 2009) 6.2. CAB was a key initiator of CARIN, the Camden Asset Recovery Inter Agency Network, which is an informal network of contacts and a cooperative group in all aspects of tackling the proceeds of crime.

[176] A Kennedy, 'An Evaluation of the Recovery of Criminal Proceeds in the United Kingdom' (2007) 33 *Journal of Money Laundering Control* 40.

[177] HM Inspectorate of Constabulary for Scotland (HMICS) and the Inspectorate of Prosecution in Scotland (IPS), *Joint Thematic Report on the Proceeds of Crime Act 2002* (Edinburgh, Scottish Government, 2009) (v).

[178] HM Inspectorate of Court Administration, *Payback Time – Joint Review of Asset Recovery since the Proceeds of Crime Act 2002* (London, HM Inspectorate of Court Administration, 2004) 10–11.

[179] House of Commons Committee of Public Accounts, *Assets Recovery Agency Fiftieth Report of Session 2006–07* (London, The Stationery Office, 2007) 5–9; Comptroller and Auditor General, n 62, 6.

[180] Assets Recovery Agency, *Annual Report 2006–07* (London, Assets Recovery Agency, 2007) Appendix B, 55.

[181] Serious Organised Crime and Police Act 2005, s 1.

[182] Serious Organised Crime Agency, *Annual Report and Accounts 2009–10* (London, Serious Organised Crime Agency, 2010) 20. These figures have not been separated into recovery and tax, and the exclusion of SOCA from the Freedom of Information Act means such details will not be revealed. Serious Organised Crime Agency, *Annual Report and Accounts 2010–11* (London, Serious Organised Crime Agency, 2011) 16; Serious Organised Crime Agency, *Annual Report and Accounts 2011–12* (London, Serious Organised Crime Agency, 2012) 15.

[183] See Serious Organised Crime Agency, *Annual Report and Accounts 2010–11*, 16; *Annual Report and Accounts 2011–12*, 15.

per year, although in 2010–11 more than £12m was recovered, and £3.5m in 2011–12.[184] Between £1m and £2m is seized in cash each year.[185]

As previously noted, a facet of the UK model which ostensibly should stimulate the vigorous pursuit of civil asset recovery is 'incentivisation'. The 'Recovered Assets Incentivisation Fund' in England and Wales distributes half of the assets recovered to the agencies involved to improve asset recovery and local crime fighting priorities.[186] Furthermore, a proportion of assets recovered in England and Wales is awarded to community projects administered by the Home Office,[187] and a similar scheme called 'Cashback for Communities' operates in Scotland.[188] In contrast to CAB in Ireland, ARA was given detailed published targets regarding recovery and a comprehensive business plan,[189] while SOCA's annual plans speak of 'strategic imperatives' with 'planned deliverables', measures and outputs, including the tackling of criminal finance and profits through asset recovery.[190] These factors may undermine the underlying rationales for the process, and the imposition of fiscal targets poses a challenge to the administration of justice, as it focuses on the revenue producing capacity of forfeiture to the potential detriment of equity or fairness, or on the key aim of the process which is to disrupt allegedly criminal behaviour.[191]

A further possible explanation for the failure of ARA when compared with the Irish CAB is that the former required a referral from a relevant police agency before acting in relation to proceeds of crime. ARA's Director was obliged to exercise his functions 'in the way which he considers is best calculated to contribute to the reduction of crime',[192] having regard to guidance given by the Secretary of State,[193] and such guidance given in 2005 stressed that the Director normally should not act without a referral from law enforcement or prosecution authorities and should consult to ensure criminal investigation or proceedings are not

---

[184] See Civil Recovery Unit, *Annual Report 2011/12* (Edinburgh, Scottish Government 2012); Crown Office Crown Office and Procurator Fiscal Service News Release, 'Proceeds of Crime Recovers Record Amount', 27 June 2011.

[185] ibid.

[186] Comptroller and Auditor General, n 62, para 2.1.

[187] See www.direct.gov.uk/en/Nl1/Newsroom/DG_178917.

[188] See www.scotland.gov.uk/Topics/Justice/public-safety/17141/cashback.

[189] ARA's 'operational targets' in 2006/07 included the disruption of between 90 and 125 criminal enterprises through the institution of criminal confiscation, civil recovery and taxation cases; the obtaining of recovery orders or voluntary settlements and the issue of tax assessments in at least 28 cases; the recovery of an amount equivalent to 100% of the agency's budget; and the realisation of at least £9.5m of receipts in civil recovery, taxation and criminal confiscation cases. Assets Recovery Agency, *Summary Annual Report 2006/07* (London, Home Office Communication Directorate, 2006) 12; and Assets Recovery Agency, *Business Plan 2006/07* (London, Home Office Communication Directorate, 2006) 16ff.

[190] Serious Organised Crime Agency, *Serious Organised Crime Agency Annual Plan 2008/09* (London, Serious Organised Crime Agency, 2008) 13ff.

[191] J Worrall, 'Addicted to the Drug War: The Role of Civil Assets Forfeiture as a Budgetary Necessity in Contemporary Law Enforcement' (2001) 29 *Journal of Criminal Justice* 171, 172; M Cheh, 'Can Something this Easy, Quick, and Profitable also be Fair? Runaway Civil Forfeiture Stumbles on the Constitution' (1994) 39 *New York Law School Law Review* 1, 43.

[192] Proceeds of Crime Act 2002, s 2(1).

[193] Proceeds of Crime Act 2002, s 2(5) and (6).

prejudiced.[194] This limited ARA's effect, given that less than 20 per cent of the relevant bodies had so referred cases by the end of August 2006[195] and given that the guidance seemed to increase the extent to which police and customs become 'territorial' about certain cases.[196] Similarly, although SOCA has been described as 'an immensely powerful statutory body',[197] like its predecessor ARA it remains dependent on external referral before initiating investigation or proceedings relating to asset recovery, differentiating it from CAB and potentially explaining its relative underuse.

VII. Further Civil Orders

Following the model of civil recovery, Part 1 of the Serious Crime Act 2007 circumvents the criminal process per se to allow serious crime prevention orders (SCPOs) to be imposed in England, Wales and Northern Ireland. These are civil orders which represent the Government in London seeking to be 'flexible and innovative' in response to 'very skilled, very intelligent and very adept' people who try to distance themselves from the actual perpetration of criminality.[198] This is a quintessential characteristic or ploy of individuals who are involved in the more senior ranks of organised crime groups, and in turn the State reacted by adapting.

SCPOs were first proposed by the Home Office in a consultation paper in 2006 as disposal orders which sought to prevent future harms and redress past harms.[199] The consultation paper stressed that 'civil orders could play a role where prosecution *is not feasible, alongside* prosecution or *as an alternative* to prosecution'.[200] In the second instance, an order could be used alongside prosecution, such as part of a deal to testify for the Crown, ensuring that the subject is bound to conditions of good behaviour; while in the latter scenario SCPOs could deal with those on the periphery of organised crime rather than constructing a prosecution case. Prior to enactment, the House of Lords Select Committee on the Constitution expressed concern about the 'wide and deep' constraints SCPOs could potentially contain and noted the possible effect on third parties.[201] Such concerns, rooted in a due process paradigm, did not dissuade the legislature from approving these measures.

[194] *Home Secretary's Guidance*, 7 February 2005, para 3.
[195] House of Commons Committee of Public Accounts, *Assets Recovery Agency Fiftieth Report of Session 2006–07* (London, The Stationery Office, 2007) 9.
[196] Kennedy, n 119, 14.
[197] *R (UMBS Online Ltd) v Serious Organised Crime Agency* [2007] EWCA Civ 406.
[198] HL Deb 7 February 2007, vol 689, col 728.
[199] Home Office, *New Powers Against Organised and Financial Crime* (London, Home Office, 2006) 28.
[200] ibid, para 3.2.
[201] House of Lords Select Committee on the Constitution, *Second Report of Session 2006–07: Serious Crime Bill* (London, Stationery Office, 2007).

Now, the High Courts in England, Wales and Northern Ireland may make a SCPO lasting for at most five years[202] if satisfied on the civil burden of proof[203] that a person over the age of 18 has been involved in serious crime[204] anywhere and it has reasonable grounds to believe that the order would protect the public by preventing, restricting or disrupting involvement by the person in serious crime in England, Wales and Northern Ireland. An application for such an order may be made by the Director of Public Prosecutions, the Director of Revenue and Customs, or the Director of the Serious Fraud Office only.[205] SCPOs may make prohibitions or restrictions on, or requirements in relation to, an individual's financial, property or business dealings or holdings, working arrangements, communications, use of premises (including private dwellings), or travel.[206] Such orders may require a person to answer questions in writing, provide information or documents (other than privileged/confidential material)[207] to a law enforcement officer, which includes a constable; a member of the staff of SOCA; an officer of Revenue and Customs; or a member of the Serious Fraud Office. However a SCPO may not require a person to answer questions, or provide information, orally.[208] Moreover, bodies corporate, partnerships and unincorporated associations may have prohibitions or restrictions placed on financial, property or business dealings or holdings of such persons; the provision of goods or services; and the employment of staff by such persons.[209]

Though the order is made on the civil burden of proof, failure to comply with a serious crime prevention order, without reasonable excuse, is an offence, punishable on indictment by up to five years imprisonment.[210] This brings the individual within the criminal justice system notwithstanding that his involvement in serious crime was never established beyond reasonable doubt, thereby circumventing due process protections. In addition to the possibility of incarceration, anything in the person's possession at the time of the offence which the court considers to have been involved in the offence may be forfeited,[211] and a company convicted may be wound up if the Director of Public Prosecutions, the Director of Revenue and Customs, or the Director of the Serious Fraud Office considers this in the public interest.[212] These weighty powers are counter-balanced to an extent by

---

[202] Serious Crime Act 2007, s 16(2).

[203] The House of Lords Select Committee on the Constitution had called for the criminal standard on the basis of the view that SCPOs amount to the determination of a criminal charge: ibid, para 17, and also see Joint Committee on Human Rights, *Twelfth Report Session 2006–07* (London, Stationery Office, 2007) para 1.14ff.

[204] Involvement in serious crime means committing a serious offence, or facilitating its commission, or behaving in such a way that is likely to facilitate its commission whether or not such an offence was committed s 2(1). See Pt 1 of Sch1 for the definition of a serious offence.

[205] Serious Crime Act 2007, s 8.

[206] s 5 contains a non-exhaustive list of the types of provision that may be made by SCPOs.

[207] Serious Crime Act 2007, ss 12–14.

[208] Serious Crime Act 2007, s 11.

[209] Serious Crime Act 2007, s 5(4).

[210] Serious Crime Act 2007, s 25.

[211] Serious Crime Act 2007, s 26.

[212] Serious Crime Act 2007, s 27.

virtue of the fact that the High Court (in England, Wales and Northern Ireland) must, on an application by a person, give him an opportunity to make representations about the making, variation or discharge of an SCPO if it considers that the proceedings would be likely to have a significant adverse effect on him.[213] Nonetheless, SCPOs remain another troubling dimension of the use of civil powers in the context of the control of organised crime.

VIII. Conclusion

Civil recovery allows the force of the State and the opprobrium of the community to be visited upon individuals who are believed to transgress the criminal law but who have otherwise evaded prosecution. In a similar manner, serious crime prevention orders represent a robust but civil approach to dealing with organised crime. The establishment of a civil recovery scheme and the imposition of serious crime prevention orders signify the development of a new policing style, in which the traditional reactive means of enforcement is usurped by more proactive policing which seeks to preclude participation in criminal enterprises by seizing the capital necessary to develop and maintain illicit markets,[214] or by prevention of certain behaviours, actions or association.

Civil recovery holds the potential to usurp ordinary police work, as a softer option to the more onerous investigative and prosecution process.[215] This indicates the importance in a due process sense of the statutory provision regarding the priority to be given to criminal prosecutions: the Proceeds of Crime Act 2002 in the UK states that 'the reduction of crime is in general best secured by means of criminal investigations and criminal proceedings'.[216] This may limit the number of people who fall within the scope of this measure. Nonetheless, as Goldstock notes, it is not apparent in a crime control sense why the requirement for the use of criminal remedies prior to the initiation of civil suits is necessary or even desirable,[217] given the widespread political and legal support for this measure. No such priority is contained in the Irish Act, although the Deputy Commissioner of the Irish police stressed that civil forfeiture operates in parallel to the normal investigating procedures of the police,[218] rather than as an alternative. Despite these intentions, asset recovery may be the preferred tactic in combating organised crime in Ireland, given the lower burden of proof and the more permissive

---

[213] Serious Crime Act 2007, s 9.

[214] S Kilcommins, I O'Donnell, E O'Sullivan and B Vaughan, *Crime, Punishment and the Search for Order in Ireland* (Dublin, Institute of Public Administration, 2004) 227.

[215] J Lea, 'Hitting Criminals where it hurts: Organised Crime and the Erosion of due Process' (2004) 35 *Cambrian Law Review* 81; Cheh, n 191.

[216] Proceeds of Crime Act 2002, s 2(6).

[217] R Goldstock, *Organised Crime in Northern Ireland: A Report for the Secretary of State* (Belfast, Northern Ireland Office, 2004) 4.17.

[218] *Gilligan*, n 71, 205.

procedural and evidential rules when contrasted with the prosecution and conviction of crime.

The Proceeds of Crime Acts in the UK and Ireland indicate a reformulation of the means of addressing organised crime, in which the needs of the State are favoured over the individual's right to due process.[219] The avoidance of the criminal law both in this respect and through the use of serious crime prevention orders symbolises an important paradigm shift, in which conventional values and procedures are relinquished in a bid to combat organised criminality. The maintenance of weighty safeguards in the criminal process becomes a moot point in this context, given the location of these processes in the civil realm which does not attract the same level of protections. There has been an irrefutable move away from due process, to a setting in which imperatives of efficiency, risk control and security are seen as superior to individual rights.

In addition, civil recovery reveals a dramatically altered conception of the role of the State: no longer is it an entity from which individuals must be protected, rather we must be shielded from each other by the State. This benign interpretation is embodied by the shift away from due process rights and rules of evidence which seek to mitigate the enormous imbalance of power between the State and the individual, towards regulations which guard us from other individuals. Moreover, the dichotomy between the ordinary decent citizen and the 'criminal' 'other', between 'us' and 'them', is drawn sharply into focus by the work of CAB, which has been described as 'moral policing'.[220]

As Pound presciently observed in the early twentieth century:

> The function of securing social interest through punitive justice seems to be insensibly slipping away from courts and hence from law and in substance, if not in form, to be coming more and more into the hands of administrative agencies.[221]

Instead of the conventional approach to criminal justice which is affected through investigation, prosecution, conviction, and imprisonment, asset recovery is realised by administrative bodies and civil processes, in the form of the Criminal Assets Bureau and the Serious Organised Crime Agency. Indeed, Kilcommins describes CAB'S means of dealing with criminality as criminal administration[222] rather than criminal justice, in which the notion of *mens rea* is circumvented.[223]

---

[219] See L Campbell, 'Theorising Asset Forfeiture in Ireland' (2007) 71 *Journal of Criminal Law* 441.

[220] Kilcommins *et al*, n 214, 229. The desire for the notion of moral policing is aptly encapsulated by the statement of the former Minister for Justice who noted that 'these people invest their money in pubs, restaurants, dancehalls, buildings, house, cars, boats, etc., to the point where it is hard to tell with whom one may be communicating in certain strata of social life. I hope that these people who are masquerading as decent upright citizens and who drive around in big cars and attend all the best social places will be found out through the efforts of the Criminal Assets Bureau and pursued relentlessly until they are convicted of their crimes'. Dáil Debates, vol 480, col 170 (9 July 1997) per Ms Owen.

[221] R Pound, 'The Future of the Criminal Law' (1921) 21 *Columbia Law Review* 1.

[222] MD Dubber, 'Policing Possession: The War on Crime and the End of the Criminal Law' (2001) 91 *Journal of Criminal Law and Criminology* 1, 93.

[223] S Kilcommins and B Vaughan, *Terrorism, Rights and the Rule of Law: Negotiating Justice in Ireland* (Cullompton, Willan, 2007) 136.

Kilcommins draws attention to Sayre's claim in 1933 that the modern conception of criminality was shifting from a basis of individual guilt to one of social danger, and his questioning of whether this signified the abandonment of the *mens rea* requirement as an essential element of criminality.[224] It appears that similar developments are evident in the use of civil recovery, given that harm, rather than culpability, is the focus.[225] Civil recovery purports to act *in rem* rather than *in personam*, and therefore may indicate a move towards 'a day when criminality will be based upon external behaviour alone irrespective of intent'.[226]

Civil asset recovery may be described as a quintessentially apersonal means of dealing with crime, in which emphasis is laid on the non-moral and regulatory aspect of the law, indicating a shift in focus away from the individual towards societal interests. It is arguable that in this context persons have a role only as nuisances to be abated or as objects of regulation.[227] The fundamental aim of the recovery process is to neutralise the threat posed to society by organised criminals, rather than attaining a just outcome in accordance with traditional principles of criminal justice. Civil recovery does not seek to impose retribution, rehabilitate or reintegrate, but rather aims to prevent the commission of further crime by seizing the assets of suspected criminals. Nonetheless, even as a civil mechanism, it involves public censure and stigma, and so may be regarded as a 'shadow criminal law'.[228]

In essence, civil recovery and other civil orders embody the favouring of crime control over due process. Although it is almost impossible to determine the effect of such orders on serious and organised criminality, political and popular support, prompted at least in part by the generation of funds for the public purse, indicate that this process will continue to be a key element in addressing organised crime in the UK and Ireland.

---

[224] ibid, 198, n 61. See FB Sayre, 'Public Welfare Offences' (1933) 55 *Columbia Law Review* 35.
[225] Kilcommins and Vaughan, n 223.
[226] ibid.
[227] Dubber, n 222, 93.
[228] *Allen v Illinois* 478 US 364 (1986) 384 per Stevens J (dissenting).

8

Revenue Matters:
Taxing Organised Crime

I. Introduction

Revenue law provides a ready if somewhat unorthodox means of targeting suspected organised criminals,[1] either through the taxing of assets or by penalisation for tax offences.[2] In the same way as asset recovery and other civil orders, the use of tax powers may overcome the impediment to justice posed when prosecution is not feasible due to lack of sufficient evidence. Moreover, taxation may be a useful supplement to the conventional prosecution process by targeting assets and capital directly. Legislative amendments in the UK and Ireland now make income deriving from criminal activity amenable to taxation, such as the income derived from trafficking or sale of illicit drugs or goods or prostitution, for example.

Since 1996 the Criminal Assets Bureau in Ireland has been able 'to take all necessary actions' under revenue legislation to ensure that the proceeds of criminal activity or suspected criminal activity are subjected to tax and that the Revenue Acts are applied fully,[3] and this power has been used extensively in addressing organised crime.[4] Similarly, the Assets Recovery Agency in the UK was accorded revenue functions by part 6 of the Proceeds of Crime Act 2002, following the recommendations in the report of the Cabinet Office Performance and Innovation Unit,[5] and these capabilities were later redistributed to the Serious Organised Crime Agency.[6] Taxing criminal assets is viewed as holding the potential to yield more economic gain than civil forfeiture and as necessary to demonstrate the fair

---

[1] The example of Al Capone is typically cited as illustrating the effectiveness of this tactic. See P Alldridge, *Money Laundering Law: Forfeiture, Confiscation, Civil Recovery, Criminal Laundering and Taxation of the Proceeds of Crime* (Oxford, Hart, 2003) 248.

[2] A Kennedy, 'An Evaluation of the Recovery of Criminal Proceeds in the United Kingdom' (2007) *Journal of Money Laundering Control* 33, 40. The latter is not considered in this work – see D Brookes, *Revenue Law: Principles and Practice* (Haywards Heath, Bloomsbury Professional, 2010).

[3] Criminal Assets Bureau Act 1996, s 5.

[4] See E Campbell, 'Taxing Illegal Assets: The Revenue Work of the Criminal Assets Bureau' (2006) 24 *Irish Law Times* 316.

[5] Cabinet Office Performance and Innovation Unit, *Recovering the Proceeds of Crime* (London, Cabinet Office, 2000) para 10.2.

[6] Serious Crime Act 2007, s 74. Powers of taxation are not devolved and so the relevant legislation applies across the UK.

application of revenue powers in society.[7] Nevertheless, despite these rationales, and as is the case regarding civil asset recovery, the ability to tax illegal assets or profits has been used less vigorously in the UK than in Ireland, apparently due to legislative and organisational factors which are explored below.

II. Taxing the Profits of Illegal Acts

Traditionally, divergent approaches were taken in Ireland and the UK regarding the taxation of the profits of illegal acts: throughout the twentieth century such profits were not taxable in Ireland on the basis that the State could not be seen to tolerate and share in the profits of crime.[8] This could be construed as implicitly condoning criminal behaviour. In contrast, the British courts rejected this logic explicitly.[9] In *Inland Revenue Commissioners v Aken* the taxation of the earnings of prostitution was permitted ostensibly on the basis that it was not illegal and constituted a trade in the sense of a provision of services for reward.[10] However, tax could not be collected in the UK if the source could not be identified, thereby rendering the proceeds and profits of organised criminality beyond the reach of taxation.

The Finance Act 1983 removed the prohibition on taxing illegal earnings in Ireland.[11] Support for this development was expressed in the Dáil on the ground that the 'weapon' of the Revenue Commissioners would to be of benefit in 'clearing up some of the big criminal operators' and 'putting them out of business altogether'.[12] Nevertheless, it was stated by a Fianna Fáil Member of Parliament that 'the very idea of putting such a provision in legislation seems to suggest an acceptance and blessing of such illegal activities' and it was suggested that instead all profits from illegal activities should be confiscated and penalties imposed on those carrying out the offences.[13] It is ironic, given such a comment, that Fianna Fáil subsequently played a central role in the enactment of the Proceeds of Crime Act 1996 and the Criminal Assets Bureau Act 1996 which facilitate the taxing of illegal profits.[14] Section 19 of the Finance Act 1983 has since been replaced by section 58 of the Taxes Consolidation Act 1997 which provides that profits or gains shall be chargeable to tax even if the source is unknown or unlawful,[15] and this

---

[7] ibid, para 10.8.

[8] *Hayes v Duggan* [1929] IR 406, 417; *Collins v Mulvey* [1956] IR 223.

[9] *Mann v Nash* [1932] 1 KB 752; *Southern (Inspector of Taxes) v AB Ltd* [1933] 1 KB 713.

[10] *Inland Revenue Commissioners v Aken* [1990] STC 497, 503–06.

[11] s 19.

[12] Dáil Debates, vol 342, cols 463–64 (5 May 1983) per Mr Molony.

[13] Dáil Debates, vol 342, col 1022 (11 May 1983) per Mr Ahern.

[14] See ch 7 for an examination of the powers of the Criminal Assets Bureau and the mechanism of civil asset recovery.

[15] Such profits or gains are described euphemistically in the tax assessment as 'miscellaneous income'.

task may be carried out by bodies other than the Revenue Commissioners.[16] As CAB possesses the ability to take all necessary actions under revenue law to ensure that the proceeds of criminal activity or suspected criminal activity are subjected to tax and that the Revenue Acts are applied fully,[17] it may issue a tax assessment of an individual, notwithstanding that the source of his income or assets may be unknown.[18] CAB may assess, demand and collect income tax, value added tax (VAT), and PAYE/PRSI,[19] and such revenue work is not limited to property which is deemed to be the proceeds of crime.[20]

The first stage in CAB's revenue actions is usually the notification of the person that the Bureau has been appointed his Inspector of Taxes,[21] and then CAB is likely to attempt to prevent the dissipation of assets upon issuing a tax assessment either by a section 2 or section 3 order under the Proceeds of Crime Act 1996[22] or a *Mareva* injunction.[23] As tax inspector, officers of CAB may require the production of accounts and books from a person who fails to deliver a statement or delivers an unsatisfactory one,[24] may enter at all reasonable times a place of employment or a place where records may be held, may ask any person to produce any records which are required for the enquiry, and may search the premises for any records.[25] No warrant is required for the exercise of such powers, indicating the wide capabilities of CAB in the context of revenue matters.[26] This is a remarkably lax scheme when compared with the strictures regarding search and seizure in the criminal process, indicating how the demands of crime control have led to the circumvention of traditional due process protections in seeking to tax the proceeds of organised crime.

CAB may apply to the Irish High Court for an order requiring a financial institution to make available for inspection the full particulars of accounts maintained by a person in that institution for the previous 10 years, and books, records or other documents in its possession which are relevant to that person's liability; or to

---

[16] Taxes Consolidation Act 1997, s 58(2).

[17] Criminal Assets Bureau Act 1996, s 5.

[18] While s 58 of the Taxes Consolidation Act 1997 is applicable to the Income Tax and Corporation Tax Acts, it does not cover the Capital Gains Tax Acts. This anomaly means that, unlike illegally earned income, illegal capital gains cannot be taxed, a distinction which is 'of potential critical relevance to criminals'. K Corrigan, *Revenue Law*, vol I (Dublin, Round Hall, 2000) 1062.

[19] Criminal Assets Bureau, *Annual Report 1999* (Dublin, Criminal Assets Bureau, 2000) 12. PAYE refers to 'pay-as-you-earn' tax which is deducted from a person's wages, while PRSI is 'pay related social insurance'.

[20] *AS v Criminal Assets Bureau* (High Court, 10 October 2005).

[21] P Hunt, 'The Criminal Assets Bureau and Taxation – Recent Developments' (2001) 14 *Irish Tax Review* 573, 574.

[22] See ch 7.

[23] In *CAB v McSweeney* (High Court, 11 April 2000), an ex parte interim *Mareva* injunction was granted to CAB. See also *Criminal Assets Bureau v Craft* [2001] 1 IR 113.

[24] Taxes Consolidation Act 1997, s 900 (as amended by the Finance Acts 1999–2008).

[25] Taxes Consolidation Act 1997, s 905 (as amended by the Finance Acts 1999–2008).

[26] The Revenue Powers Group Report recommended that this power should be subject to a District Court warrant. Revenue Powers Group, *Report to the Minister for Finance* (Dublin, Stationery Office, 2003) 110, Recommendation 10.

give any reasonably required information or explanations.[27] Furthermore, a High Court judge may make an order prohibiting the transfer of or dealing with any assets or moneys of a person that are in the custody of the financial institution.[28]

In the UK, the revenue functions of the Serious and Organised Crime Agency may be exercised if SOCA has reasonable grounds to suspect that income arising or a gain accruing to a person may be subject to income tax and that income or gain arises as a result of any person's criminal conduct.[29] This is conduct which would constitute an offence in the UK but does not include conduct constituting an offence relating to a matter under the care and management of the Board of HM Revenue and Customs, such as tax fraud.[30] SOCA then notifies the person, stating its intention to carry out its revenue functions,[31] and may make an assessment for income tax, capital gains tax or corporation tax;[32] in other words SOCA may carry out taxation functions of Her Majesty's Revenue and Customs (HMRC). In so doing, SOCA must apply all interpretations of the law and concessions published by the Board of HMRC.[33] Crucially, it is immaterial if SOCA cannot identify a source for any income,[34] a legislative change originally recommended in the Cabinet Office Performance and Innovation Unit report on *Recovering the Proceeds of Crime.*[35] However, this provision is construed strictly: in *Rose v Director of the Assets Recovery Agency*[36] the assessment was specifically made on the basis of drug dealing (as 'trading income' rather than 'other income') and so when this could not be established on the balance of probabilities the tax assessments were quashed.

SOCA may require a person to make a personal tax return complete with relevant accounts, statements and documents as are reasonably required to establish the chargeable and payable amounts for a year of assessment,[37] after which SOCA may give a notice of the intention to enquire into this return.[38] Furthermore, SOCA, as the assessor of tax, may require the taxpayer to produce accounts, books and other information which are reasonably required for the purpose of determining if the tax return is incorrect or incomplete.[39] An inspector of tax may

---

[27] Taxes Consolidation Act 1997, s 908, as amended by s 207 of the Finance Act 1999.

[28] Taxes Consolidation Act 1997, s 908(8) (as amended). Importantly, sub-s 9 allows the judge to exclude the name or address of the authorised officer from an affidavit or order which is to be made available to the taxpayer, the financial institution or their solicitors, and to hold cross-examination out of sight. Corrigan argues that this protection of identity indicates that '[i]t is clearly envisaged that section 908 will be invoked only in the most serious of cases', that is, cases concerning CAB. Corrigan, n 18, 431.

[29] Proceeds of Crime Act 2002, s 317(1).

[30] Proceeds of Crime Act 2002, s 326.

[31] Proceeds of Crime Act 2002, s 317(2).

[32] Taxes Management Act 1970, s 29(1).

[33] Proceeds of Crime Act 2002, s 324(3).

[34] Proceeds of Crime Act 2002, s 319(1).

[35] Cabinet Office Performance and Innovation Unit, n 5, para 10.22.

[36] *Rose v Director of the Assets Recovery Agency* [2006] STC (SCD) 472 [19]–[21].

[37] Taxes Management Act 1970, ss 8 and 12.

[38] Taxes Management Act 1970, s 9A.

[39] Taxes Management Act 1970, s19A.

require any person to deliver or make available to him documents which in the inspector's reasonable opinion contain, or may contain, information relevant to a tax liability of that or another person.[40] This aspect of the work of the Assets Recovery Agency and SOCA has generated case law which is favourable to the State. For example, in *Harper v Director of the Assets Recovery Agency*, the Special Commissioners found that ARA's method of assessment was sound, and that the applicant had not dislodged the burden of proof when he claimed that the lodgements were in fact legitimate pension and compensation deposits.[41] However, in *Forbes v Director of the Assets Recovery Agency* certain years of assessment were challenged successfully on the basis that there was no evidence of any trade or income by the subject for those years,[42] and the 'inflation increments' used by ARA were criticised and rejected.[43]

These revenue capabilities do not permit applications for and use of warrants to enter and search premises in the UK.[44] Moreover, SOCA's investigative powers do not apply in the context of revenue matters.[45] In other words, not only does SOCA have more limited powers of investigation than the equivalent Irish agency, CAB, it is also more constrained than is HMRC. SOCA's capacities are in marked contrast to those of CAB, which, as outlined in chapter seven, possesses considerable investigative powers, such as that of entry and search, and has extraordinary abilities in comparison to domestic Revenue authorities in Ireland.[46] Whilst in Ireland Revenue officials must carry identification cards when on revenue business, members of CAB who are also officials of the Revenue Commissioners are not required to produce authorisation cards or otherwise identify themselves when they are carrying out CAB business and are accompanied by a police officer.[47] This truly is a 'Kafkaesque' situation, whereby unidentified individuals representing the State may enter and search a person's property.[48] In this vein, in the UK the report of the Cabinet Office Performance and Innovation Unit recommended that revenue officers accompanying law enforcement officers on searches or field operations should not be under an obligation to identify themselves except as representatives of the Inland Revenue (now HMRC),[49] though this suggestion has yet to be implemented in the UK.

Furthermore, SOCA's revenue functions do not include the prosecution of offences.[50] In contrast, Garda Bureau Officers, on the directions of the Irish

[40] Finance Act 2008, Sch 36.
[41] *Harper v Director of the Assets Recovery Agency* [2005] STC (SCD) 874 [34]–[38].
[42] *Forbes v Director of the Assets Recovery Agency* [2007] STC (SCD) 1 [16] and [29].
[43] ibid, [20].
[44] Proceeds of Crime Act 2002, s 323(3)(e).
[45] Proceeds of Crime Act 2002, Pt 8.
[46] A Donnelly and M Walsh, *Revenue Investigations and Enforcement* (Dublin, Butterworths, 2002) 12. Section 8(8) of the Criminal Assets Bureau Act 1996 provides that a member of the Garda Síochána, an officer of the Revenue Commissioners or of the Minister for Social Welfare who is a bureau officer retains the powers or duties that accrue to her from that role in carrying out CAB business.
[47] Criminal Assets Bureau Act 1996, s 10(2).
[48] See F Kafka, *The Trial* (London, Penguin, 2000).
[49] Cabinet Office Performance and Innovation Unit, n 5, Conclusion 52.
[50] Proceeds of Crime Act 2002, s 323(3)(b) and (e).

Director of Public Prosecutions, will often charge or have significant input in the institution of prosecutions for knowingly or wilfully failing to make tax returns.[51] As Kennedy notes, the position that SOCA cannot institute its own criminal prosecution for tax evasion may have been influenced by the fear that to legislate otherwise could compromise the civil classification of asset recovery proceedings, but he feels that organisational design warrants having tax assessment and prosecution vested with the same agency.[52]

As noted in chapter seven, a CAB officer in Ireland may impart information to officers of the Revenue Commissioners;[53] indeed, Donnelly and Walsh describe '[c]ommunication and the exchange of information between Revenue and CAB . . . [as] an essential precursor to the investigations conducted by CAB'.[54] Information held by HMRC in the UK may be disclosed to CAB or a specified public authority to assist it in the exercise of any of its functions regarding the proceeds of crime.[55] Further disclosure of such information is only allowed regarding proceeds of crime work and with the consent of HMRC.[56] Similarly, SOCA in the UK may receive information in this regard from other agencies,[57] and may disclose information to HMRC.[58]

III. Appeals against Tax Assessments

In the UK, when the Proceeds of Crime Act 2002 was enacted an appeal in respect of revenue functions by SOCA lay to the Special Commissioners whose determination was final and conclusive.[59] In general, the Special Commissioners heard complex appeals arising from tax assessments relating to income tax, capital gains tax and corporation tax. The Tax Chamber of the First-tier Tribunal replaced the Special Commissioners in 2009,[60] and the Chamber now hears appeals against SOCA's assessments. In Ireland appeal against an income or corporation tax

---

[51] Taxes Consolidation Act 1997, s 1078 (as amended). See Criminal Assets Bureau, *Annual Report 2007* (Dublin, Criminal Assets Bureau, 2008) para 4.32.

[52] Kennedy, n 2, n 50.

[53] Criminal Assets Bureau Act 1996, s 8(7). Furthermore, s 1 of the Disclosure of Certain Information for Taxation and Other Purposes Act 1996, which inserted s 63A2 into the Criminal Justice Act 1994, permits the exchange of information between the Garda Síochána and the Revenue Commissioners. This Act was welcomed on the basis that it ended 'an extraordinary system of effective legislative gagging which has been imposed over the years on Revenue officials, gardaí and certain other people in the public service'. Seanad Debates, vol 148, col 1452 (26 July 1996) per Mr Roche.

[54] Donnelly and Walsh, n 46, 106–07.

[55] Serious Crime Act 2007, s 85.

[56] Serious Crime Act 2007, s 85(4).

[57] Proceeds of Crime Act 2002, s 436 (see *Khan v Director of the Assets Recovery Agency* [2006] STC (SCD) 154).

[58] Proceeds of Crime Act 2002, s 438(a).

[59] Proceeds of Crime Act 2002, s 320(1).

[60] Transfer of Tribunal Functions and Revenue and Customs Appeals Order 2009.

assessment is to the Appeal Commissioners,[61] and to the Revenue Commissioners for a VAT determination.[62]

The Irish courts have constrained the exercise of CAB's powers in the context of tax matters to a certain degree. In *Criminal Assets Bureau v KB*, records and cash relating to the defendant's business had been seized in a police investigation into money laundering.[63] CAB had raised a tax assessment in respect of miscellaneous income of the defendant but the seizure of his assets allegedly precluded his accountants from quantifying the tax liability. CAB refused to accept this as a reason for not complying with the need to specify the amount due and to make a payment. The High Court held that while the defendant did not attempt within the relevant appeal period to obtain copies of the necessary documents which were in the hands of the State, it was questionable whether there was sufficient time to do so and to enable his accountants to submit a return based on those documents. In addition, a *Mareva* injunction in Ireland and a world-wide injunction had been imposed on the defendant's assets, and the Court found that there was some substance in the allegation that it probably would not have been possible to have them lifted or varied within the 30-day appeal period, and thus it would have been impossible for the defendant to comply with the requirements for appealing the assessment. Therefore, the Court concluded that there was a reasonable probability that the respondent had a real and bona fide defence in this regard and so was entitled to a plenary hearing to determine the legitimacy of his defences. Moreover, in *CAB v Craft and Hunt* it was emphasised that CAB must serve a demand on a taxpayer prior to the stage in the process when the assessment becomes final and conclusive and proceedings for collection commence.[64] This demonstrates that CAB's abilities are constrained by strict judicial interpretation of the law, again underlining the courts' position as guardian of due process in the context of an expansive yet oblique means of crime control.

IV. Challenges to Revenue Powers

The nature of the revenue process carried out by the Assets Recovery Agency was contested in *Khan v Director of the Assets Recovery Agency*, where the Special Commissioners rejected the contention that Article 6 of the ECHR (European Convention on Human Rights) which protects the right to a fair trial was engaged and breached, and concluded that the process did not involve a criminal charge.[65] The Special Commissioners drew on civil recovery jurisprudence to reach this conclusion: 'If Part 5 civil recovery proceedings are not protected as criminal

---

[61] Taxes Consolidation Act 1997, s 933(1)(a) (as amended).
[62] Value-Added Tax Act 1972, s 25 (as amended).
[63] *Criminal Assets Bureau v KB* [2001] IEHC 93.
[64] *Criminal Assets Bureau v Craft and Hunt* [2003] 2 IR 168.
[65] *Khan v Director of the Assets Recovery Agency* [2006] STC (SCD) 154.

charges by article 6, tax assessment proceedings relating to Part 6 general Revenue functions do not involve criminal charge status either'.[66] Furthermore, the qualifying condition for the exercise of ARA's revenue powers of 'reasonable grounds to suspect' did not require proof of criminal conduct but only a genuine suspicion which was objectively reasonable.[67] Similarly, in *Criminal Assets Bureau v PS*, the Irish High Court emphasised that proceedings to recover tax bear none of the hallmarks of a criminal trial.[68] Nevertheless, Mumford and Alldridge have claimed that these taxation powers are not equivalent to the 'general power to tax' but rather constitute the application of the taxation system to a specific individual for specific or general deterrence.[69] This academic criticism has not held weight judicially.

Moreover, it was held in *Khan v Director of the Assets Recovery Agency* that the tax assessments did not engage Article 7 ECHR which precludes retrospective punishment, as there was no determination that the applicant was guilty of a criminal offence nor was a criminal penalty imposed.[70] Finally, while the assessments did involve deprivation of the appellant's possessions within Article 1 of the First Protocol of the ECHR which protects the right to private property, this was within the wide margin of appreciation of contracting states.[71]

Furthermore, the House of Lords held that the privilege against self-incrimination is not available in response to requests from tax authorities, on the basis that all tax collection requires declaration of income to the State which may enforce sanctions for failure to do so.[72] This conclusion was echoed by the European Commission on Human Rights which found that Article 6 was not breached by compulsory tax statements, noting that the right not to incriminate oneself is concerned primarily with respecting the will of an accused person to remain silent in the context of criminal proceedings.[73] Nonetheless, as the European Court emphasised in *Saunders v UK*, the right of the accused not to incriminate himself under Article 6(1) will be breached by the reliance at trial on statements which were obtained compulsorily.[74] This was followed by the Irish courts in *CG v Appeal Commissioners* where the applicant was assessed by CAB for income tax for 1994–2001 and was also simultaneously charged with failing to deliver tax returns for the years 1994–96.[75] He appealed against CAB's tax assessments to the Appeal Commissioners and sought adjournment of these appeals pending the determination of the criminal charges on the basis that they related to the same years.[76] When adjournment was refused, the

---

[66] ibid, [27].
[67] ibid, [39]. See n 30.
[68] *Criminal Assets Bureau v PS* (High Court, 19 October 2004).
[69] A Mumford and P Alldridge, 'Taxation as an Adjunct to the Criminal Justice System: The New Assets Recovery Agency Regime' (2002) *British Tax Review* 458, 462.
[70] *Khan*, n 65, paras 46–47.
[71] ibid, para 43.
[72] *R v Allen* (2002) 1 AC 509, 543.
[73] *Allen v United Kingdom* (2002) 35 EHRR CD 289.
[74] *Saunders v UK* (1997) 23 EHRR 313.
[75] *CG v Appeal Commissioners* [2005] 2 IR 472.
[76] ibid, [6].

applicant argued that this infringed his right to silence and privilege against self-incrimination, on the ground that he could reveal incriminating evidence in his appeal against the Commissioners' decision. The High Court held that the particular facts of the case did not suggest that he would be required to give self-incriminating evidence at the appeal.[77] However, the Court noted that in this case there was agreement between the parties that no evidence given at the tax appeal by the applicant would lead to any further line of enquiry by CAB in relation to the pending charges, but that different considerations may apply if there were no such agreement.[78] Indeed, Corrigan claims more generally that information disclosed in annual tax returns should not be available to the prosecuting authorities of the State in relation to a trial for a criminal offence.[79] In the UK, the current guidance from the Secretary of State does not prohibit a criminal investigation being carried out at the same time as a tax investigation, but these may never occur simultaneously in relation to the same criminality.[80]

V. Interplay between Civil Recovery and Revenue Powers

Whether civil recovery and taxation are seen as complementary or mutually exclusive approaches to dealing with the proceeds of organised crime differs in the comparator jurisdictions. Ireland takes an expansive approach which arguably is more effective in terms of crime control though more invasive as regards individual rights. Priority is given to civil recovery in the UK: 'The director will operate a hierarchy of options . . . Only when those other approaches have been exhausted will the taxation functions arise'.[81] In contrast, both tactics may operate in tandem in Ireland, notwithstanding potential hardship to the individual involved.

The intersection between the asset recovery dimension of CAB's work and its revenue capacities was explored in *CAB v Kelly*, where the Irish Supreme Court rejected the appellant's claim that he was unable to make the appropriate tax return to CAB's assessments because his monies were subject to an interim order under section 2 of the Proceeds of Crime Act 1996.[82] The Court emphasised that

---

[77] ibid, [28].

[78] ibid, [29].

[79] Corrigan, n 18, 1064. This follows the reservation expressed by Moriarty J in *M v D* [1998] 3 IR 175, 181, and McGuinness J in *Gilligan v Criminal Assets Bureau* [1998] 3 IR 185, 233 concerning s 9 of the Proceeds of Crime Act 1996.

[80] Attorney-General, *Guidance to Prosecuting Bodies on their Asset Recovery Powers under the Proceeds of Crime Act 2002* (London, Attorney-General, 2009) available at www.attorneygeneral.gov.uk/Publications/Pages/AttorneyGeneralissuedguidancetoprosectuingbodiesontheirassetrecoverypowersunder.aspx, points 9 and 10.

[81] House of Commons, Standing Committee B, 15 January 2002, col 928 per Mr Ainsworth.

[82] *Criminal Assets Bureau v Kelly*, Supreme Court, October 11, 2002.

while section 2(3)(a) allows for the discharge or vary of an order, the defendant did not qualify for this remedy. Section 6 also allows for the interim order to be varied or discharged so as to enable the defendant to pay 'necessary expenses', and this is broad enough to include liabilities to income tax.[83] In addition, a late notice of appeal against a tax assessment is permitted within 12 months due to 'reasonable cause',[84] but the Court concluded that the appellant was not denied access to his funds in such a way as would prevent him from exercising his right of appeal.

Thus, it may be seen that the imposition of an interim or interlocutory order under the Proceeds of Crime Act 1996 does not preclude CAB from making a tax assessment, nor does it absolve an individual from making tax returns. This ensures that the different facets of CAB's work may operate in conjunction, so as to improve the effectiveness of Irish State powers used against organised crime.

VI. Conclusion

In Ireland, the application of the Revenue Acts by CAB has proved to be effective against organised crime insofar as it deprives persons of the benefit of such activity.[85] Revenue gathered in this way far outweighs that acquired under CAB's recovery powers:[86] €6,769,218 in tax was collected in 2000,[87] and a threefold climb was noted in 2001 to €23,561,666,[88] although this has decreased gradually to somewhere between €4 and €5 million since 2008.[89] In contrast to civil recovery, which generally takes seven years in the absence of party consent, is a long and complicated process, and may involve third party rights, CAB's revenue work attracts fewer safeguards and has a limited time frame within which an individual may appeal against the assessment. Indeed, the returns gained through tax assessment lends credence to the observation of Considine and Kilcommins that CAB has grown to rely more heavily on the power to tax rather than the powers it was granted to seize the assets of suspected criminals.[90]

---

[83]   ibid.

[84]   Taxes Consolidation Act 1997, s 933(7)(a).

[85]   F Murphy and B Galvin, 'Targeting the Financial Wealth of Criminals in Ireland' (1999) 9 *Irish Criminal Law Journal* 133, 158.

[86]   See ch 7.

[87]   Criminal Assets Bureau, *Annual Report 2000* (Dublin, Criminal Assets Bureau, 2001) 13, table 7.

[88]   Criminal Assets Bureau, *Annual Report 2001* (Dublin, Criminal Assets Bureau, 2002) ch 3, table 7. See Department of Justice, Equality and Law Reform Press Release, 'Criminal Assets Bureau Annual Report Shows Threefold Increase in Taxes Collected on Profits from Criminal Activity', Dublin, 2002.

[89]   Criminal Assets Bureau, *Annual Report 2008* (Dublin, Criminal Assets Bureau, 2009) 20; *Annual Report 2010* (Dublin, Criminal Assets Bureau, 2011) 19.

[90]   J Considine and S Kilcommins, 'The Importance of Safeguards on Revenue Powers: Another Perspective' (2006) 19 *Irish Tax Review* 49, 50.

In the UK SOCA has seized proportionately less than CAB. In 2011–12 £18.7 million was recovered in the confiscation process, in recovery settlements and tax settlements.[91] No disaggregated figure for tax alone is available. Possible explanations for this level lie in the construction of legislation[92] (the Proceeds of Crime Act 2002 limits the investigative powers of SOCA when compared with CAB in the context of its revenue work), bad organisational commitment to this tactic, and poor organisational cooperation. The absence of documentary evidence as a result of 'spend as you go' criminals who do not retain much of their profits may preclude the assessment of records and ultimate taxation,[93] although this has not posed insurmountable problems in Ireland. In a bid to remedy the perceived flaws in the UK model, HMRC has created a multi-disciplinary Criminal Taxes Unit which will seek to improve 'information flows'.[94]

Despite the divergence in terms of relative success, the use of revenue laws in this manner in both the UK and Ireland is an equivalent departure from the criminal justice process per se to a speedier means of recovering profits and proceeds of suspected criminality. Taxation of potentially criminal profits seeks to neutralise organised crime rather than identifying, proving or addressing the individual culpability of the actors involved. It is a quintessential adaptive response to organised criminality, yet less problematic in a rights' sense than civil recovery given that the stigma of the criminal label is not accorded to those subject to revenue laws. Nonetheless, CAB in particular is accorded significant investigative powers which impinge to a great deal on the privacy of the individual. This is a prototypical crime control approach, with considerable discretion accorded to an administrative agency. While taxing illegal assets may be seen as the State sanctioning or condoning the accrual of illegitimate gains, in fact it is an archetypal pragmatic response, and merely results in tax laws being applied to all, regardless of the nature of the 'work' or income involved. Furthermore, its appeal to policy makers is unlikely to wane, given the recouping of substantial funds, and the lower evidential burden on the authorities.

[91] Serious Organised Crime Agency, *Annual Report and Accounts 2011–12* (London, Serious Organised Crime Agency, 2012) 108. Regrettably these figures have not been separated into recovery and tax, and the exclusion of SOCA from the Freedom of Information Act means such details will not be revealed.

[92] See House of Commons Northern Ireland Affairs Committee, *Organised Crime in Northern Ireland*, vol I (Third Report of Session 2005–06) (London, The Stationery Office, 2006) 54.

[93] A Kennedy, 'Winning the Information Wars: Collecting, Sharing and Analysing Information in Asset Recovery Investigations' (2007) *Journal of Financial Crime* 372, 378.

[94] HMRC, *Criminal Finances Strategic Framework* available at www.hmrc.gov.uk/about/criminal-finances-strategy.pdf, paras 90, 93.

9

Conclusion

I. Introduction

Though the parameters of the term and concept 'organised crime' are nebulous, it is treated as encompassing a cohesive, homogeneous and recognisable form of crimes and criminal actors, warranting novel and expansive legal powers. Overall, organised crime is systematic illegal behaviour, carried out by or on behalf of a group, motivated by profit, and underpinned by the threat or use of violence: throughout, witnesses are intimidated, jurors manipulated and the law's loopholes employed so as to evade justice.[1] Consequently a combative stance is taken by the State in rhetoric, in law-making, and in practice, as the threat of organised crime is sought to be addressed in the traditional way in the criminal justice system as well as through more novel civil means and revenue powers. Some of these measures are problematic in a rights' sense, others are dubious in terms of their effectiveness, and others are implemented in an inconsistent and uneven manner.

II. Explaining the Dominant Narrative

The foremost narrative in popular and political discourse is that the police are hampered in their ability to investigate crime, that the rules of the criminal process constrain unnecessarily the prosecution of organised criminals, and that, even if convicted, such persons cannot be punished sufficiently and effectively given existing sentencing practices. Various factors account for the impression that the detection, punishment, prevention and control of organised crime is stymied by the protective rights of the accused and that new and robust measures therefore are warranted. The growing rates of certain types of crime, the nature of organised crime, and the political milieu and tenor of debate all contribute to this belief, underlining the perceived need to introduce and use innovative means to counter organised crime.

---

[1] J Landesco, *Organized Crime in Chicago* (Chicago, University of Chicago Press, 1968) 107.

A key factor influencing the drive to expand State powers against organised crime lies in the irrefutable rise in crime rates in recent decades in the UK and Ireland. While statistics for certain crimes have plateaued or are falling,[2] this does not negate the fact that rates remain at levels unprecedented before the 1960s in the UK and the 1980s in Ireland, and that some offences involving firearms and drugs in particular have increased significantly.[3] Moreover, the prosecution and conviction rates for murders involving firearms are below the average for other homicides.[4] This provokes feelings of vulnerability on the part of the general public and undercuts confidence in the justice system as it exists currently. Furthermore, the intrinsic qualities of organised crime set the apparent failings of the current system into sharp relief: the difficulty in detecting such crimes, the intimidation of those who may witness such behaviour, the complicity of the public in certain aspects by providing a market for illegal goods or services, the limitations of imprisonment in terms of prevention of further criminality, and the generation and accrual of vast resources.

Legitimate fears about crime rates and the features of organised crime influence and coalesce with a policy discourse in which public protection is venerated, risk is to be avoided at all costs, and a sense of crisis is generated and heightened; this facilitates the creeping erosion of due process rights, often, unfortunately, to no good end. Ultimately, the politicisation of law and order ensures that crime in general continues to be a central issue in policy and law-making, and this phenomenon prompts the belief that the criminal process as traditionally conceived is incapable of dealing with organised crime in particular. There is no divergence among the leading political parties across the UK and Ireland regarding the need for tough strategies; generally speaking such sentiment is echoed by the media and thus focuses popular attention and maintains public concern on the matter. Moreover, the political drive to amend central due process precepts is founded on a perceived democratic mandate which sees public protection as paramount and the rights of community as disregarded unjustifiably.

While the prevalent perspective sees the criminal process as weighted unduly in favour of the individual to the detriment of the investigation and prosecution of crime and the conviction and punishment of offenders, this belief is not substantiated by the range of legal powers currently available to the States in the UK and Ireland. Contrary to popular and political representation, these States are endowed with significant capabilities and entitlements during pre-trial investigation and interrogation, at the court hearing, and post-conviction, and such abilities are being enhanced continually as standard practices, norms and rules are amended to address organised criminality.

[2] See ch 2.
[3] ibid.
[4] See Dáil Debates, vol 668, col 106 (19 November 2008). In response to a parliamentary question the UK Secretary of State noted that detection rates for specific offences involving firearms is not available centrally (HC WA 29 October 2008, col 1086W per Jacqui Smith).

At the pre-trial stage of the criminal process, surveillance powers have been extended, lengthy detention periods are permitted, and the right to silence has been eroded. While these changes may indeed improve the detection and investigation of organised crime, in doing so traditional protective rights and restrictions on State interference and intervention have been attenuated. Similarly, at the criminal trial, conventional norms have been amended to improve the likelihood of successful prosecution of organised crime: non-jury trials are held, evidence from accomplices is used, and previous inconsistent statements are admissible in court. Then, at the post-trial facet of the process, a marked divergence from traditional norms of proportionality in sentencing towards a more mechanical and offence-centred model may be seen with the use of presumptive sentences which impinge on judicial discretion and indicate the growing involvement of public representatives in sentencing, so as to deter and punish organised crime robustly.

This litany of capabilities at all stages of the criminal process gives the lie to the common feeling that the present legal framework precludes the effective investigation, prosecution and punishment of organised crime. As outlined, traditional norms, principles and safeguards have been changed extensively because of the danger posed by organised crime and the complexities in successfully prosecuting such cases. Furthermore, the attempt to address organised crime has extended beyond the criminal justice process: the work of the Serious Organised Crime Agency, the Criminal Assets Bureau and the Scottish Ministers, with their ability to confiscate and forfeit assets in a civil process and to tax assets, reinforces the States' abilities and resituates them outside of the criminal process. The significance of such measures in a crime control sense cannot be denied; the encroachment on due process values is more contentious.

III. Recalibrating the Criminal Justice Process

It is difficult to identify a coherent logic to the legal reactions adopted to address organised criminality. Overall, and crudely speaking, developments across the UK and Ireland relating to organised crime are indicative of a re-evaluation by legislators and policy makers of the norms of due process and its importance, and an associated elevation of the notions of security and public protection. While one should not overstate the issue, in certain respects political discourse and legislative action involves a move away from rights and liberties towards a more utilitarian and consequentialist way of thinking. Diminishing concern for process is matched by a concomitant growth in result-oriented justice.

The current trajectory of the criminal process demonstrates a move from fundamental liberal standards which highlight the primacy of the individual and the need to limit State power, to a community-focused outlook in which public protection and the rights of the community are emphasised. Notwithstanding the potentially positive aspects of communitarian ways of thinking, the moral author-itarian interpretation that is taking root in respect of penal and criminal policy may undermine individual protections, by seeking to equate the interests of the community with the rights of the citizen. This is facilitated by virtue of the fact that few are concerned about the civil liberties of suspected organised criminals, who are seen as beyond the bounds of civil society.

In essence, it seems that the challenges posed by organised crime, coupled with a range of social, political and cultural features, are causing a shift in the criminal process from a rights-based and process-oriented model towards an approach which focuses more on results, public protection and the control of crime, not-withstanding the threat to deontological liberties. While this trend is not homog-enous or inexorable, it nonetheless embodies convincingly the developments in the criminal process precipitated by the threat of organised criminality. However, changes in the criminal process are not depicted by policy makers as involving a move away from due process rights.[5] Constitutional and procedural rights are not being taken away; on the contrary, they are 'updated'[6] to make the situation 'fairer' for society and the law-abiding public,[7] and the system is merely being 'rebalanced'.[8]

In addition to this benign portrayal, scant regard is given to the expansion of some of these amendments to apply to a broader range of offences of lesser grav-ity. Although many new provisions are aimed primarily at organised criminals, such as those permitting lengthy detention periods and presumptive sentences, some may also be used in proceedings relating to other offences. Like the seepage of anti-subversive measures into the 'ordinary' criminal realm, organised crime now drives the erosion of protections for the accused and the expansion of State powers, which may then be employed against less serious criminality.

What is notable about some of the laws available to address organised crime is the limited degree of their use in practice. In some instances, this may demon-strate a careful and cautious approach on the part of the investigating authorities, the prosecution, or the judiciary, predicated on a tightly drawn legislative provi-sion. This is evident, for example, in relation to the holding of non-jury trials in England and Wales. While a narrowly constructed legal rule may restrict the use of certain State powers, failure to apply the law may also exemplify a tension between different arms of the State, as is apparent in the sentencing of drugs offences in Ireland with the use of the exception provisions to bypass presumptive

---

[5] A Ashworth, *Human Rights, Serious Crime, and Criminal Procedure* (London, Sweet & Maxwell, 2002) 115.

[6] Department of Justice, Equality and Law Reform Speech, 'Address by the Tánaiste' (Criminal Law Conference, Royal College of Surgeons, 25 November 2006).

[7] See Dáil Debates, vol 629, col 1670 (14 December 2006) per Minister for Justice, Mr McDowell.

[8] eg see Home Office, *Criminal Justice System Review: Rebalancing the Criminal Justice System in Favour of the Law-abiding Majority* (London, Home Office, 2006); Balance in the Criminal Law Review Group, *Final Report of the Balance in the Criminal Law Review Group* (Dublin, Department of Justice, 2007) 3ff; and Dáil Debates, vol 597, col 1276 (15 February 2005) per Minister for Justice, Mr McDowell.

minimums. Moreover, implementation may be constrained as a result of conflict between State agencies, or at least poor cooperation, such as occurred in relation to confiscation and asset recovery in the UK. Furthermore, the pronounced gap between political rhetoric on the one hand and police and prosecutorial practice on the other manifests itself in the lack of use of post-conviction orders and extended detention in Ireland.

IV. Key National Differences

In responding to organised crime, there exist and remain key distinguishing factors between the comparator jurisdictions. What is politically and legally palatable in Ireland in this context is shaped by cultural and legal contingencies, most notably the terrorist legacy: akin to Cole's remark in relation to terrorism laws in the US, Ireland is 'repeating history' in an unfortunate manner.[9] Counter-terrorism measures have provided a model in Ireland both in legislative substance and in terms of pushing the boundaries of what is regarded as permissible in addressing organised crime. Moreover, politics and policy-making in Ireland are characterised by a marked pragmatism, and the criminal justice realm in particular has been bereft of any empirical or theoretical grounding until very recently. Indeed the tenor of official policy documents betrays a sensationalist sentiment such as in the use of inflammatory terms such as 'gangland' crime.[10] Levi and Maguire noted in 2004 the absence in England and Wales of major evaluative research studies despite considerable legislative effort aimed at opposing organised crime and money laundering during the 1990s;[11] such a paucity of analysis still characterises the development of counter-organised crime policy in Ireland. There exist few novel or progressive measures; instead the laws transpose or emulate existing domestic measures, or imitate legislation from across the Irish Sea. While Ireland forged a path in terms of the introduction of civil recovery which was imitated by the UK and other jurisdictions in Europe, again this derived from the counter-terrorist legislative canon.

Rights have been attenuated at every stage of the criminal process; nonetheless the constitutional protection in Ireland of the right to due process, and also to liberty and bodily integrity provides a critical safeguard, insofar as the judiciary may stop or slow the drive to more repressive or punitive measures. Generally speaking, the Irish Supreme Court affirms due process values and has tempered the effect of presumptive sentences. Moreover, a sense of constitutional due

---

[9] D Cole and J Dempsey, *Terrorism and the Constitution: Sacrificing Civil Liberties in the Name of National Security* (New York, New Press, 2002) 150.

[10] See, eg Department of Justice, Equality and Law Reform, *White Paper on Crime: Organised and White Collar Crime* (Dublin, Department of Justice, Equality and Law Reform, 2010).

[11] M Levi and M Maguire, 'Reducing and Preventing Organised Crime: An Evidence-based Critique' (2004) 41 *Crime, Law & Social Change* 397, 407.

process appears to have permeated into the legislative psyche with the notable absence of tactics such as anonymous witness evidence. This is comparable to the situation in the United States where both the presence of a written Constitution and the judicial framework regarding the invalidation of unconstitutional measures reins in the punitive tendencies of the legislature. Conversely, the judicial *imprimatur* for non-jury trials and civil recovery legitimates such reactions both legally and culturally, and thereby concretises radical approaches which contravene liberal constitutional values. The persistent presence of a measure such as non-jury trials for subversive crime and its approval by the courts themselves means that there is no public and therefore no political discomfort with the extended use of such a mechanism in Ireland.

Similarly, England, Wales and Northern Ireland have readily adopted a robust model in addressing organised crime, with, inter alia, expansive powers of surveillance, the use of anonymous witnesses, non-jury trials, and punitive sentencing rules. However, the introduction and use of indeterminate sentences exemplifies the legislature and judiciary operating in harmony, demonstrating the effect of parliamentary supremacy and a rather different attitude from the Irish judiciary regarding sentencing practice. Akin to the situation in Ireland, the precursors for some such measures derived from the attempt to deal with subversive and terrorist activity related to the political struggle in Northern Ireland, for example the drawing of inferences from silence, the use of accomplice evidence, and anonymous witnesses.

A tradition of progressive criminal justice and penal policies appears to have protected Scotland to some extent from some of the more populist and punitive means of addressing organised crime. Broadly speaking, Scotland has a more entrenched communitarian and progressive approach to criminal justice, evident in the Children's Hearing System, for example.[12] McAra identified, prior to devolution, the strength and influence of 'elite policy networks' in the development of criminal justice in Scotland,[13] and this has served to insulate Scotland from the pandering to populist demand that is often evident elsewhere.[14] Since devolution, however, it seems that Scotland has taken a more punitive turn, at least in a rhetorical sense, and this is evident as regards organised criminality especially. Indeed, legislation such as the Criminal Justice and Licensing (Scotland) Act 2010 encapsulates the tension in policy creation in Scotland – the proposed measures seek to address organised crime through an overly expansive definition, despite lengthy evidence opposing this being given by interest groups, non-governmental organisations and academics. Though ostensibly such interventions indicate a

[12] See Lord Kilbrandon, *Children and Young Persons Scotland. Report by the Committee by the Secretary of State for Scotland by Command of Her Majesty* (Edinburgh, Her Majesty's Stationery Office, 1964); C McDiarmid, 'Perspectives on the Children's Hearings System' in J Scoular (ed), *Family Dynamics: Contemporary Issues in Family Law* (London, Butterworths, 2001) 29–48.

[13] L McAra, 'The Politics of Penality: An Overview of the Development of Penal Policy in Scotland' in P Duff and N Hutton (eds), *Criminal Justice in Scotland* (Aldershot, Ashgate, 1999) 355–80.

[14] See J Pratt, *Penal Populism* (London, Routledge, 2007).

246 Conclusion

desire to base policy development on academic research and practical insights, this did not lead to significant amendment of the legislation itself.

Misuse of drugs and firearms are not devolved matters for the Scottish Parliament as they are included as reserved matters in the Scotland Act 1998. Thus UK-wide legislation is relevant, reducing the impact of the Scottish Parliament and making it less likely that there is a distinctively Scottish reaction to organised crime. Indeed, despite the independence borne of devolution, approval from the Scottish Parliament has been given to a range of measures which fall within the purview of the devolved administration yet have been legislated for in London. Moreover, while Scotland has not adopted radical measures such as non-jury trials, it has acquiesced in or imitated measures like anonymous witnesses and civil asset forfeiture which derive from Acts of the Westminster Parliament.

V. Concluding Remarks

As outlined, the drive to deal adequately and robustly with organised crime has tested and sometimes compromised the value of due process rights and protective norms in the criminal processes across the UK and Ireland. The perception that the State is impotent and that urgent legal action is required rests on a range of factors, including the growth in specific crime rates, to a more nebulous mood of vulnerability, and the politicisation of law and order. To be sure, certain criminal actors and acts, which fall within the umbrella term 'organised crime', pose an unquestionable and grave danger to the safety of the public and to the administration of justice. Although this threat is often dramatised and sensationalised in the media, it remains a real one, and one which may indeed merit some revision of traditional approaches to crime control. The innate features of organised crime and the level and nature of the danger to society, in particular to those laypersons involved in the criminal process, may in fact warrant the reconsideration of certain norms and rights. Thus, it is necessary to accept that as some rights are derogable or negotiable, so the interpretation of certain liberties in society and rules of the criminal process may need to be updated or altered, given the shifting character of crime. Nevertheless, any adjustments must be grounded on careful and considered political and popular debate, must be in the public interest, and must involve minimal limitation of the particular right.

Limiting and redefining rights should be done with reluctance, to the lowest extent possible, and only if such a move is based on adequate evidence of both the need to act and the likely efficacy of the proposal, if that can be ascertained.[15] This is not necessarily how legal reactions to organised crime develop or are

---

[15] In fact, the State cannot determine the pervasiveness or strength of organised crime before or after the introduction of new laws. See J Jacobs with C Panarella and J Worthington, *Busting the Mob: United States v Cosa Nostra* (New York, New York University Press, 1994) 23.

constructed: in reality they are often crisis-driven, and prompted by political and media furore. Moreover, the expressive facet of these measures is often central rather than being predicated on rigorous academic research as to their likely efficacy. Indeed, the purpose of some of these new policies is questionable when they are not used regularly, such as the periods of prolonged detention in Ireland, and when some are implemented in such a way as to be less effective than their potential, such as asset recovery in England and Wales.

The unanimity of major political parties on the need for more powers in this respect implies that yet future incursions on rights are possible and that existing safeguards are not impermeable to circumscription. In determining the extent of the problem of organised crime and the appropriate response, a macro-analysis must be adopted which does not lose sight of overarching precepts of a liberal democracy which values individual rights and limited State power. It is crucial to reflect on the type of society to which we aspire and the apposite rules of the constitutive legal system before rights are restricted or abrogated in the pursuit of crime control. The significance of rights in society and in the criminal process must be considered in both an abstract and an individually grounded sense, that is, in terms of their importance on a conceptual level and the actual consequences of their existence.

Rights are open to the charge that they are elitist and imposed on society from above through their enforcement by the courts[16] rather than developing from the community itself, and this claim is underlined by general public support for punitive legislation and for a reassessment of the criminal process and procedural rights. Nevertheless, popular approval does not justify a swing away from procedural rights. The erosion of rights affects particular members of society more than others, given that the majority of citizens are unlikely to be questioned or charged with a crime and so may disregard the importance of procedural protections. However, incursions on key facets of the criminal process affect all members of a society that purports to protect the individual against the might of the State. The danger of limiting rights and augmenting State powers in the context of the criminal process involves the possibility of more interference in the private lives of citizens, a move towards result- rather than process-oriented justice, an increased risk of improper or unsafe convictions, and harsher and more punitive sentences.

The rationale behind limited State and police abilities and the concomitant elevation of the rights of the accused derives from the disparity of power between the parties in a criminal case. Although it may be argued that this gap has narrowed, given the wealth of some criminal suspects, the State retains resources and authority which cannot be equalled by an individual defendant, and therefore the need for protective devices remains. Moreover, the restriction of due process rights, which were introduced as individual protections and to guard against the danger of unfair convictions, does not necessarily further the fight against

---

[16] See C Gearty, *Can Human Rights Survive?* (Cambridge, Cambridge University Press, 2006) 69ff for a consideration of the false division, as Gearty sees it, between human rights and politics.

organised criminality and in fact may compromise the safety of the individual, as well as challenging the norms on which our society is based.

The UK (both as an homogenous entity and its constituent jurisdictions) and Ireland now have considerable legislative powers to deal with the phenomenon of organised crime through the usual criminal justice channels, as well as by means of more innovative tactics. Such abilities apply across the different stages of the criminal process, and are being ever expanded. While the underlying rationale for the increase in State capacities is understandable, predicated as it is on risk aversion and the desire to protect the public, this neglects to acknowledge the significance of due process, the underuse of existing laws, and the limitations of law as a primary means of dealing with the illusive yet potent notion of organised crime.

INDEX